FAIRY TAIL

50

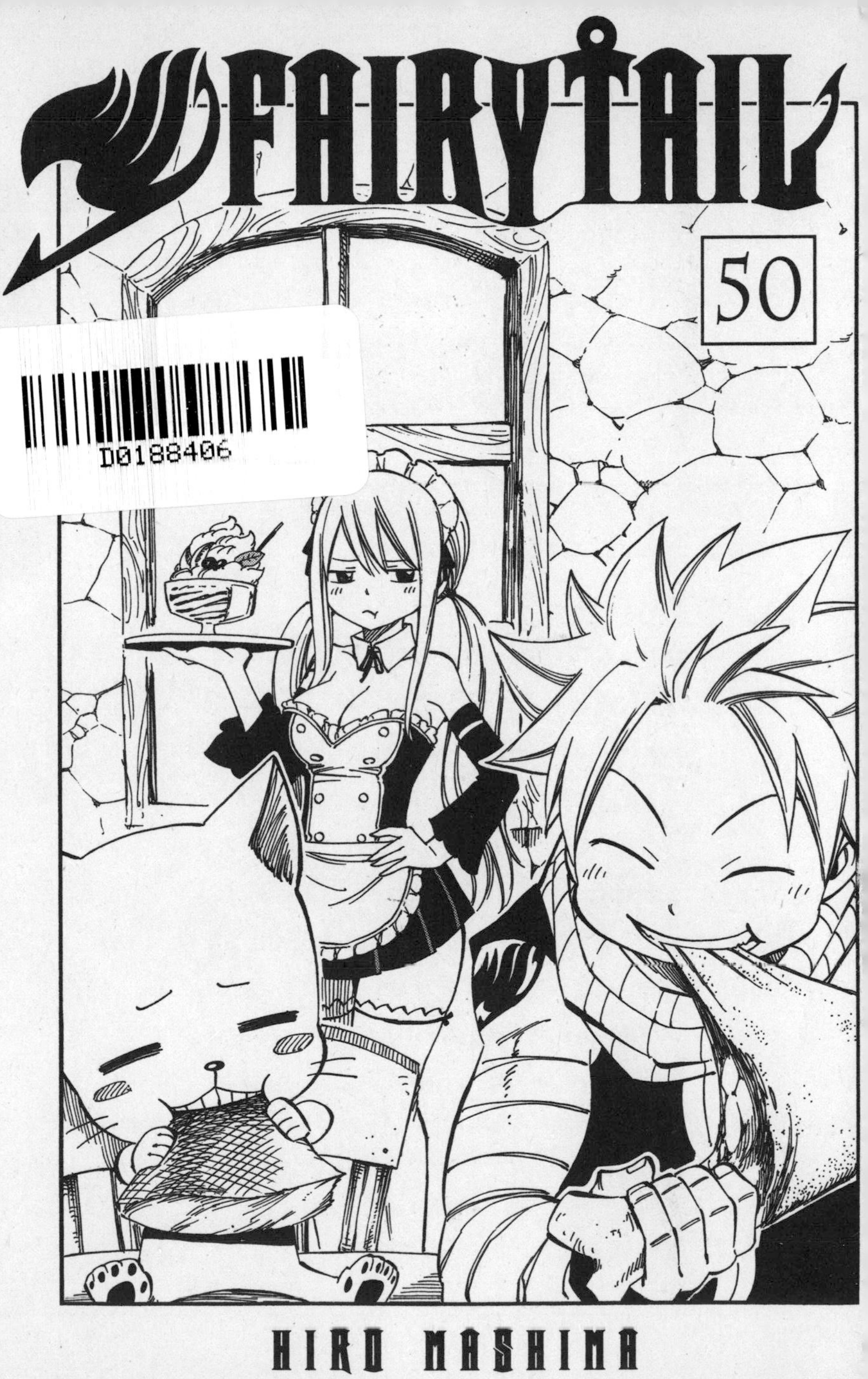

HIRO MASHIMA

FAIRY TAIL 50
CONTENTS♥

FAIRY TAIL

フェアリーテイル

Chapter 421: Wendy and Sherria

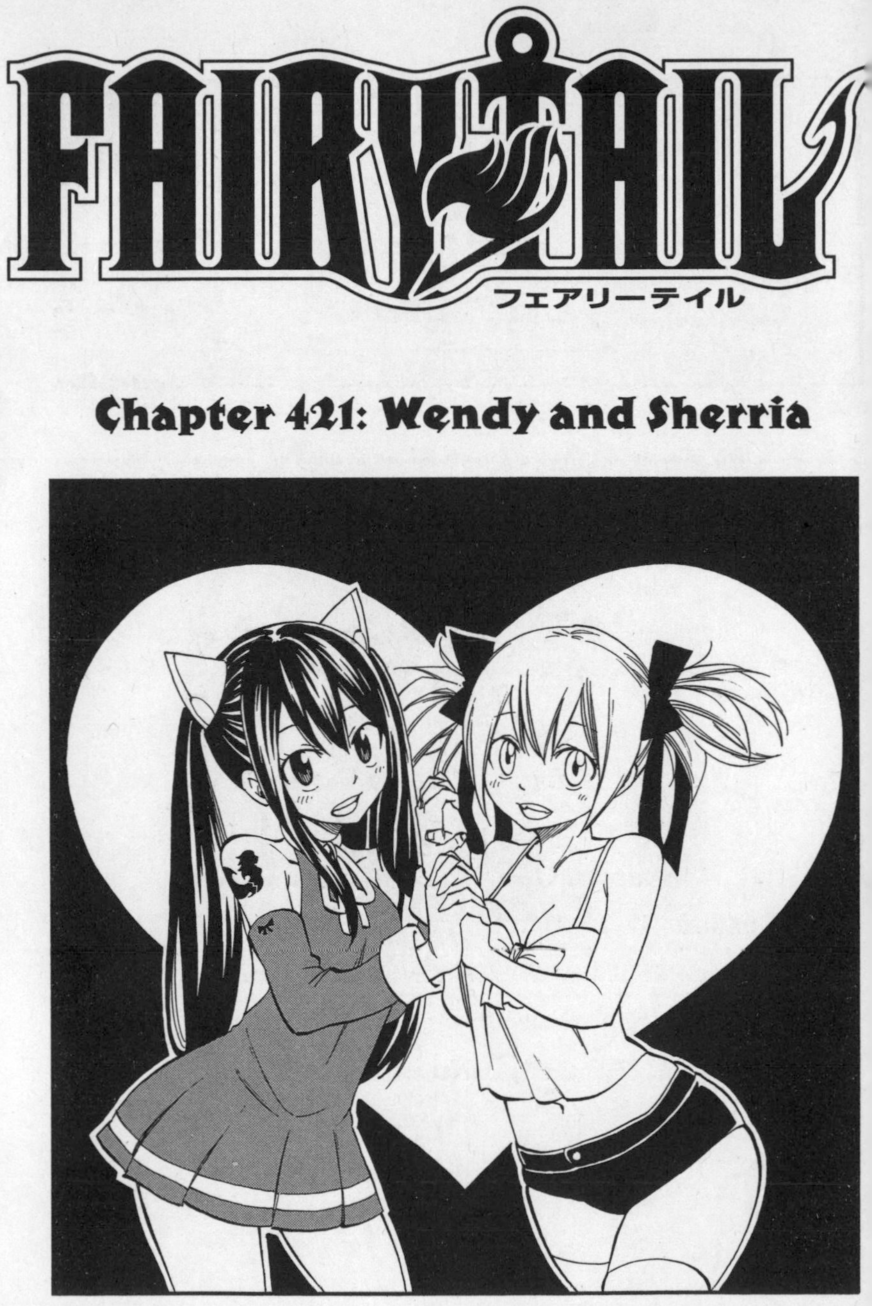

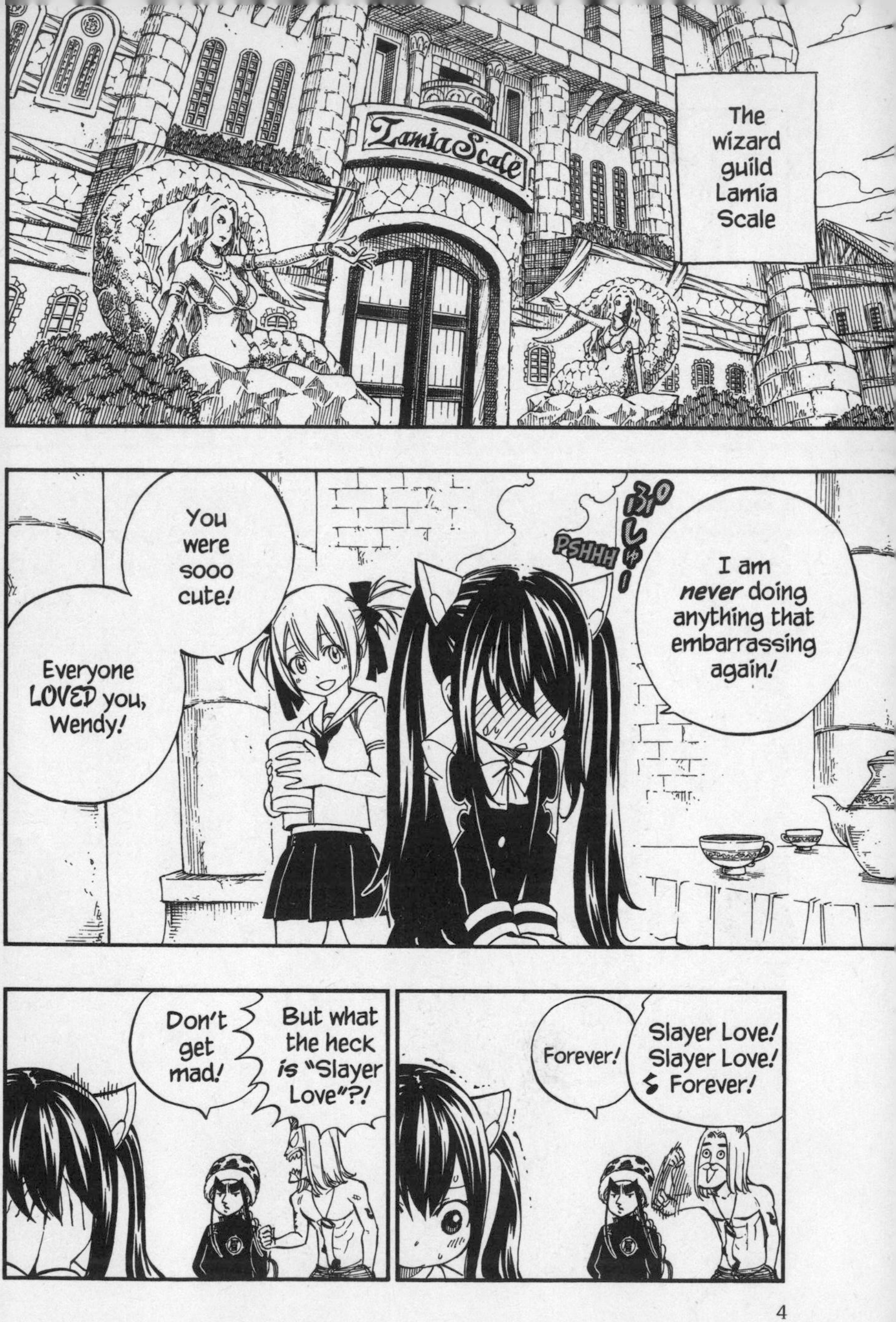
Lamia Scale
The wizard guild Lamia Scale
I am *never* doing anything that embarrassing again!
PSHHH
You were sooo cute!
Everyone LOVED you, Wendy!
Slayer Love! Slayer Love! Forever!
Forever!
But what the heck *is* "Slayer Love"?!
Don't get mad!

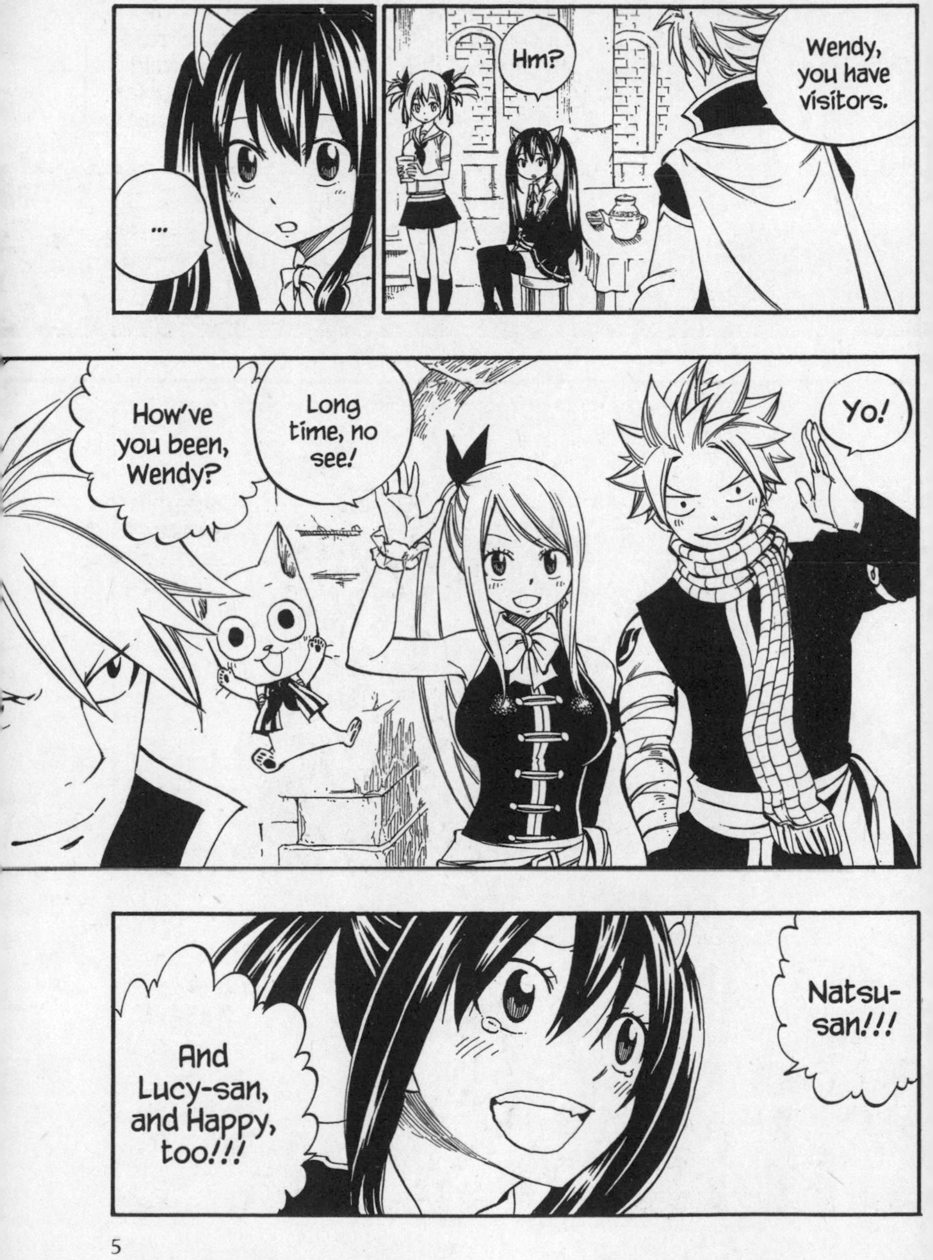
Wendy, you have visitors.
Hm?
...
Yo!
Long time, no see!
How've you been, Wendy?
Natsu-san!!!
And Lucy-san, and Happy, too!!!

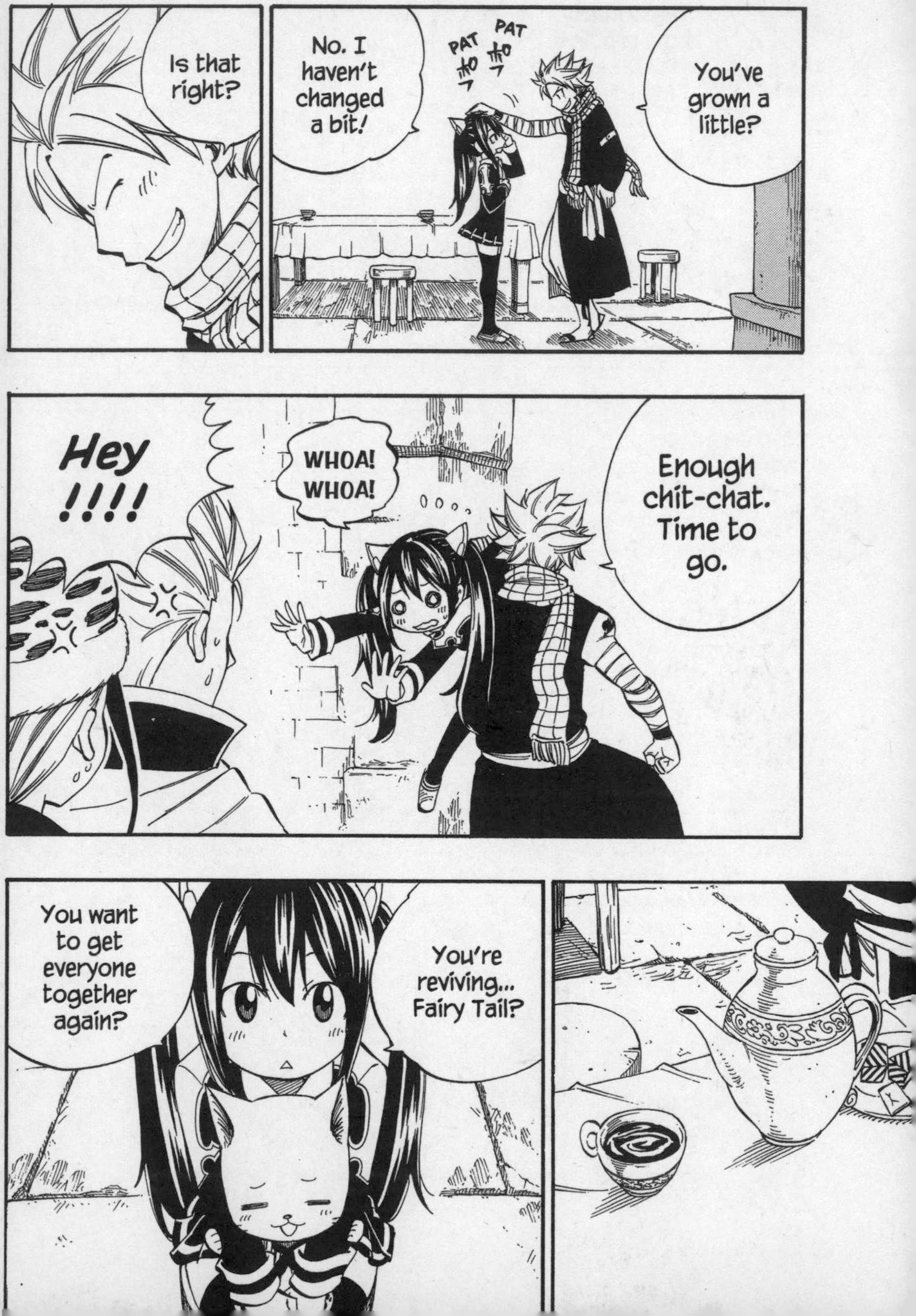
You've grown a little?
PAT PAT
No. I haven't changed a bit!
Is that right?
Enough chit-chat. Time to go.
WHOA! WHOA!
Hey !!!!
You're reviving... Fairy Tail?
You want to get everyone together again?

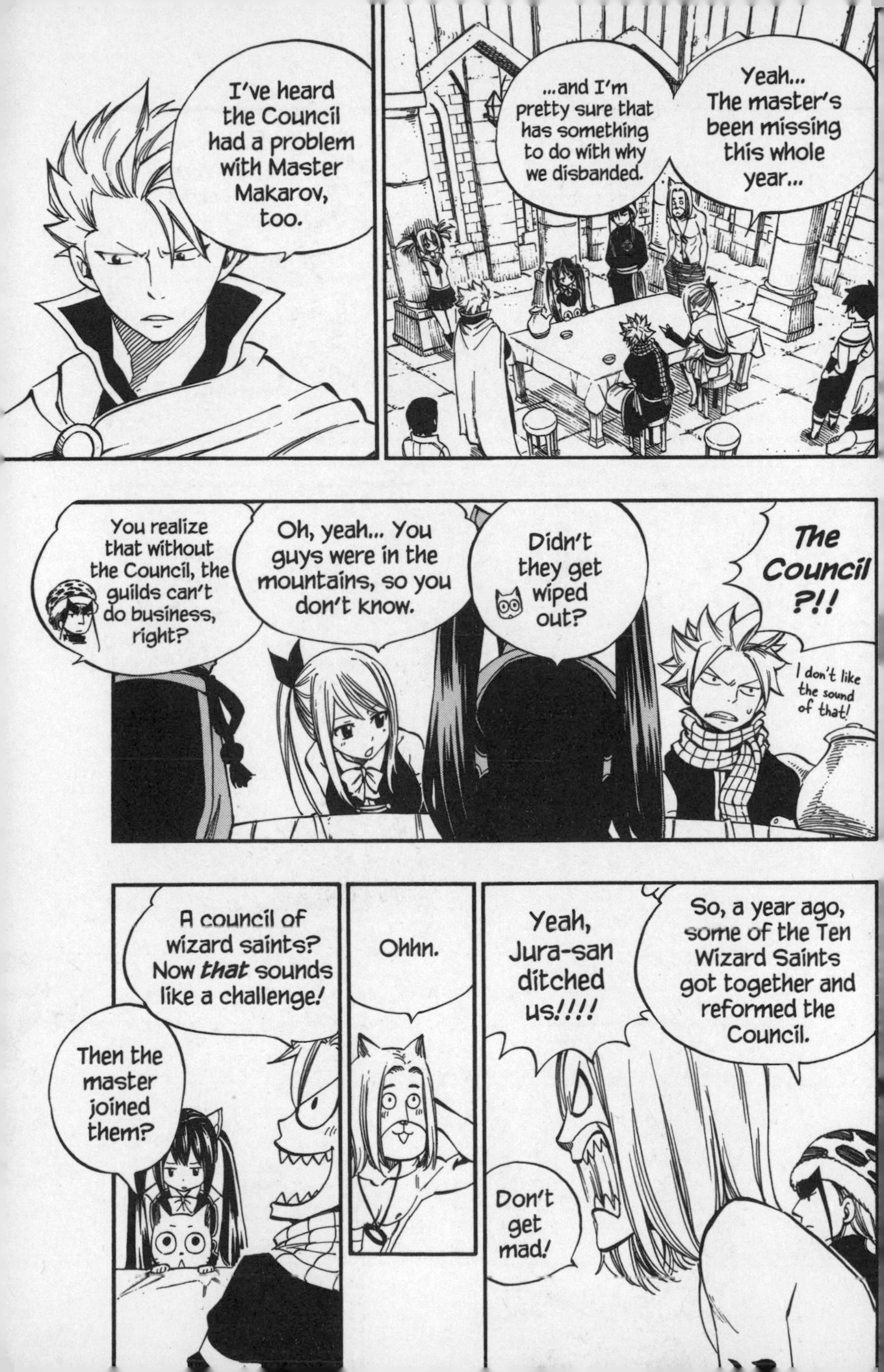
Yeah... The master's been missing this whole year...
...and I'm pretty sure that has something to do with why we disbanded.
I've heard the Council had a problem with Master Makarov, too.
The Council ?!!
I don't like the sound of that!
Didn't they get wiped out?
Oh, yeah... You guys were in the mountains, so you don't know.
You realize that without the Council, the guilds can't do business, right?
So, a year ago, some of the Ten Wizard Saints got together and reformed the Council.
Yeah, Jura-san ditched us!!!!
Don't get mad!
Ohhn.
A council of wizard saints? Now *that* sounds like a challenge!
Then the master joined them?

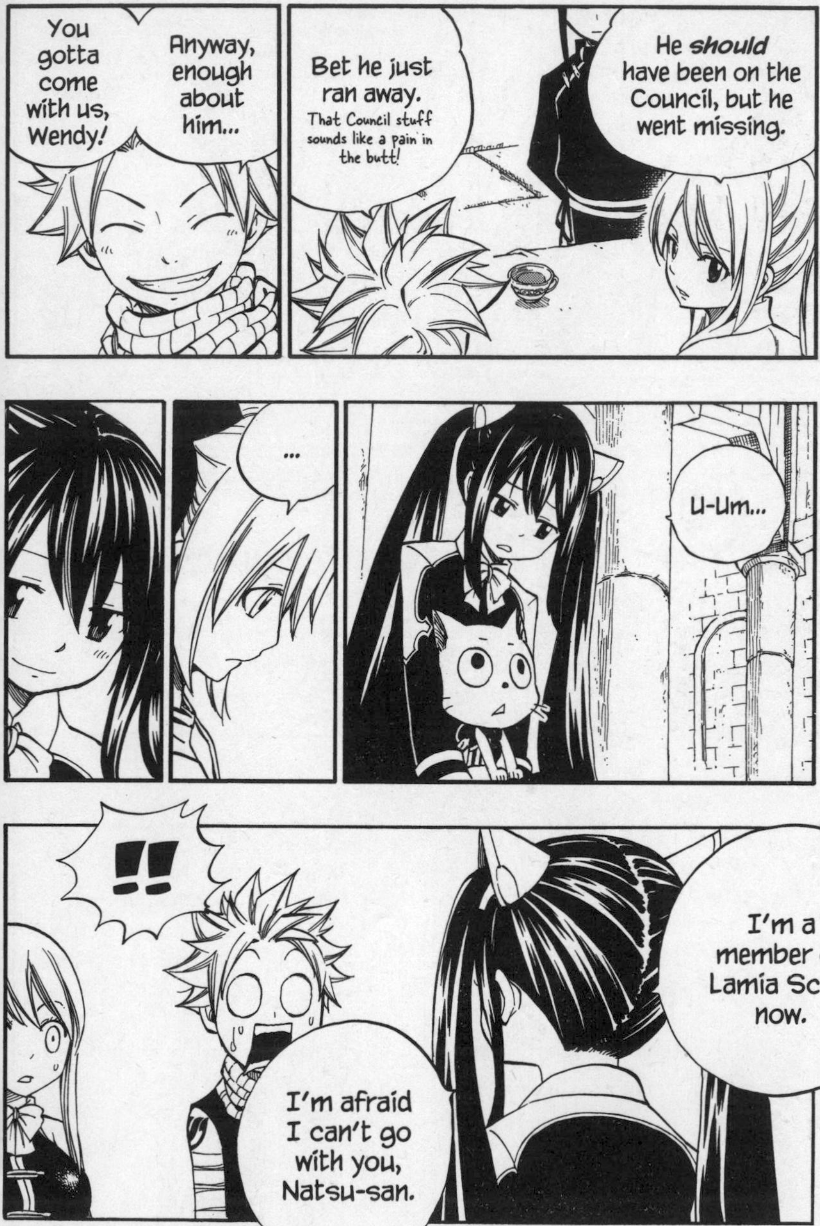
He *should* have been on the Council, but he went missing.
Bet he just ran away.
That Council stuff sounds like a pain in the butt!
Anyway, enough about him...
You gotta come with us, Wendy!
U-Um...
...
I'm a member of Lamia Scale now.
!!
I'm afraid I can't go with you, Natsu-san.

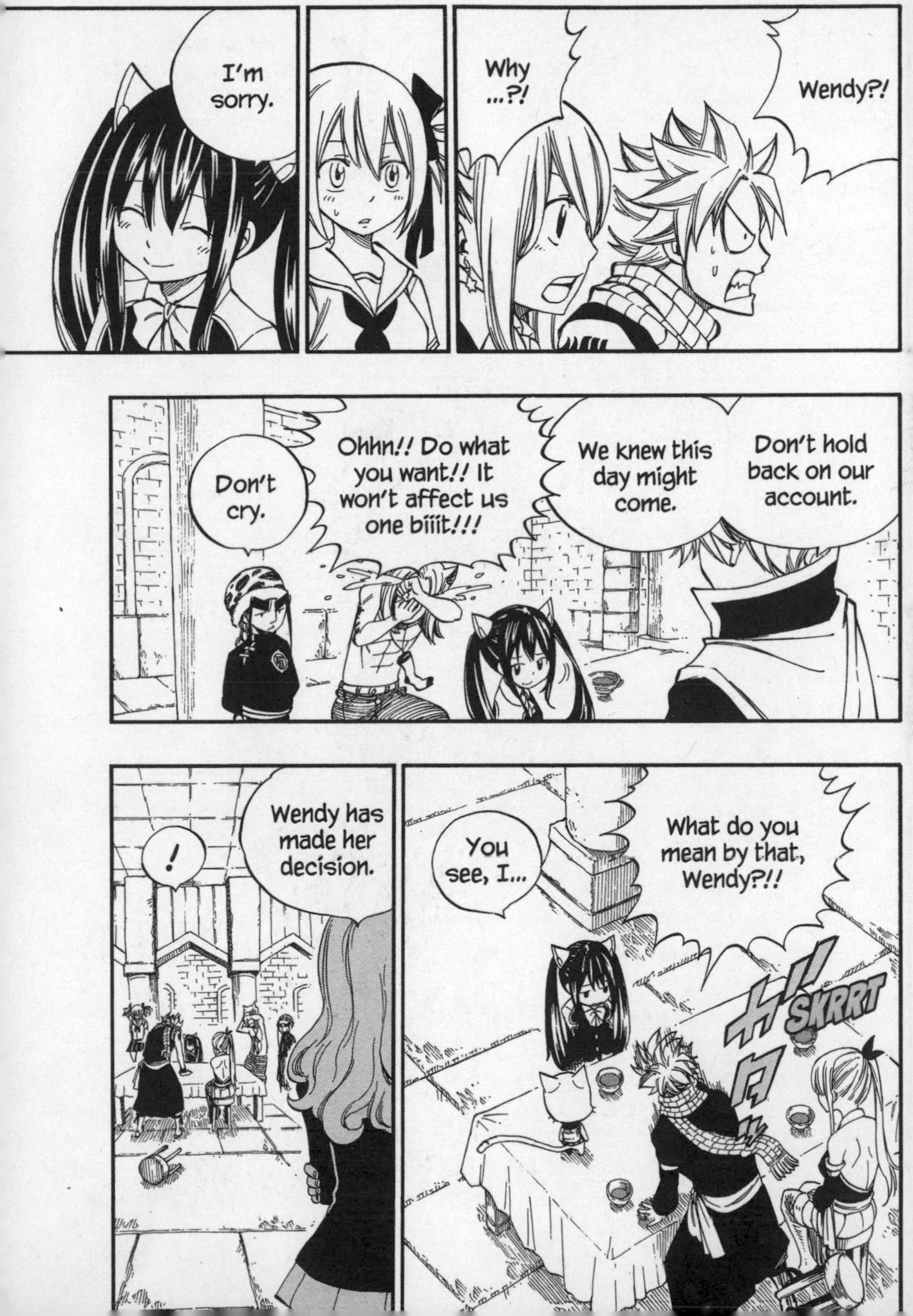
Wendy?!
Why ...?!
I'm sorry.
Don't hold back on our account.
We knew this day might come.
Ohhn!! Do what you want!! It won't affect us one biiit!!!
Don't cry.
What do you mean by that, Wendy?!!
SKRRT
You see, I...
Wendy has made her decision.
!

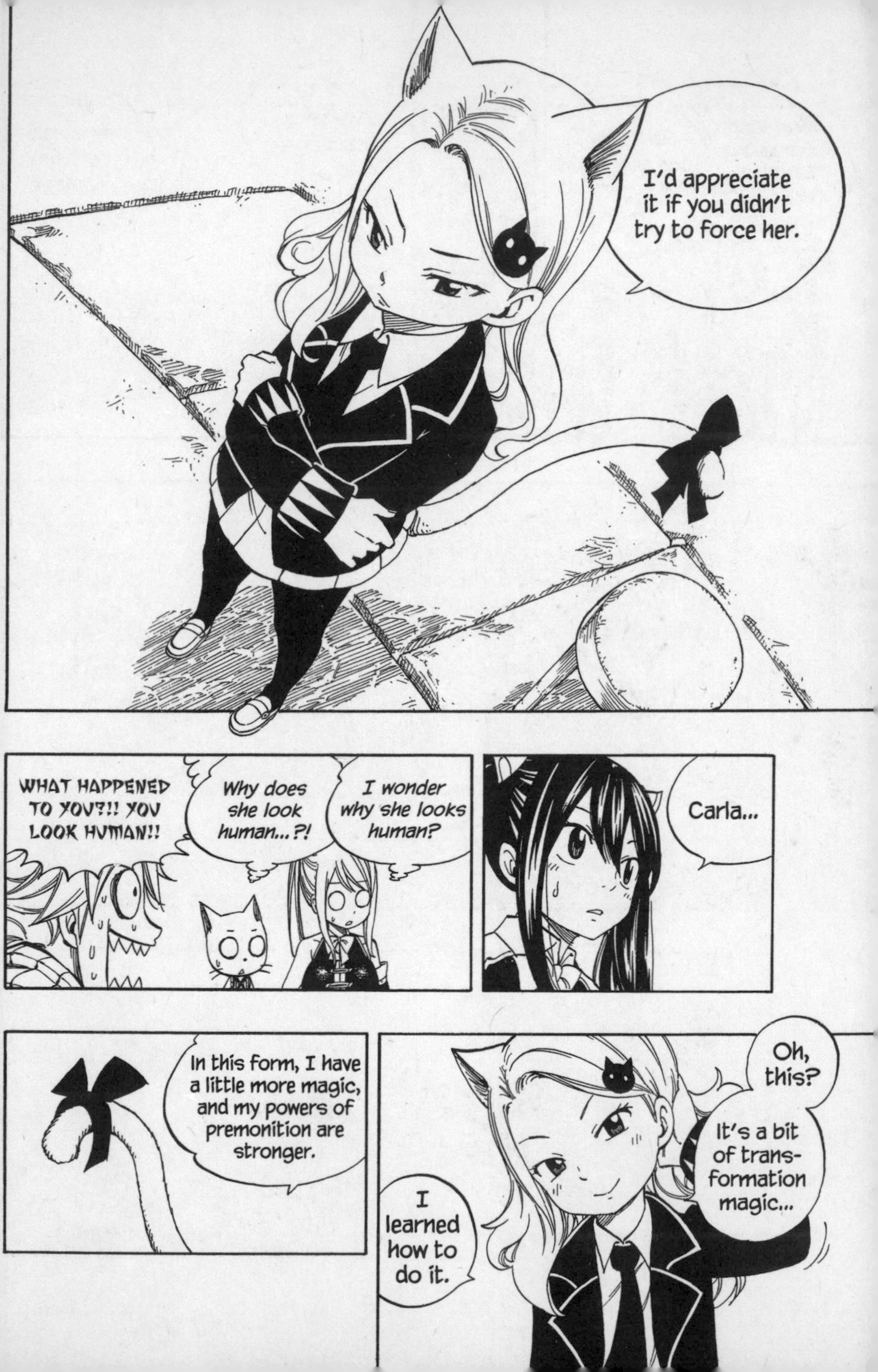

I'd appreciate it if you didn't try to force her.
Carla...
I wonder why she looks human?
Why does she look human...?!
WHAT HAPPENED TO YOU?!! YOU LOOK HUMAN!!
Oh, this?
It's a bit of trans-formation magic...
I learned how to do it.
In this form, I have a little more magic, and my powers of premonition are stronger.

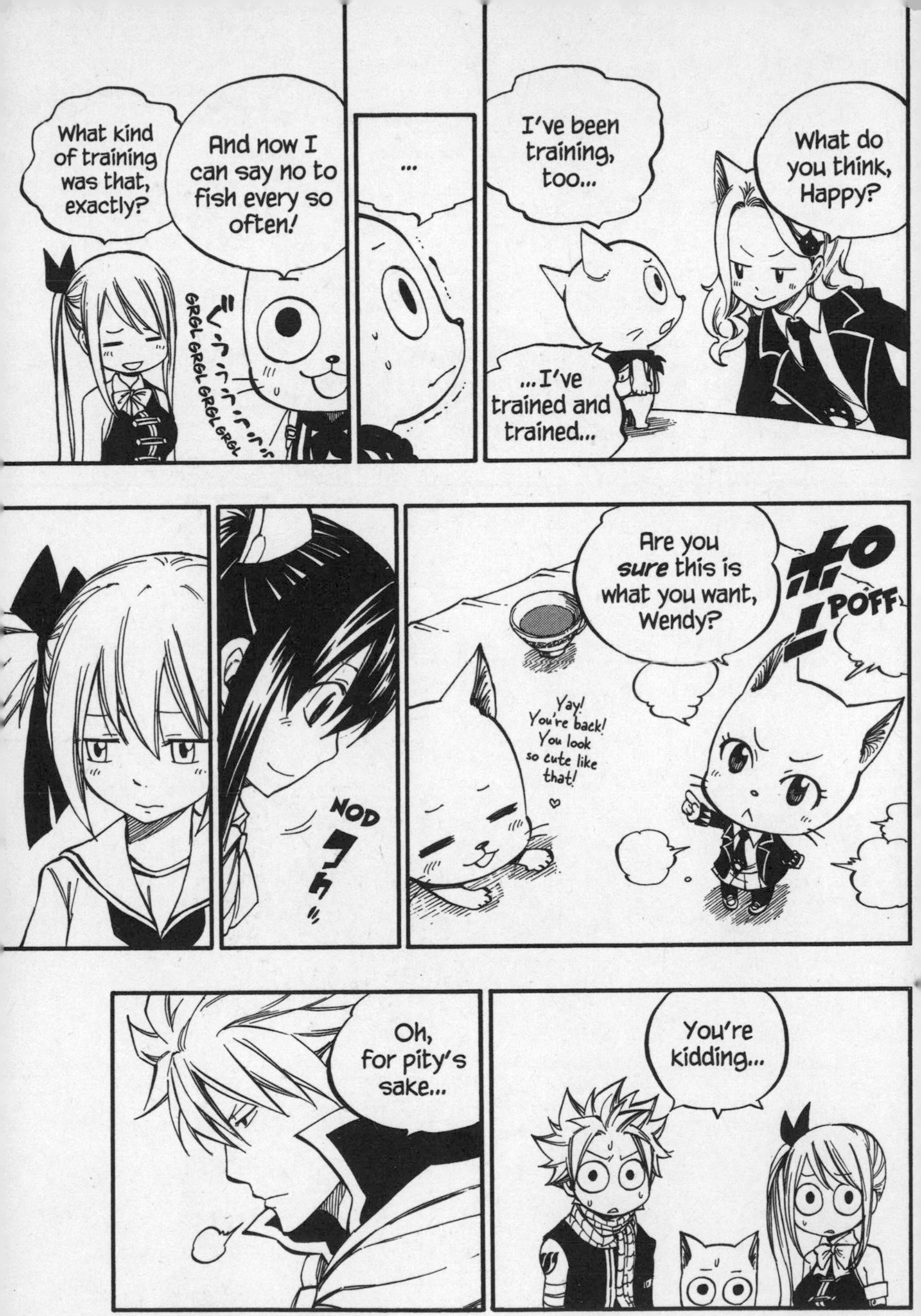
What do you think, Happy?
I've been training, too...
...I've trained and trained...
...
And now I can say no to fish every so often!
GRGL GRGL GRGL GRGL
What kind of training was that, exactly?
POFF
Are you *sure* this is what you want, Wendy?
Yay! You're back! You look so cute like that!
NOD
You're kidding...
Oh, for pity's sake...

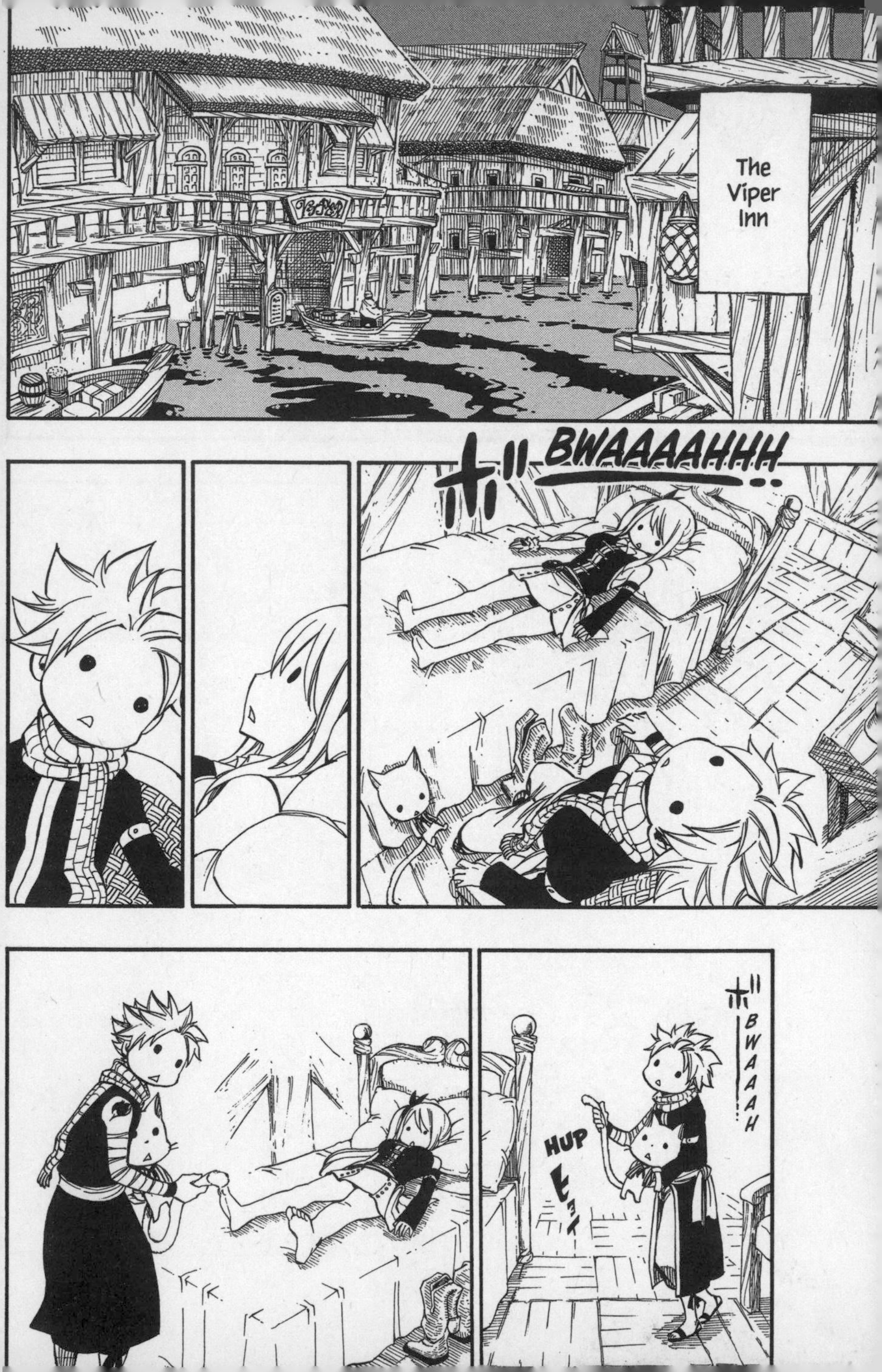
The Viper Inn
BWAAAAHHH!!
BWAAAAH!!
HUP

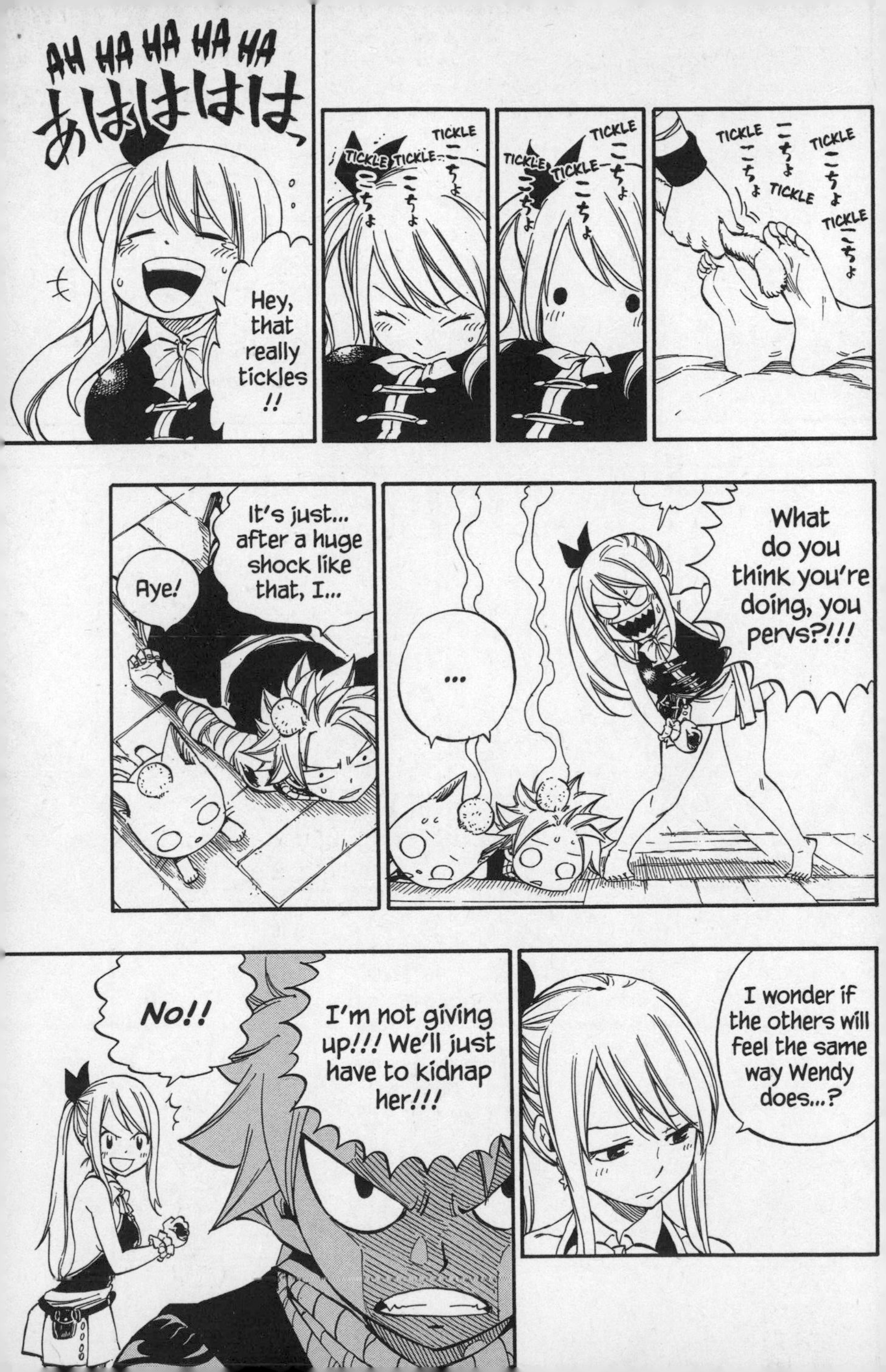
TICKLE こちょ
TICKLE こちょ
TICKLE こちょ
TICKLE こちょ
TICKLE こちょ
TICKLE こちょ
TICKLE こちょ
TICKLE こちょ
TICKLE こちょ
TICKLE こちょ
AH HA HA HA HA あはははは
Hey, that really tickles!!
What do you think you're doing, you pervs?!!!
...
It's just... after a huge shock like that, I...
Aye!
I wonder if the others will feel the same way Wendy does...?
I'm not giving up!!! We'll just have to kidnap her!!!
No!!

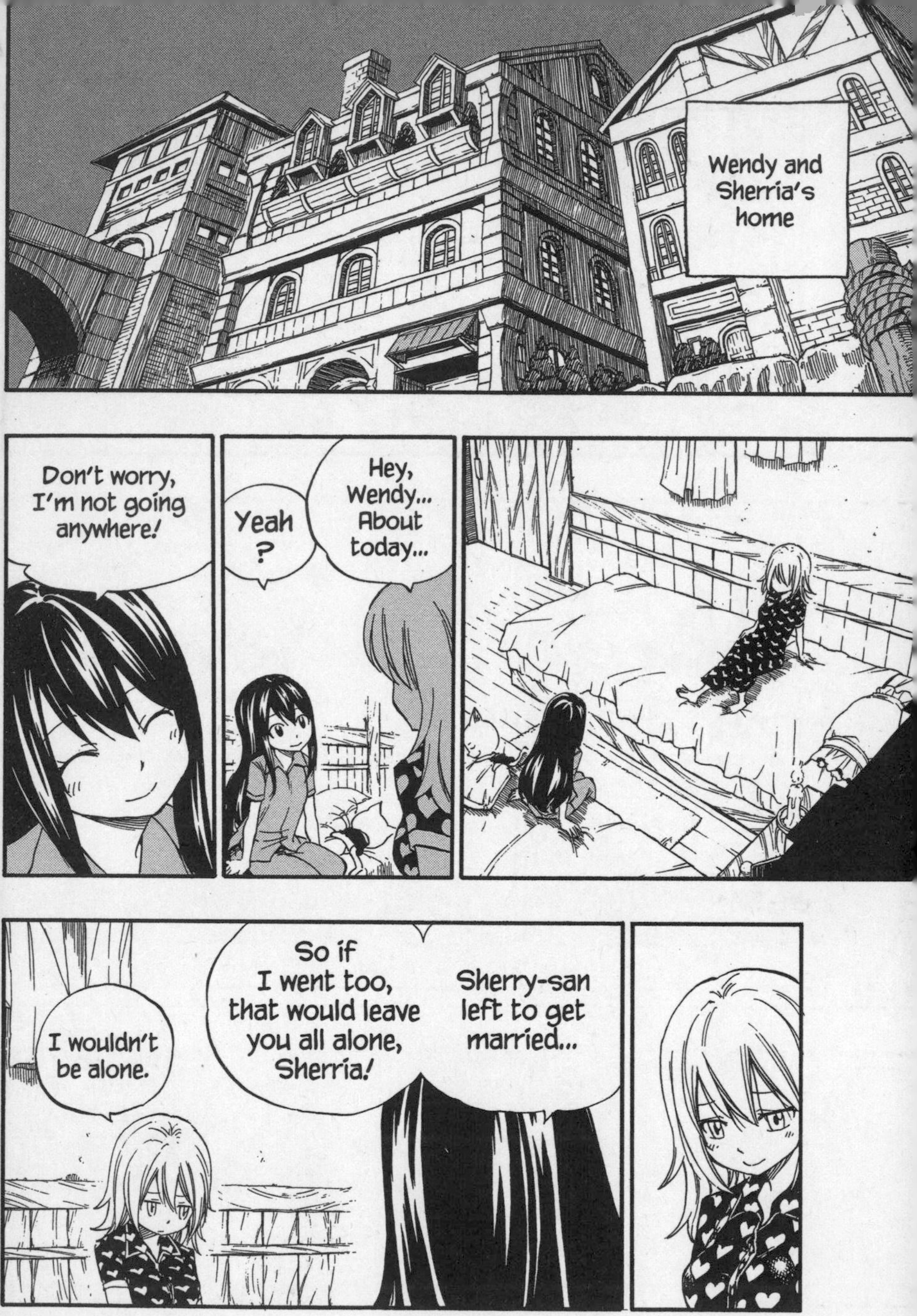
Wendy and Sherria's home
Hey, Wendy... About today...
Yeah?
Don't worry, I'm not going anywhere!
Sherry-san left to get married...
So if I went too, that would leave you all alone, Sherria!
I wouldn't be alone.

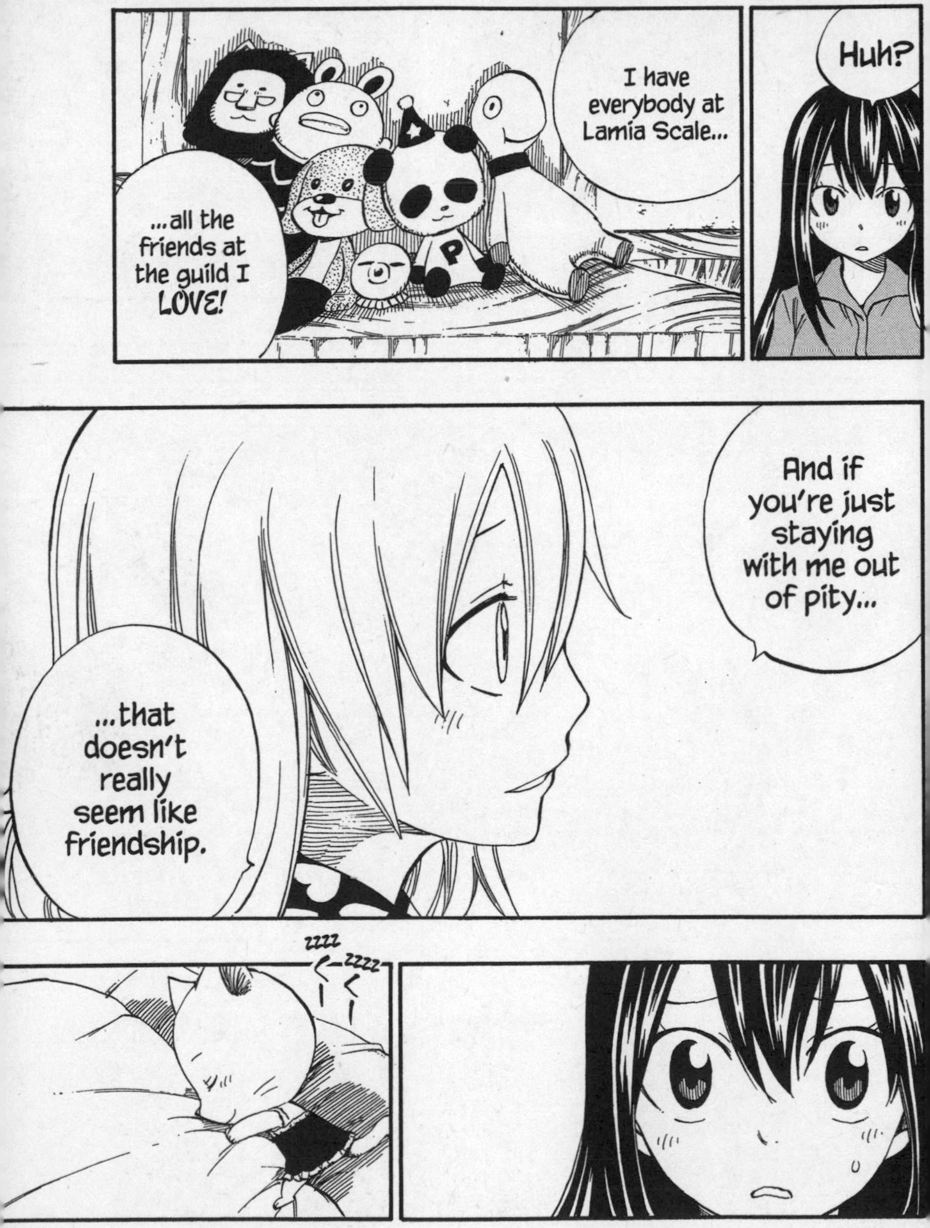
Huh?
I have everybody at Lamia Scale...
...all the friends at the guild I LOVE!
And if you're just staying with me out of pity...
...that doesn't really seem like friendship.
zzzz
zzzz

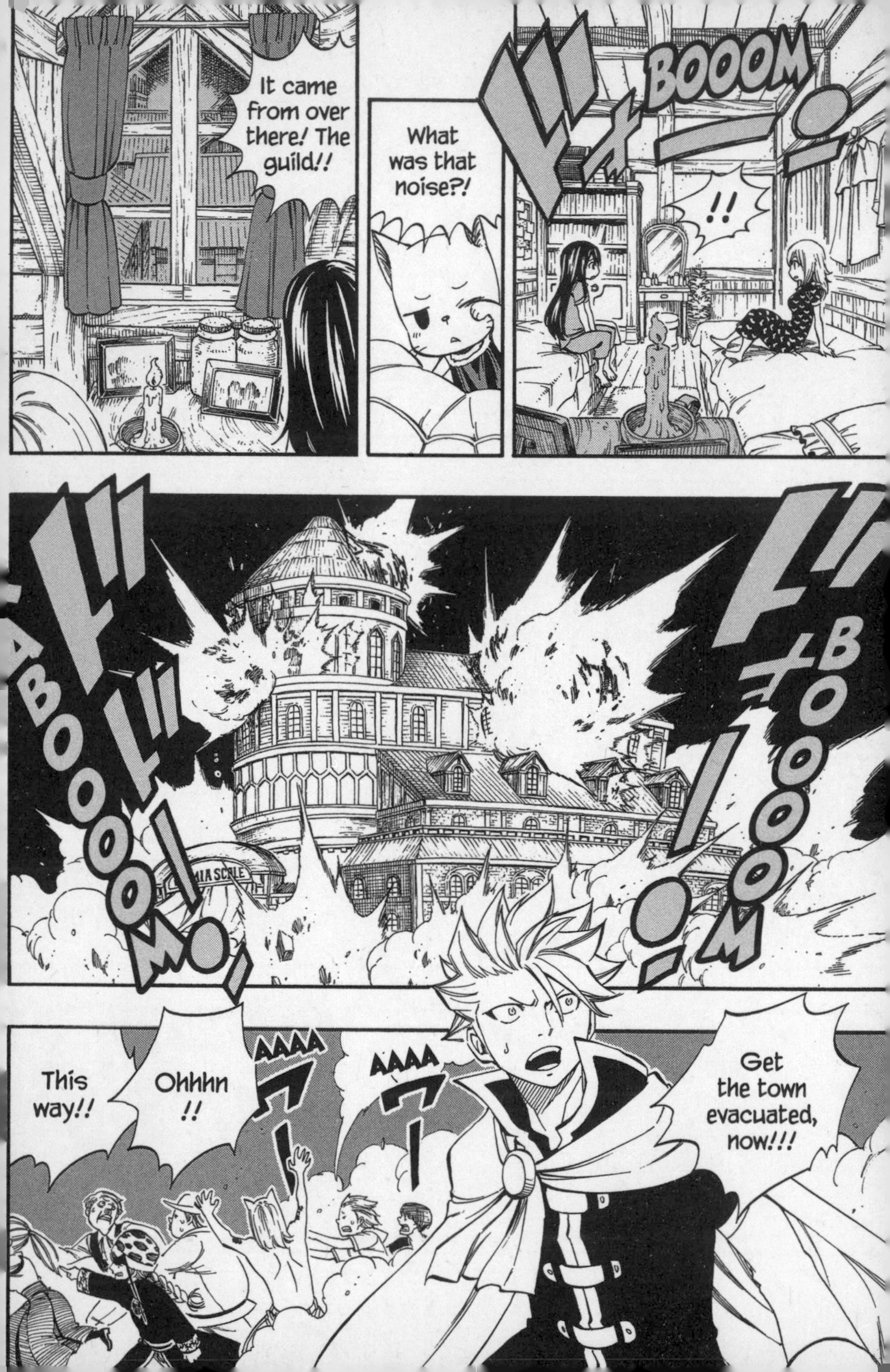
BOOOM
!!
What was that noise?!
It came from over there! The guild!!
BOOOOOM
ABOOOOOM
Get the town evacuated, now!!!
AAAA
AAAA
Ohhhn !!
This way!!

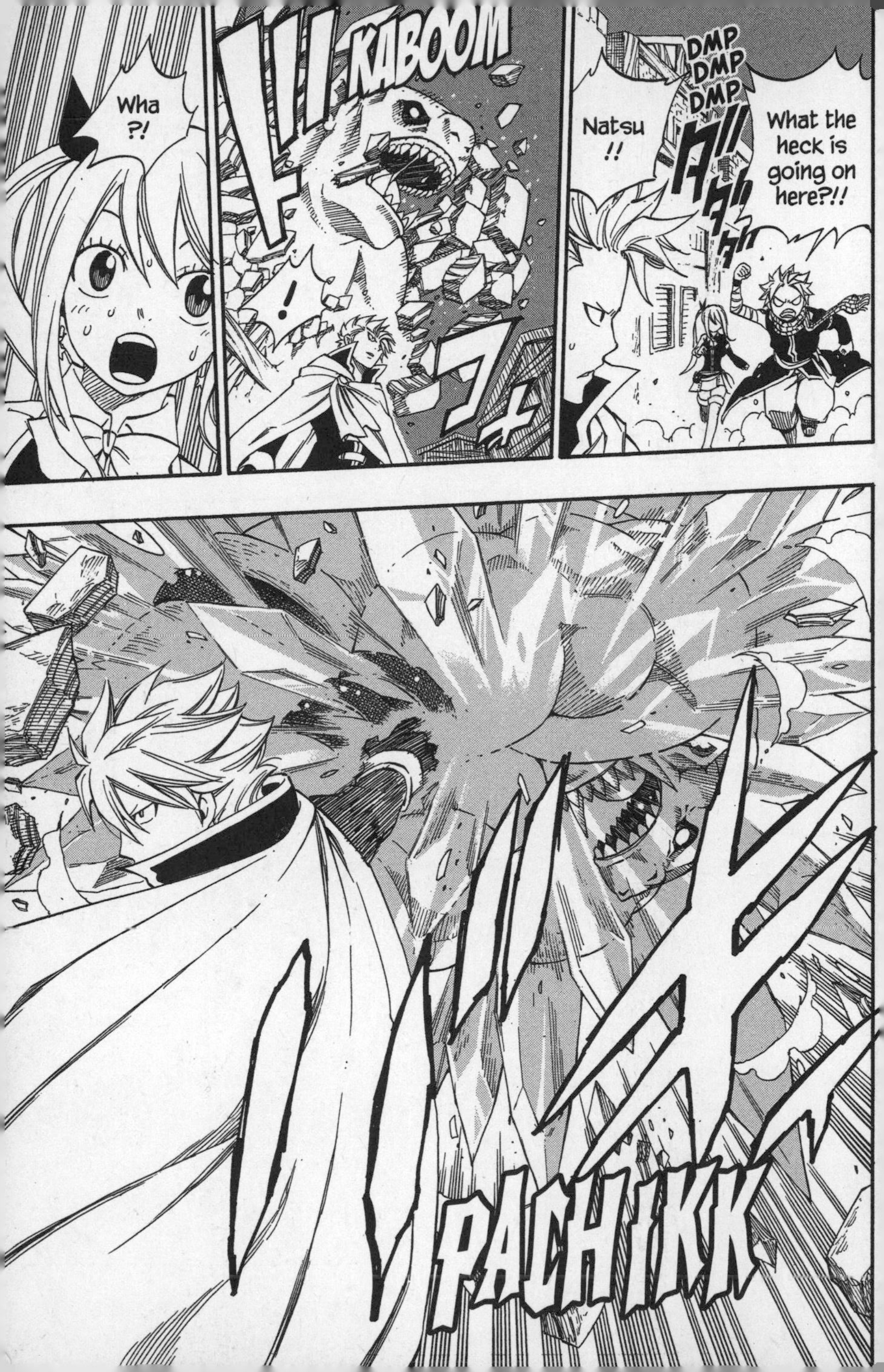
DMP
DMP
DMP
What the heck is going on here?!!
Natsu !!
KABOOM
!
Wha ?!
PACHIKK

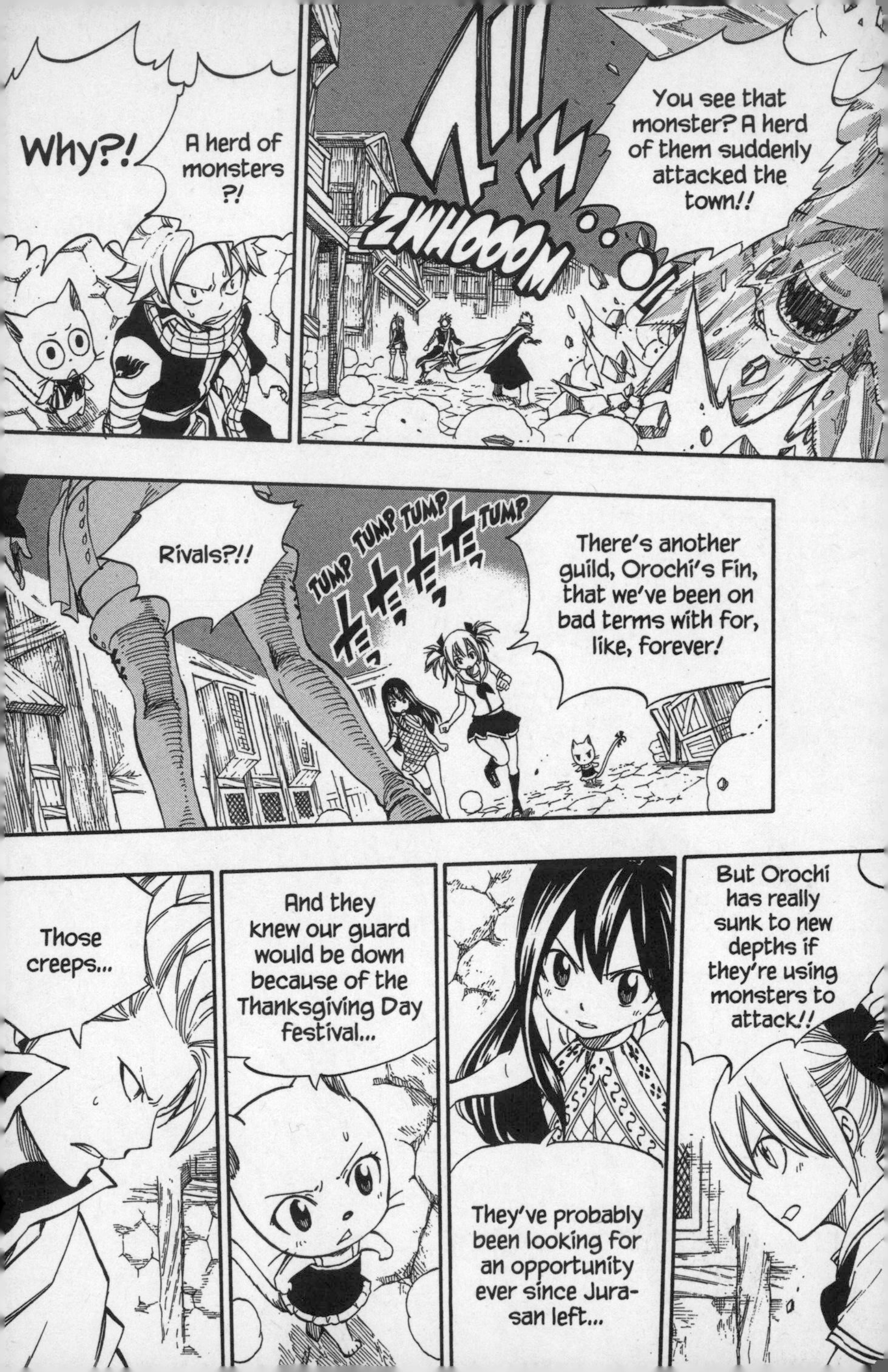

You see that monster? A herd of them suddenly attacked the town!!
ZWHOOOM
A herd of monsters ?!
Why?!
There's another guild, Orochi's Fin, that we've been on bad terms with for, like, forever!
TUMP TUMP TUMP TUMP
Rivals?!!
But Orochi has really sunk to new depths if they're using monsters to attack!!
They've probably been looking for an opportunity ever since Jura-san left...
And they knew our guard would be down because of the Thanksgiving Day festival...
Those creeps...

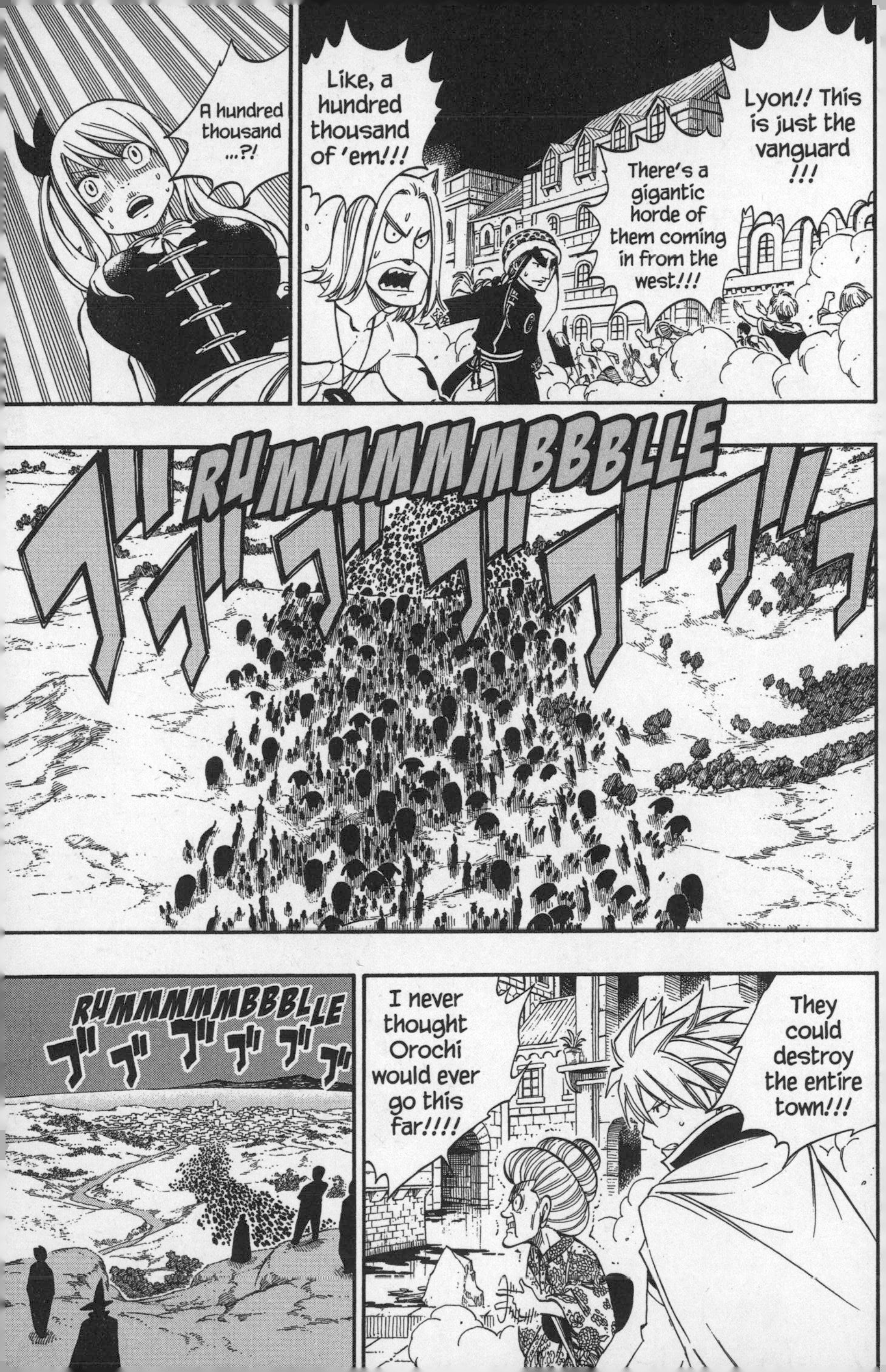
Lyon!! This is just the vanguard!!!
There's a gigantic horde of them coming in from the west!!!
Like, a hundred thousand of 'em!!!
A hundred thousand ...?!
RUMMMMMMMBBBLLE
They could destroy the entire town!!!
I never thought Orochi would ever go this far!!!!
RUMMMMMMBBBLLE

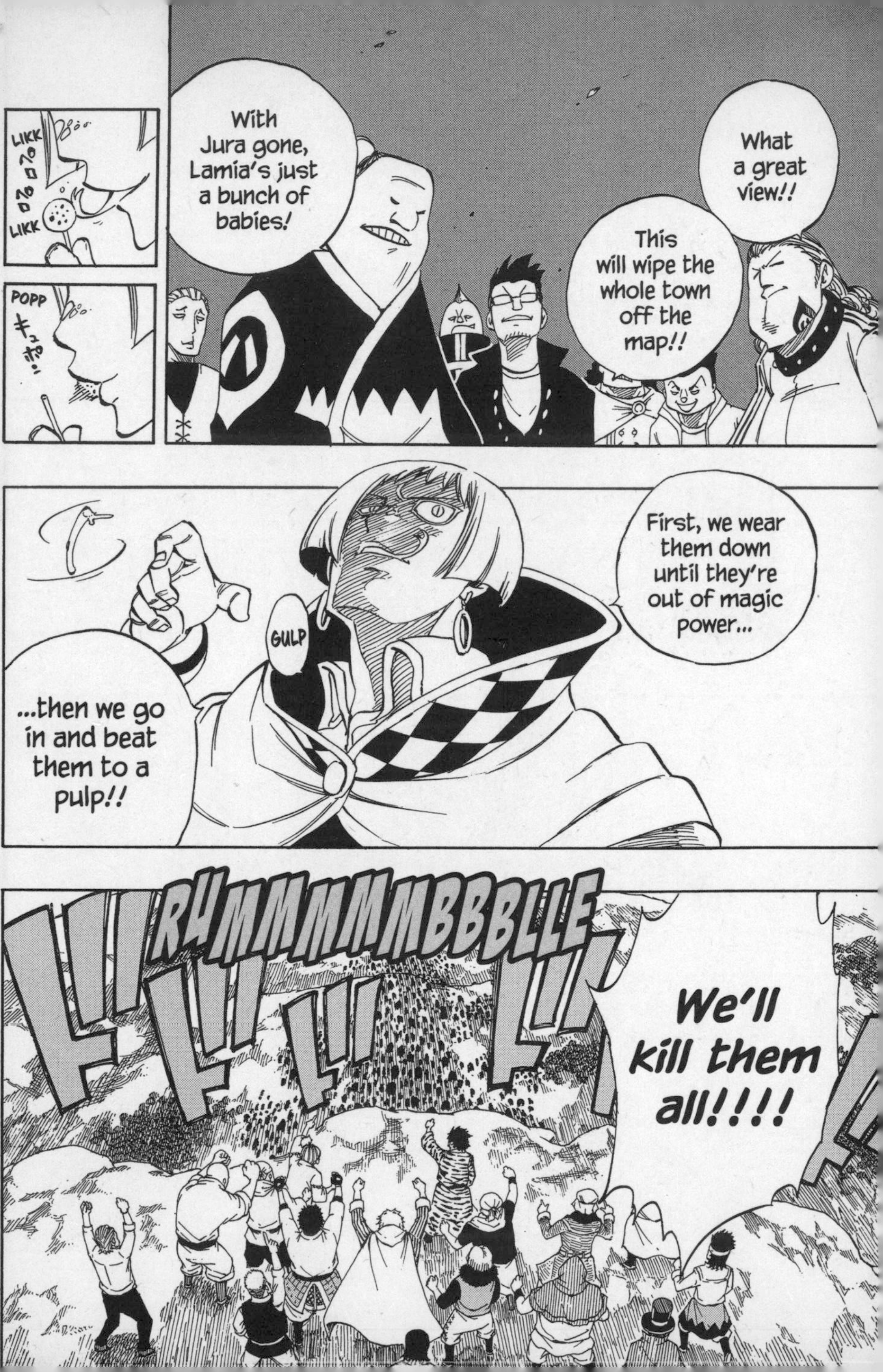
What a great view!!
This will wipe the whole town off the map!!
With Jura gone, Lamia's just a bunch of babies!
LIKK LIKK
POPP
First, we wear them down until they're out of magic power...
GULP
...then we go in and beat them to a pulp!!
We'll kill them all!!!!
RUMMMMMMBBBLLE

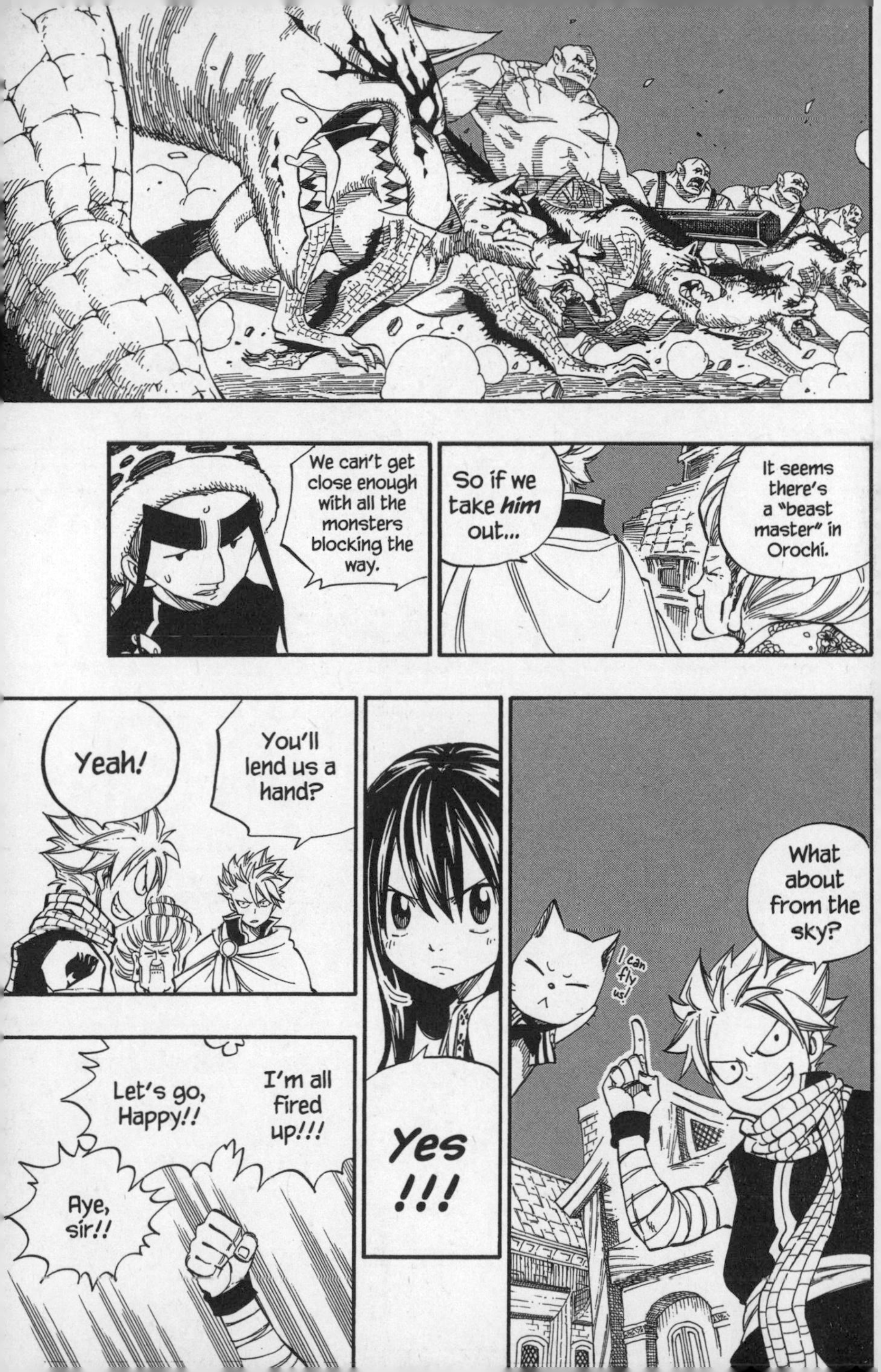
It seems there's a "beast master" in Orochi.
So if we take *him* out...
We can't get close enough with all the monsters blocking the way.
What about from the sky?
I can fly us!
Yes !!!
You'll lend us a hand?
Yeah!
I'm all fired up!!!
Let's go, Happy!!
Aye, sir!!

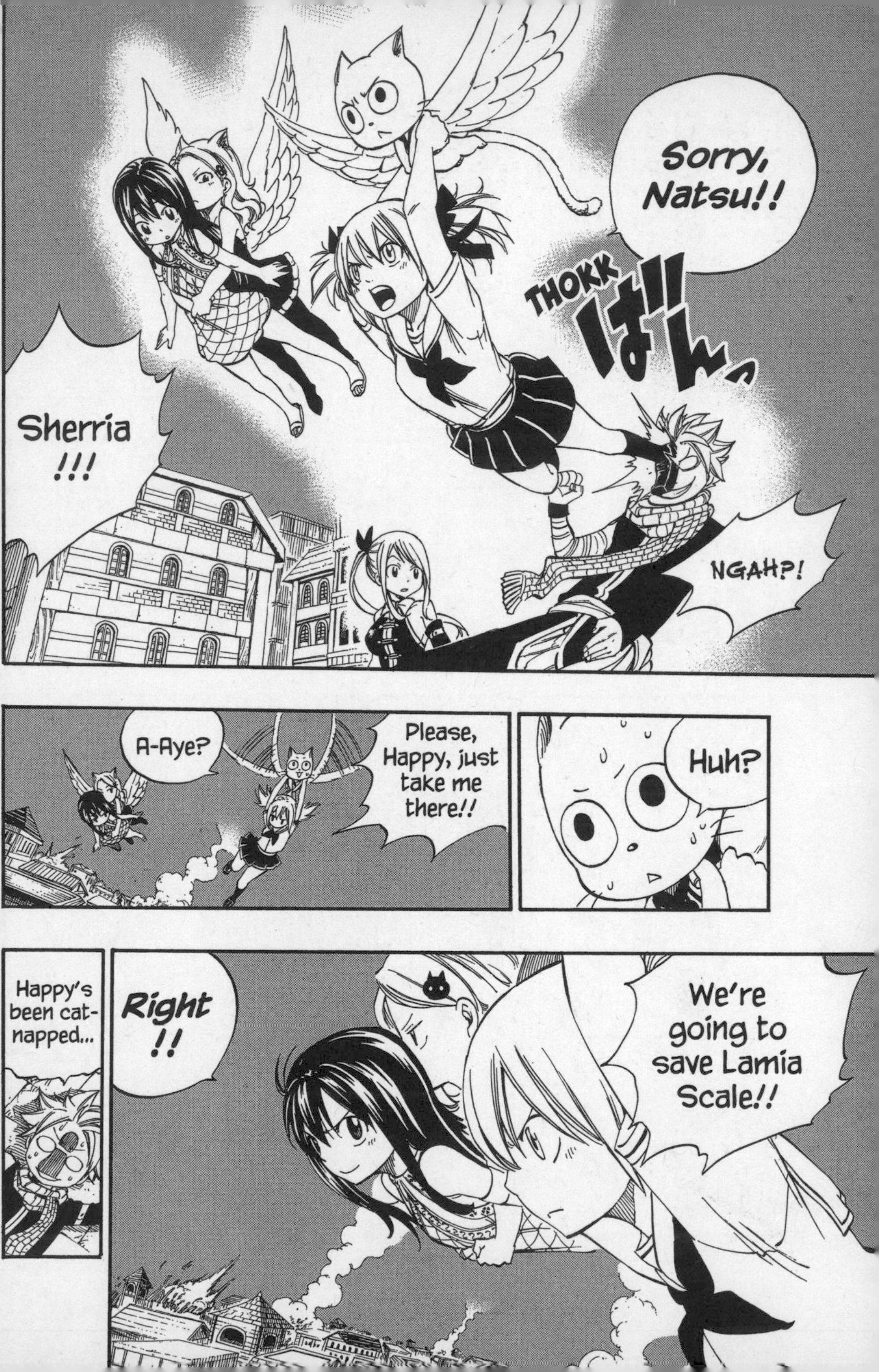
Sorry, Natsu!!
THOKK
ばん
NGAH?!
Sherria !!!
Huh?
Please, Happy, just take me there!!
A-Aye?
We're going to save Lamia Scale!!
Right !!
Happy's been cat-napped...

FAIRY TAIL

フェアリーテイル

Chapter 422: Orochi's Fin

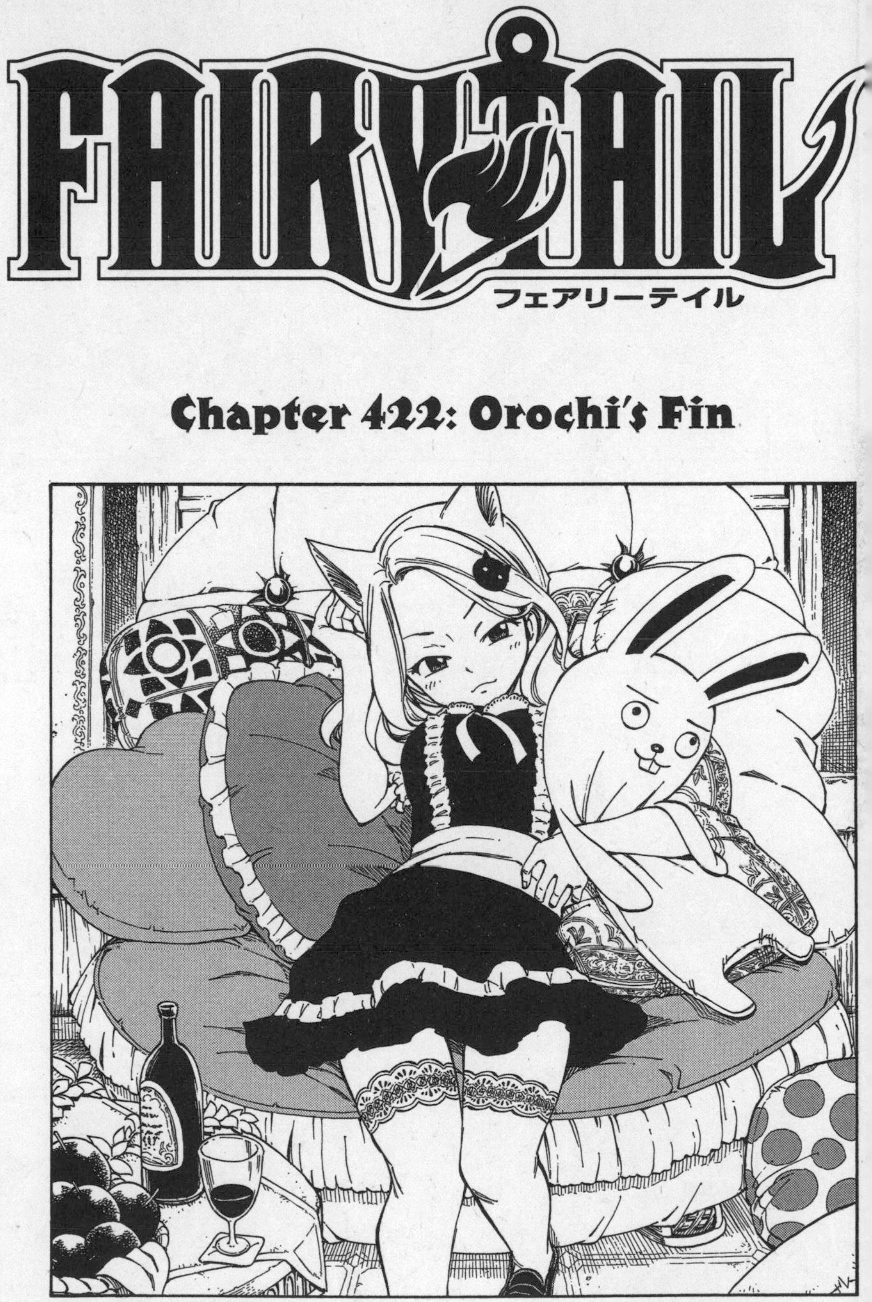

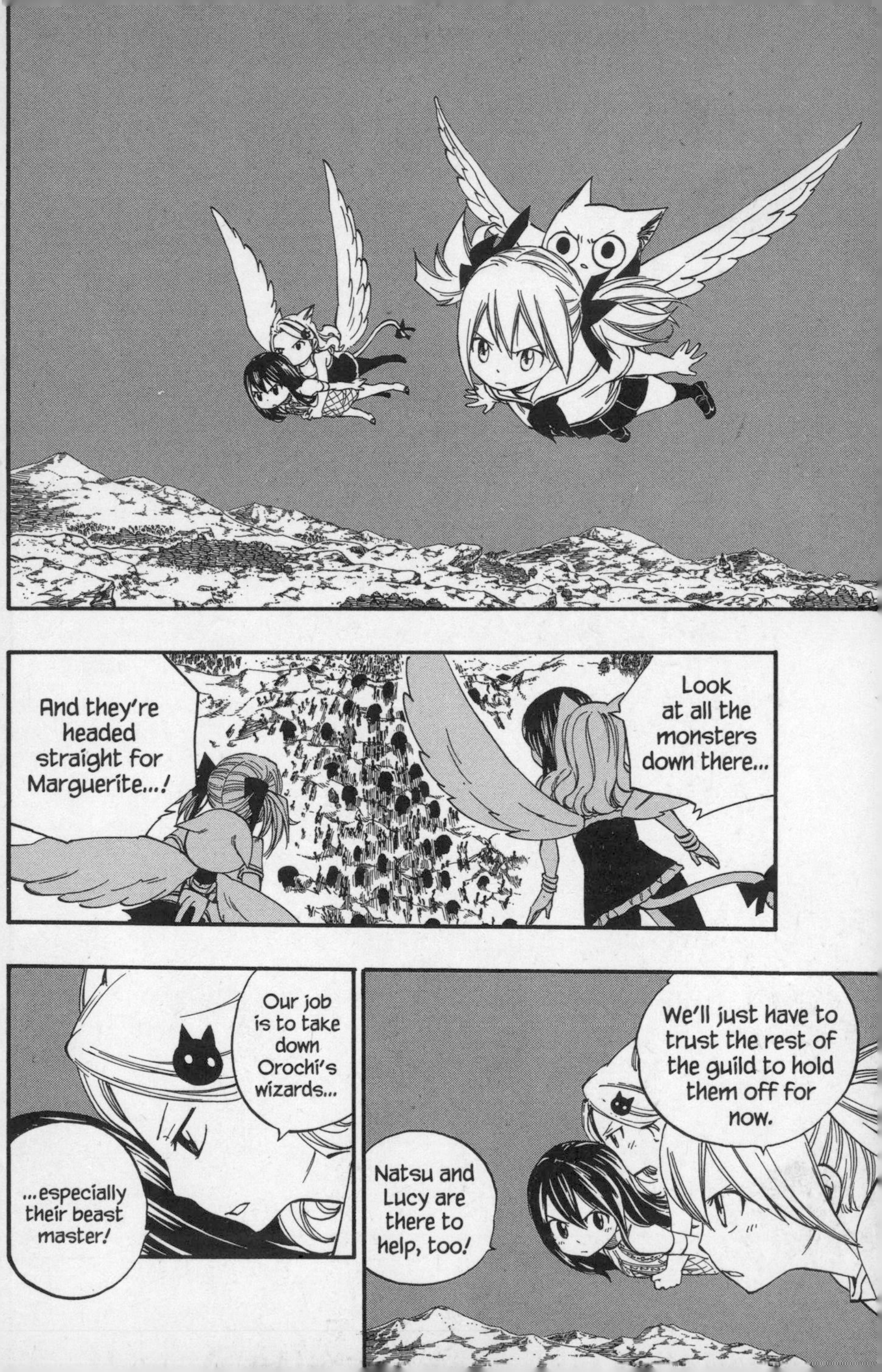
Look at all the monsters down there...
And they're headed straight for Marguerite...!
We'll just have to trust the rest of the guild to hold them off for now.
Natsu and Lucy are there to help, too!
Our job is to take down Orochi's wizards...
...especially their beast master!

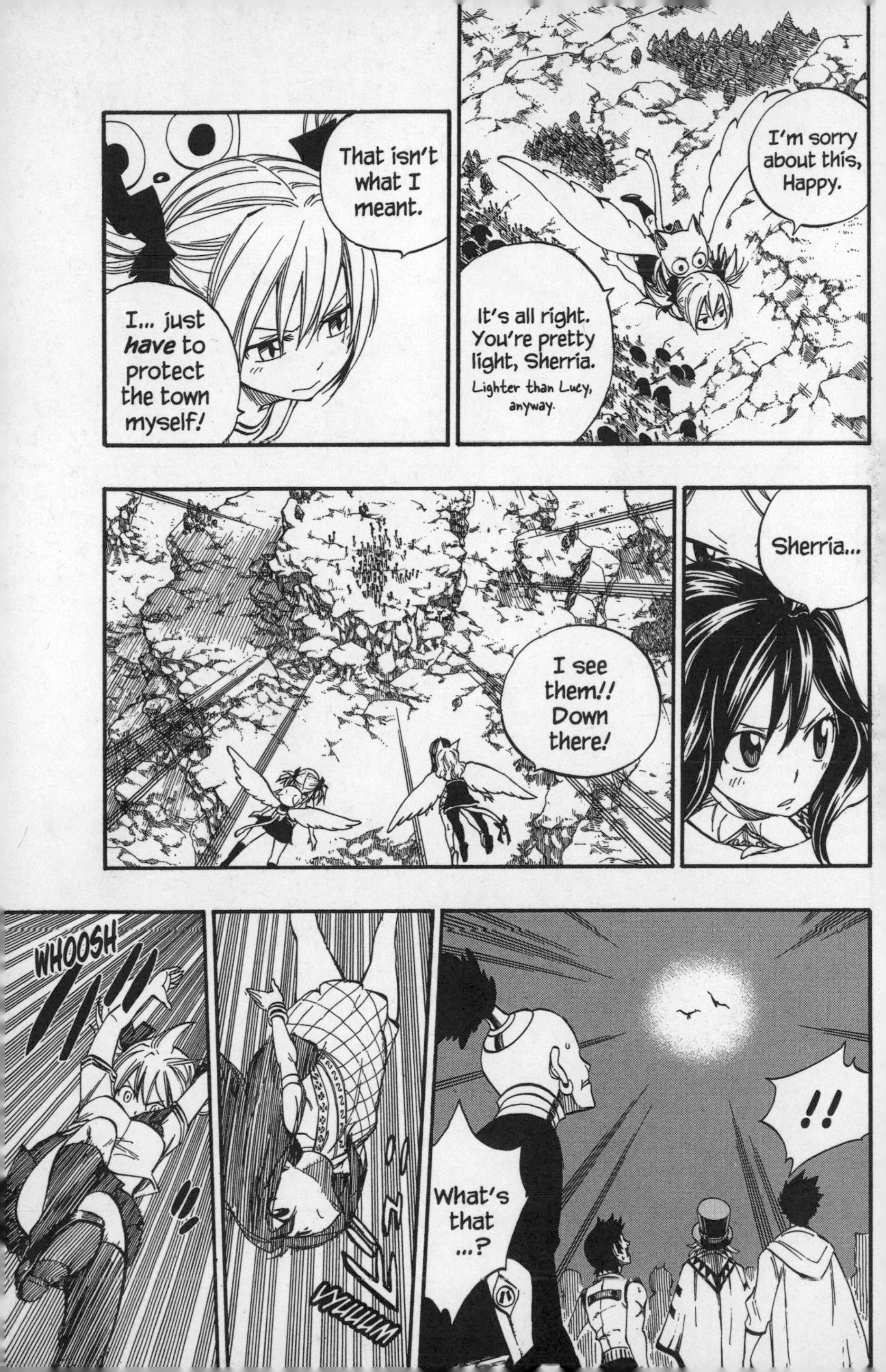
I'm sorry about this, Happy.
It's all right. You're pretty light, Sherria.
Lighter than Lucy, anyway.
That isn't what I meant.
I... just *have* to protect the town myself!
Sherria...
I see them!! Down there!
!!
What's that ...?
WHOOSH
!!

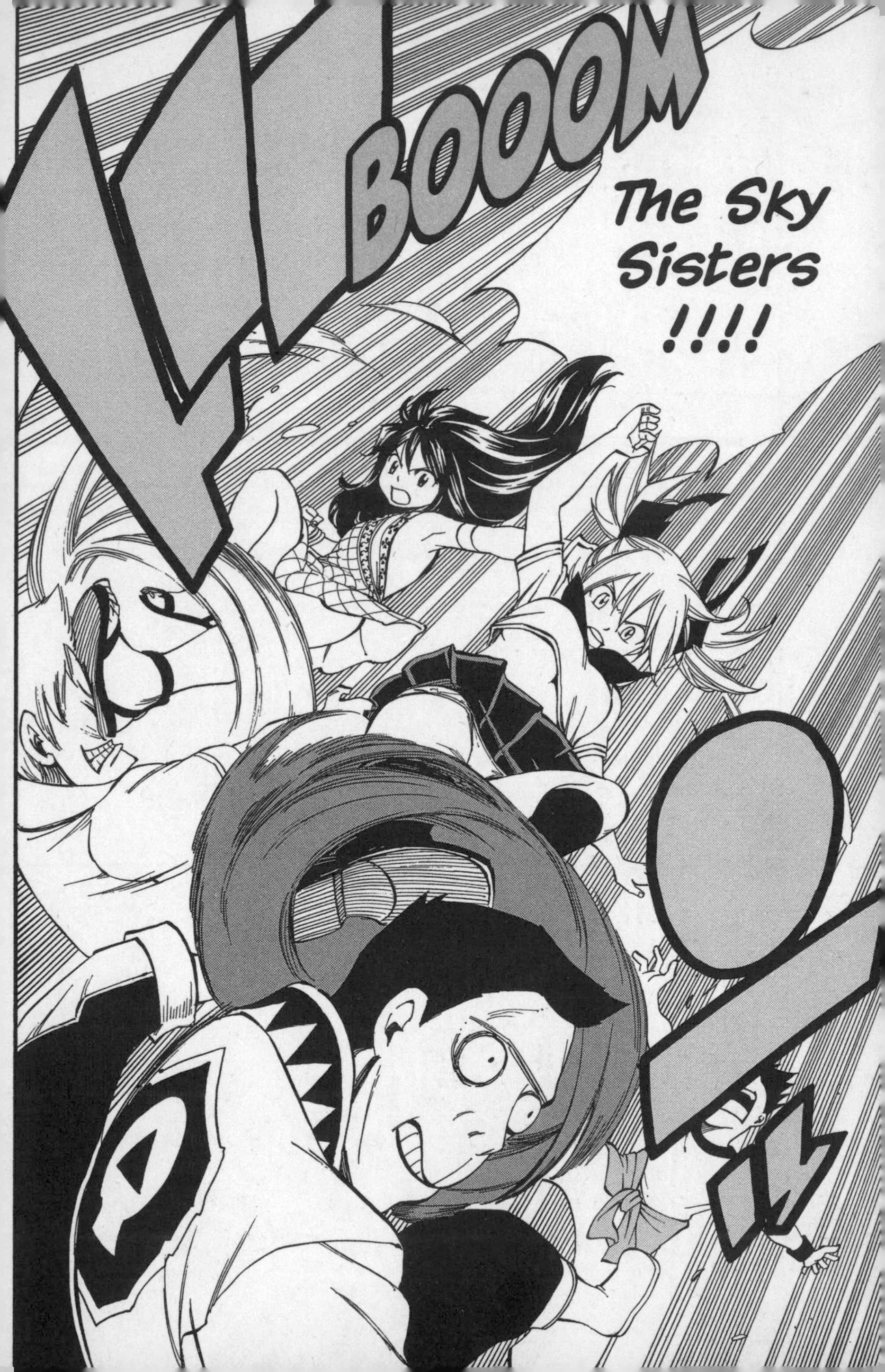
BOOOM
The Sky Sisters !!!!

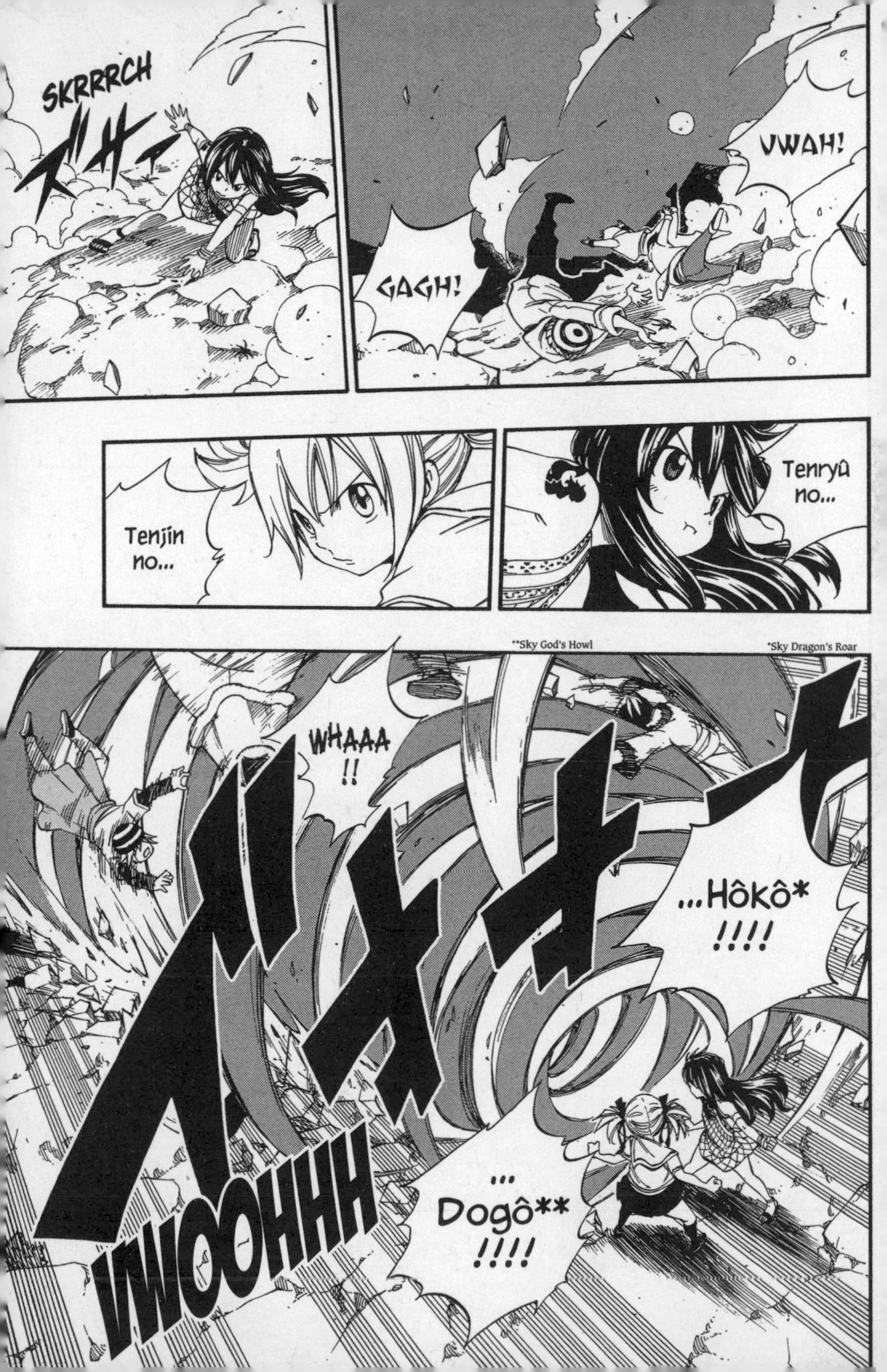
VWAH!
GAGH!
SKRRRCH
Tenryû no...
Tenjin no...
WHAAA !!
...Hôkô* !!!!
... Dogô** !!!!
VWOOHHH

*Sky Dragon's Roar

**Sky God's Howl

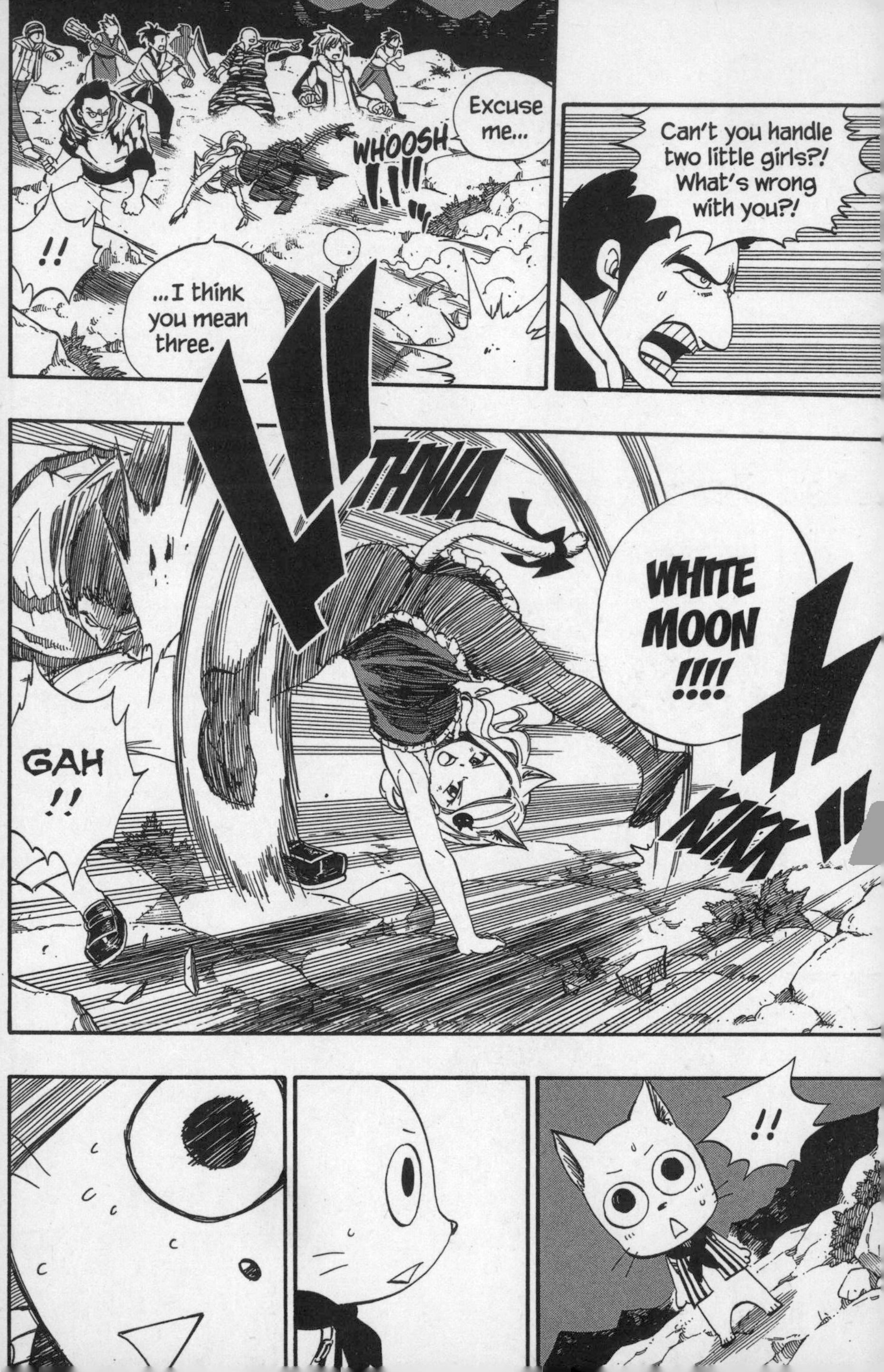
Can't you handle two little girls?! What's wrong with you?!
Excuse me...
WHOOSH!!!!
!!
...I think you mean three.
THWA
WHITE MOON!!!!
KIKK!!
GAH!!
!!

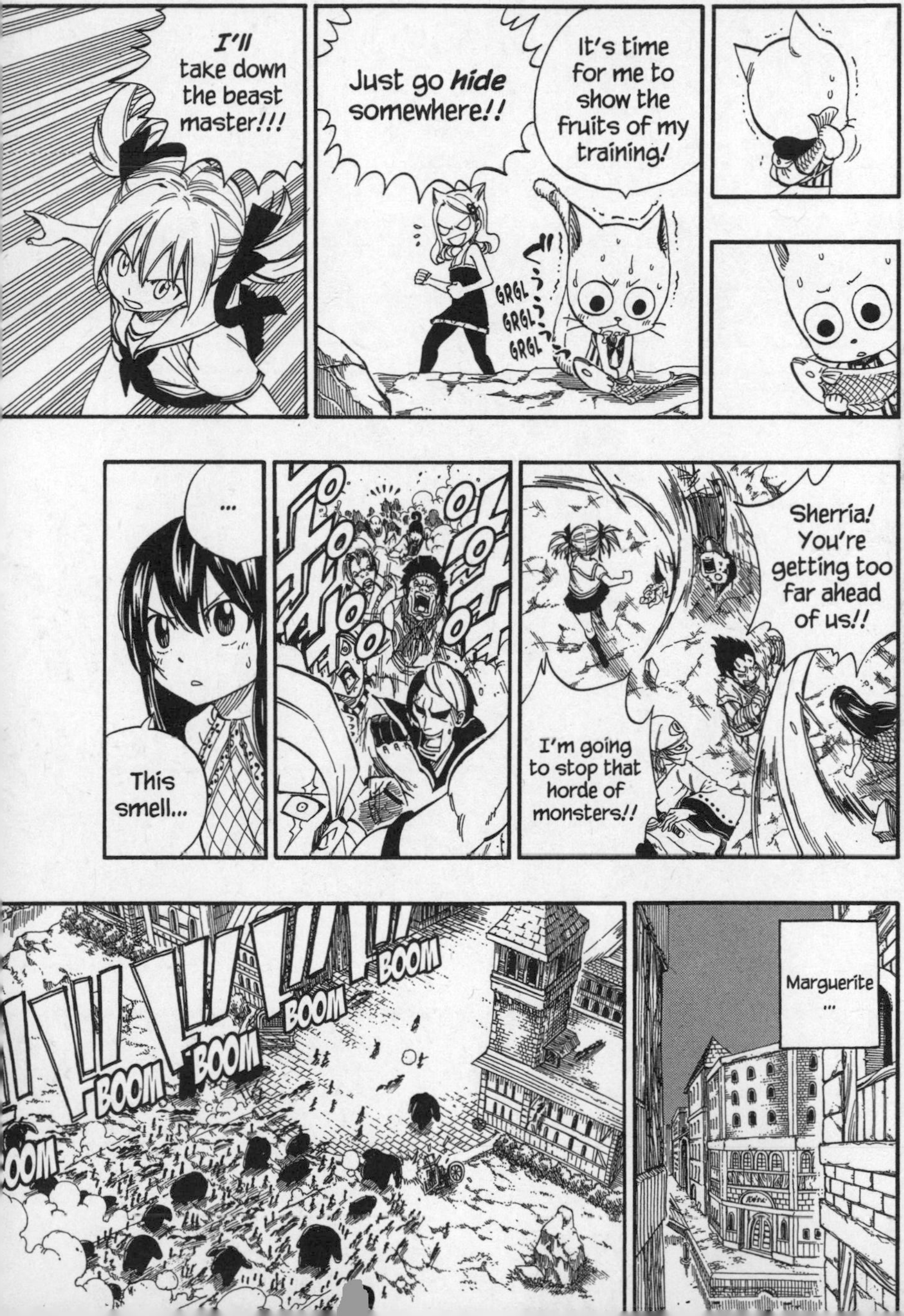
It's time for me to show the fruits of my training!
Just go *hide* somewhere!!
GRGL GRGL GRGL
I'll take down the beast master!!!
Sherria! You're getting too far ahead of us!!
I'm going to stop that horde of monsters!!
...
This smell...
Marguerite ...
BOOM
BOOM
BOOM
BOOM
OOM

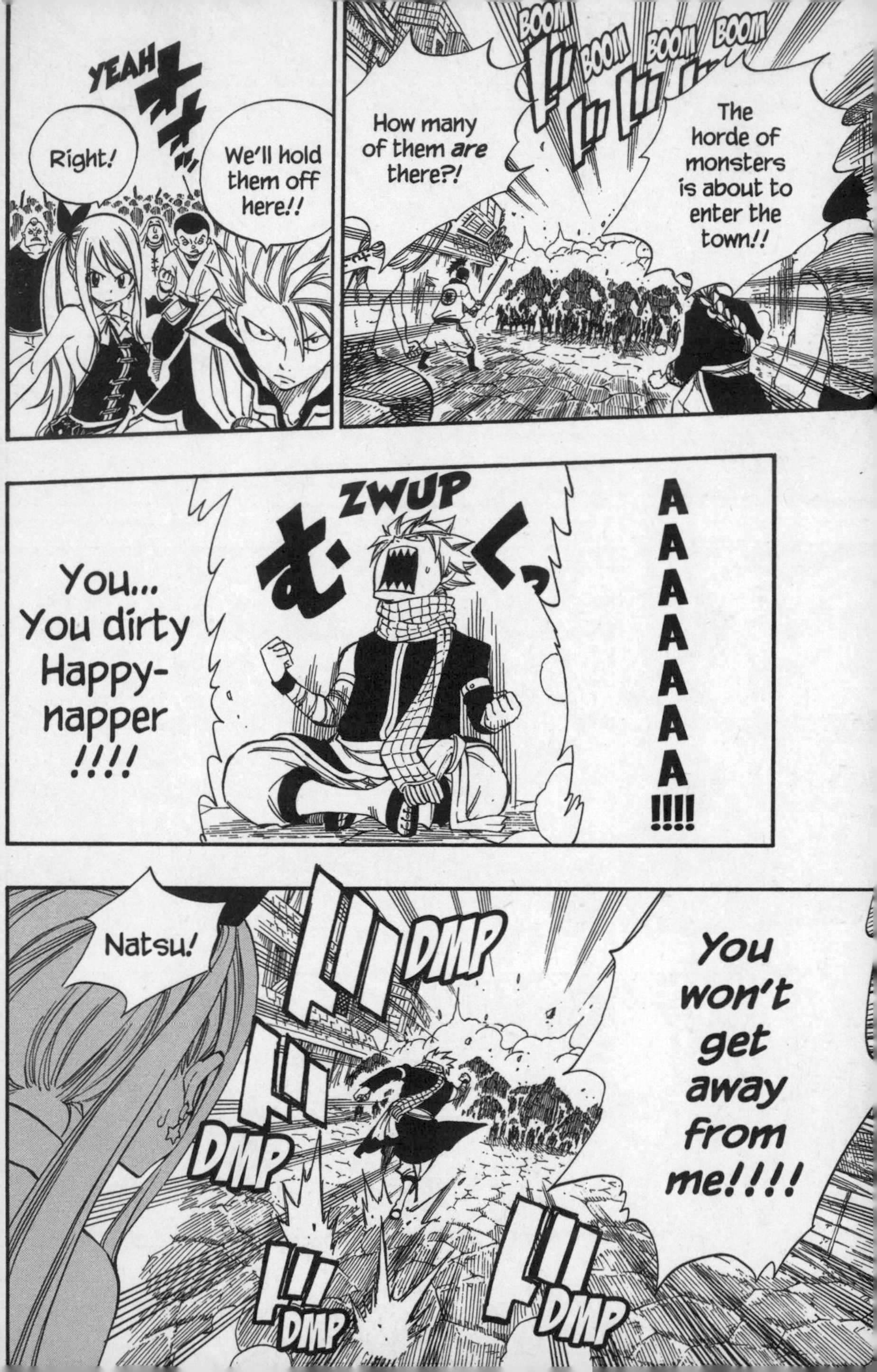
BOOM BOOM BOOM BOOM
The horde of monsters is about to enter the town!!
How many of them are there?!
YEAH
We'll hold them off here!!
Right!
AAAAAAAAA!!!!
ZWUP
むくっ
You... You dirty Happy-napper!!!!
You won't get away from me!!!!
DMP
DMP
DMP
DMP
Natsu!

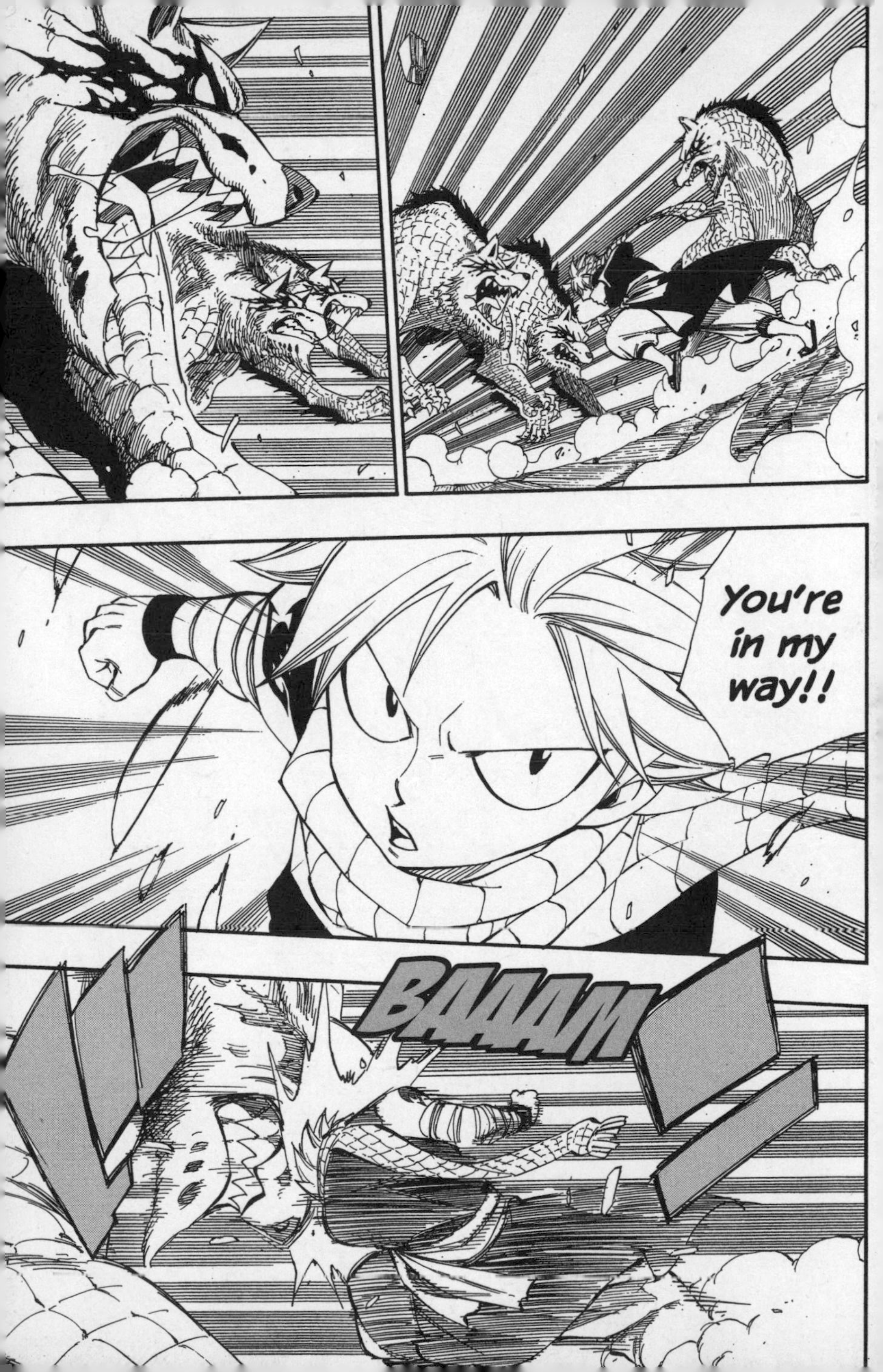
You're in my way!!
BAAAM

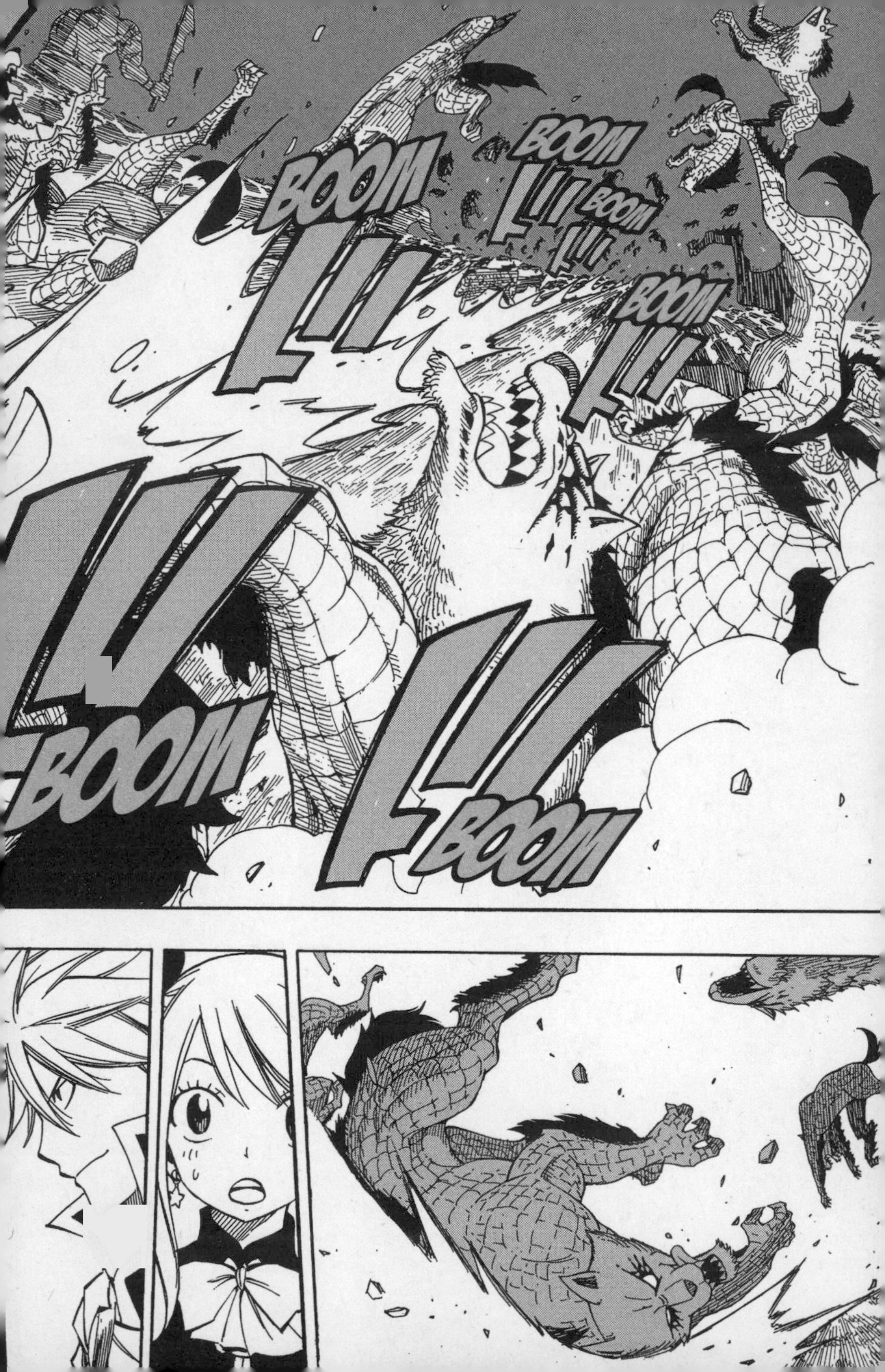
BOOM
BOOM
BOOM
BOOM
BOOM
BOOM

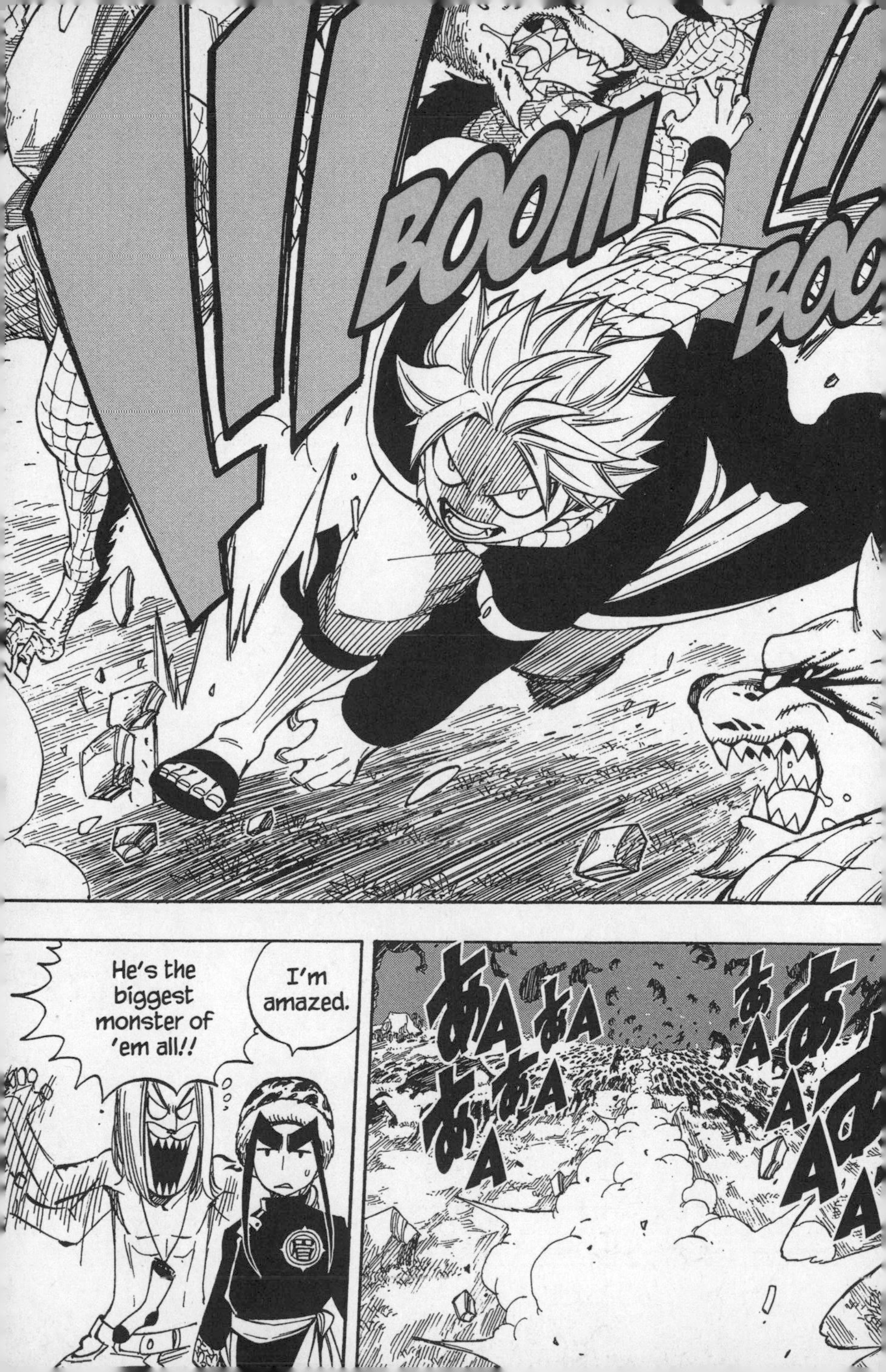
BOOM
あA
あA
I'm amazed.
He's the biggest monster of 'em all!!

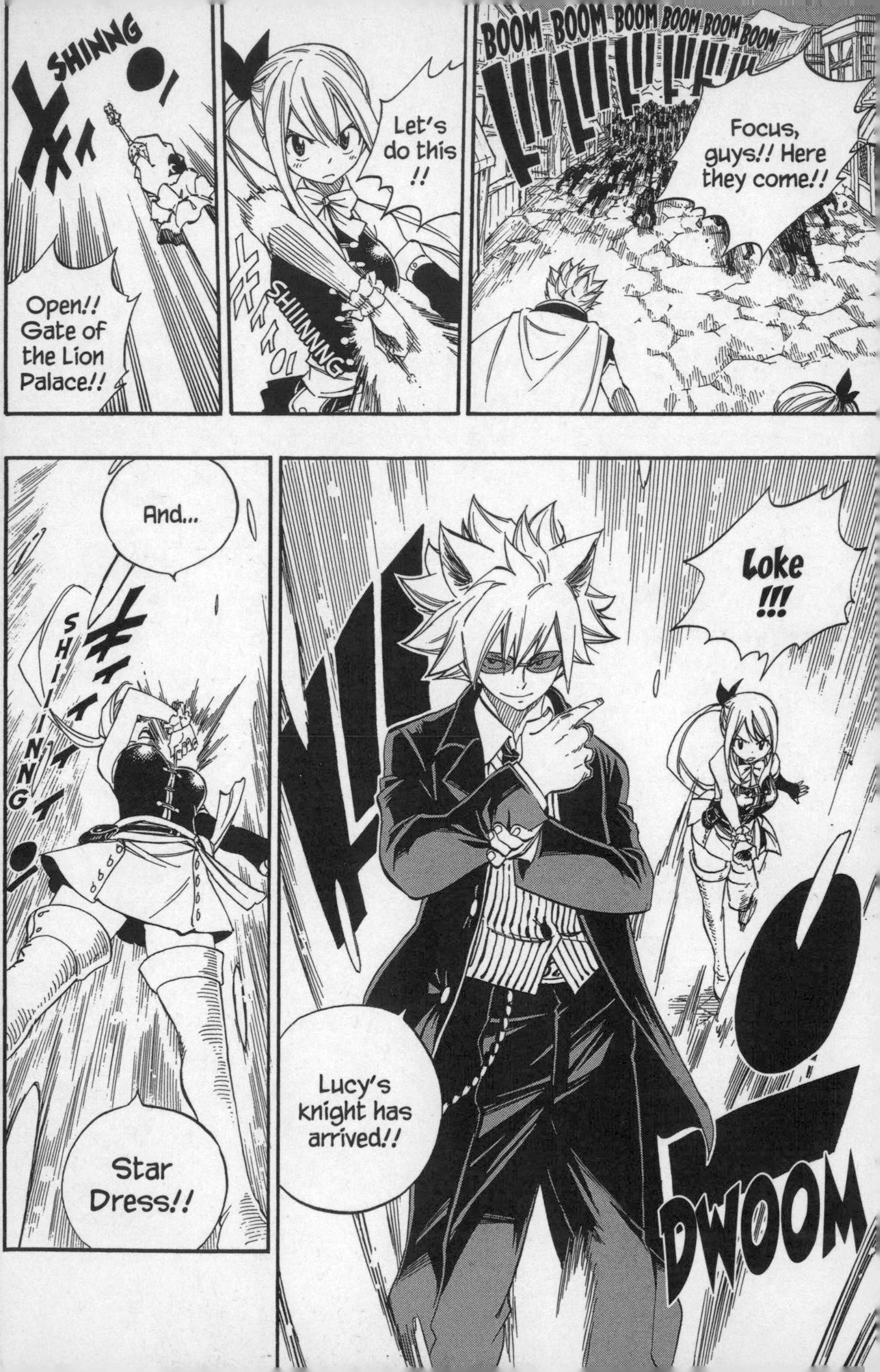
BOOM BOOM BOOM BOOM BOOM BOOM
Focus, guys!! Here they come!!
Let's do this!!
SHIIINNNG
SHINNG
Open!! Gate of the Lion Palace!!
Loke!!!
Lucy's knight has arrived!!
DWOOM
And...
SHIIINNNG
Star Dress!!

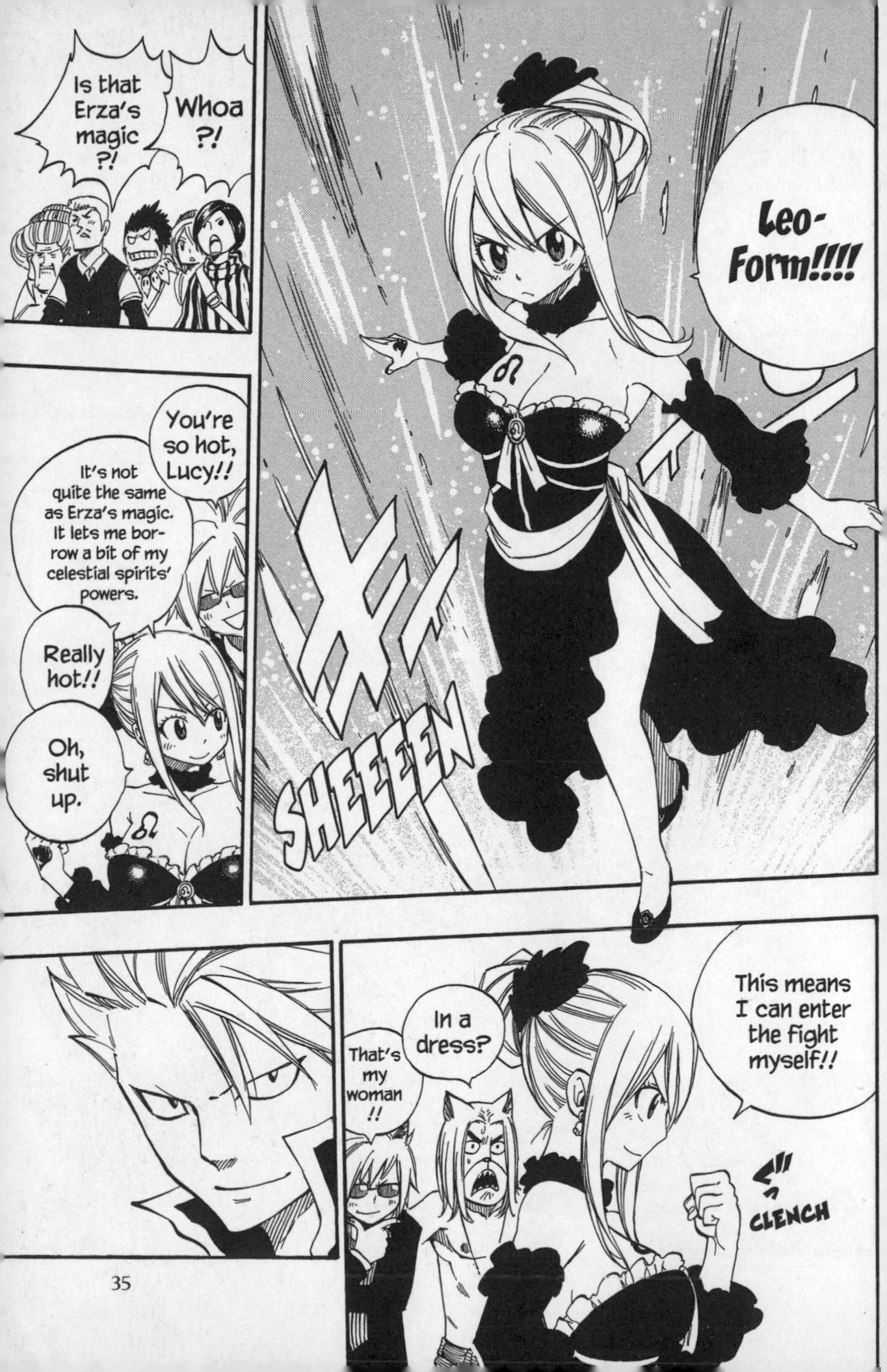
Leo-Form!!!!
SHEEEEN
Whoa ?!
Is that Erza's magic ?!
You're so hot, Lucy!!
It's not quite the same as Erza's magic. It lets me borrow a bit of my celestial spirits' powers.
Really hot!!
Oh, shut up.
This means I can enter the fight myself!!
CLENCH
In a dress?
That's my woman !!

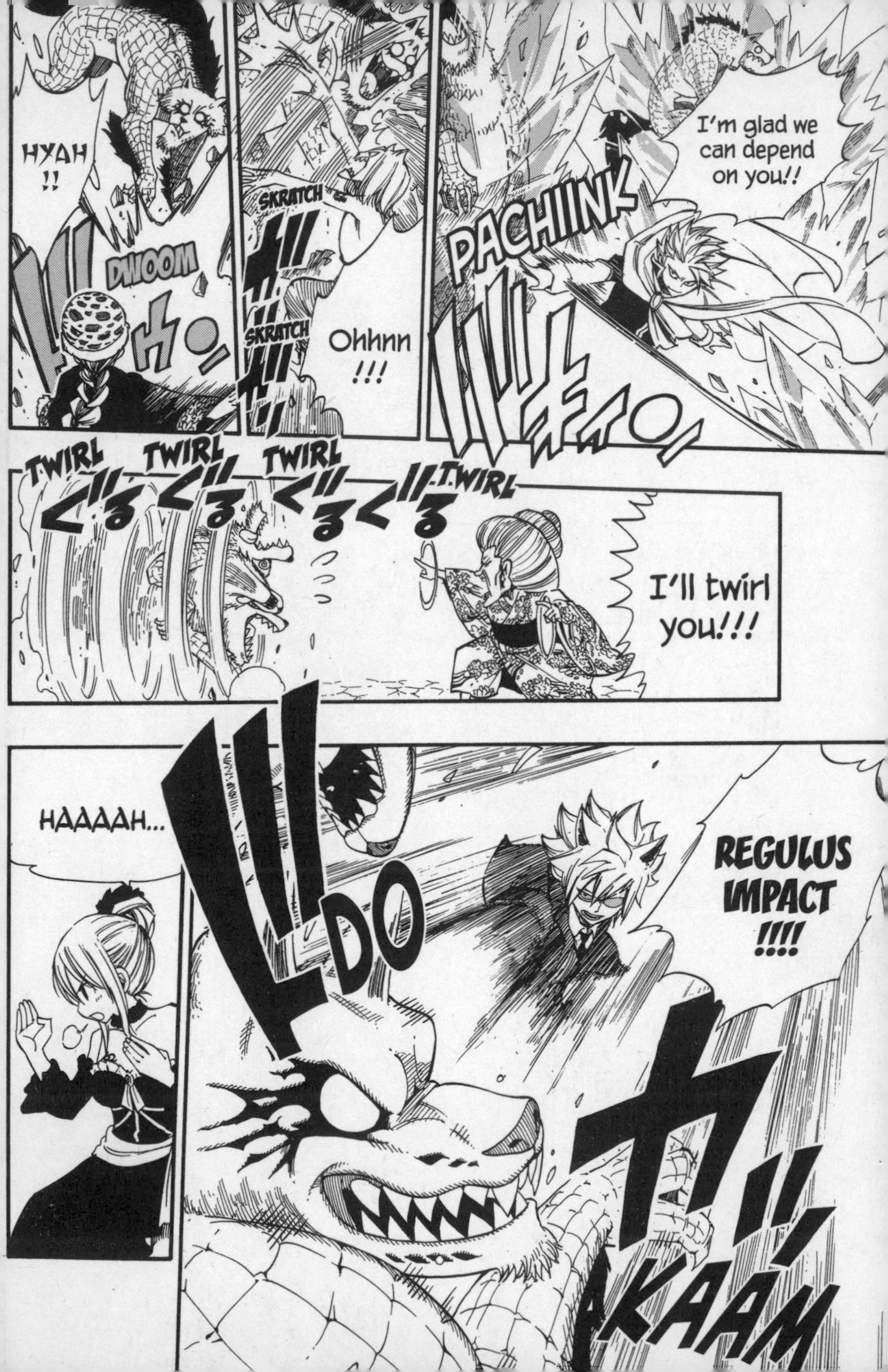
I'm glad we can depend on you!!
PACHIINK
SKRATCH
SKRATCH
Ohhnn !!!
HYAH !!
DWOOM
I'll twirl you!!!
TWIRL
TWIRL
TWIRL
T.WIRL
REGULUS IMPACT !!!!
DO
KAAM
HAAAAH...

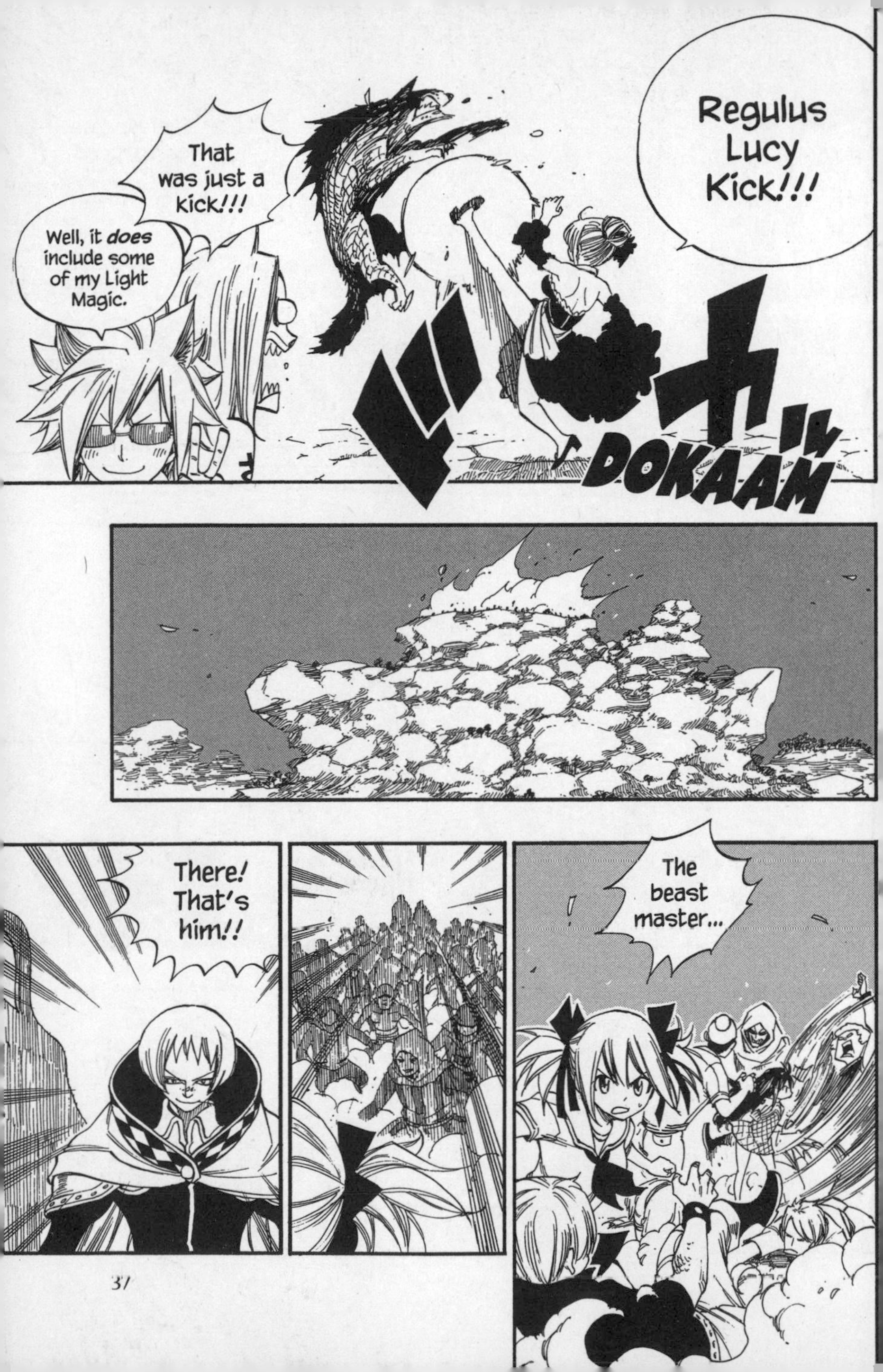
Regulus Lucy Kick!!!
DOKAAM
That was just a kick!!!
Well, it *does* include some of my Light Magic.
The beast master...
There! That's him!!

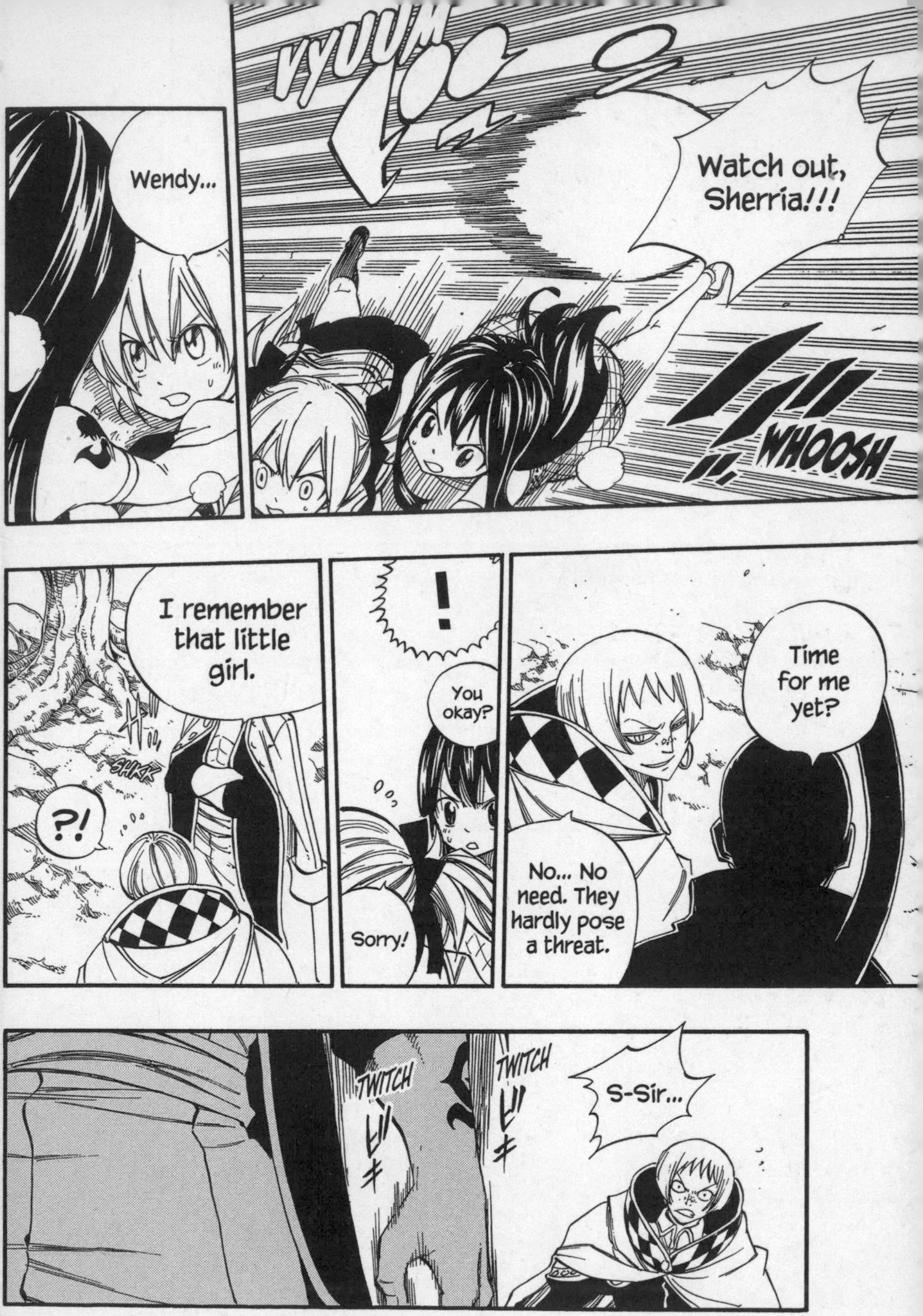

VYUUM
Watch out, Sherria!!!
WHOOSH
Wendy...
Time for me yet?
No... No need. They hardly pose a threat.
!
You okay?
Sorry!
I remember that little girl.
SHKK
?!
TWITCH
TWITCH
S-Sir...

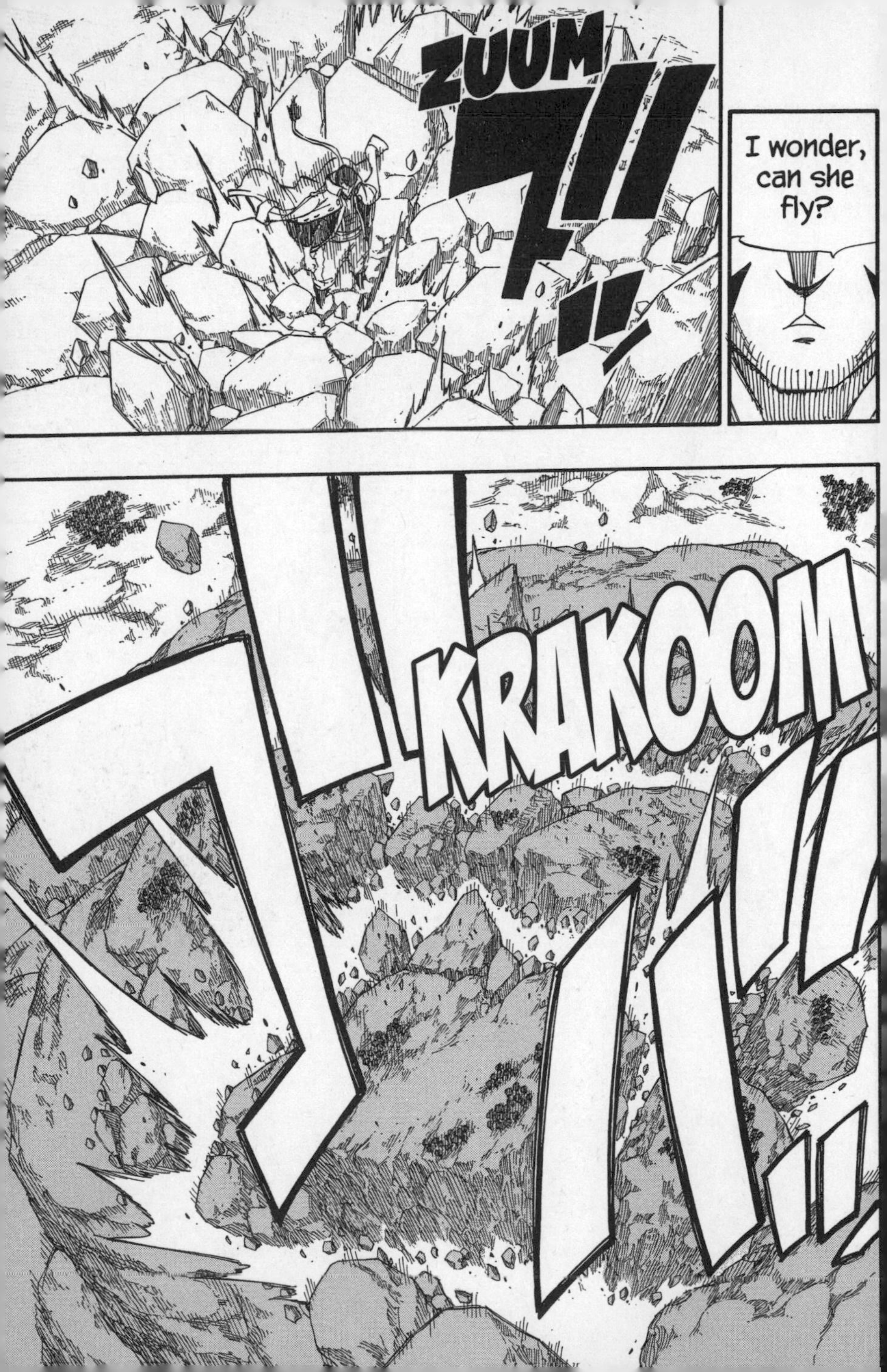
I wonder, can she fly?
ZUUM
KRAKOOM

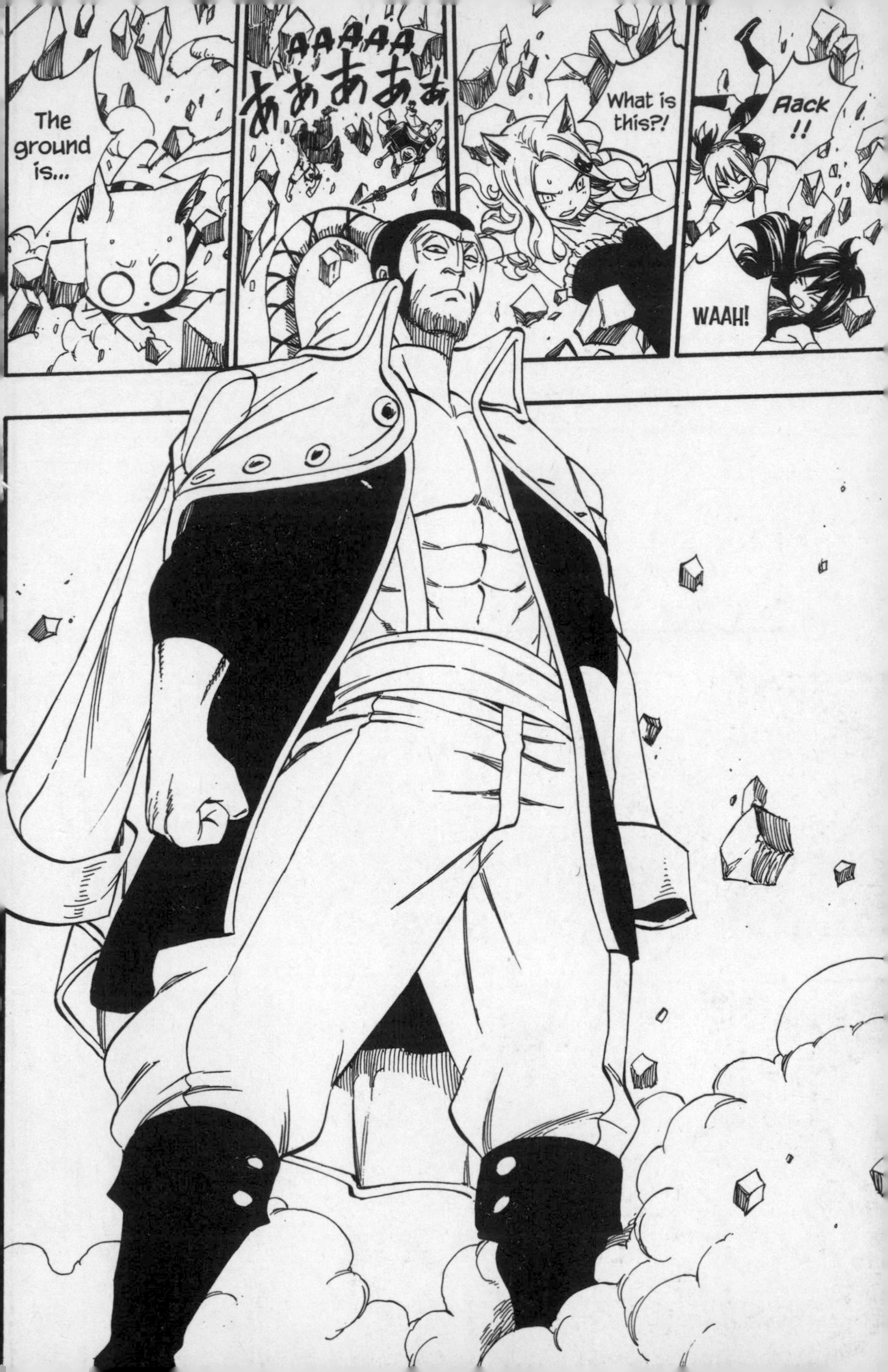
Aack !!
WAAH!
What is this?!
AAAAA
あああああ
The ground is...

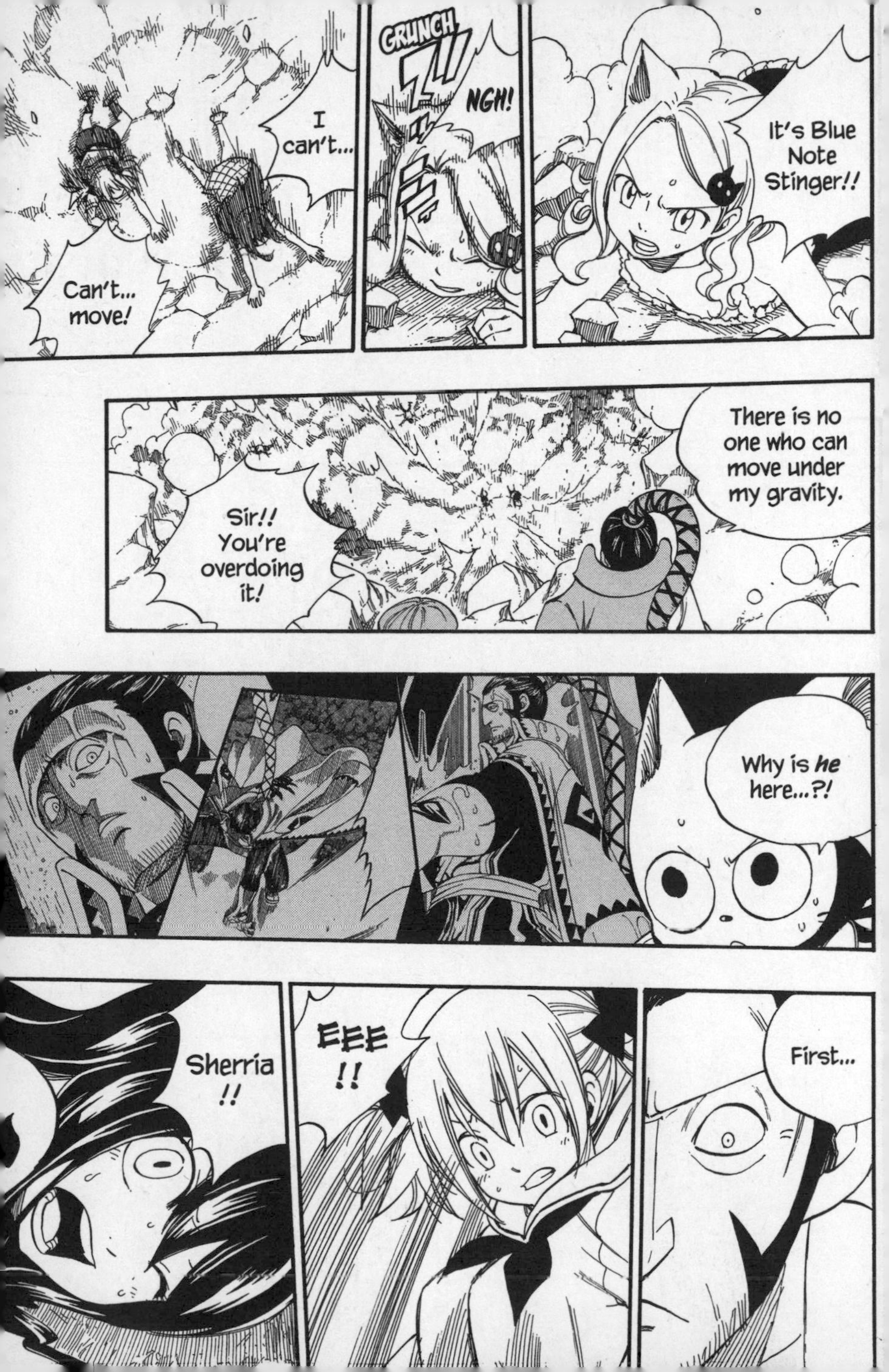
It's Blue Note Stinger!!
GRUNCH
NGH!
I can't...
Can't... move!
There is no one who can move under my gravity.
Sir!! You're overdoing it!
Why is *he* here...?!
First...
EEE !!
Sherria !!

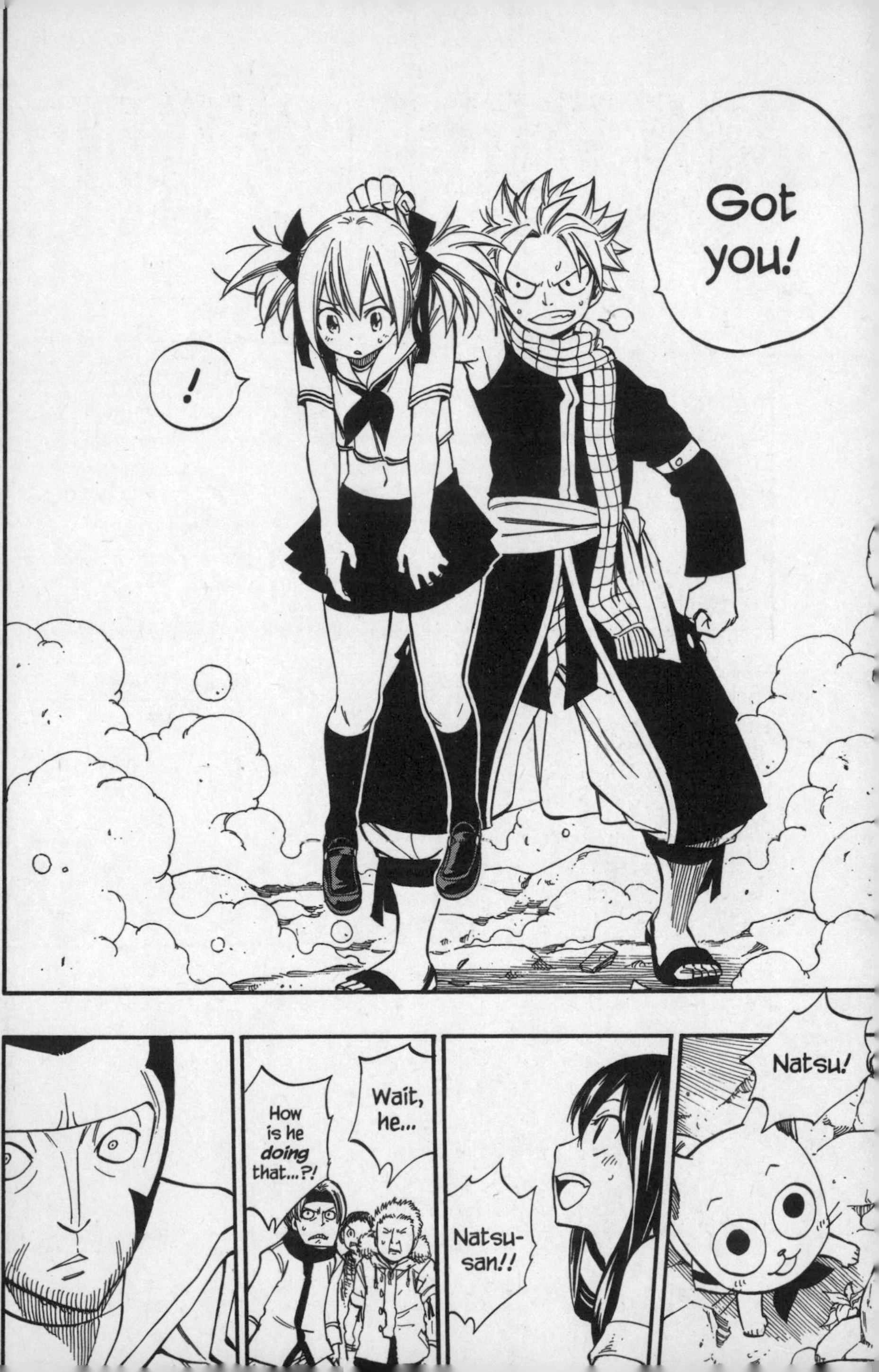
Got you!
!
Natsu!
Natsu-san!!
Wait, he...
How is he *doing* that...?!

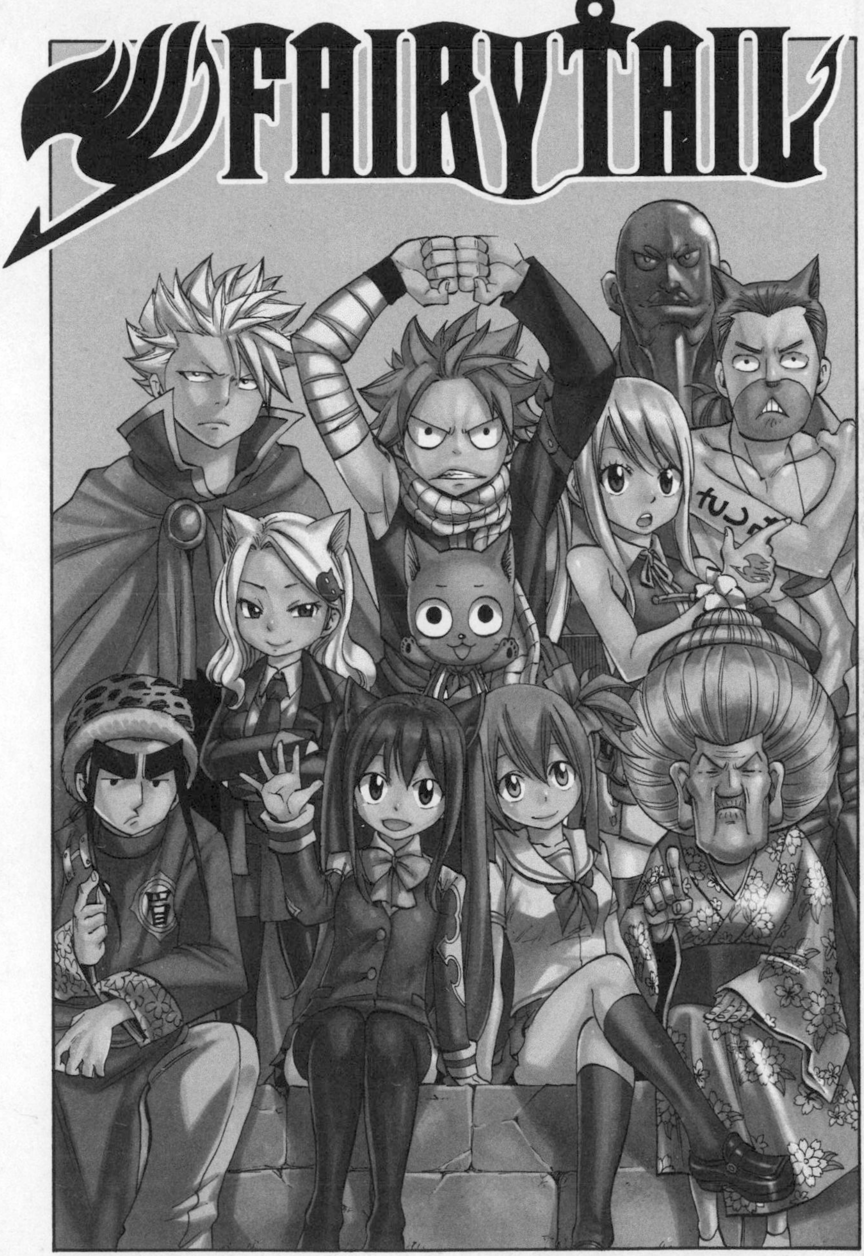
FAIRY TAIL

Chapter 423: Do It All for Love

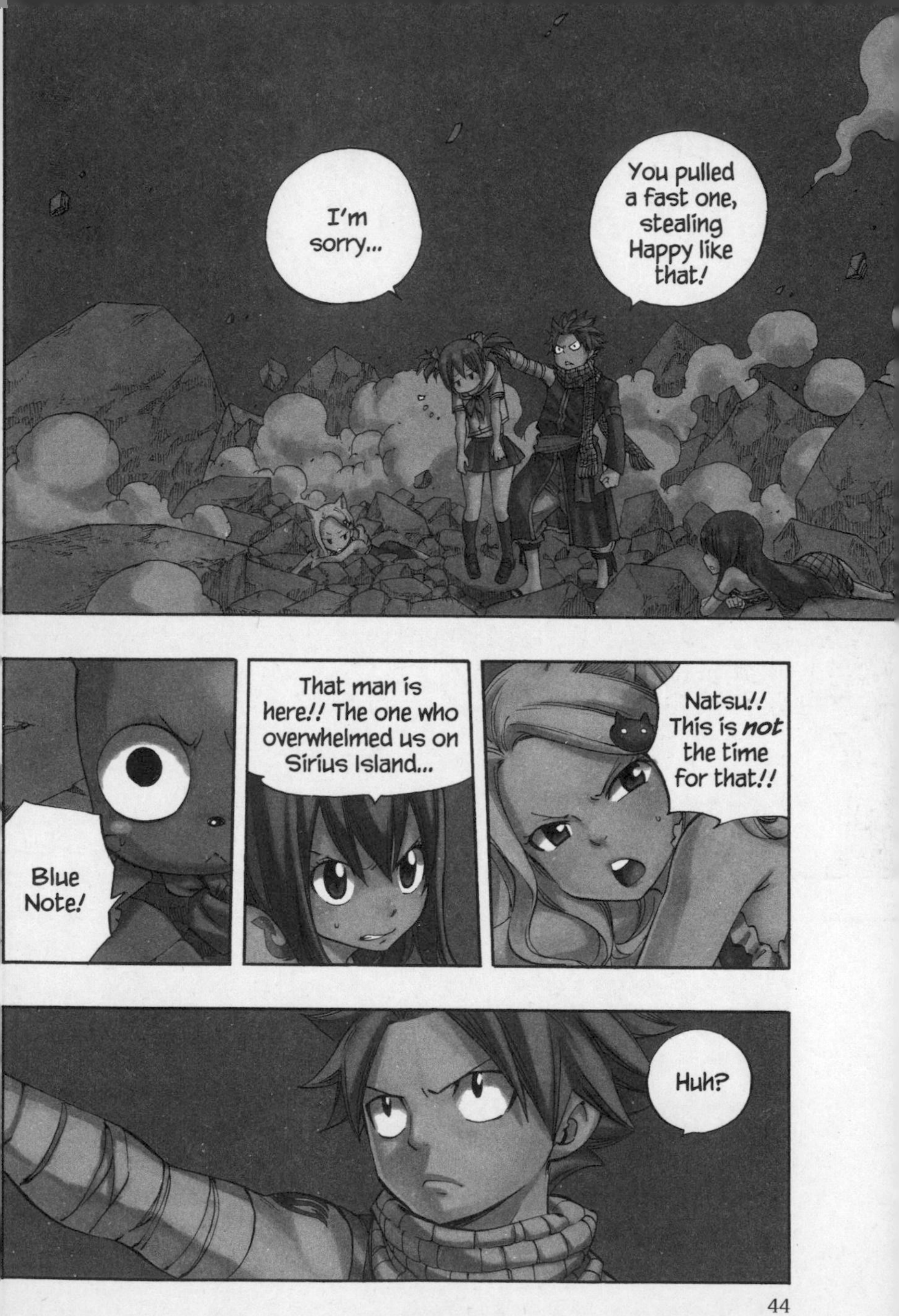
You pulled a fast one, stealing Happy like that!
I'm sorry...
Natsu!! This is *not* the time for that!!
That man is here!! The one who overwhelmed us on Sirius Island...
Blue Note!
Huh?

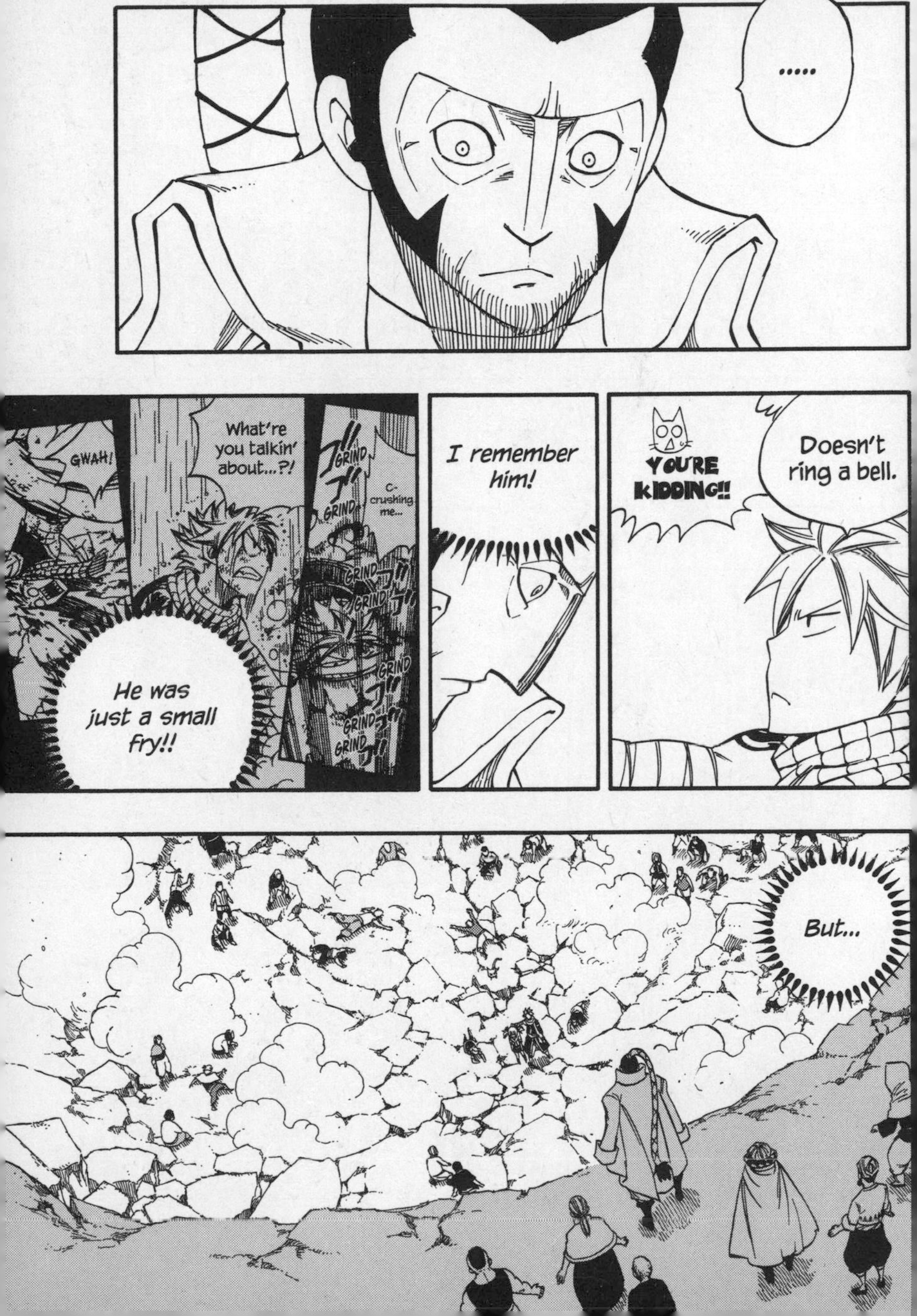
.....
Doesn't ring a bell.
YOU'RE KIDDING!!
I remember him!
GRIND GRIND GRIND GRIND GRIND GRIND GRIND
C-crushing me...
What're you talkin' about...?!
GWAH!
He was just a small fry!!
But...

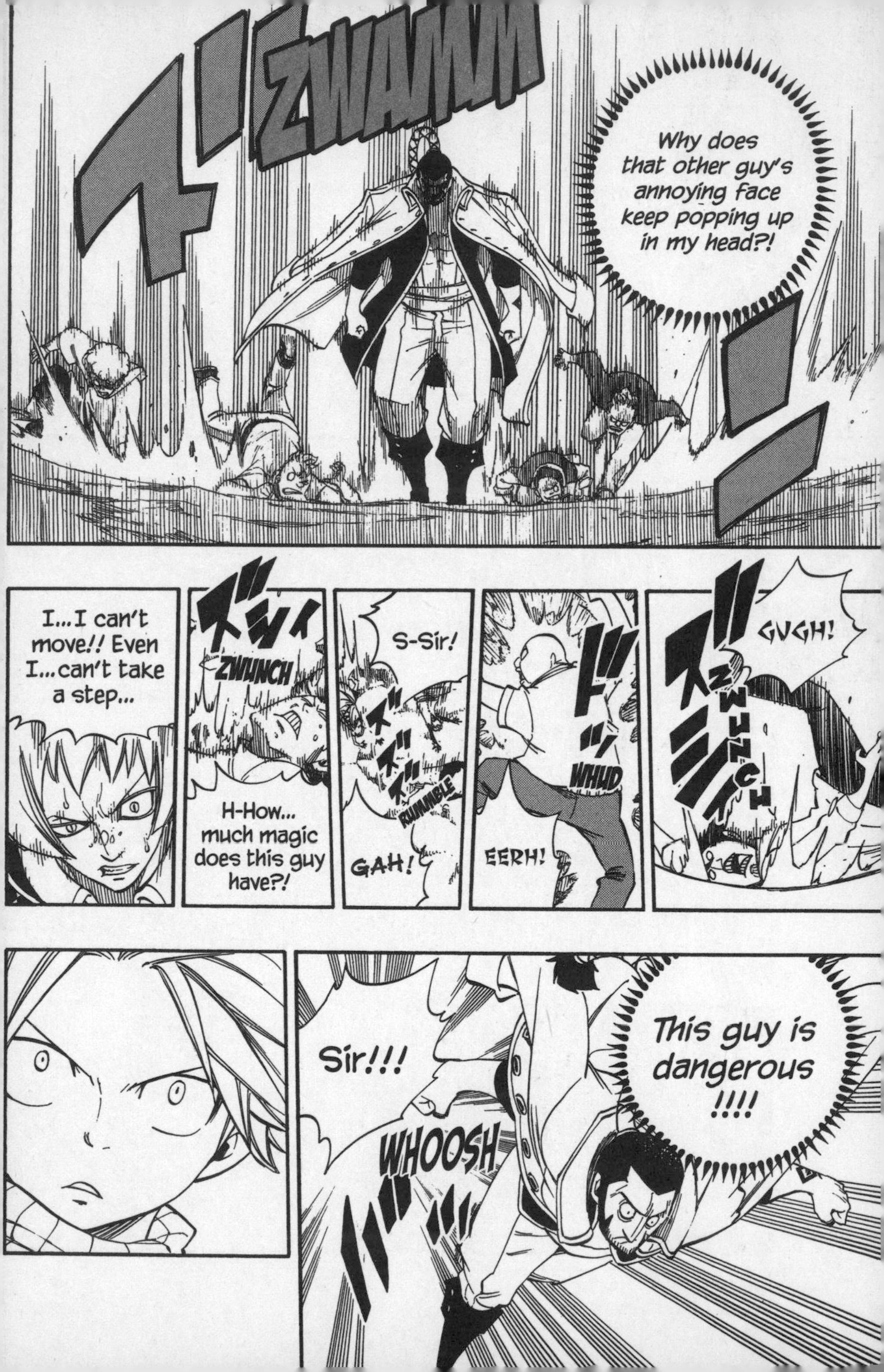
ZWAMM
Why does that other guy's annoying face keep popping up in my head?!
GUGH!
ZWUNCH
EERH!
WHUD
S-Sir!
RUMMBLE
GAH!
ZWUNCH
H-How... much magic does this guy have?!
I...I can't move!! Even I...can't take a step...
This guy is dangerous!!!!
Sir!!!
WHOOSH

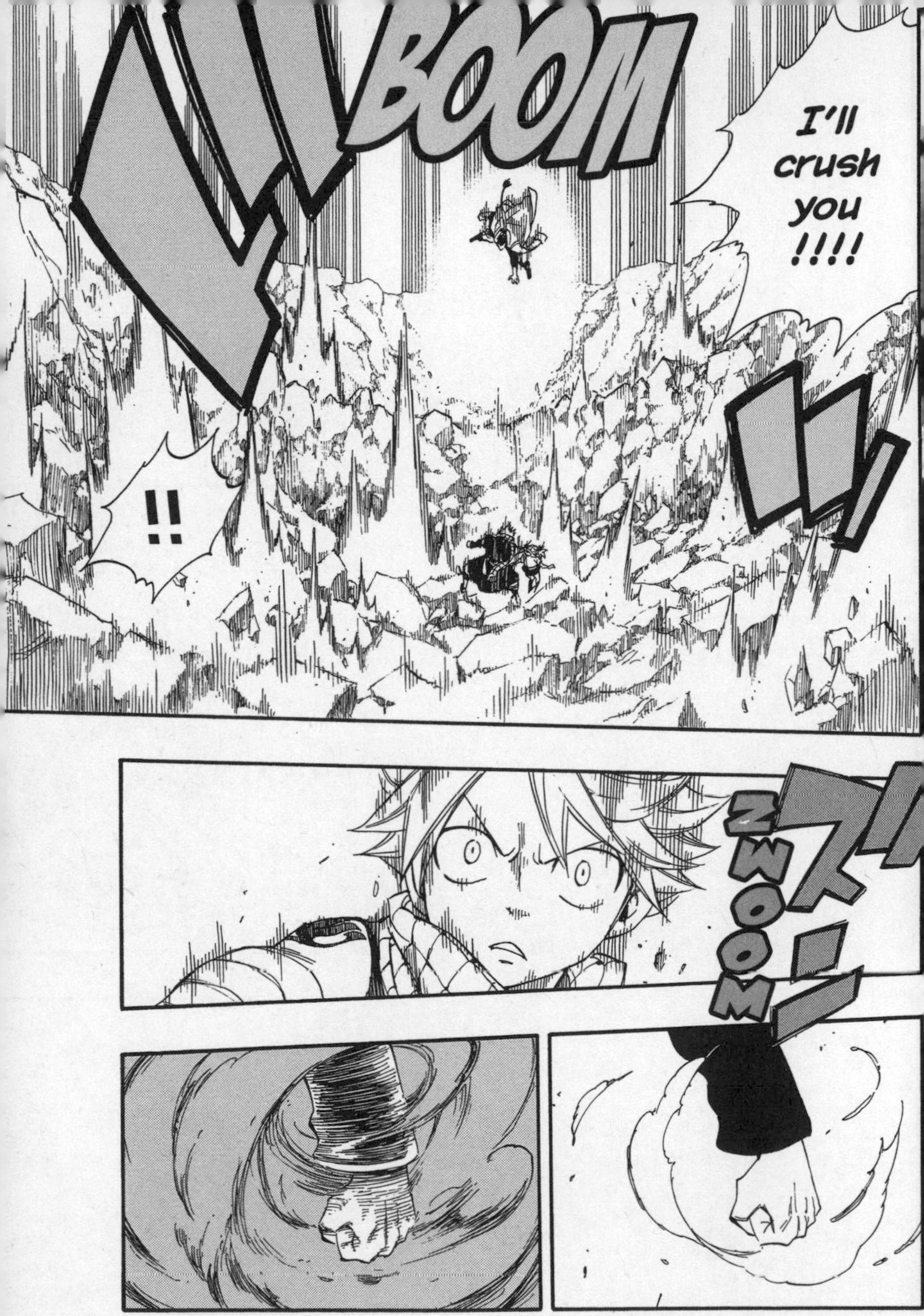
I'll crush you !!!!
BOOM
!!
ZWOOM

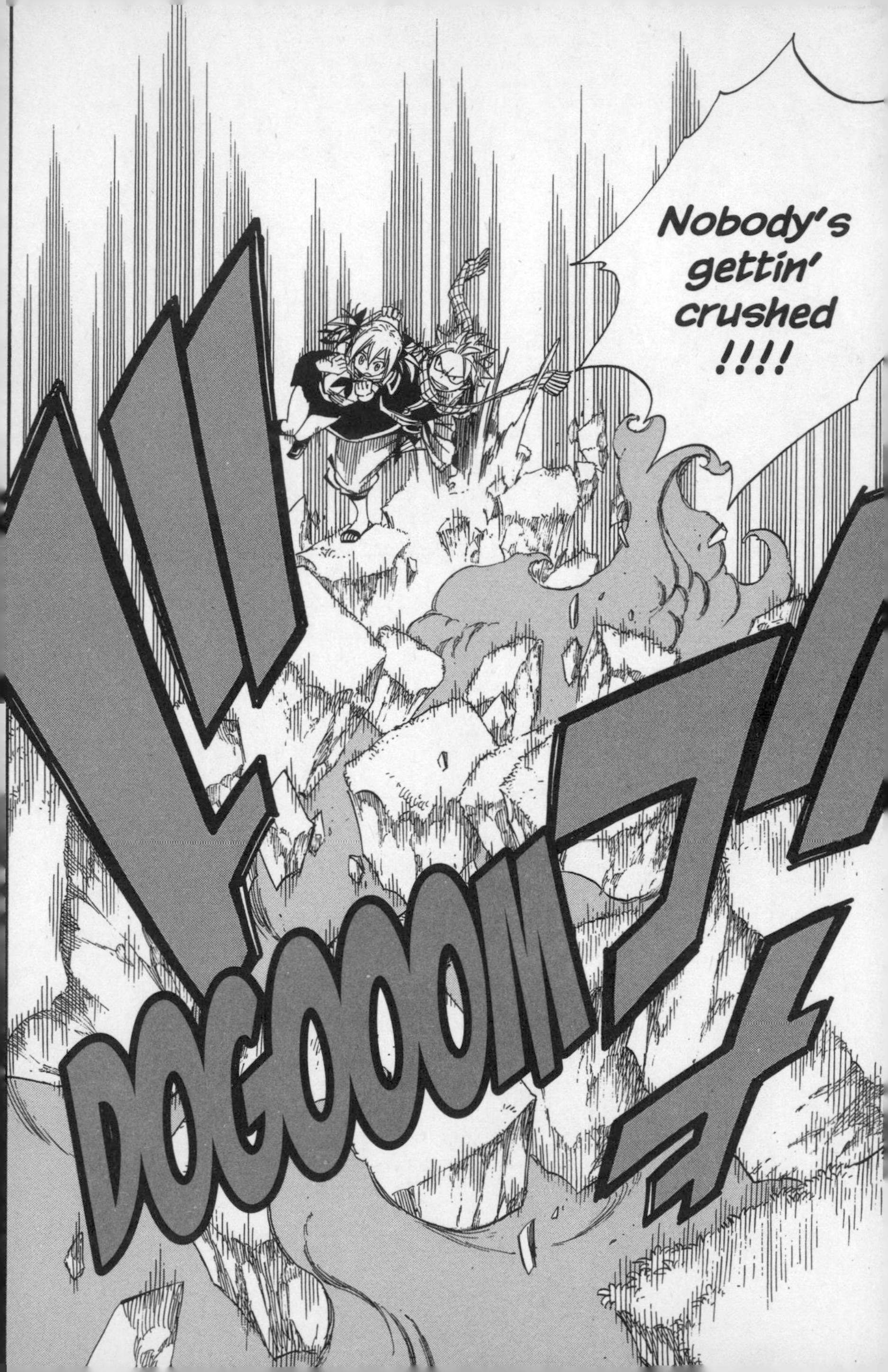
Nobody's gettin' crushed !!!!
DOGOOOM

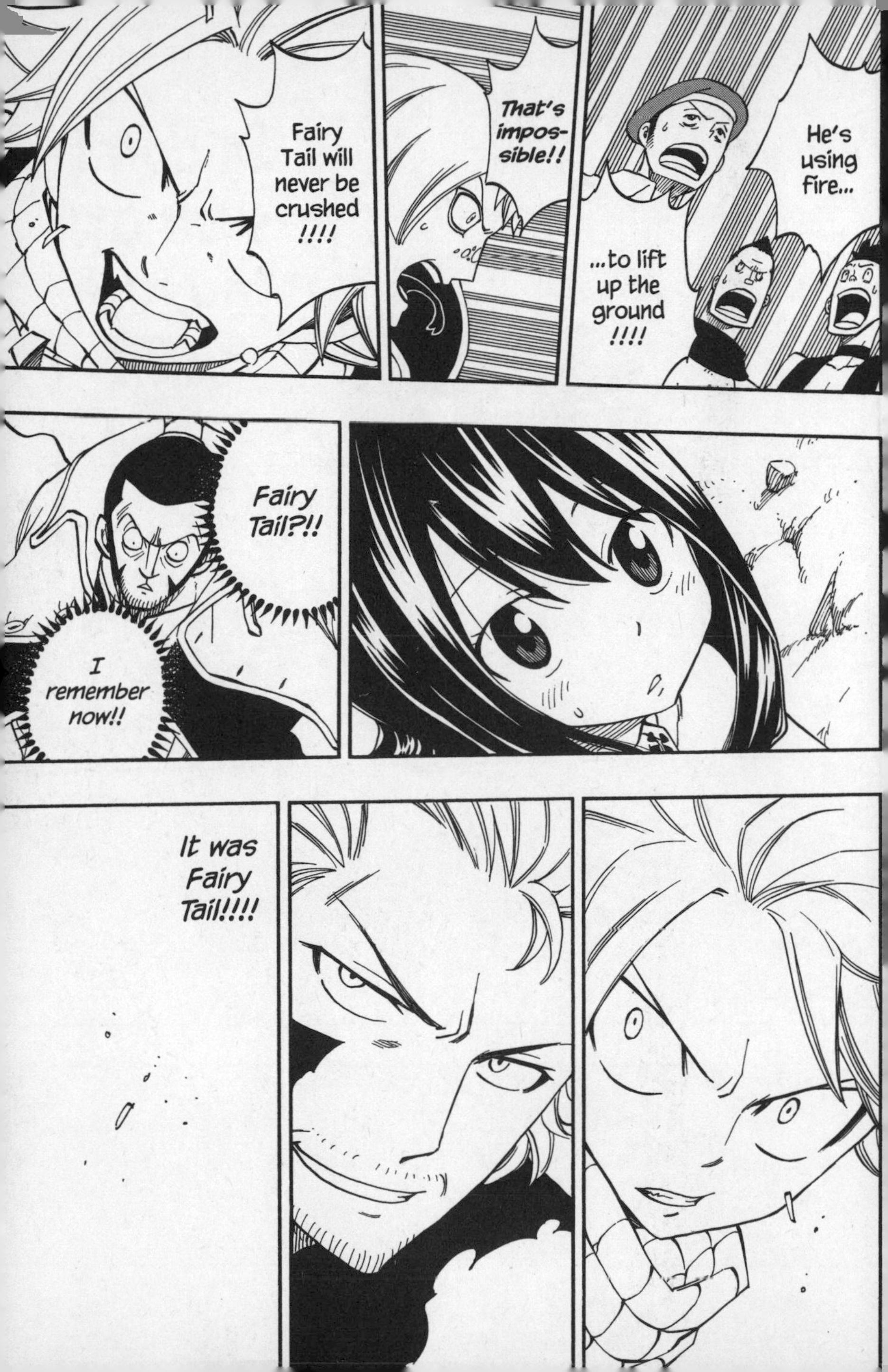
He's using fire...
...to lift up the ground !!!!
That's impos-sible!!
Fairy Tail will never be crushed !!!!
Fairy Tail?!!
I remember now!!
It was Fairy Tail!!!!

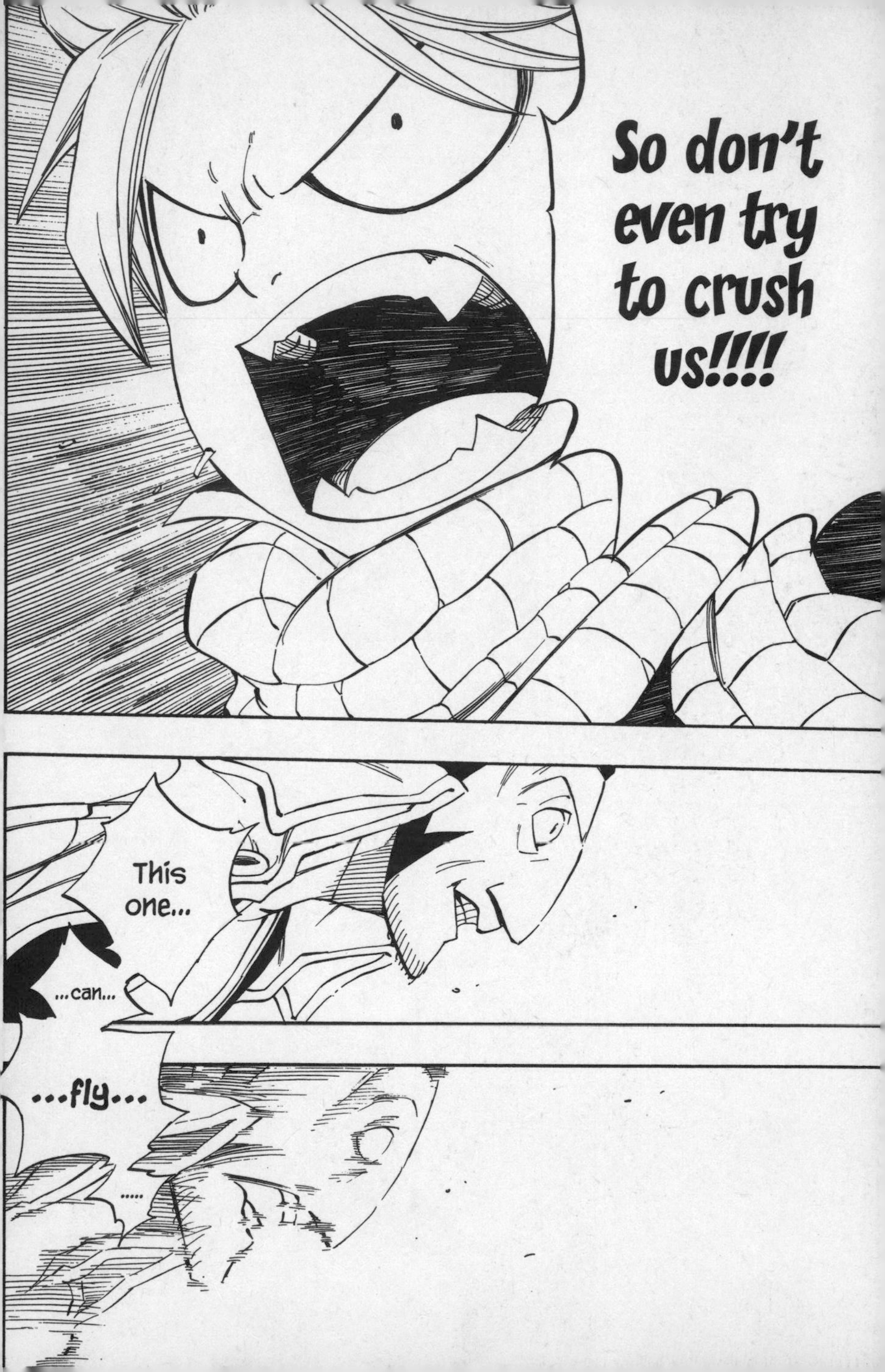
So don't even try to crush us!!!!
This one...
...can...
...fly...
.....

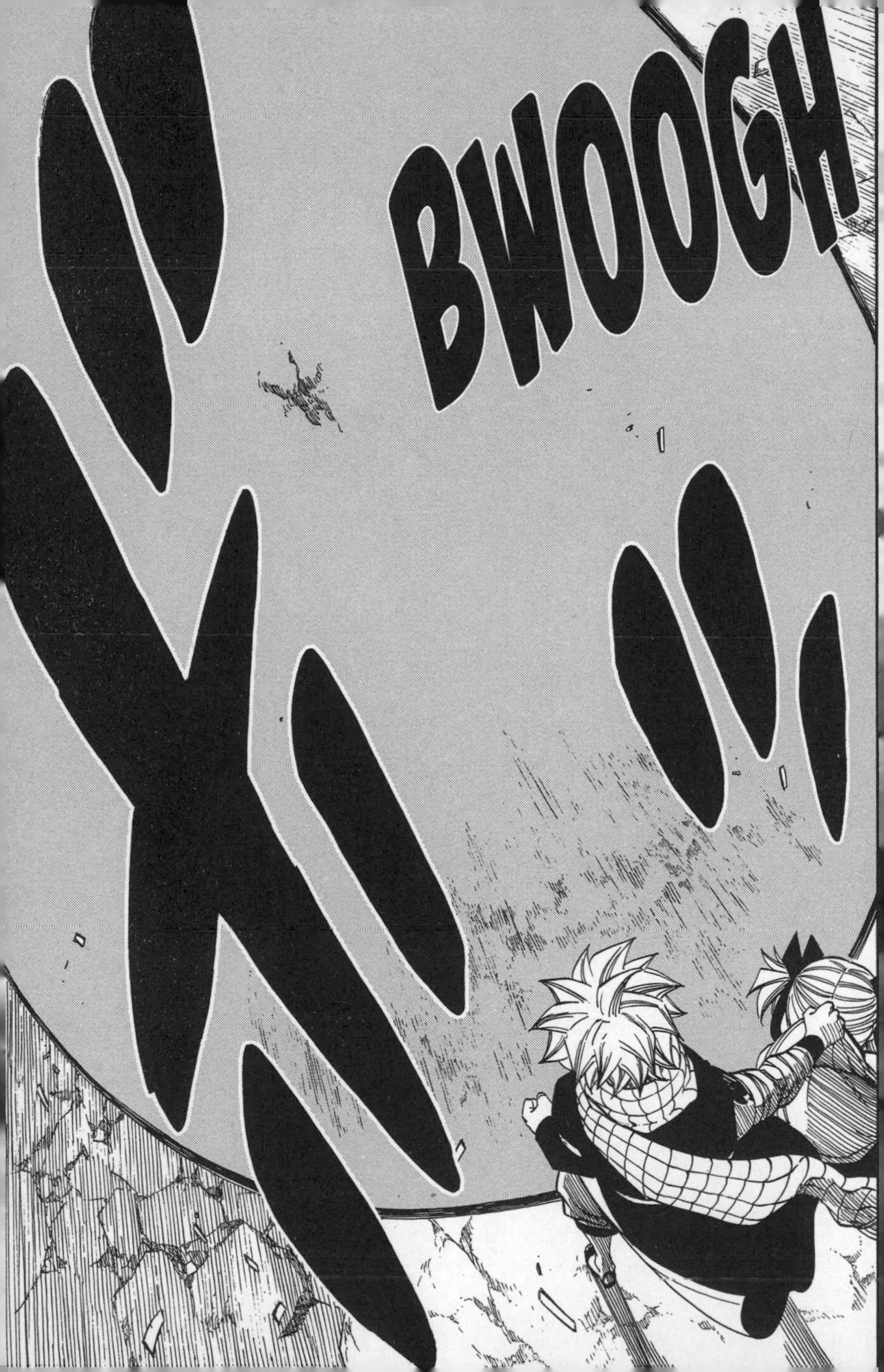
BWOOGH

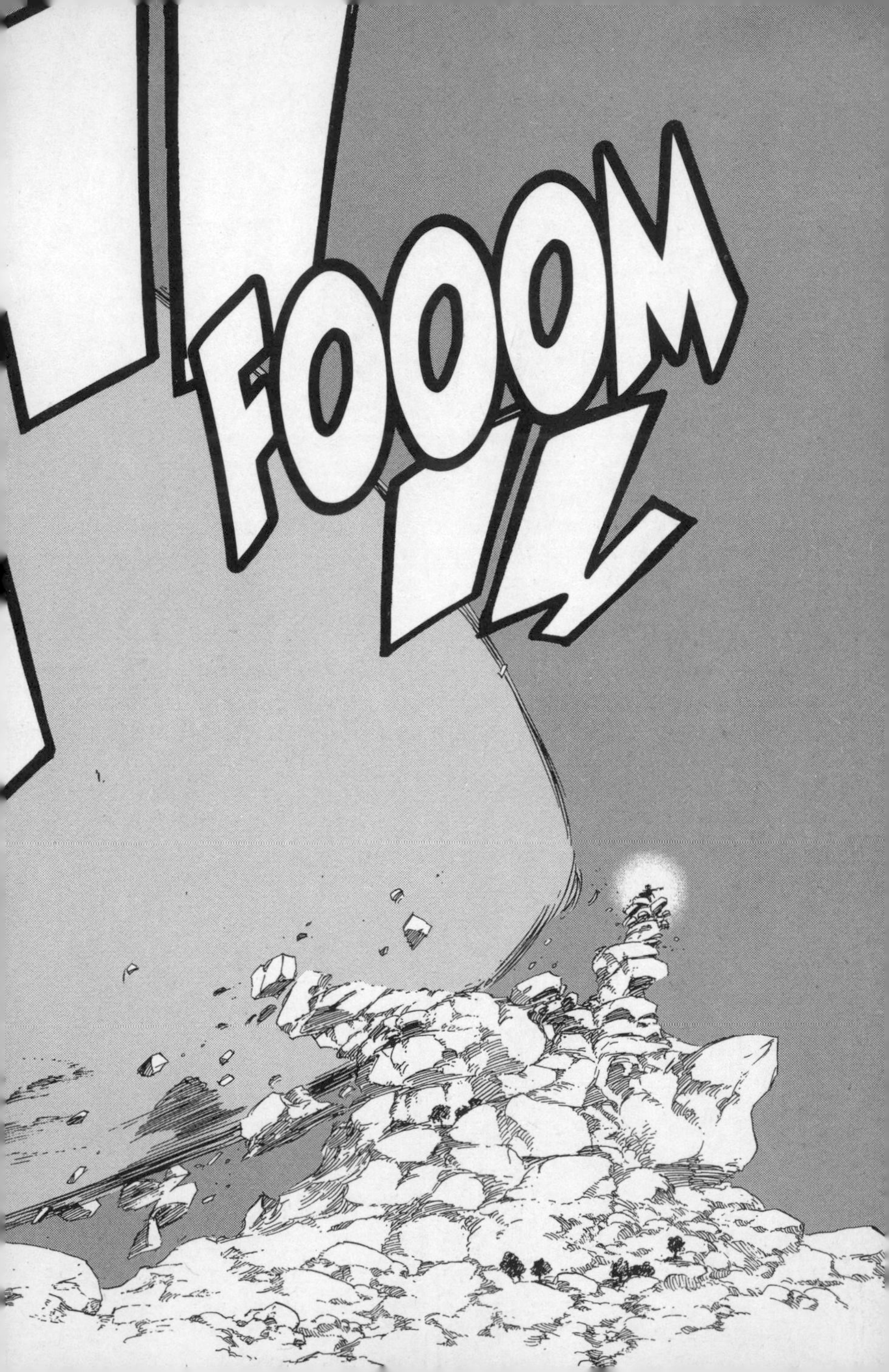
FOOOM

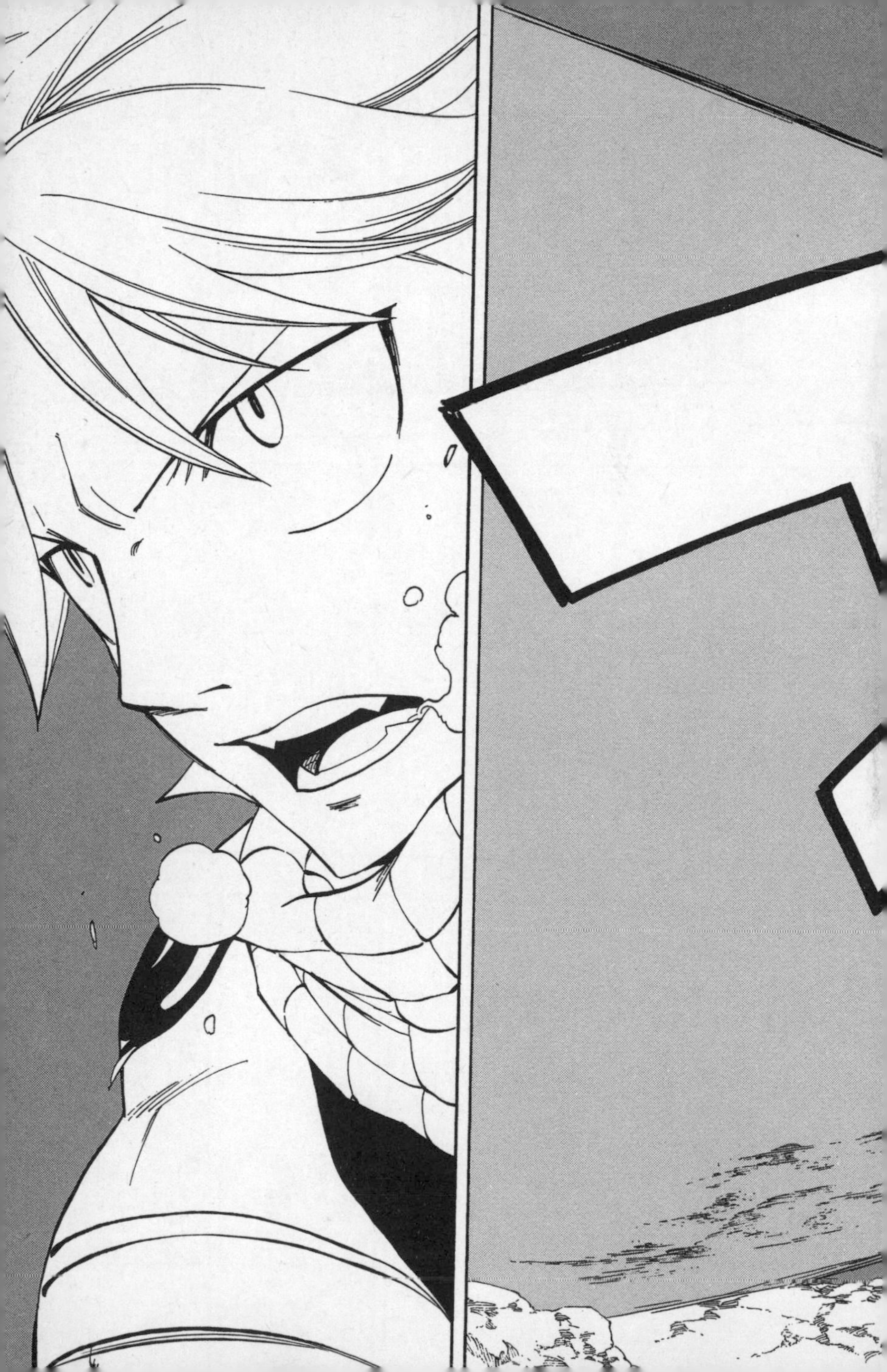

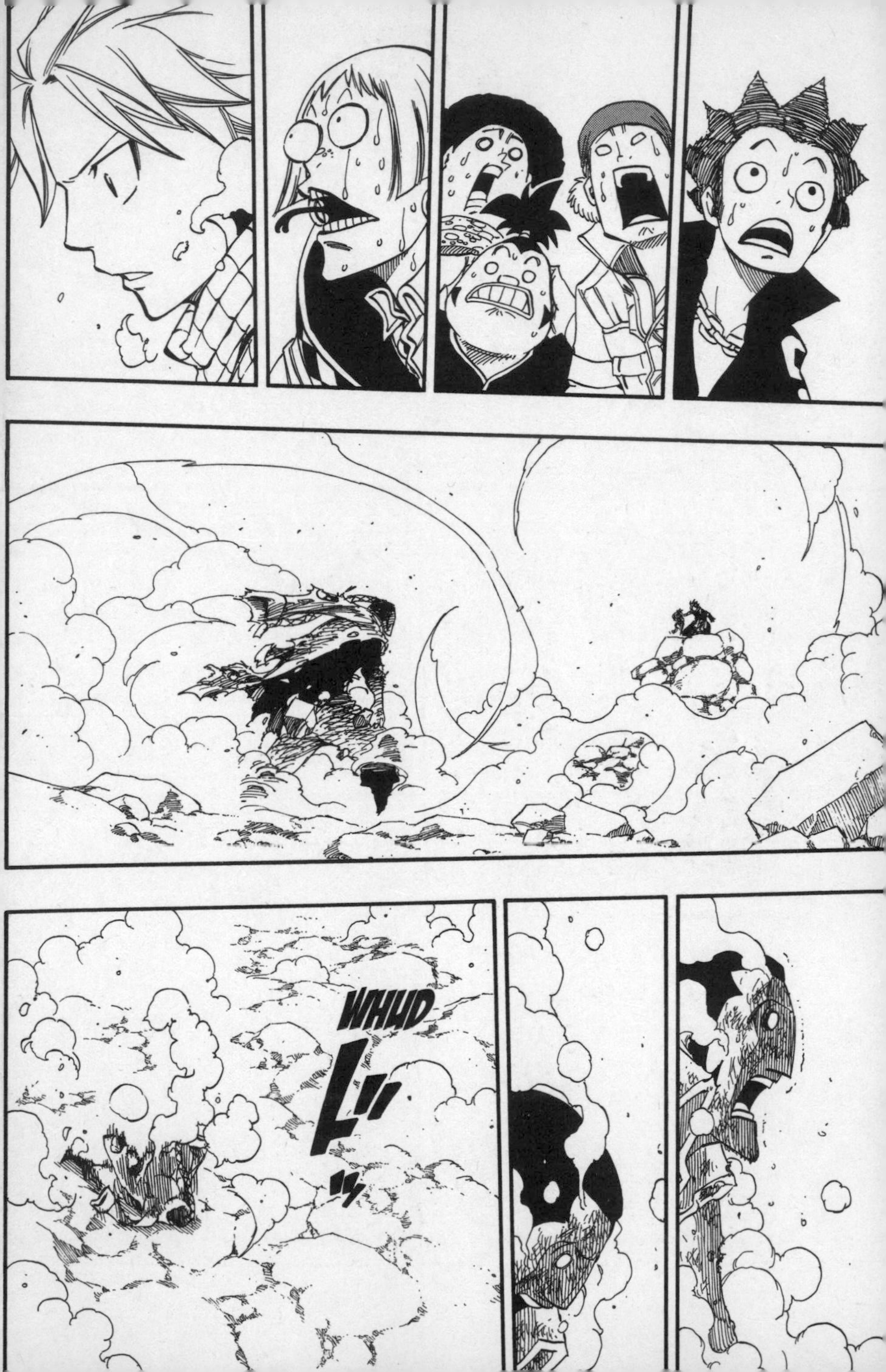
WHUD

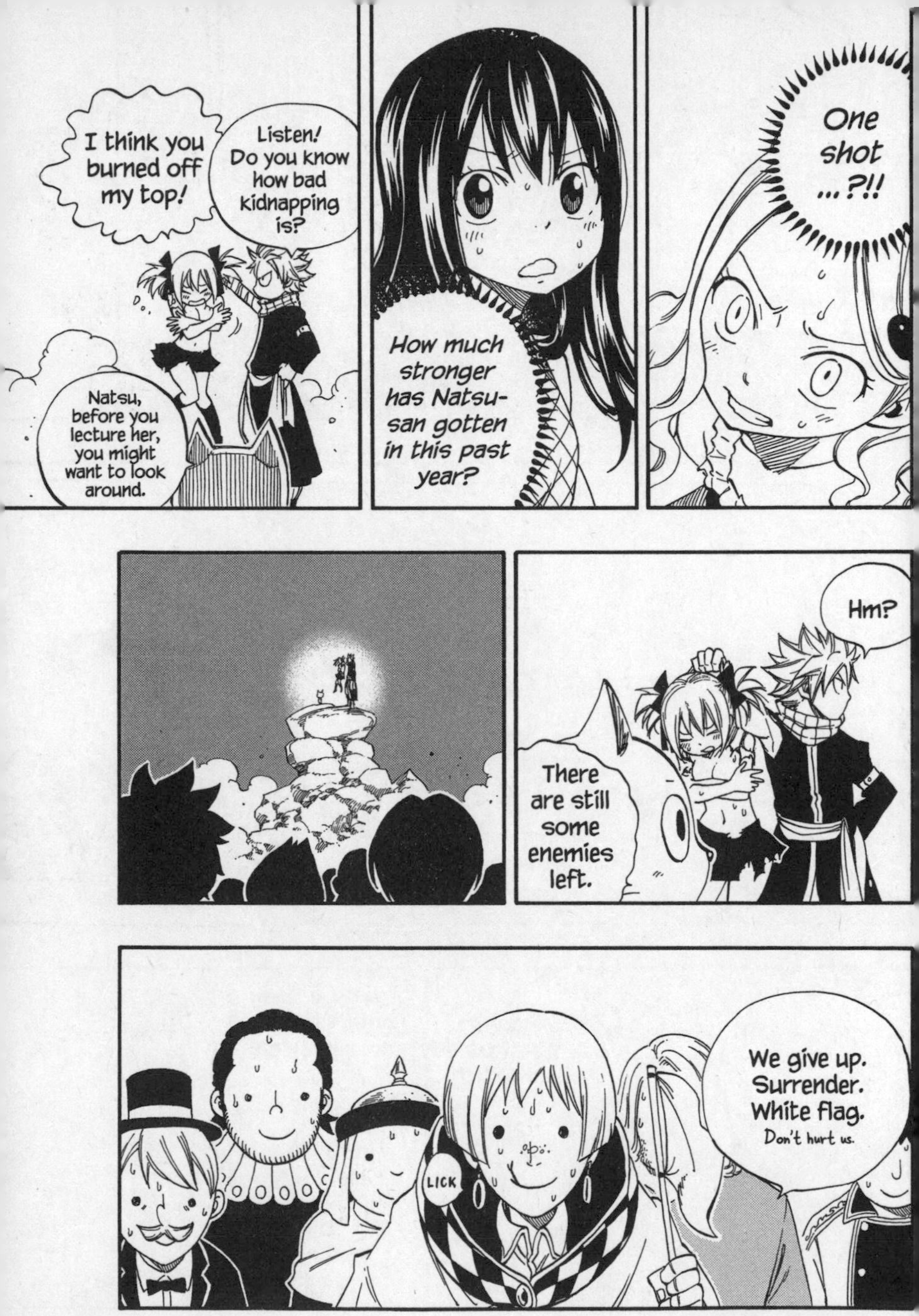
One shot ...?!!
How much stronger has Natsu-san gotten in this past year?
Listen! Do you know how bad kidnapping is?
I think you burned off my top!
Natsu, before you lecture her, you might want to look around.
Hm?
There are still some enemies left.
We give up. Surrender. White flag. Don't hurt us.
LICK

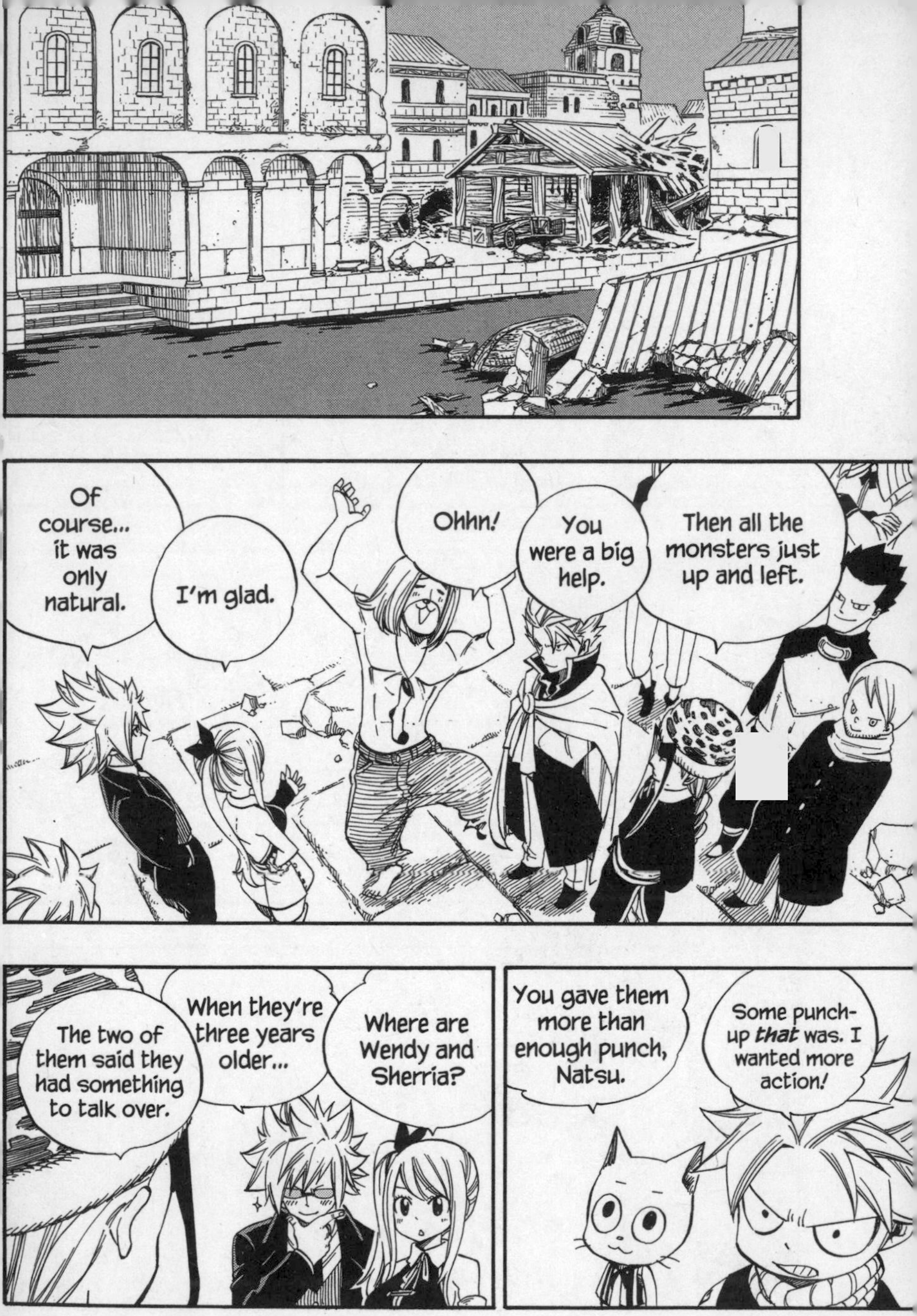
Then all the monsters just up and left.
You were a big help.
Ohhn!
I'm glad.
Of course... it was only natural.
Some punch-up *that* was. I wanted more action!
You gave them more than enough punch, Natsu.
Where are Wendy and Sherria?
When they're three years older...
The two of them said they had something to talk over.

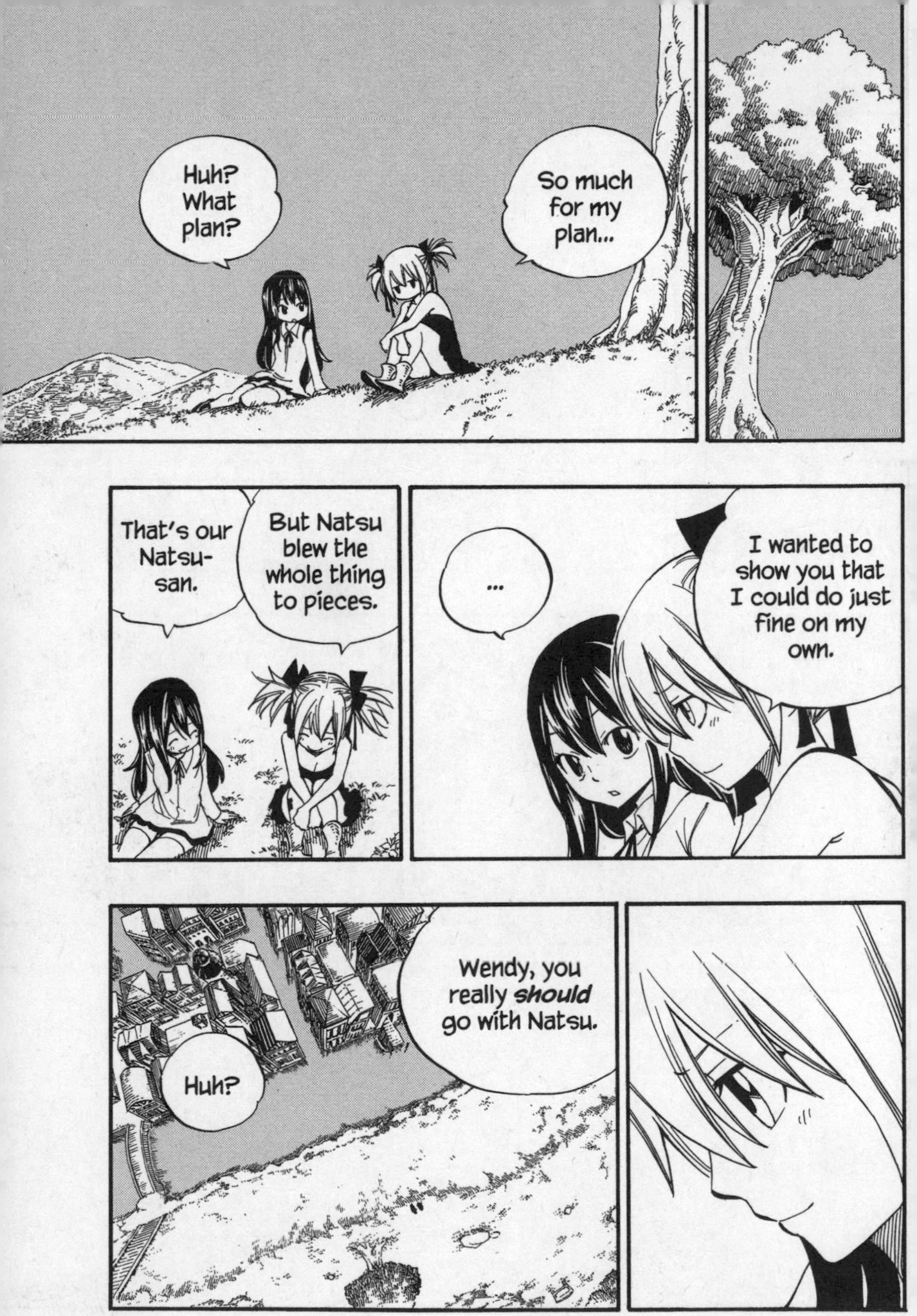
So much for my plan...
Huh? What plan?
I wanted to show you that I could do just fine on my own.
...
But Natsu blew the whole thing to pieces.
That's our Natsu-san.
Wendy, you really *should* go with Natsu.
Huh?

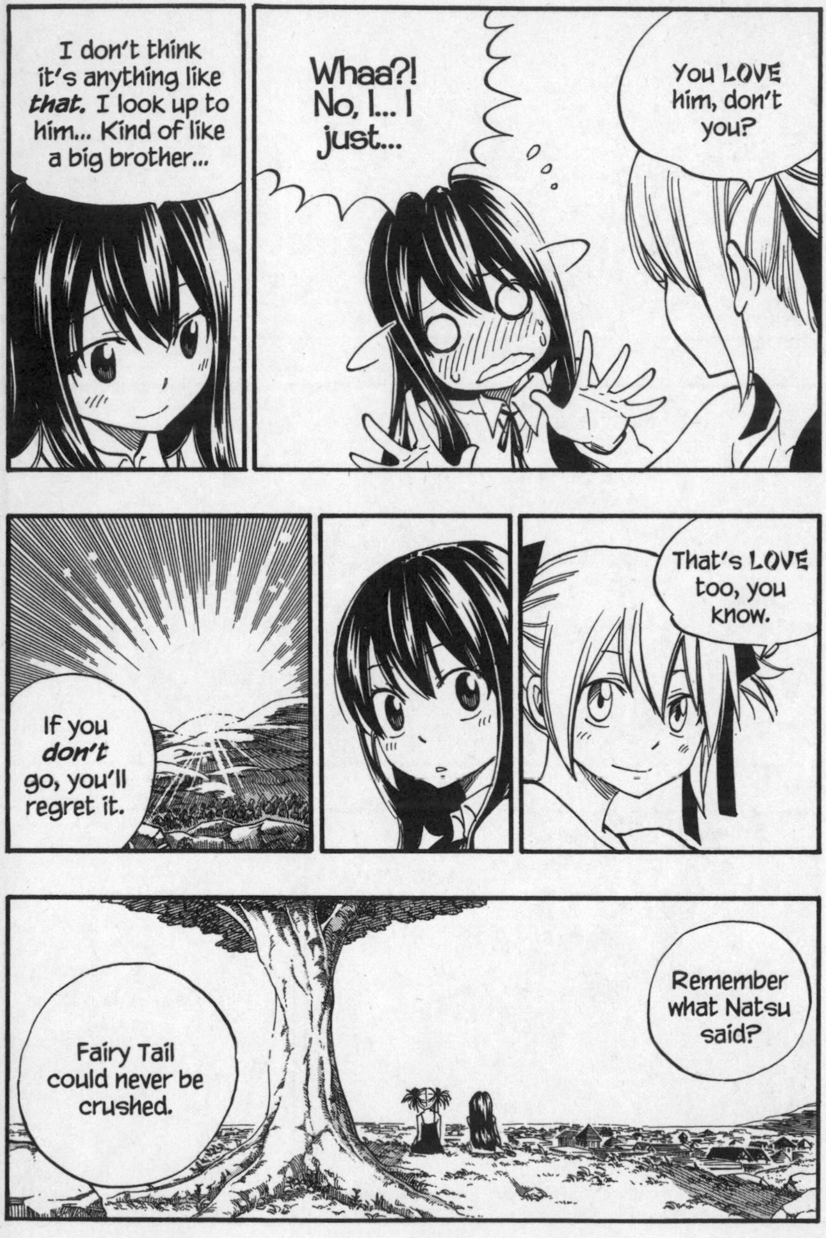
You LOVE him, don't you?
Whaa?! No, I... I just...
I don't think it's anything like *that.* I look up to him... Kind of like a big brother...
That's LOVE too, you know.
If you *don't* go, you'll regret it.
Remember what Natsu said?
Fairy Tail could never be crushed.

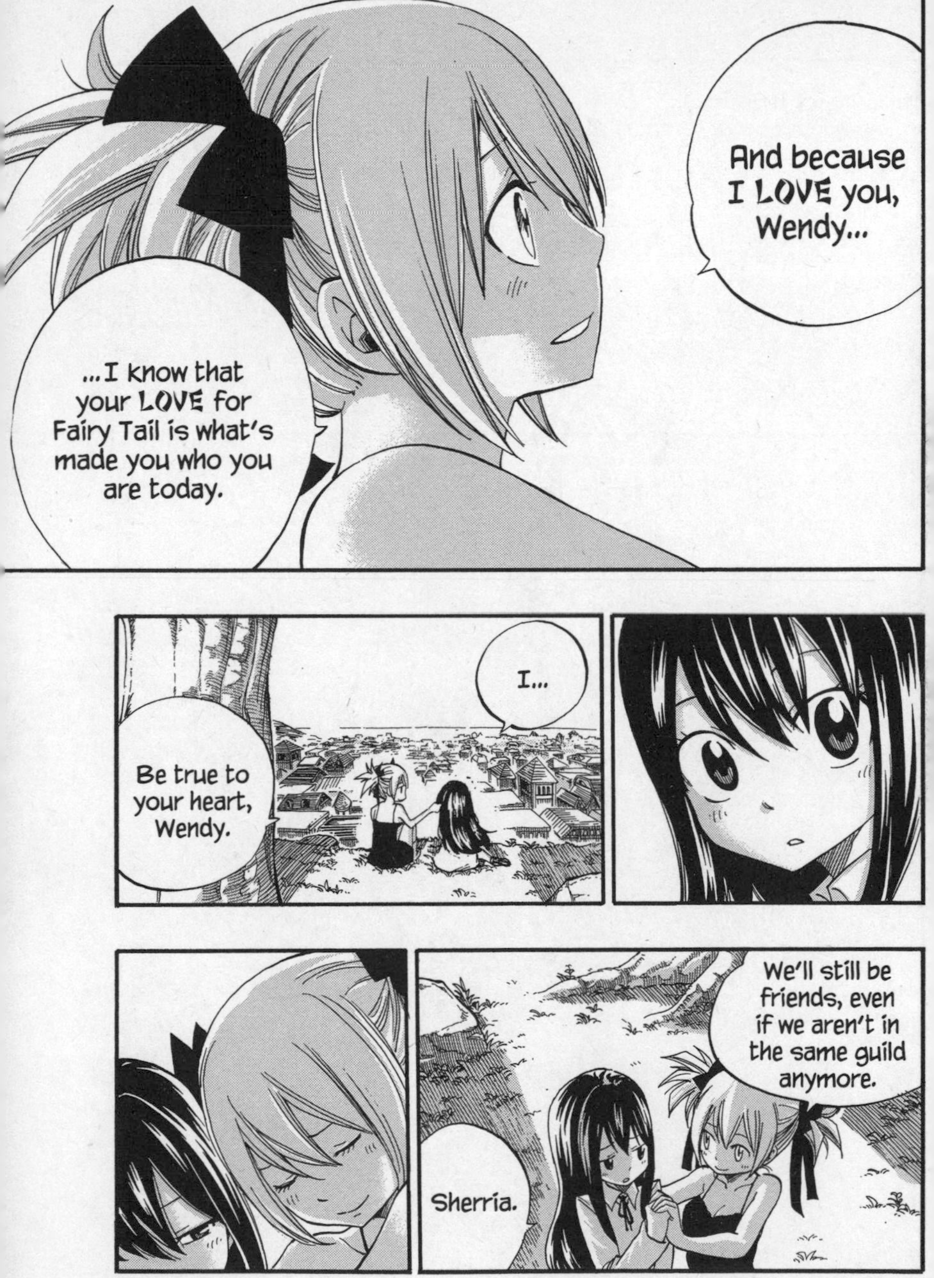
And because I LOVE you, Wendy...
...I know that your LOVE for Fairy Tail is what's made you who you are today.
I...
Be true to your heart, Wendy.
We'll still be friends, even if we aren't in the same guild anymore.
Sherria.

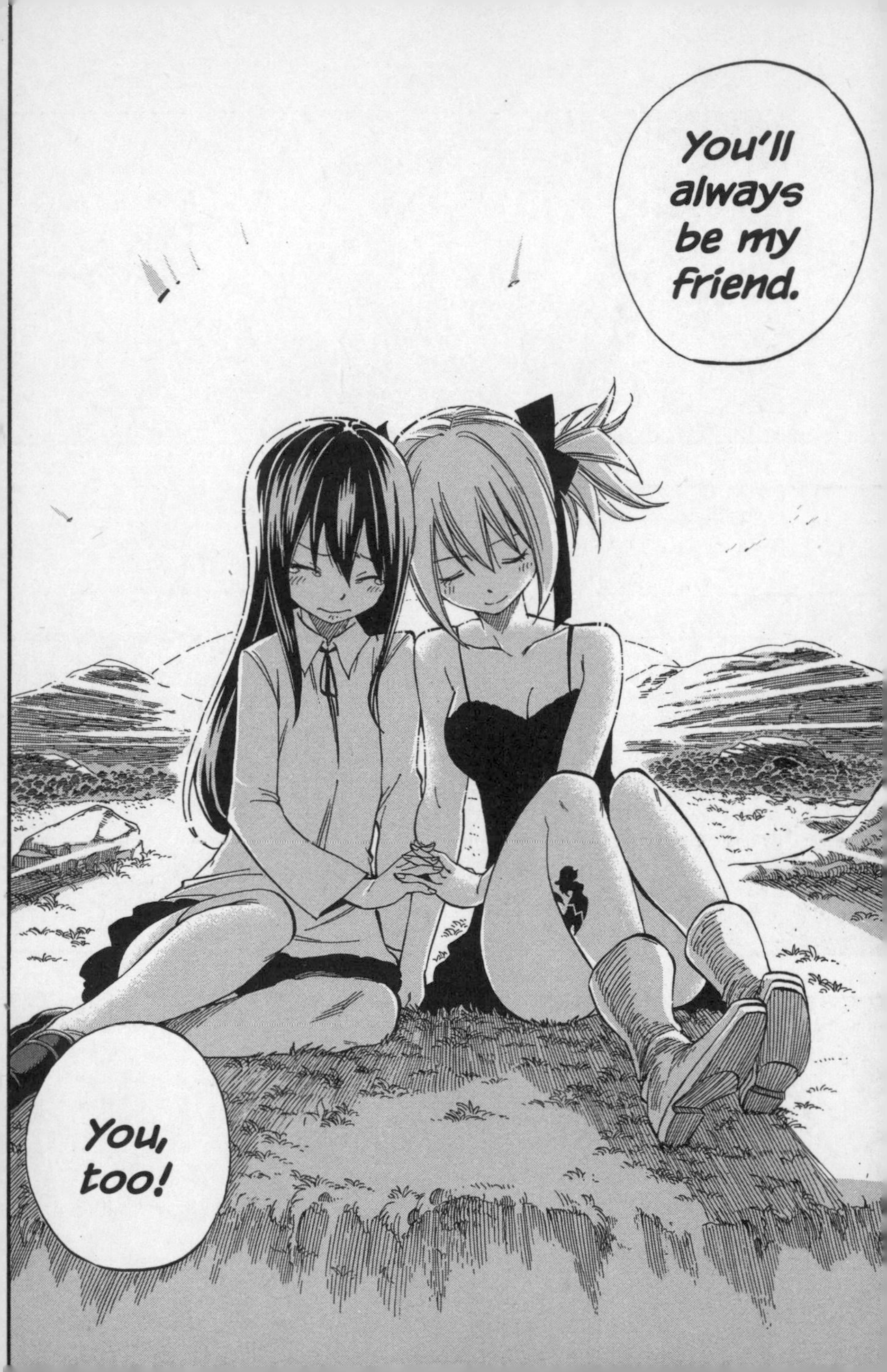
You'll always be my friend.
You, too!

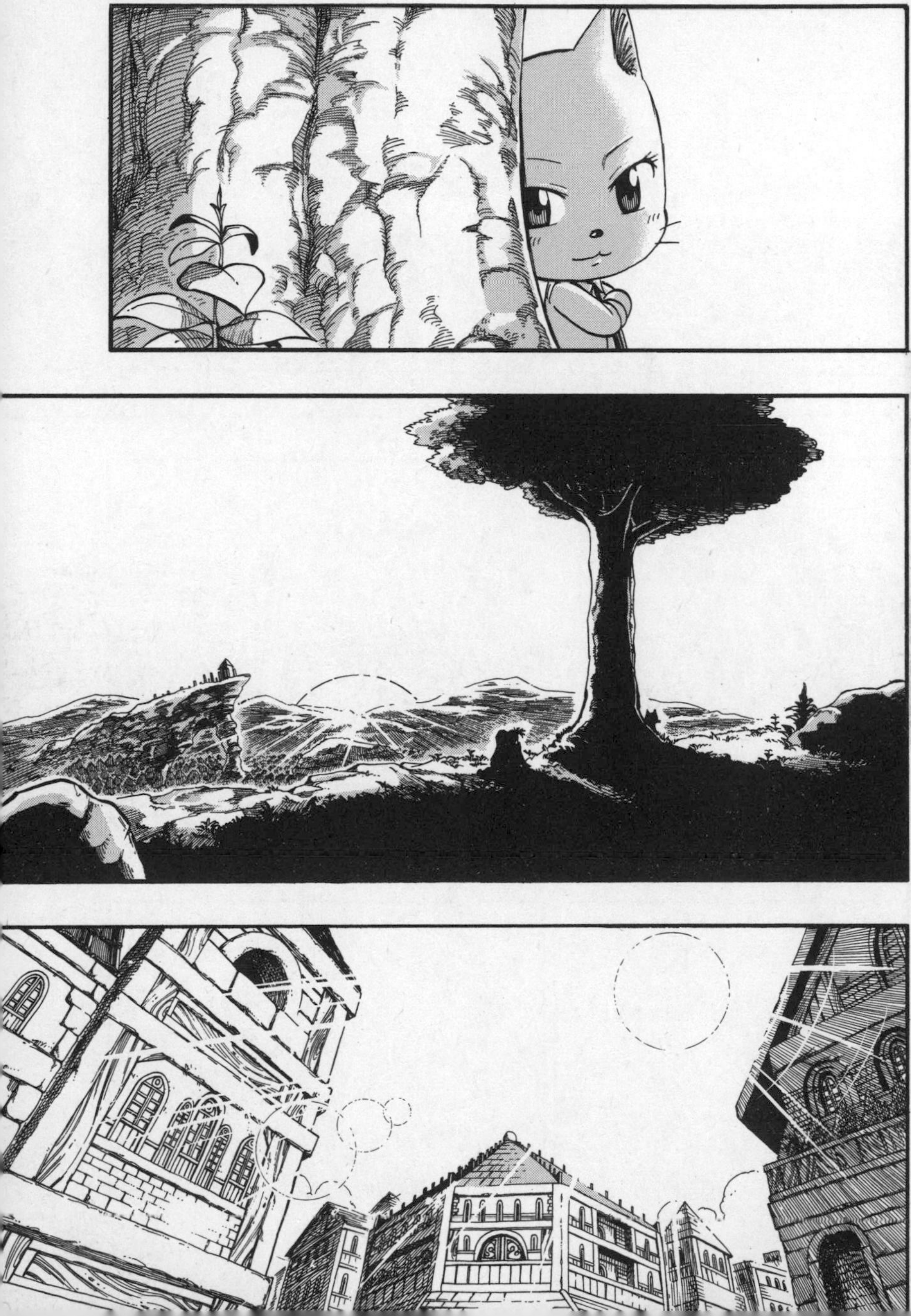

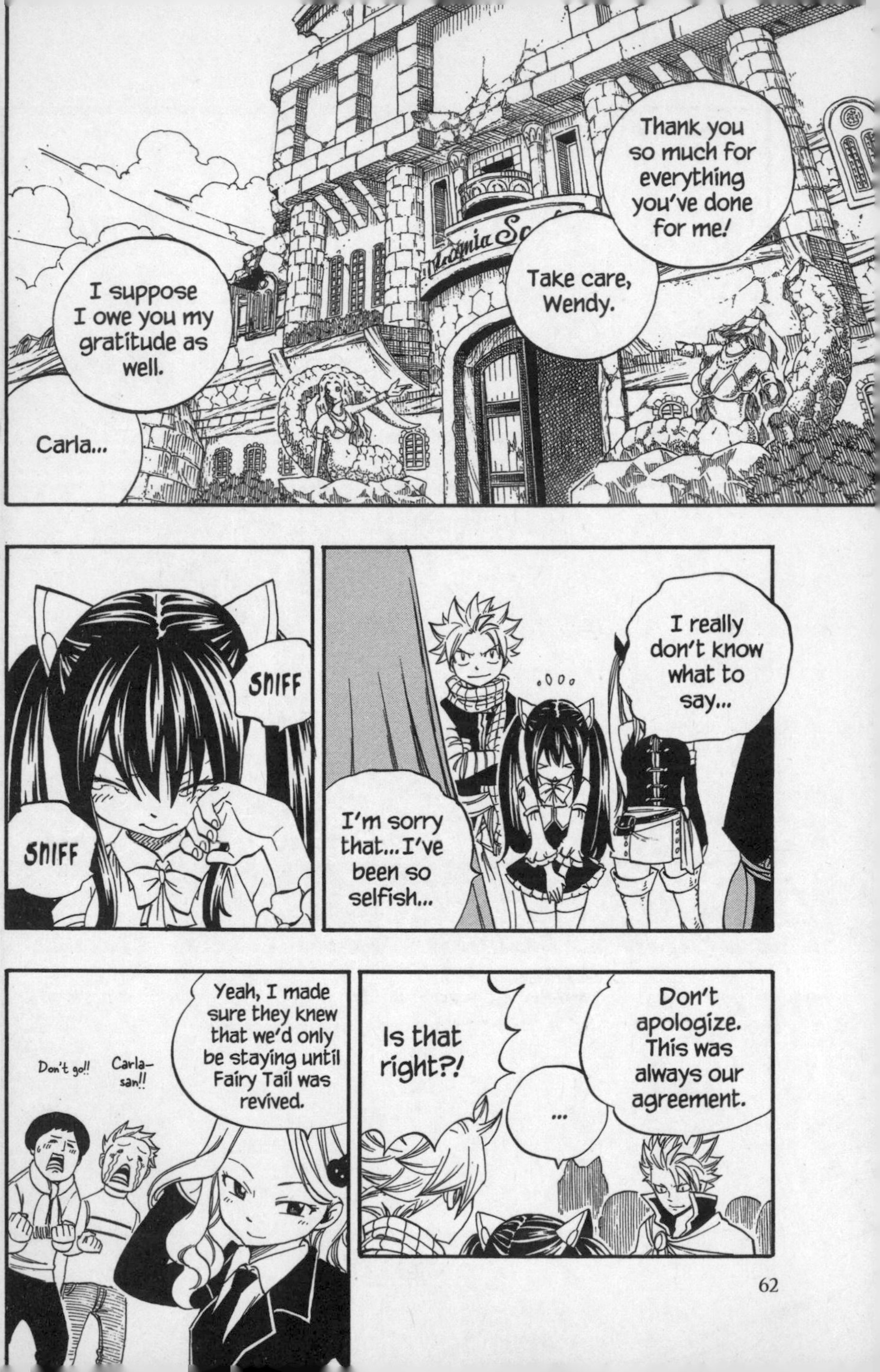
Thank you so much for everything you've done for me!
Take care, Wendy.
I suppose I owe you my gratitude as well.
Carla...
I really don't know what to say...
I'm sorry that...I've been so selfish...
SNIFF
SNIFF
Don't apologize. This was always our agreement.
...
Is that right?!
Yeah, I made sure they knew that we'd only be staying until Fairy Tail was revived.
Carla-san!!
Don't go!!

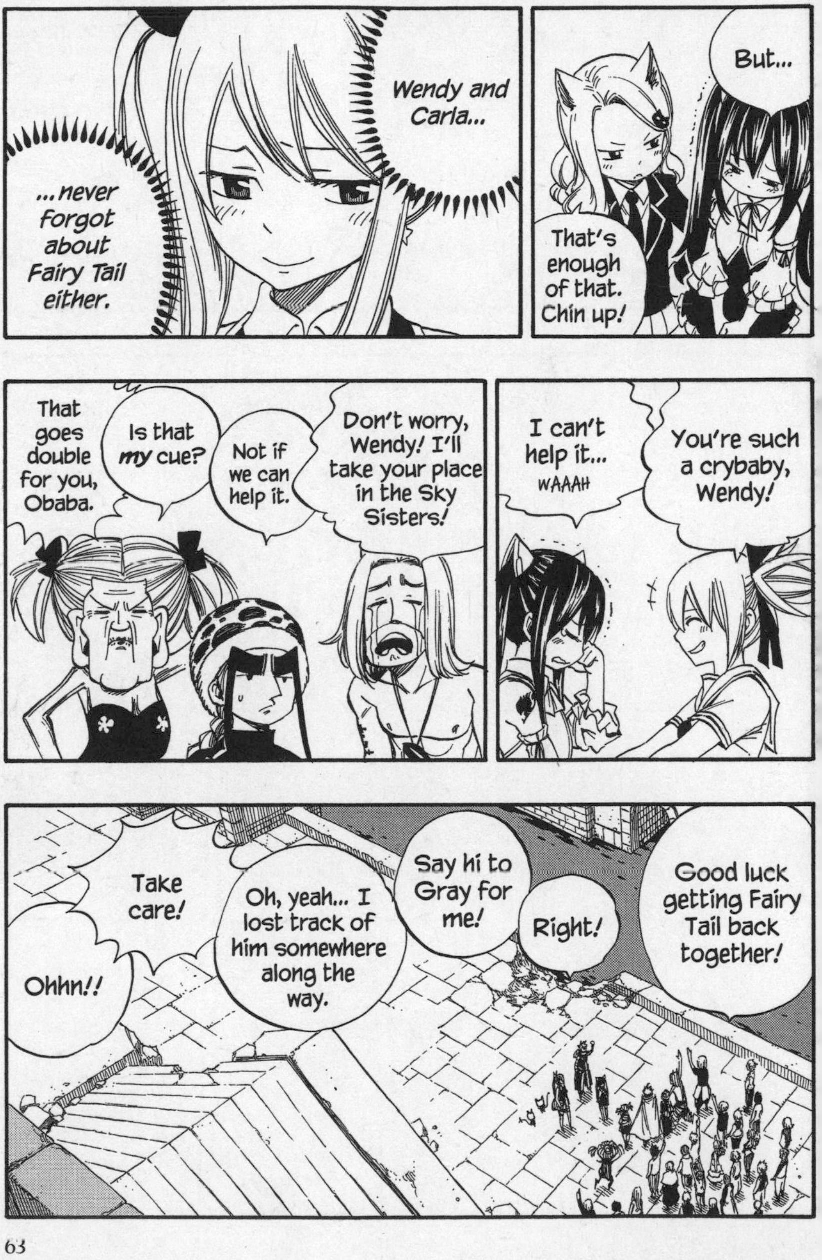

But...
That's enough of that. Chin up!
Wendy and Carla...
...never forgot about Fairy Tail either.
You're such a crybaby, Wendy!
I can't help it...
WAAAH
Don't worry, Wendy! I'll take your place in the Sky Sisters!
Not if we can help it.
Is that *my* cue?
That goes double for you, Obaba.
Good luck getting Fairy Tail back together!
Right!
Say hi to Gray for me!
Oh, yeah... I lost track of him somewhere along the way.
Take care!
Ohhn!!

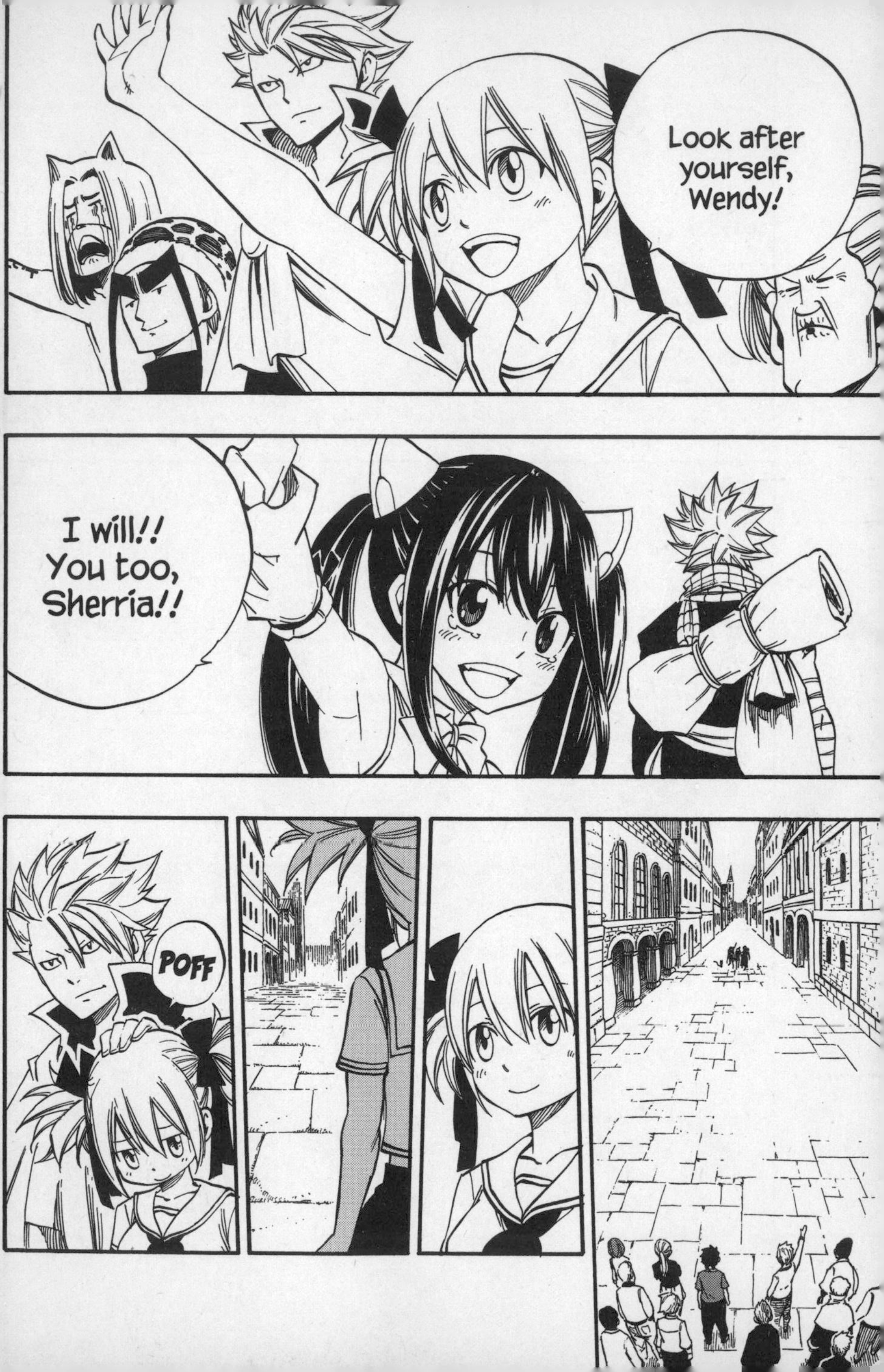
Look after yourself, Wendy!
I will!! You too, Sherria!!
POFF

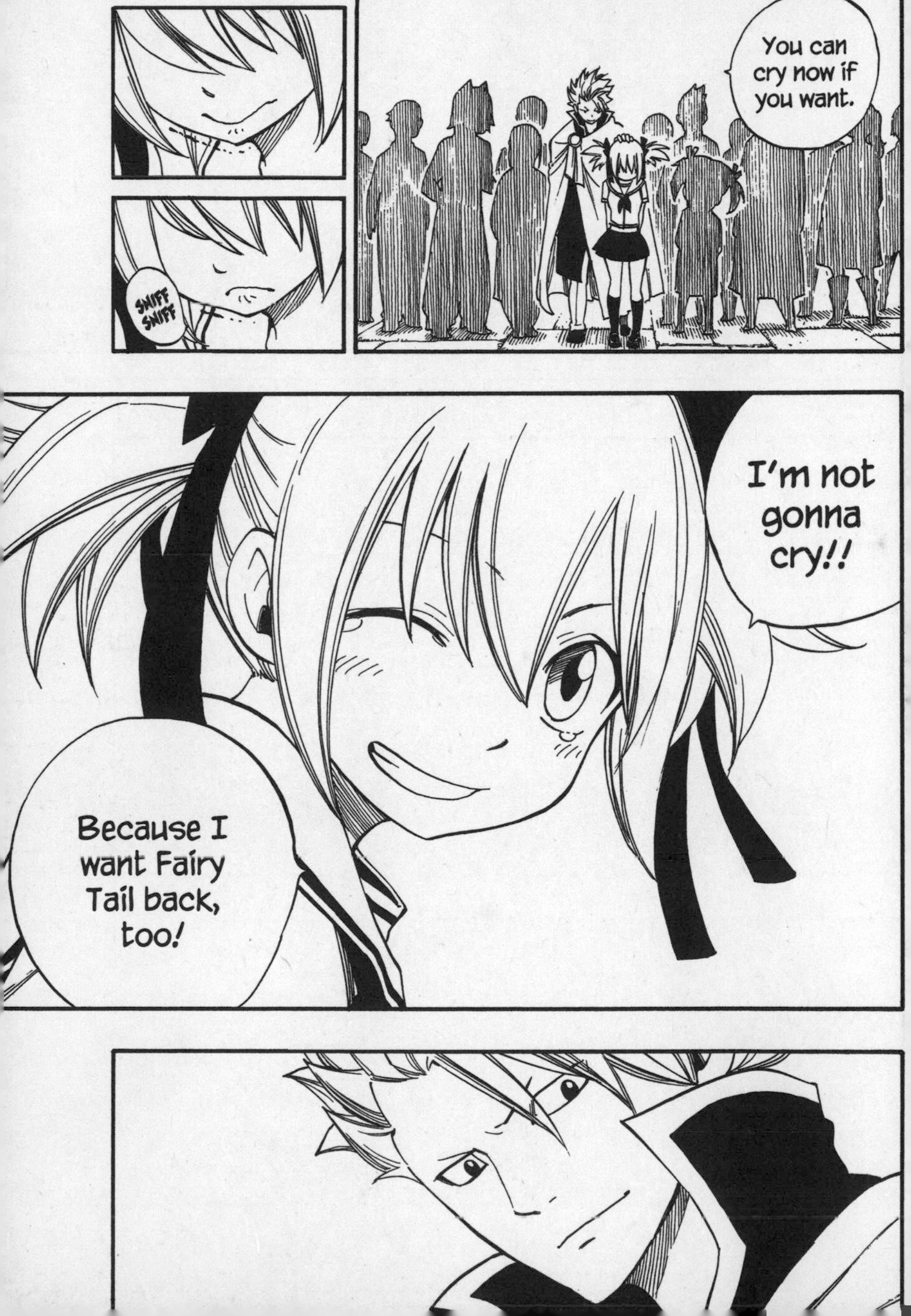
You can cry now if you want.
SNIFF SNIFF
I'm not gonna cry!!
Because I want Fairy Tail back, too!

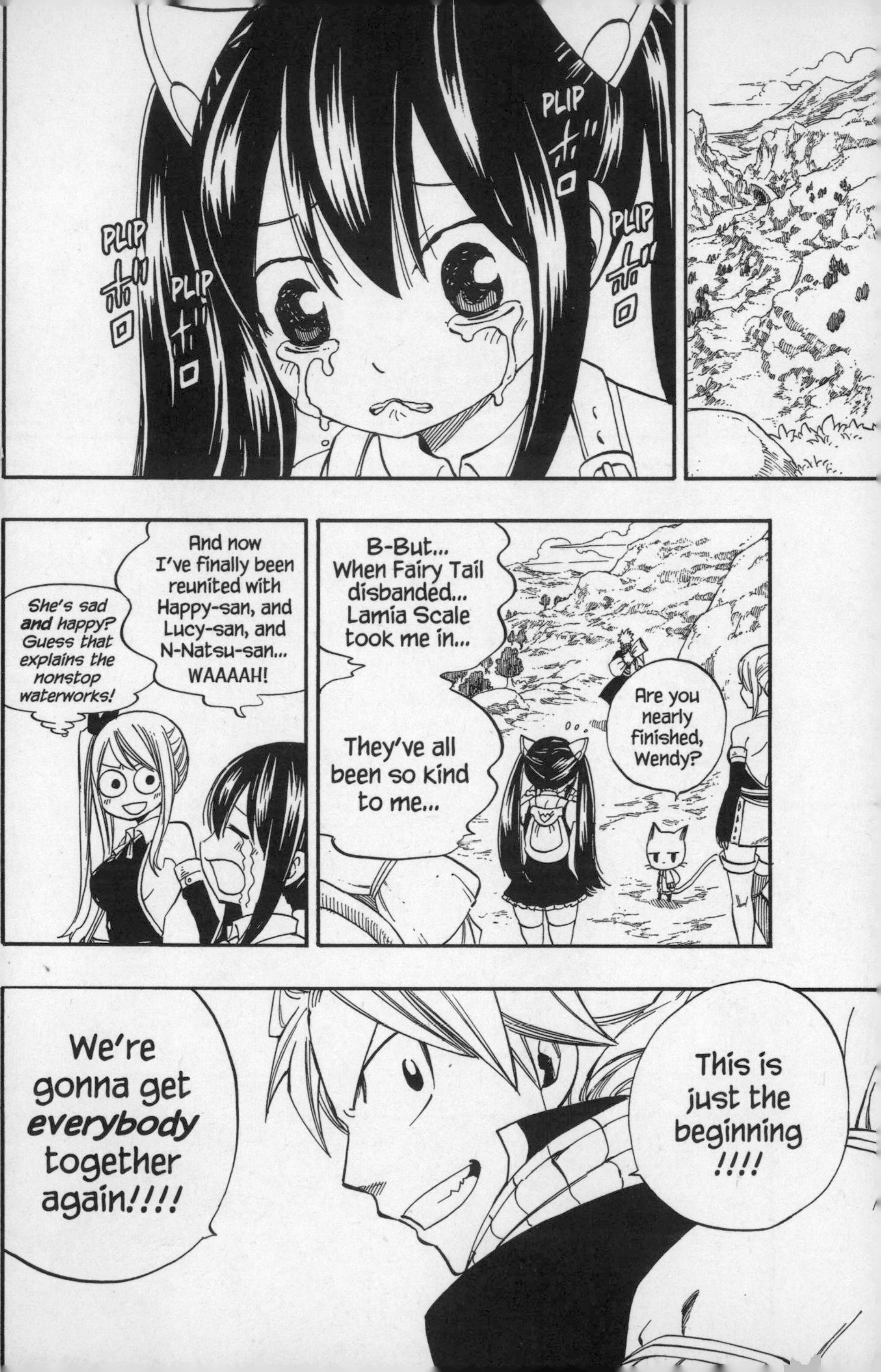
PLIP
PLIP
PLIP
PLIP
B-But... When Fairy Tail disbanded... Lamia Scale took me in...
They've all been so kind to me...
Are you nearly finished, Wendy?
And now I've finally been reunited with Happy-san, and Lucy-san, and N-Natsu-san... WAAAAH!
She's sad *and* happy? Guess that explains the nonstop waterworks!
This is just the beginning !!!!
We're gonna get *everybody* together again!!!!

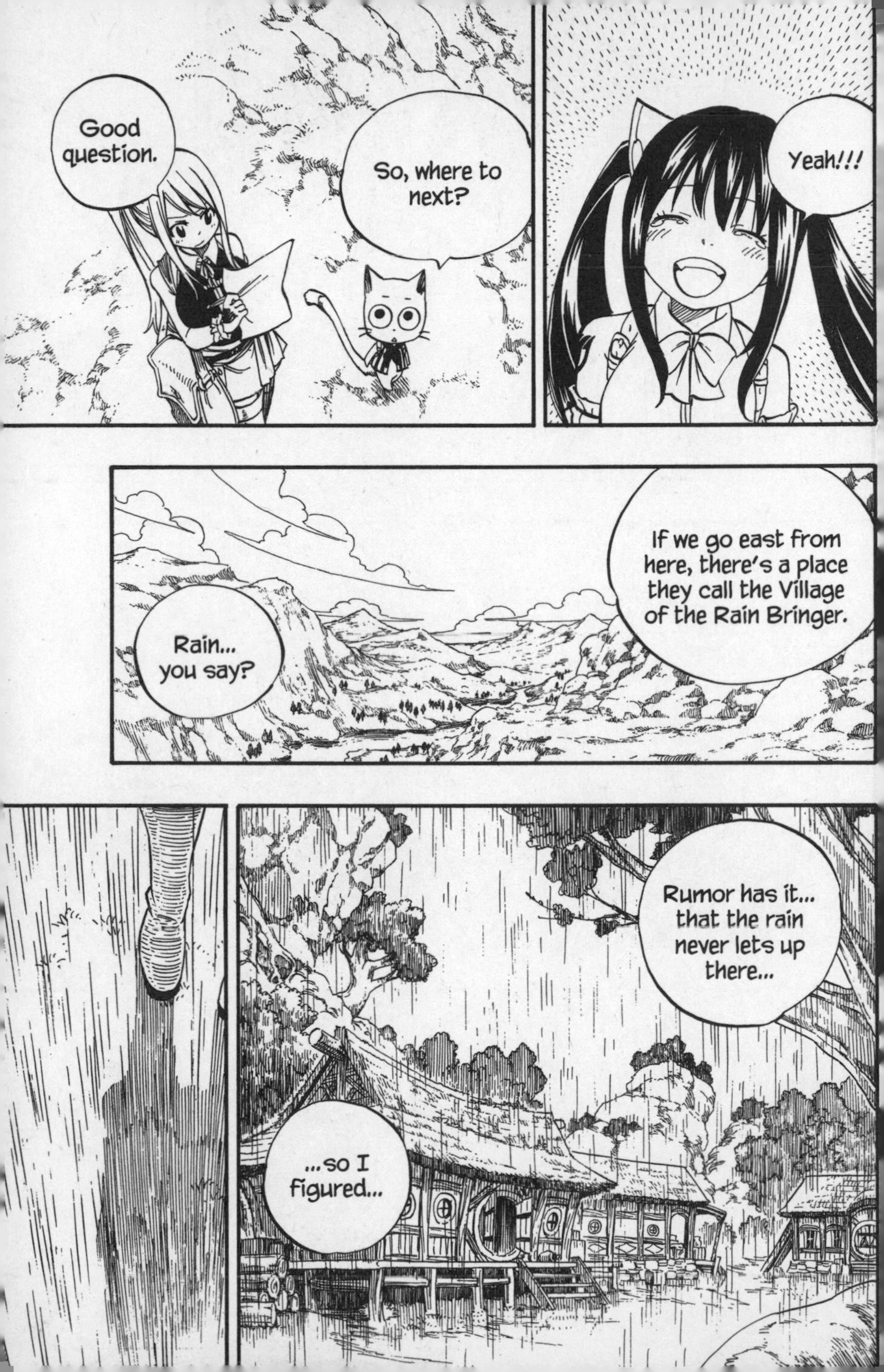
Yeah!!!
So, where to next?
Good question.
If we go east from here, there's a place they call the Village of the Rain Bringer.
Rain... you say?
Rumor has it... that the rain never lets up there...
...so I figured...

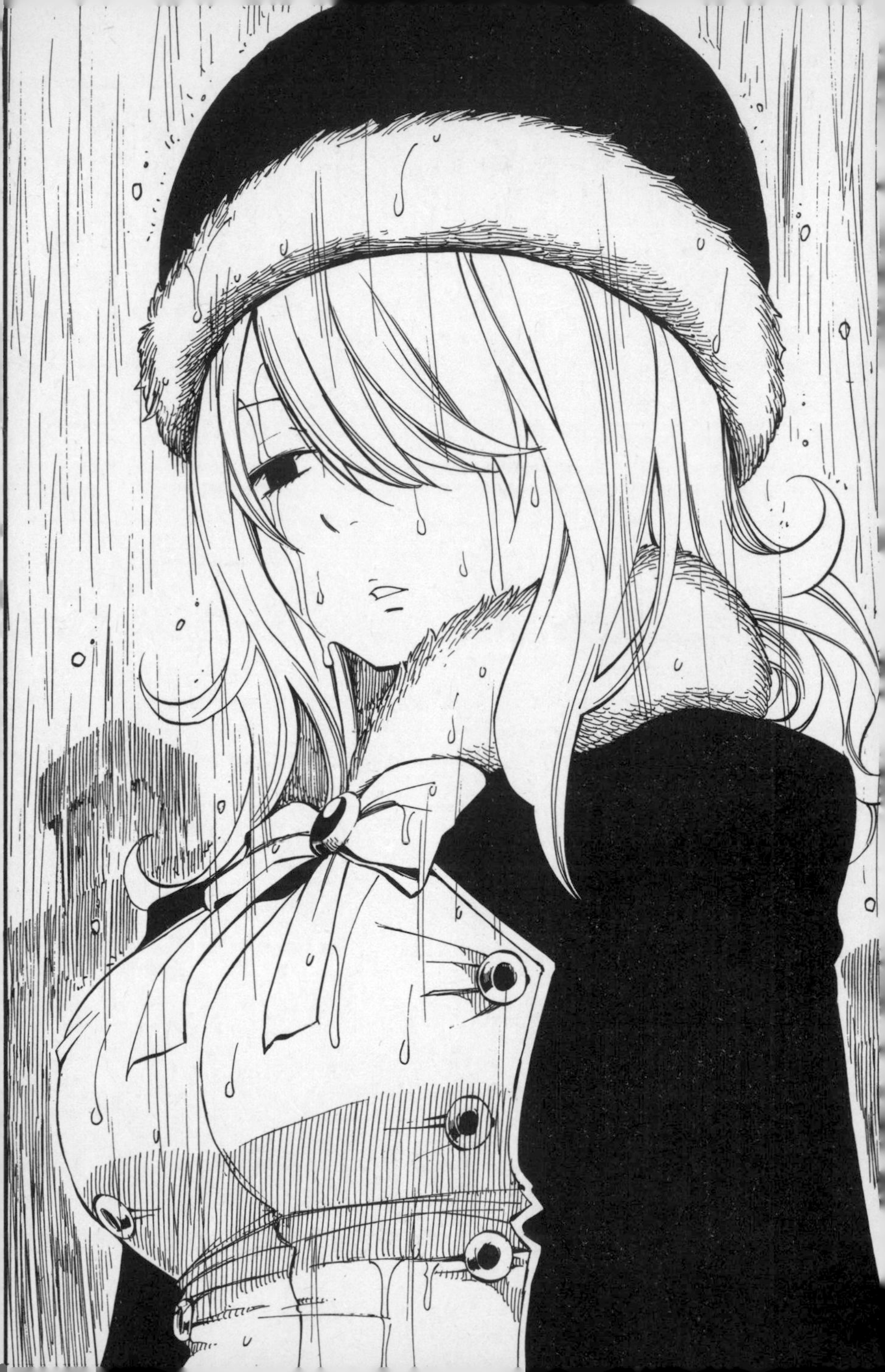

FAIRY TAIL
フェアリーテイル

Chapter 424: Avatar

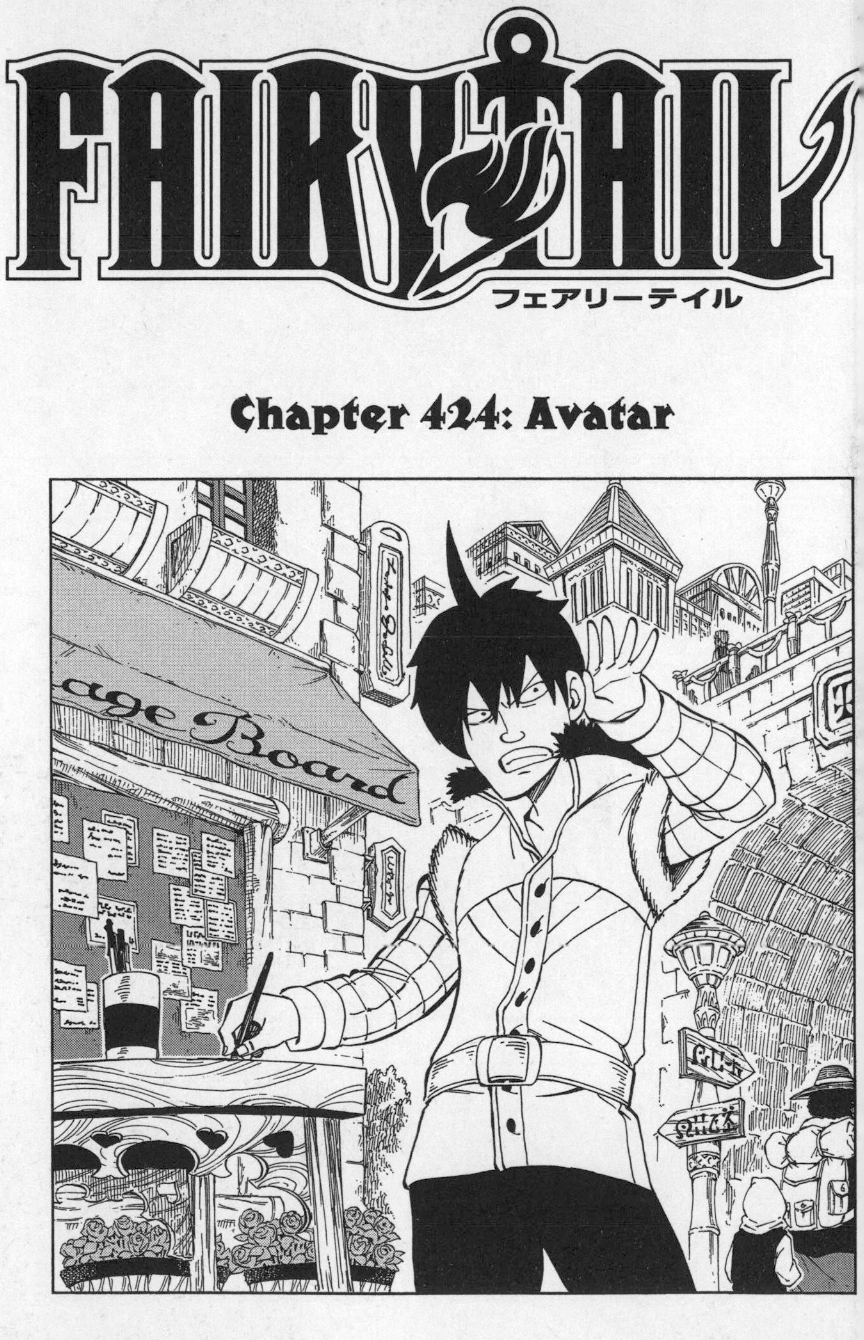
age Board

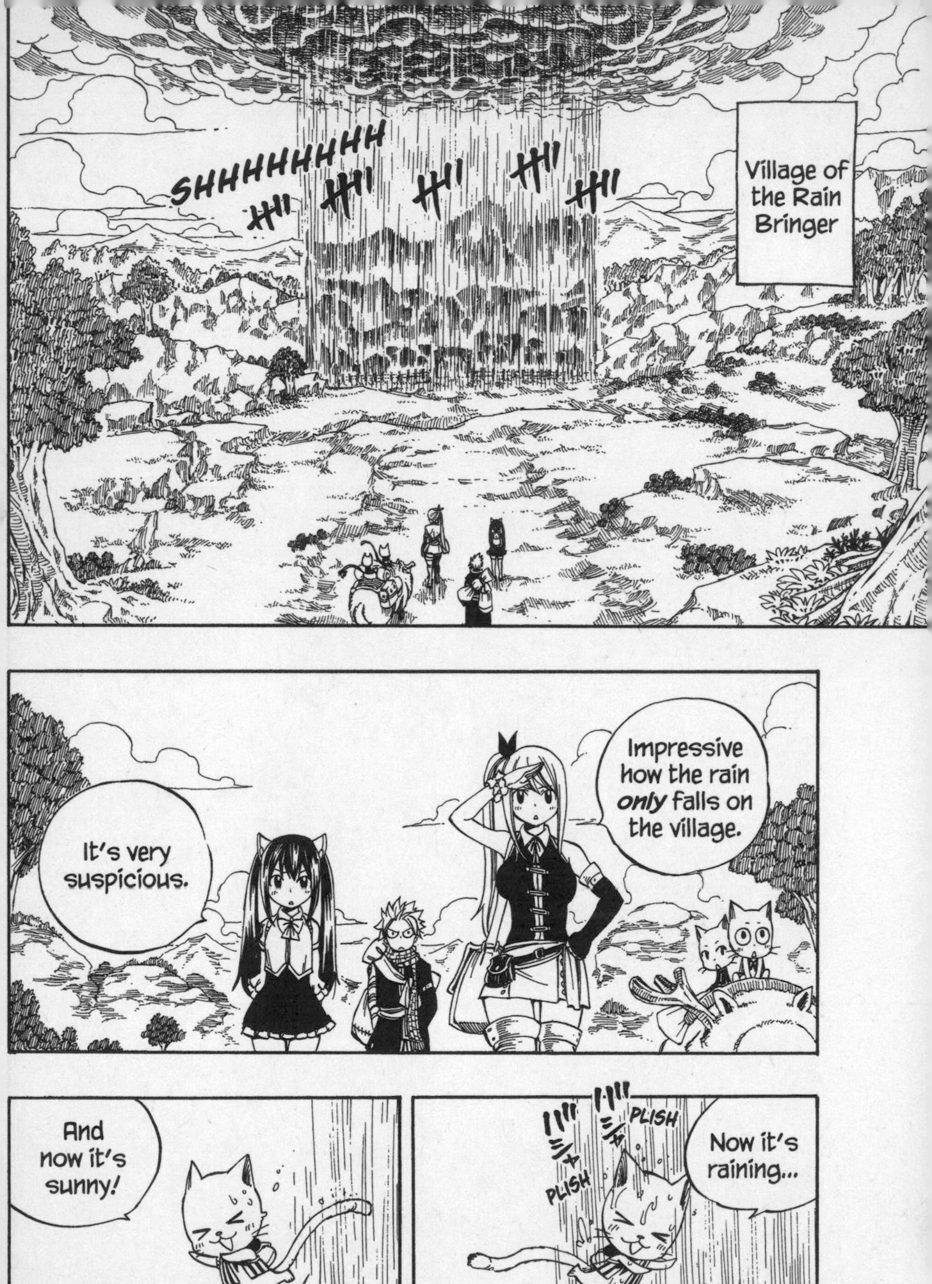
Village of the Rain Bringer
SHHHHHHHH
Impressive how the rain *only* falls on the village.
It's very suspicious.
PLISH
PLISH
Now it's raining...
And now it's sunny!

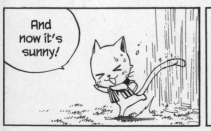

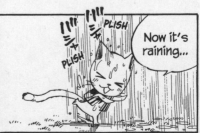

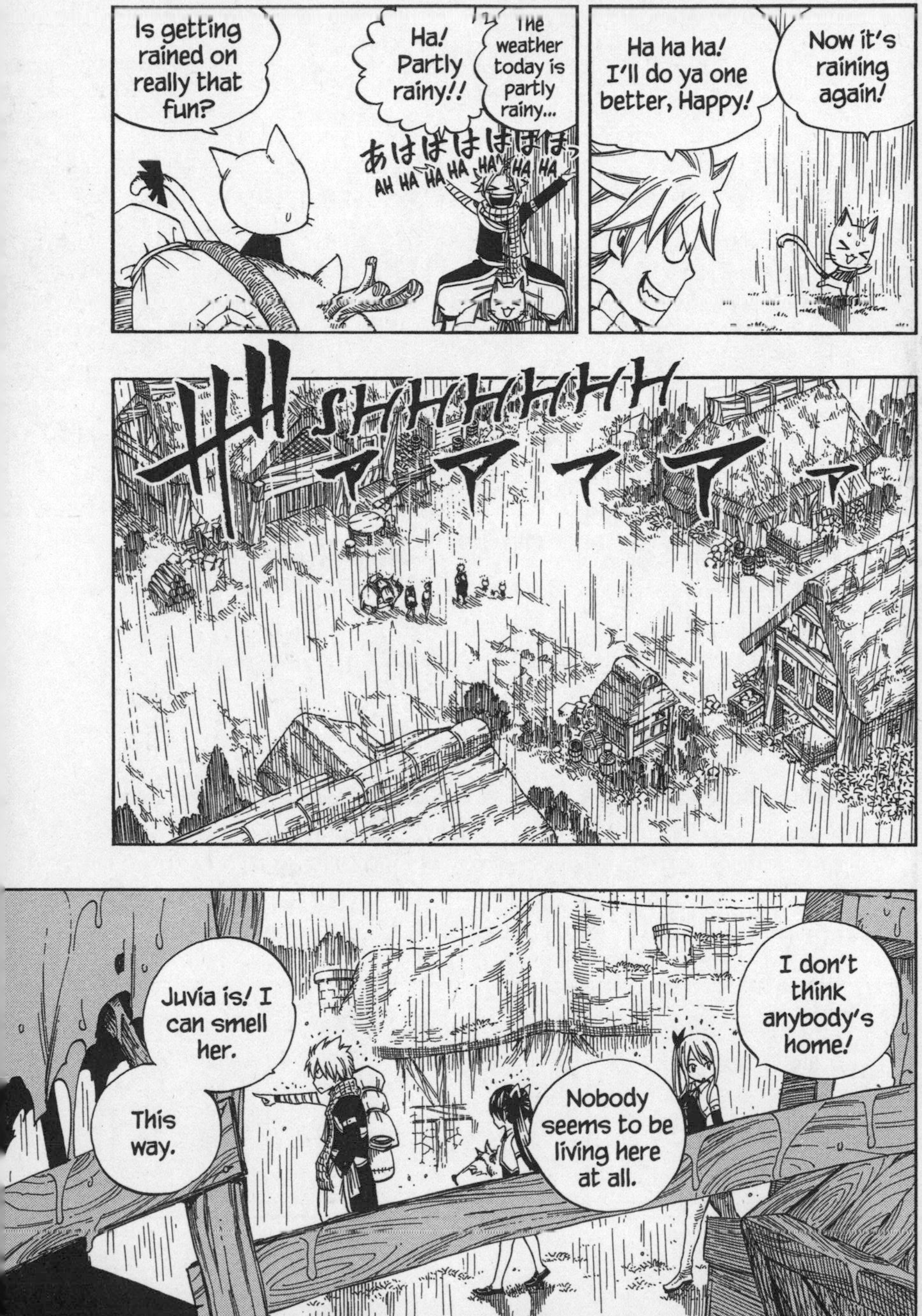
Now it's raining again!
Ha ha ha! I'll do ya one better, Happy!
The weather today is partly rainy...
Ha! Partly rainy!!
あはははははっ
AH HA HA HA HA HA HA
Is getting rained on really that fun?
ザァァァァ
HSHHHHHH
I don't think anybody's home!
Nobody seems to be living here at all.
Juvia is! I can smell her.
This way.

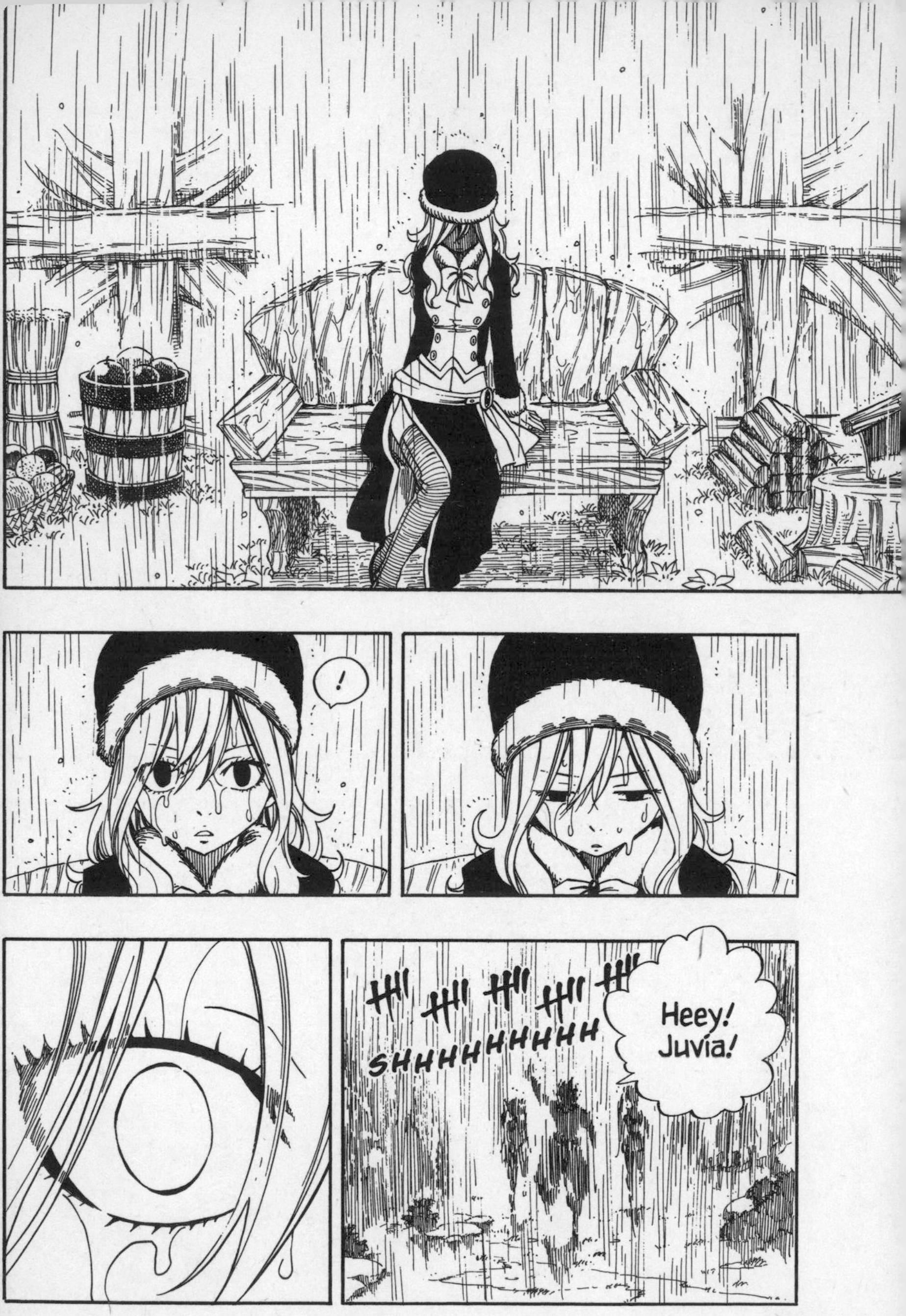
!
Heey! Juvia!
SHHHHHHHHH

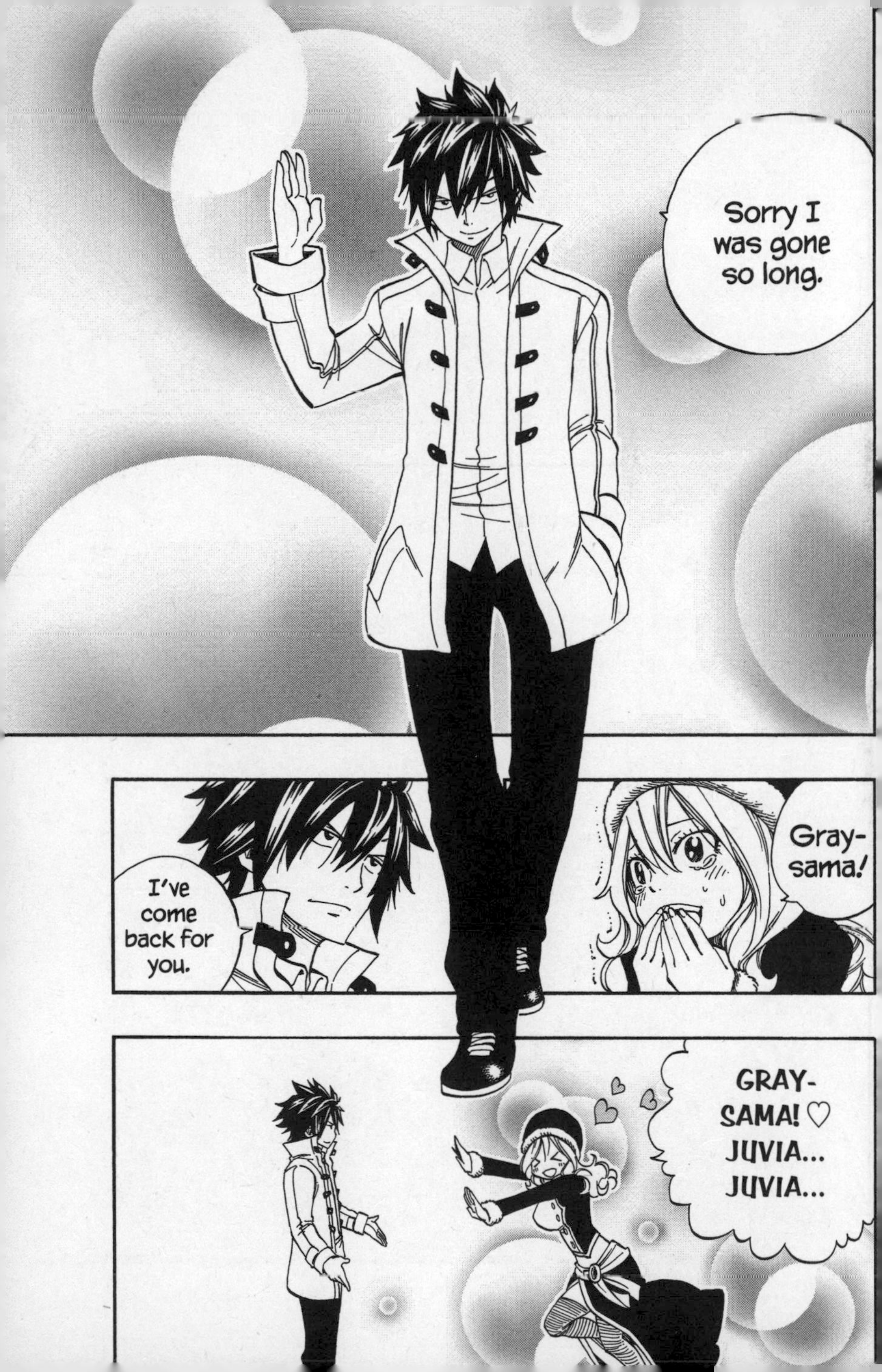
Sorry I was gone so long.
Gray-sama!
I've come back for you.
GRAY-SAMA! ♡ JUVIA... JUVIA...

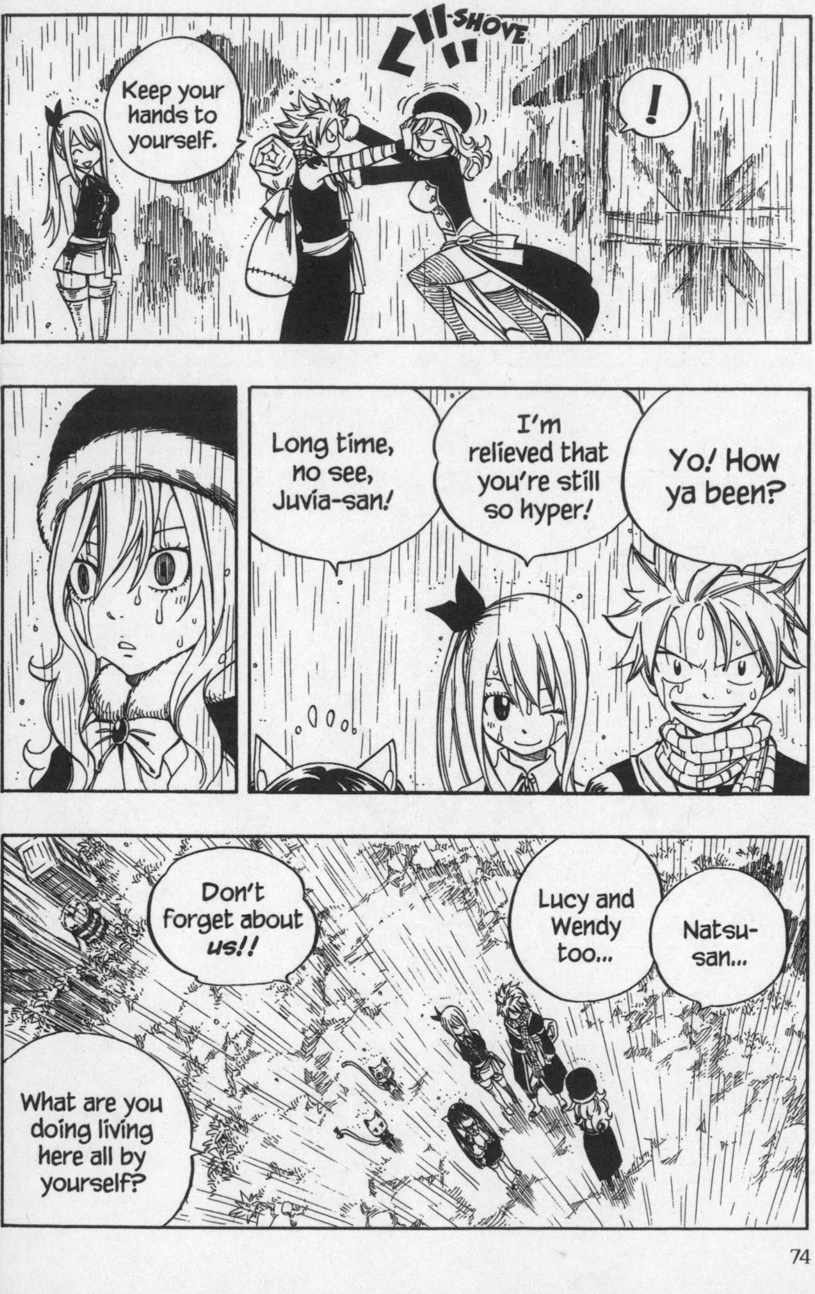
!
SHOVE
Keep your hands to yourself.
Yo! How ya been?
I'm relieved that you're still so hyper!
Long time, no see, Juvia-san!
Natsu-san...
Lucy and Wendy too...
Don't forget about us!!
What are you doing living here all by yourself?

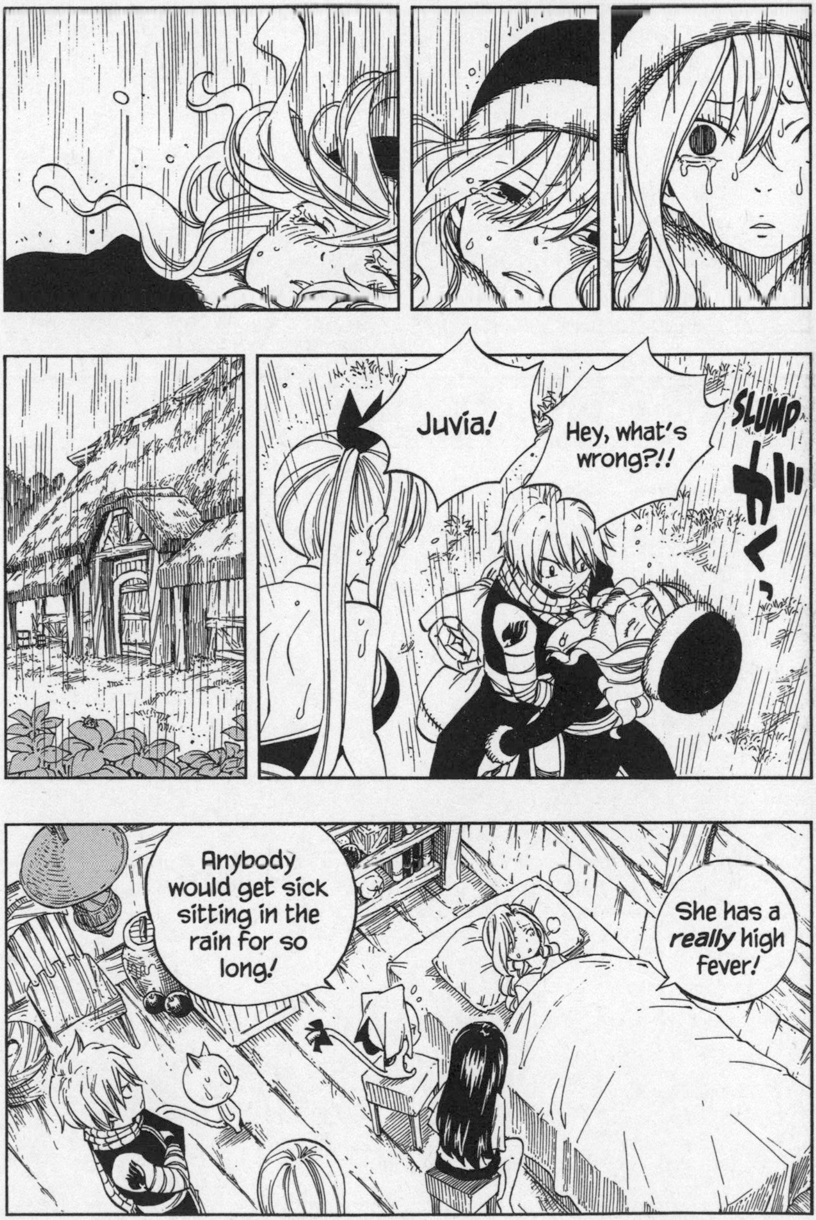
SLUMP
がくっ
Hey, what's wrong?!!
Juvia!
She has a *really* high fever!
Anybody would get sick sitting in the rain for so long!

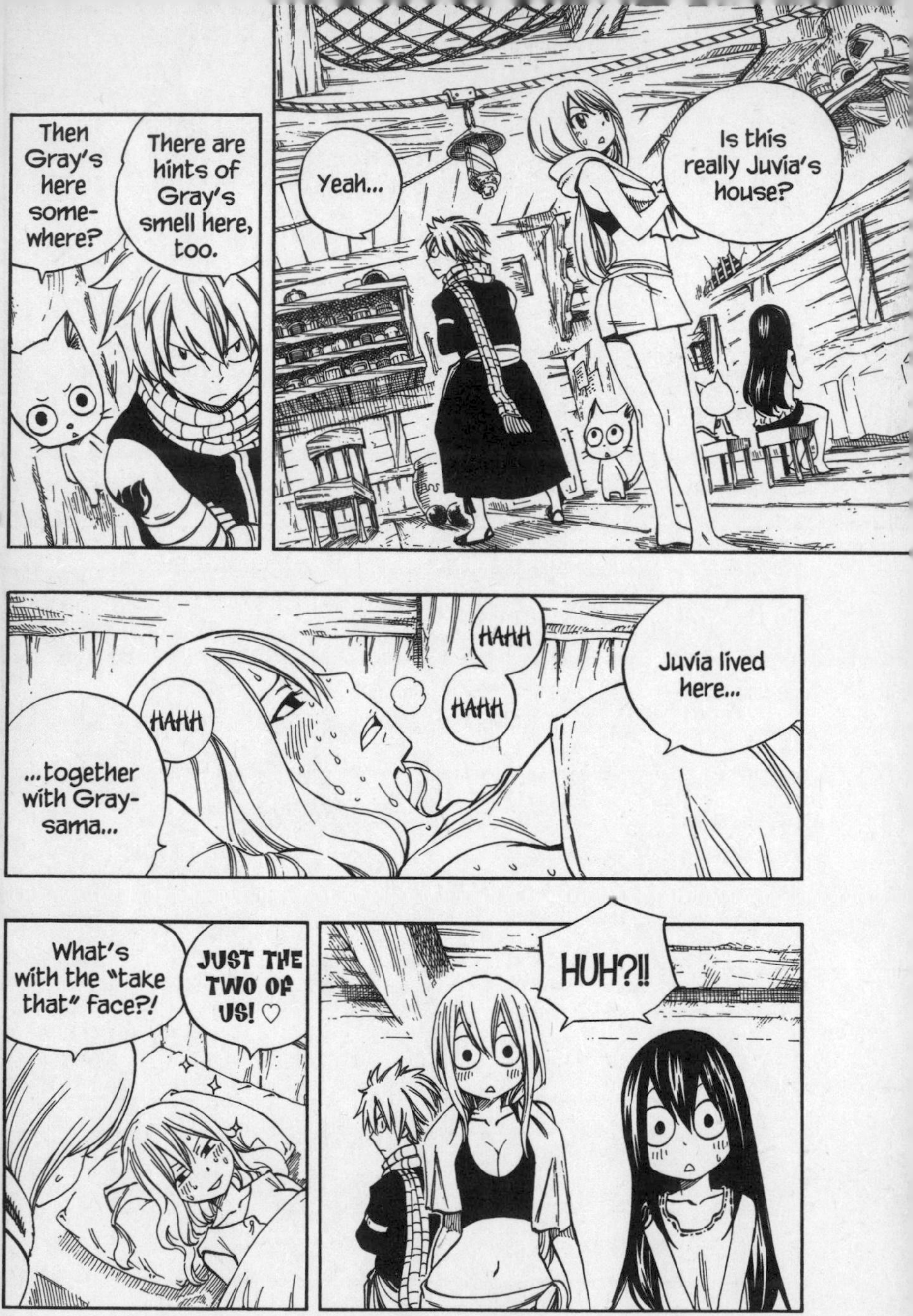
Is this really Juvia's house?
Yeah...
There are hints of Gray's smell here, too.
Then Gray's here somewhere?
Juvia lived here...
HAHH
HAHH
HAHH
...together with Gray-sama...
HUH?!!
JUST THE TWO OF US! ♡
What's with the "take that" face?!

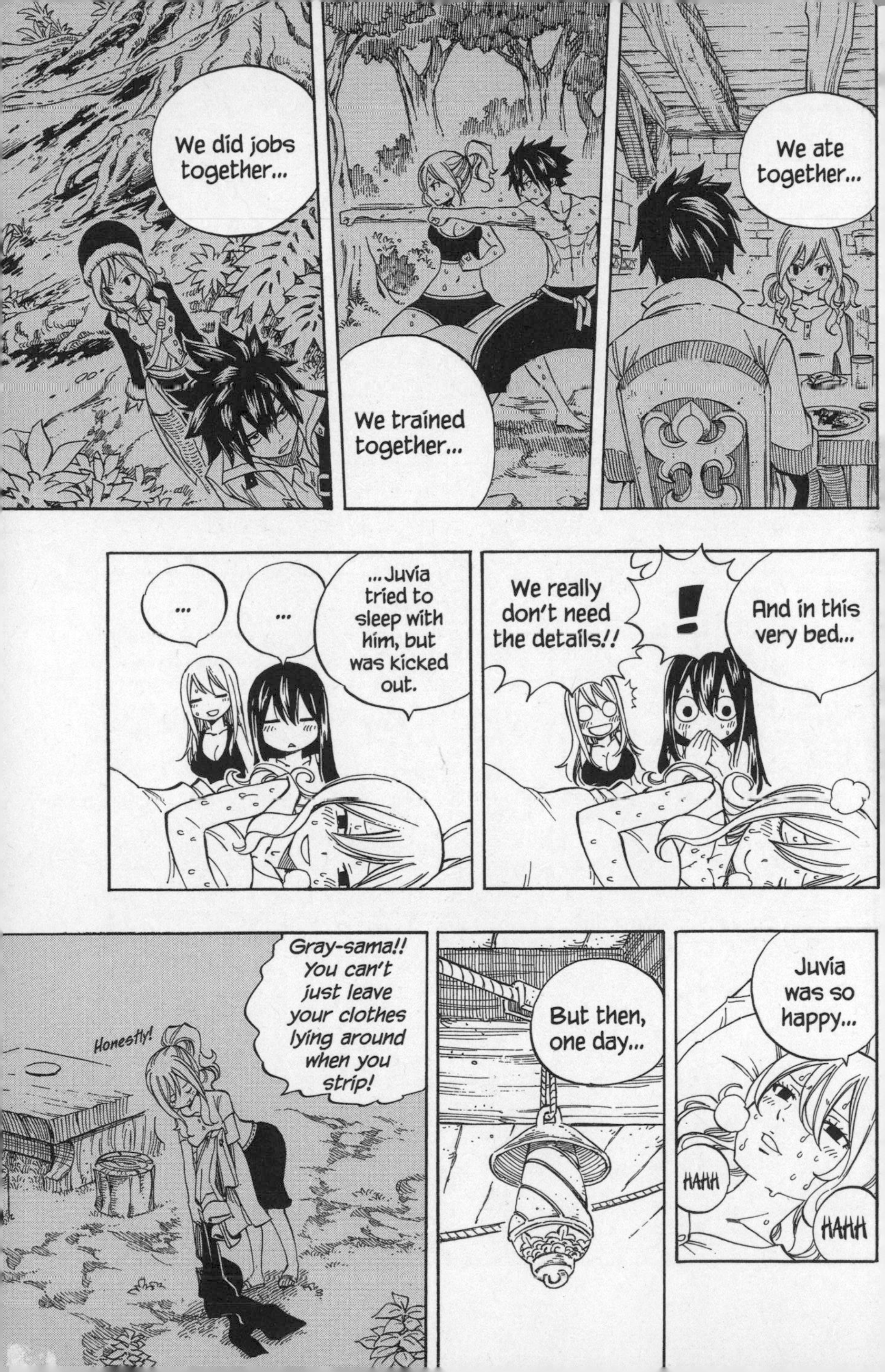
We ate together...
We trained together...
We did jobs together...
And in this very bed...
!
We really don't need the details!!
...Juvia tried to sleep with him, but was kicked out.
...
...
Juvia was so happy...
HAHH
HAHH
But then, one day...
Gray-sama!! You can't just leave your clothes lying around when you strip!
Honestly!

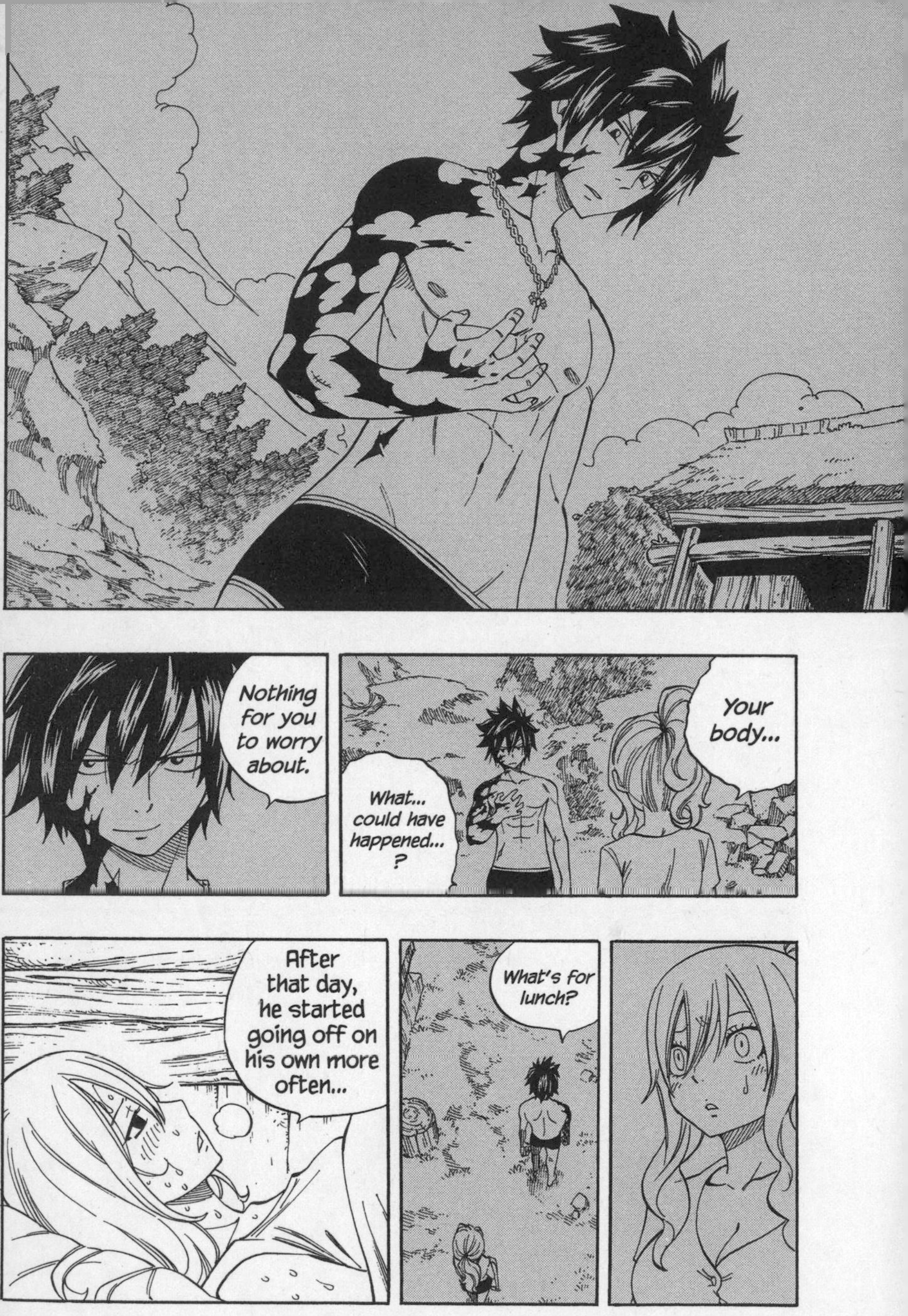
Your body...
What... could have happened...?
Nothing for you to worry about.
What's for lunch?
After that day, he started going off on his own more often...

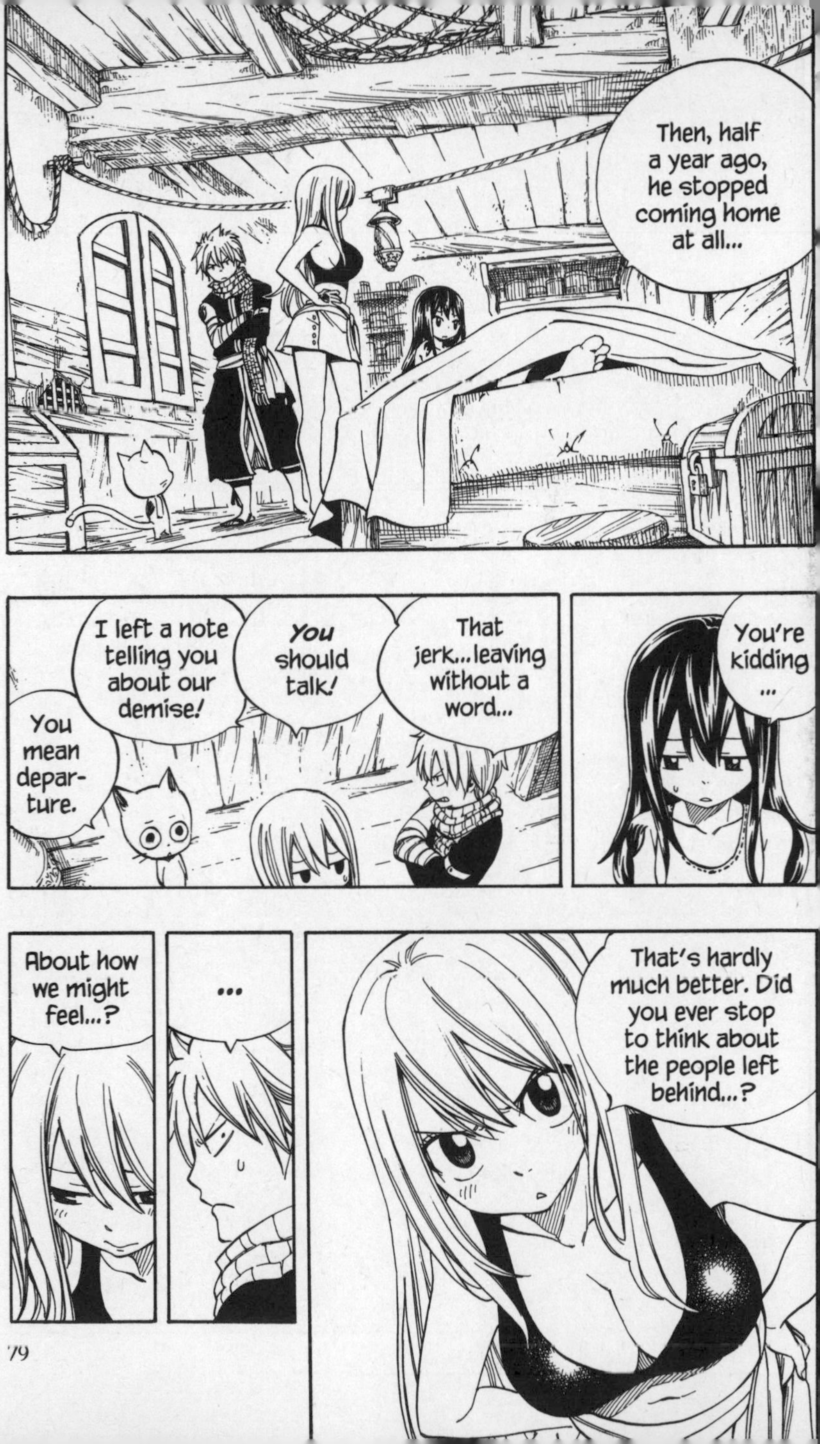

Then, half a year ago, he stopped coming home at all...
You're kidding ...
That jerk...leaving without a word...
You should talk!
I left a note telling you about our demise!
You mean departure.
That's hardly much better. Did you ever stop to think about the people left behind...?
...
About how we might feel...?

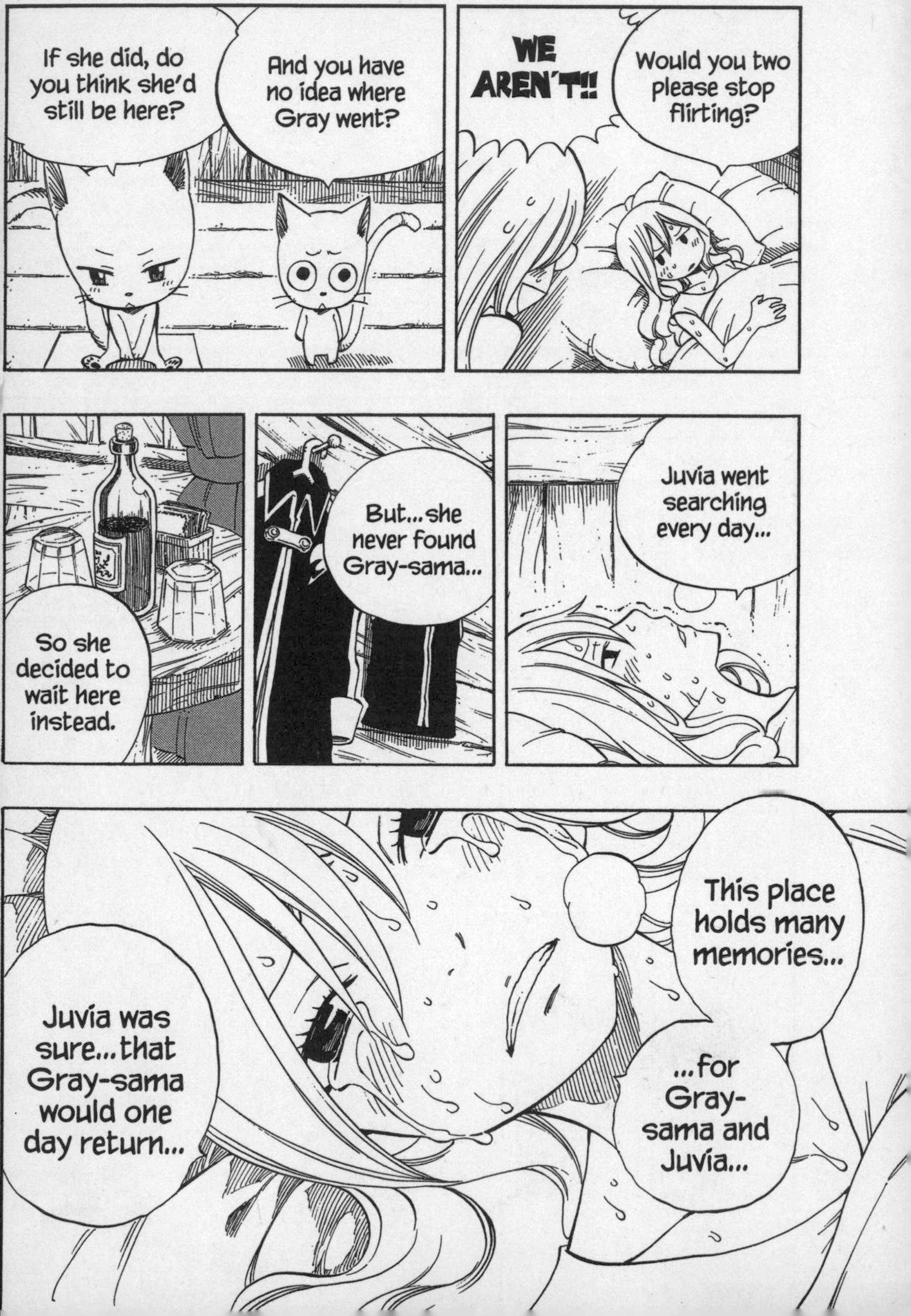
Would you two please stop flirting?
WE AREN'T!!
And you have no idea where Gray went?
If she did, do you think she'd still be here?
Juvia went searching every day...
But...she never found Gray-sama...
So she decided to wait here instead.
This place holds many memories...
...for Gray-sama and Juvia...
Juvia was sure...that Gray-sama would one day return...

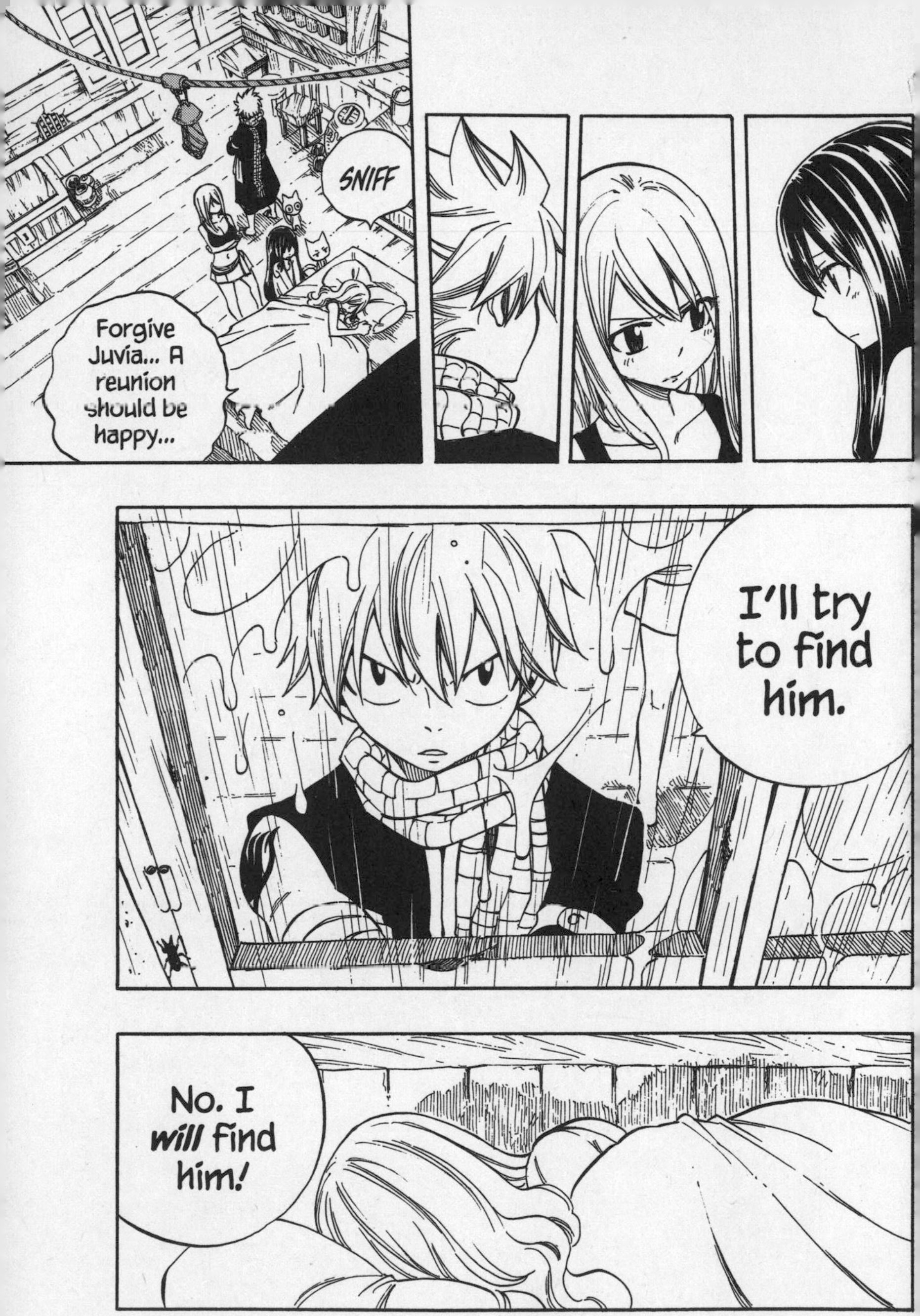
SNIFF
Forgive Juvia... A reunion should be happy...
I'll try to find him.
No. I *will* find him!

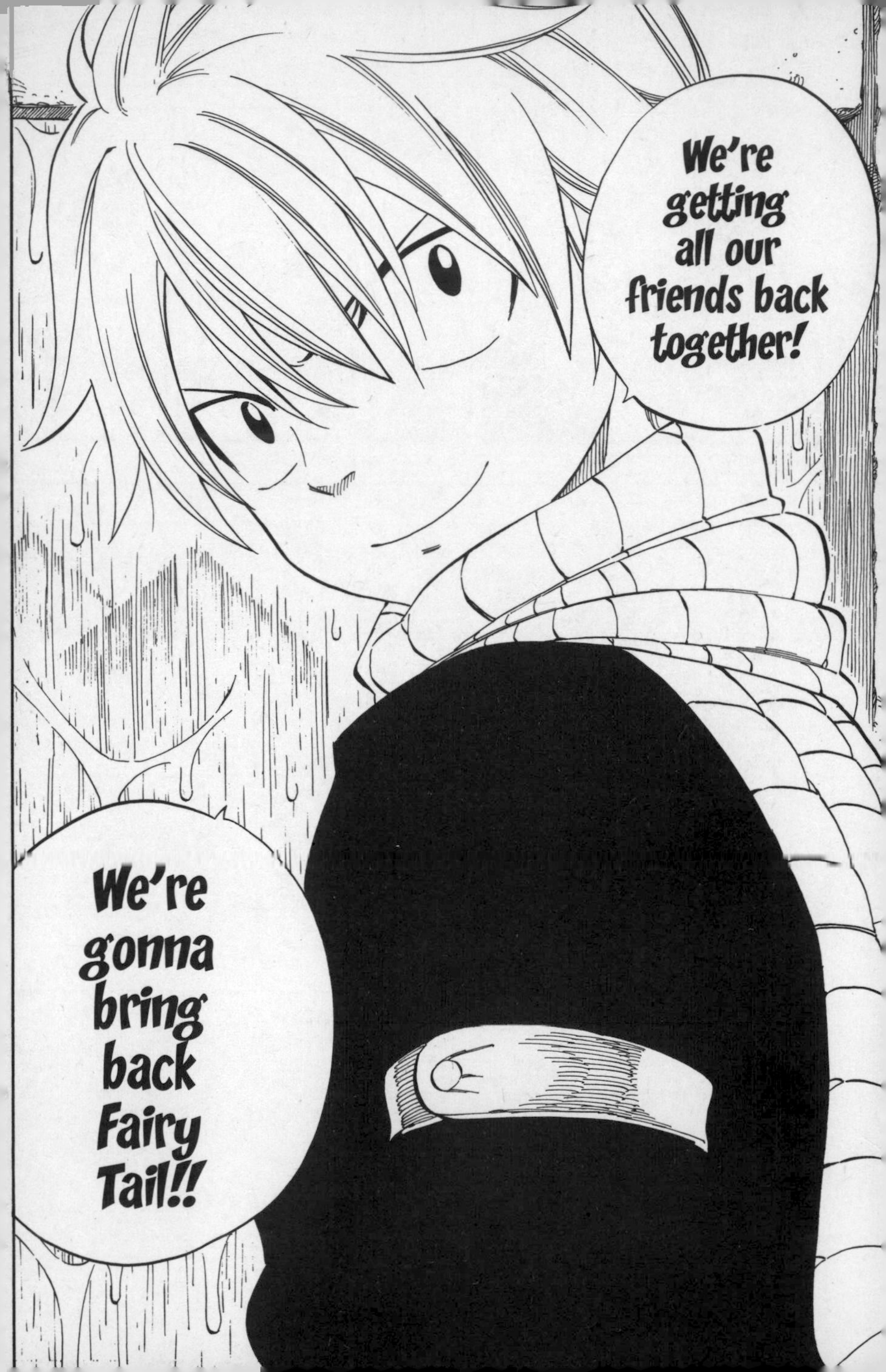
We're getting all our friends back together!
We're gonna bring back Fairy Tail!!

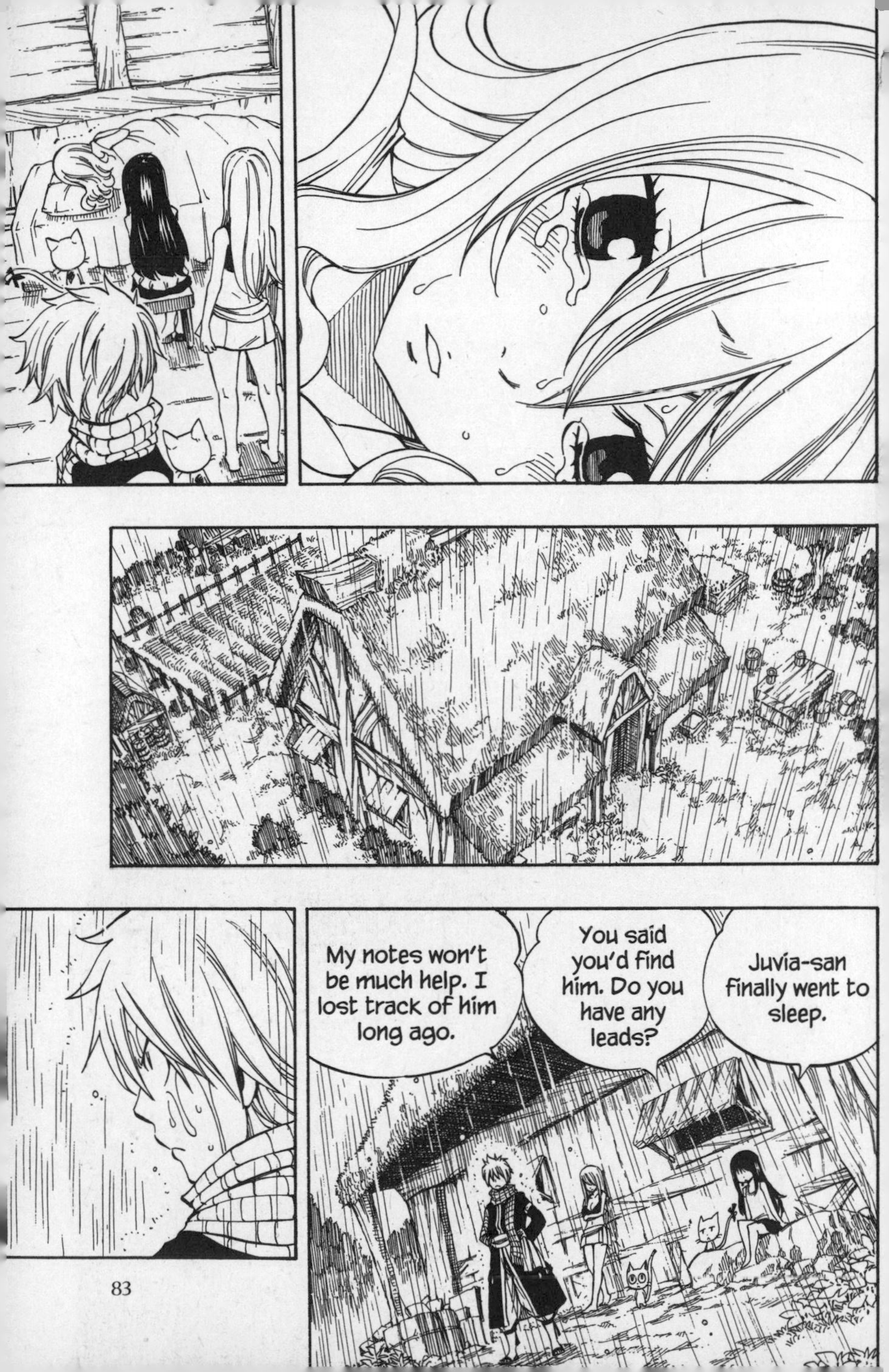
Juvia-san finally went to sleep.
You said you'd find him. Do you have any leads?
My notes won't be much help. I lost track of him long ago.

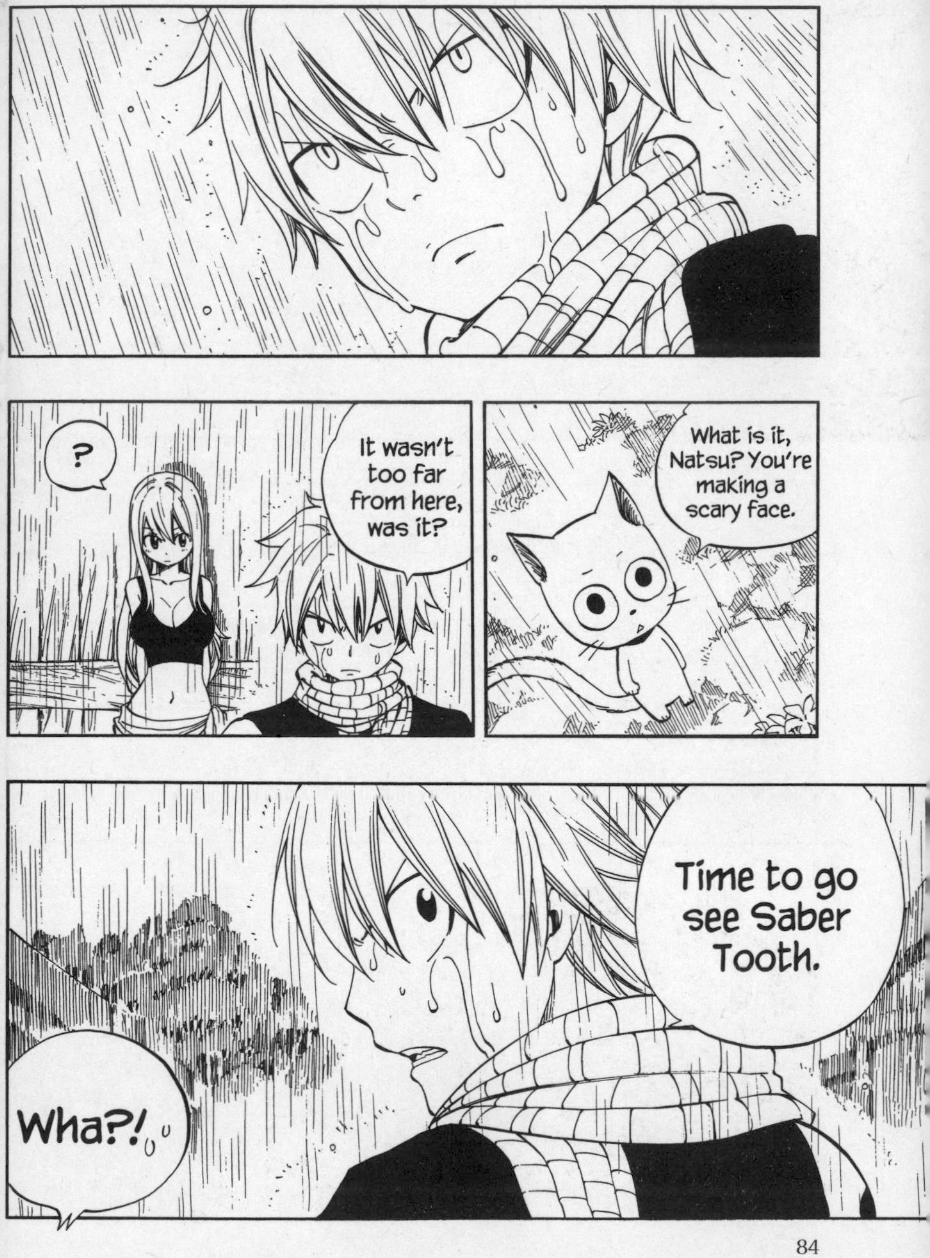
What is it, Natsu? You're making a scary face.
It wasn't too far from here, was it?
?
Time to go see Saber Tooth.
Wha?!

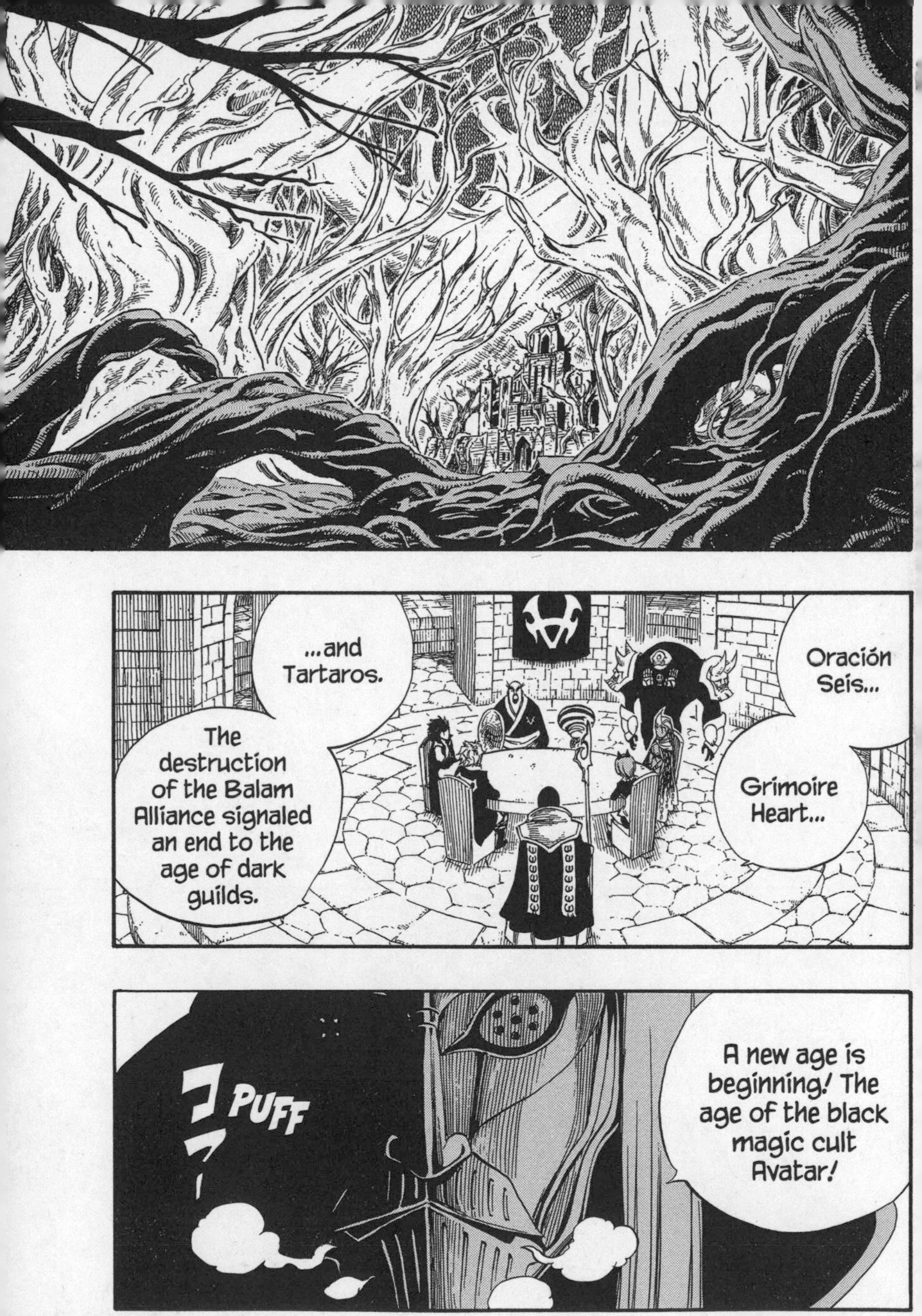
Oración Seis...
Grimoire Heart...
...and Tartaros.
The destruction of the Balam Alliance signaled an end to the age of dark guilds.
A new age is beginning! The age of the black magic cult Avatar!
PUFF

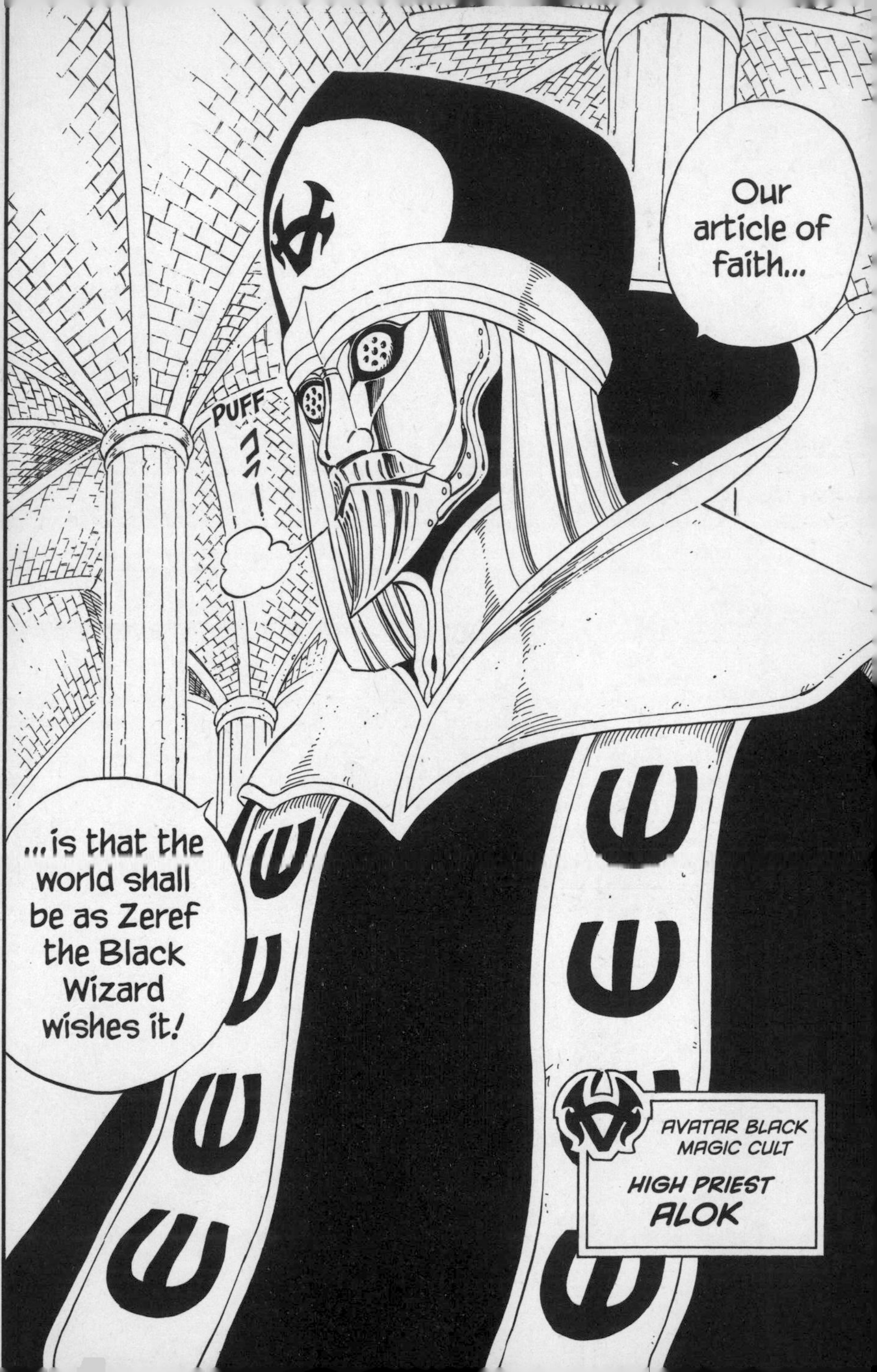
Our article of faith...
PUFF
...is that the world shall be as Zeref the Black Wizard wishes it!
AVATAR BLACK MAGIC CULT
HIGH PRIEST ALOK

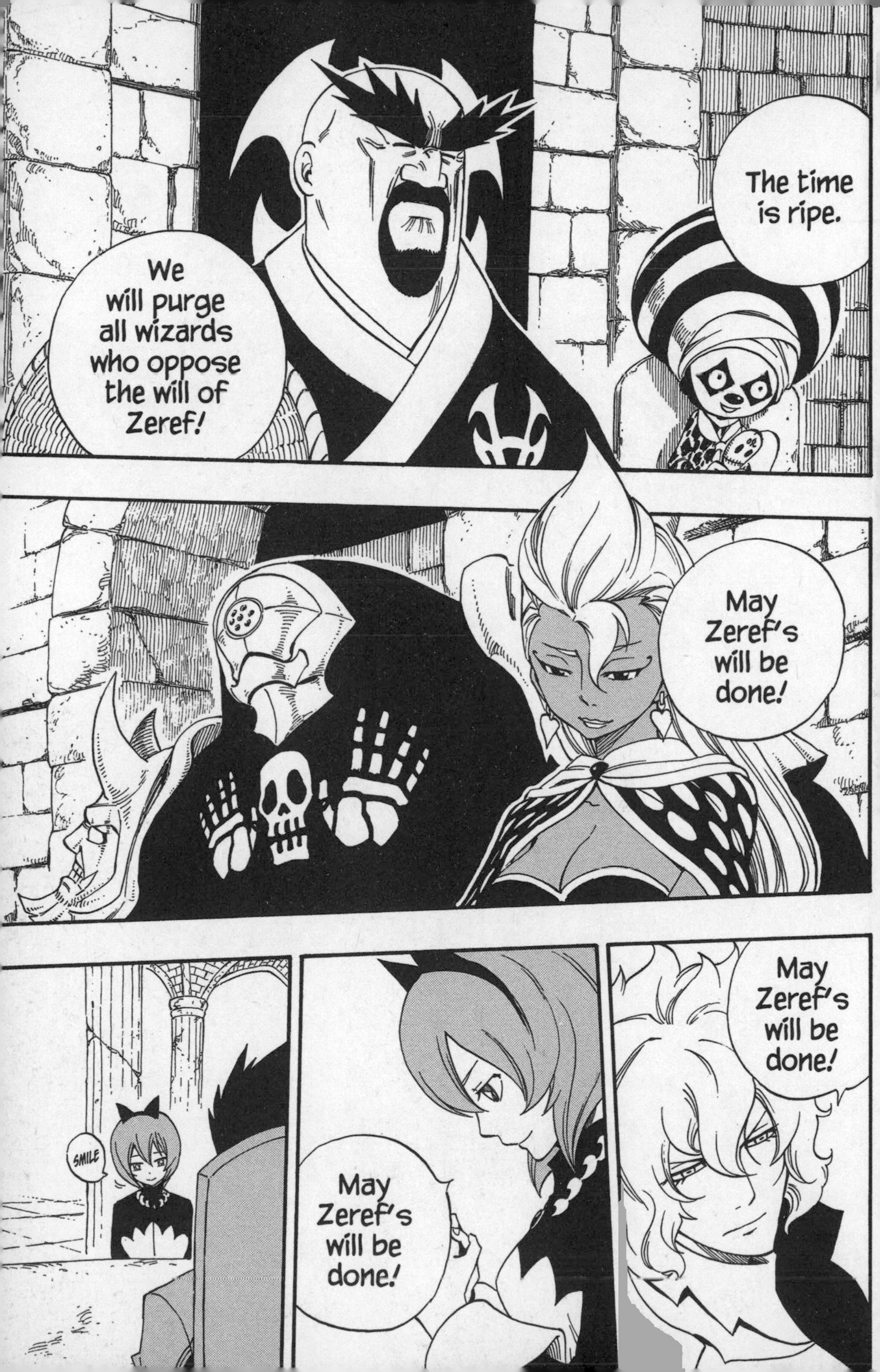
The time is ripe.
We will purge all wizards who oppose the will of Zeref!
May Zeref's will be done!
May Zeref's will be done!
May Zeref's will be done!
SMILE

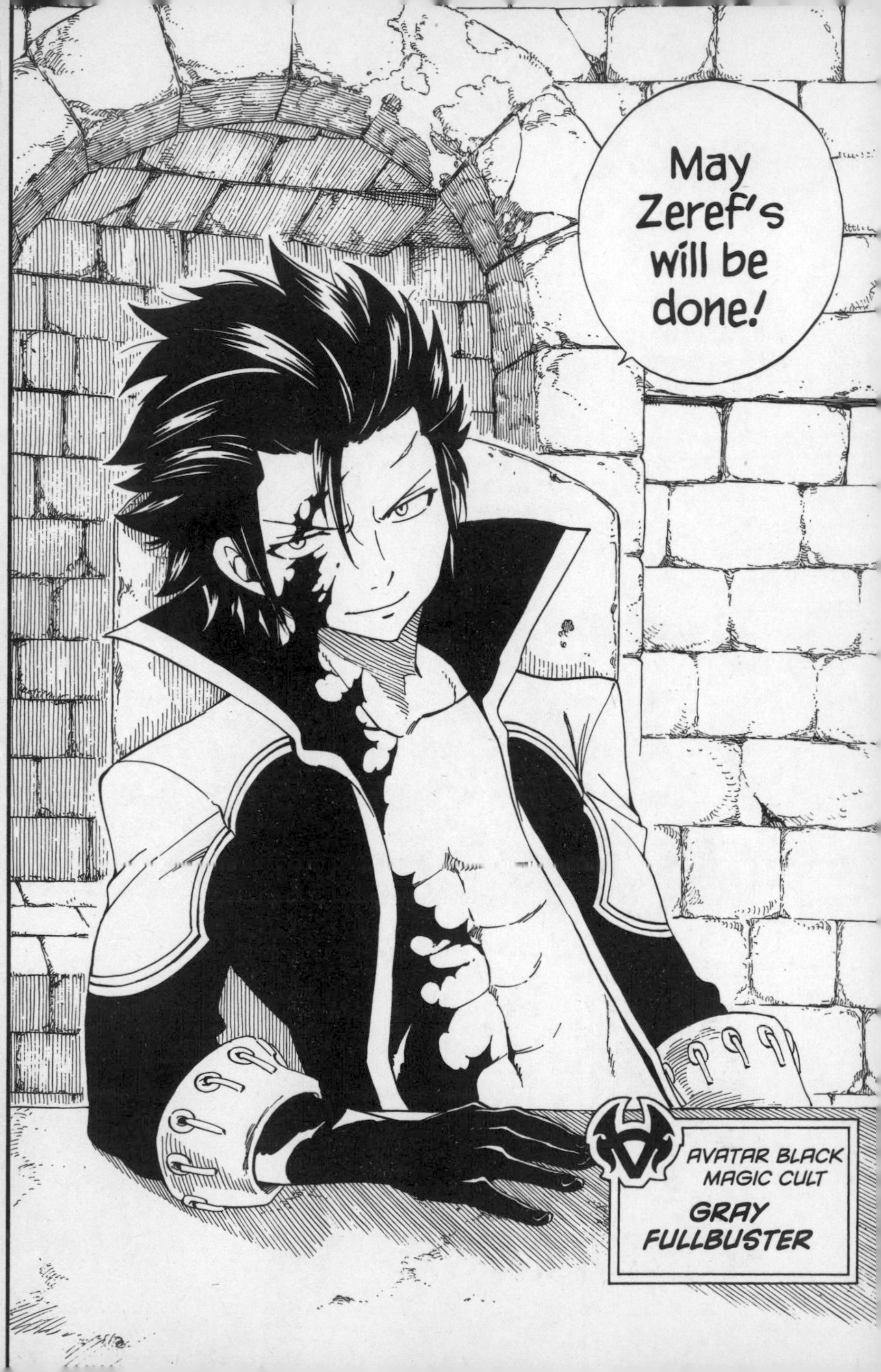

May Zeref's will be done!
AVATAR BLACK MAGIC CULT
GRAY FULLBUSTER

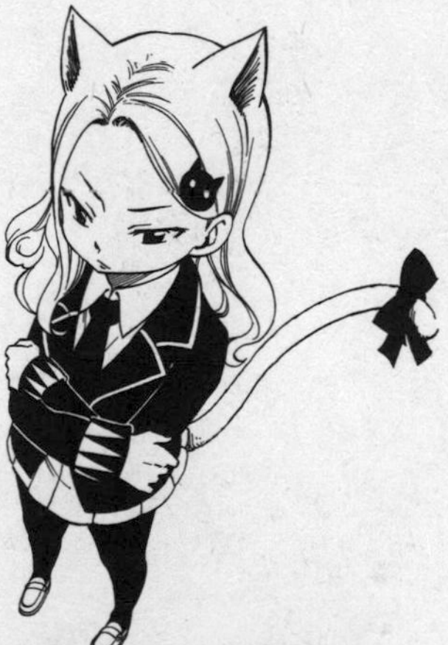

FAIRY TAIL

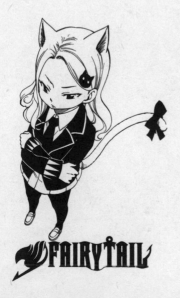

Chapter 425: Saber Tooth X792

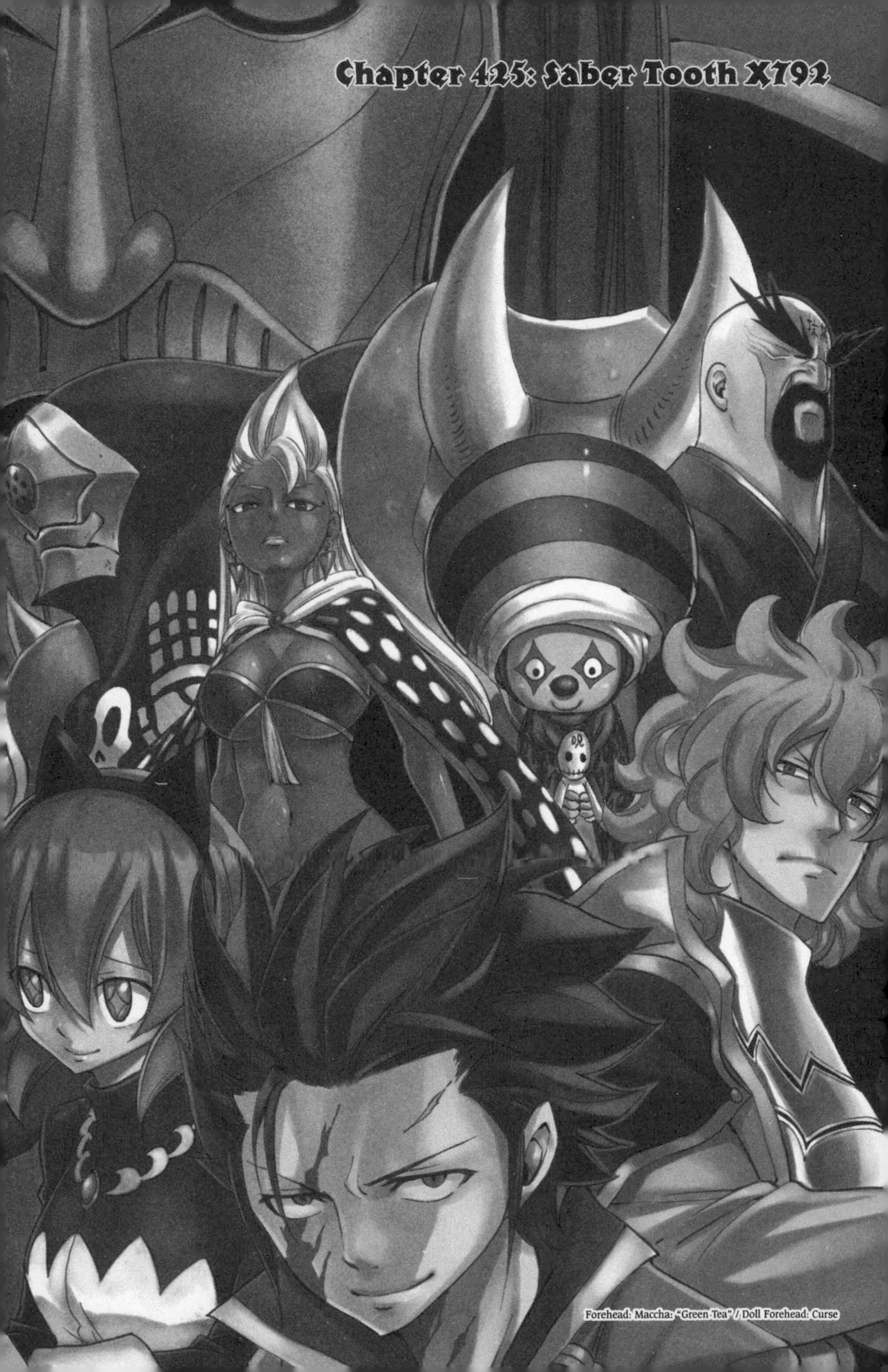

Forehead: Maccha: "Green Tea" / Doll Forehead: Curse

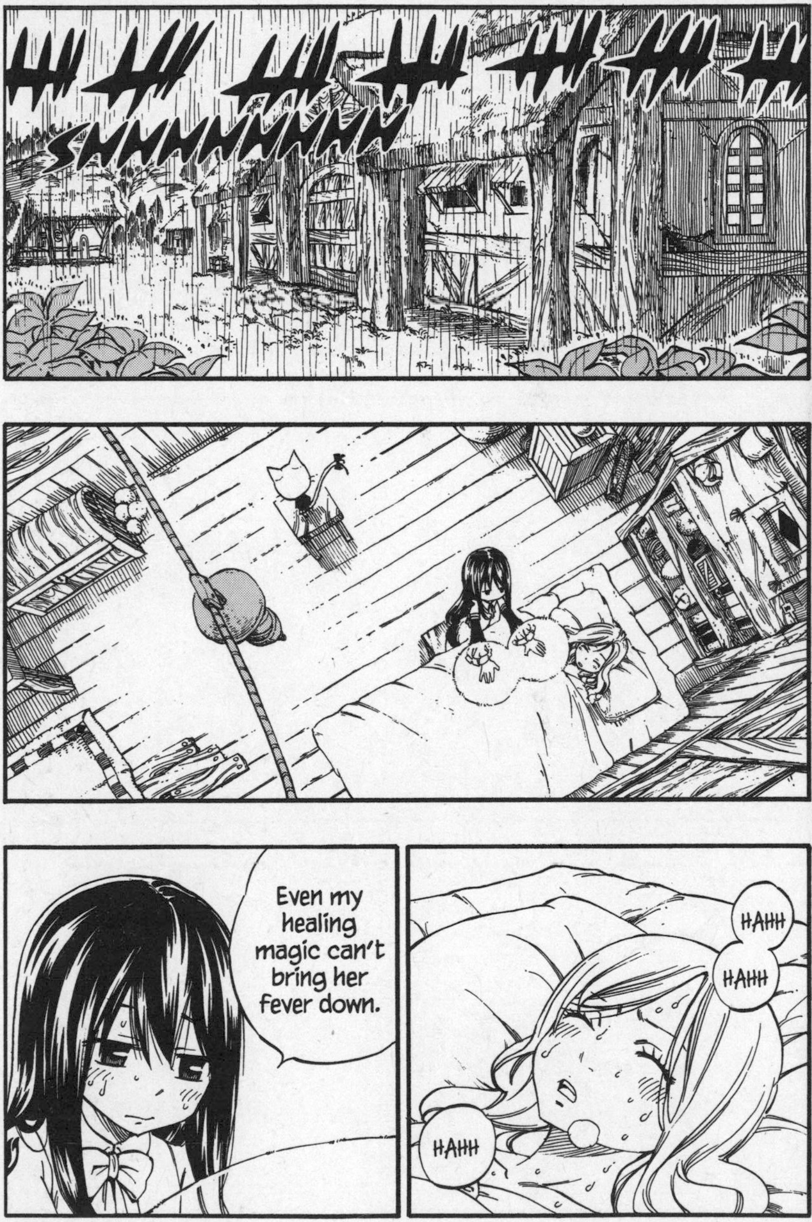
HAHH
HAHH
HAHH
Even my healing magic can't bring her fever down.

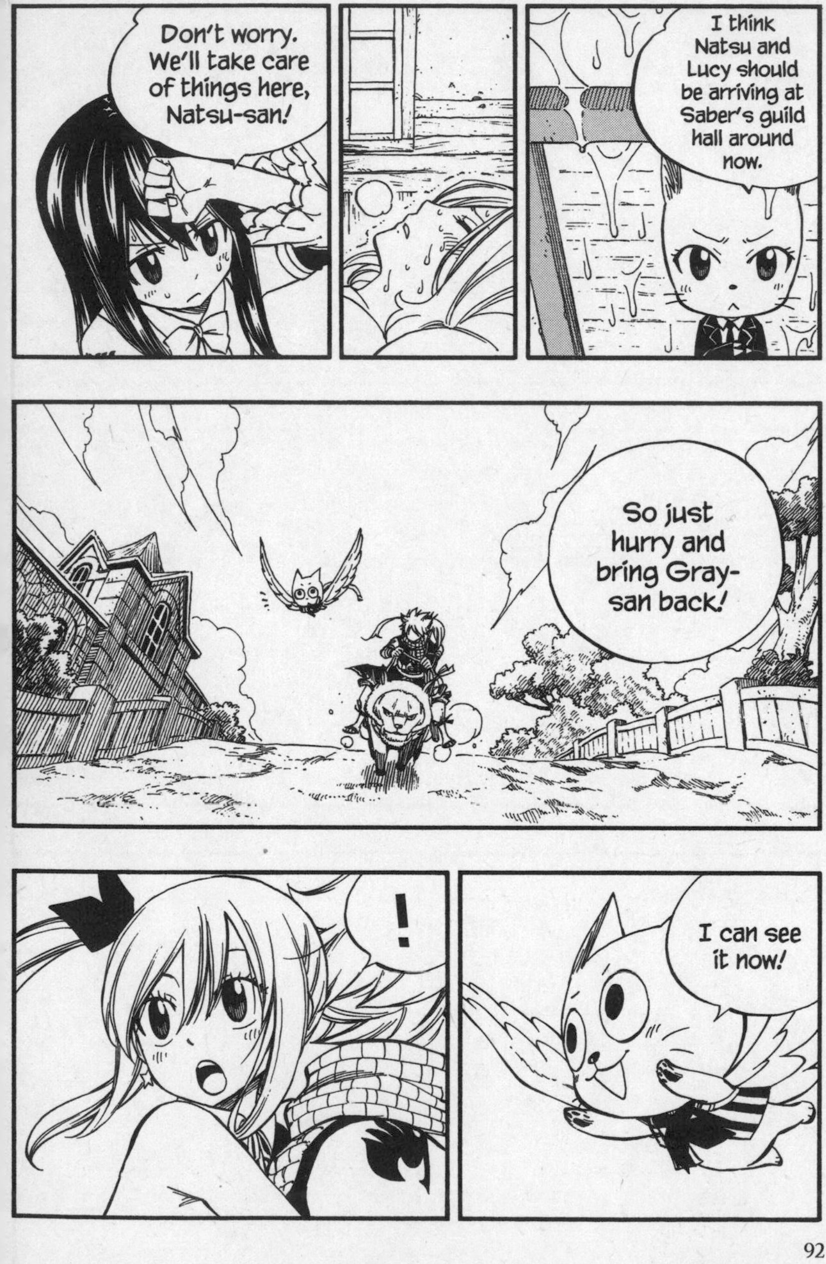

I think Natsu and Lucy should be arriving at Saber's guild hall around now.
Don't worry. We'll take care of things here, Natsu-san!
So just hurry and bring Gray-san back!
I can see it now!
!

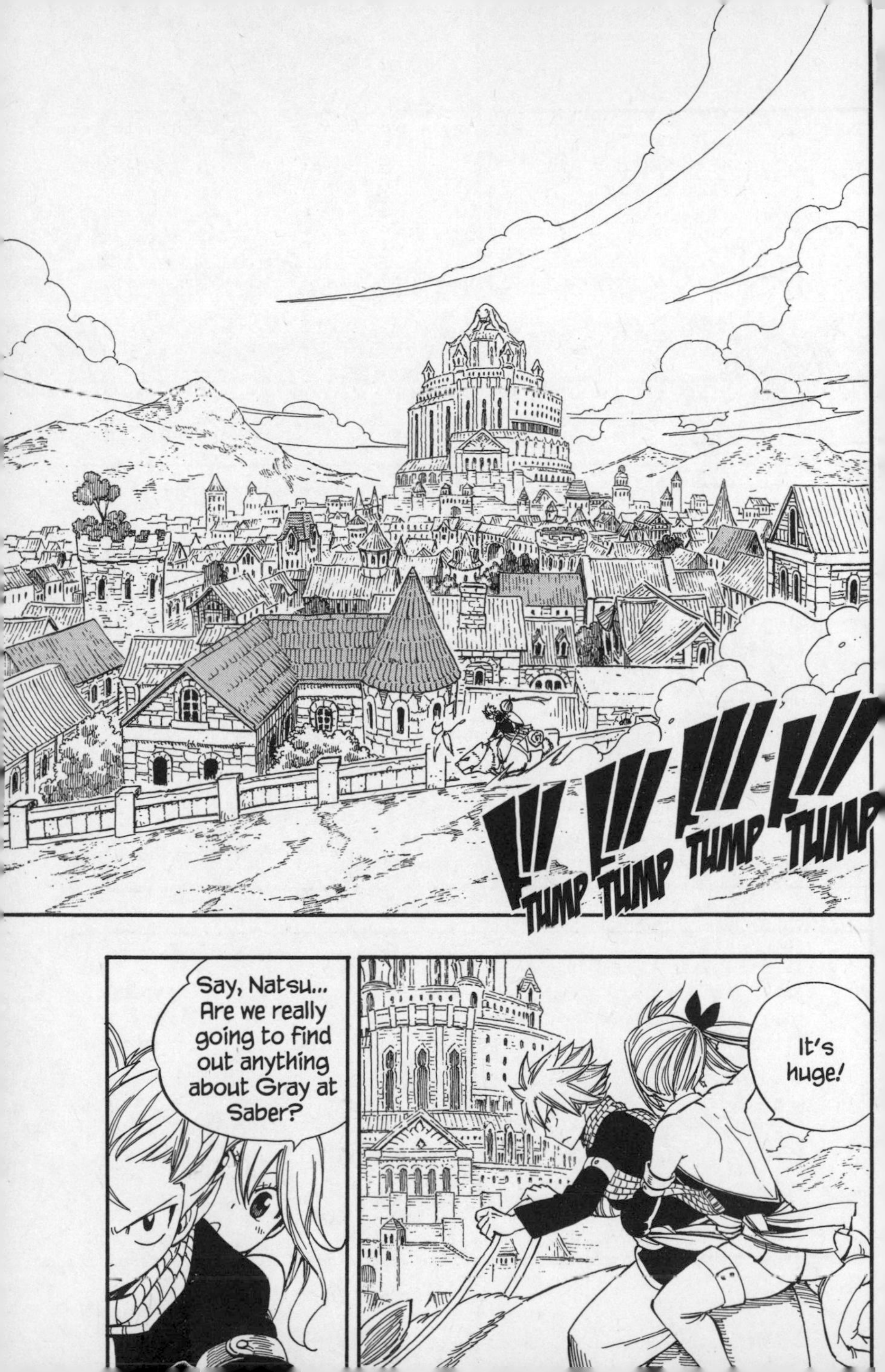
TUMP TUMP TUMP TUMP
It's huge!
Say, Natsu... Are we really going to find out anything about Gray at Saber?

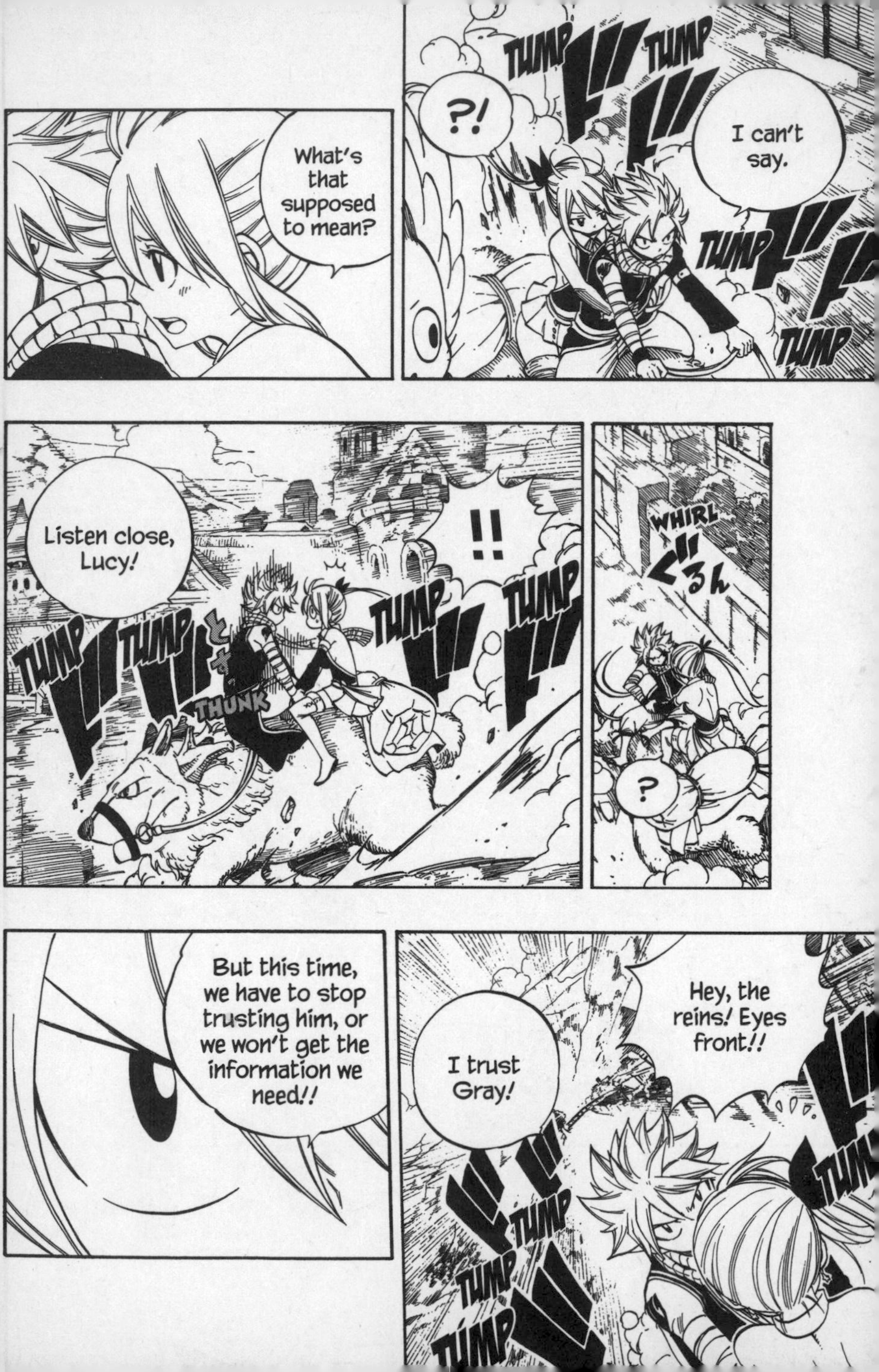

TUMP
TUMP
?!
I can't say.
TUMP
TUMP
What's that supposed to mean?
WHIRL
?
!!
TUMP
TUMP
Listen close, Lucy!
TUMP
TUMP
THUNK
Hey, the reins! Eyes front!!
I trust Gray!
TUMP
TUMP
TUMP
TUMP
But this time, we have to stop trusting him, or we won't get the information we need!!

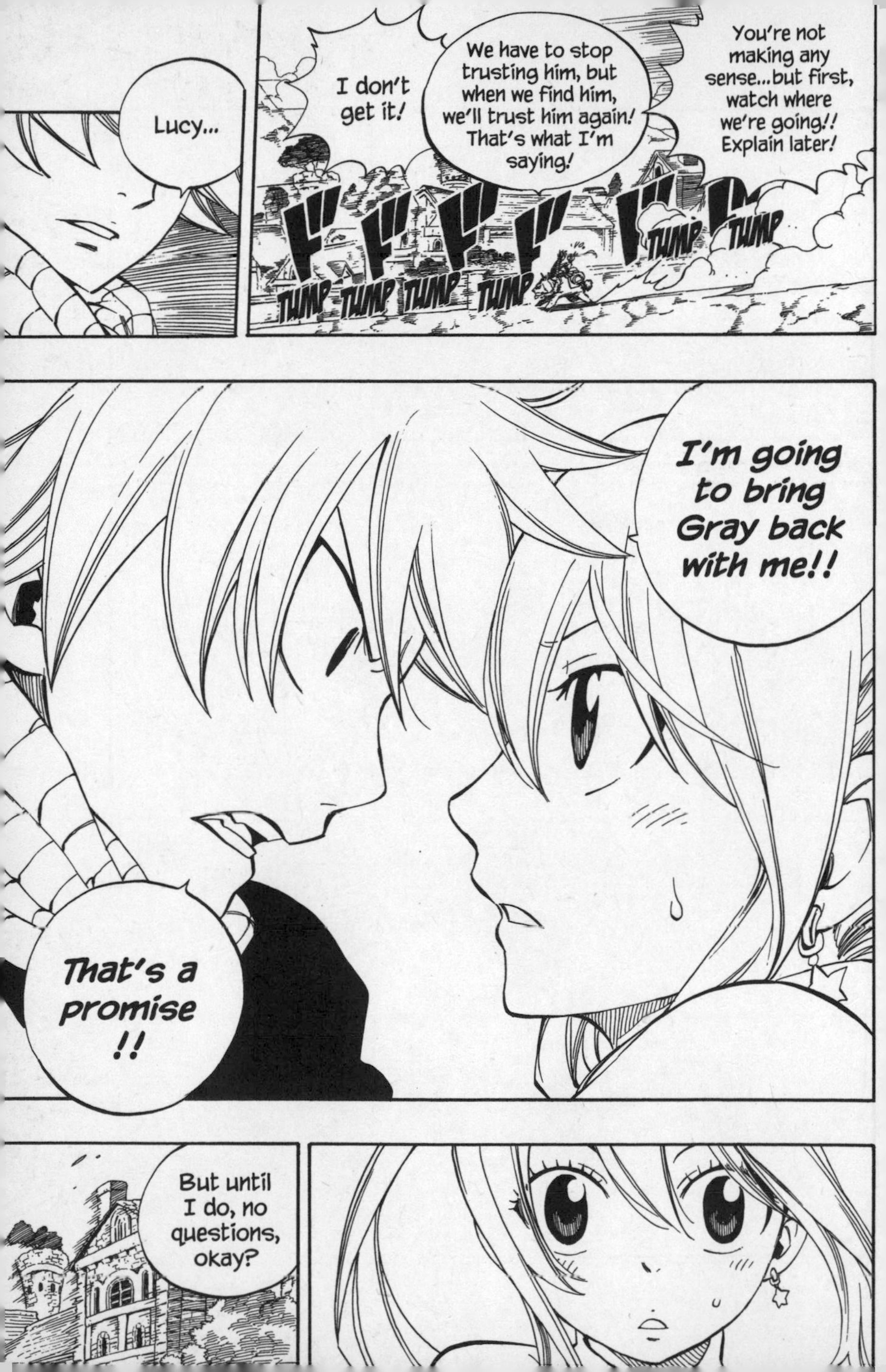
You're not making any sense...but first, watch where we're going!! Explain later!
We have to stop trusting him, but when we find him, we'll trust him again! That's what I'm saying!
I don't get it!
TUMP
TUMP
TUMP
TUMP
TUMP
TUMP
Lucy...
I'm going to bring Gray back with me!!
That's a promise !!
But until I do, no questions, okay?

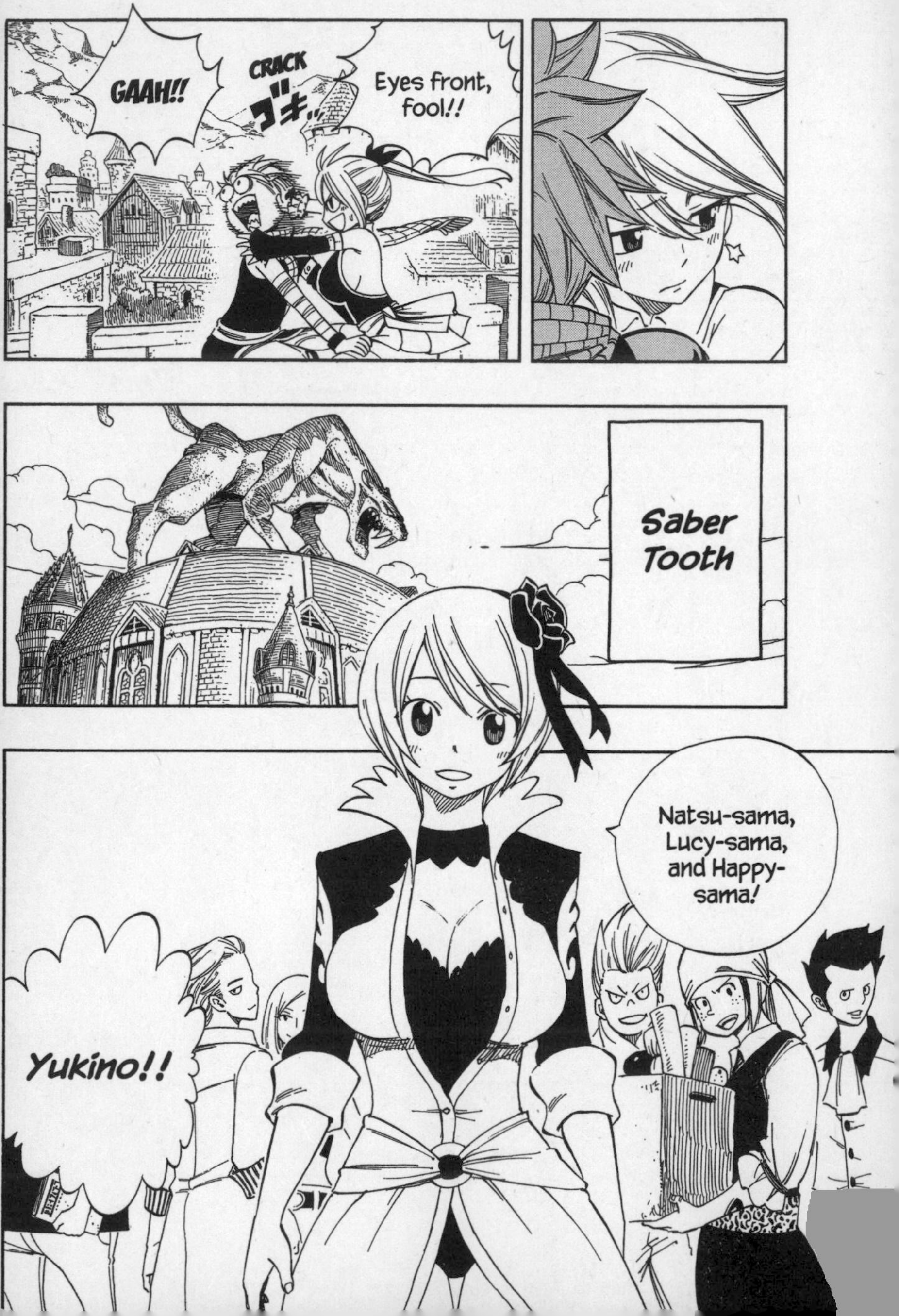
Eyes front, fool!!
CRACK
ゴキ..
GAAH!!
Saber Tooth
Natsu-sama, Lucy-sama, and Happy-sama!
Yukino!!

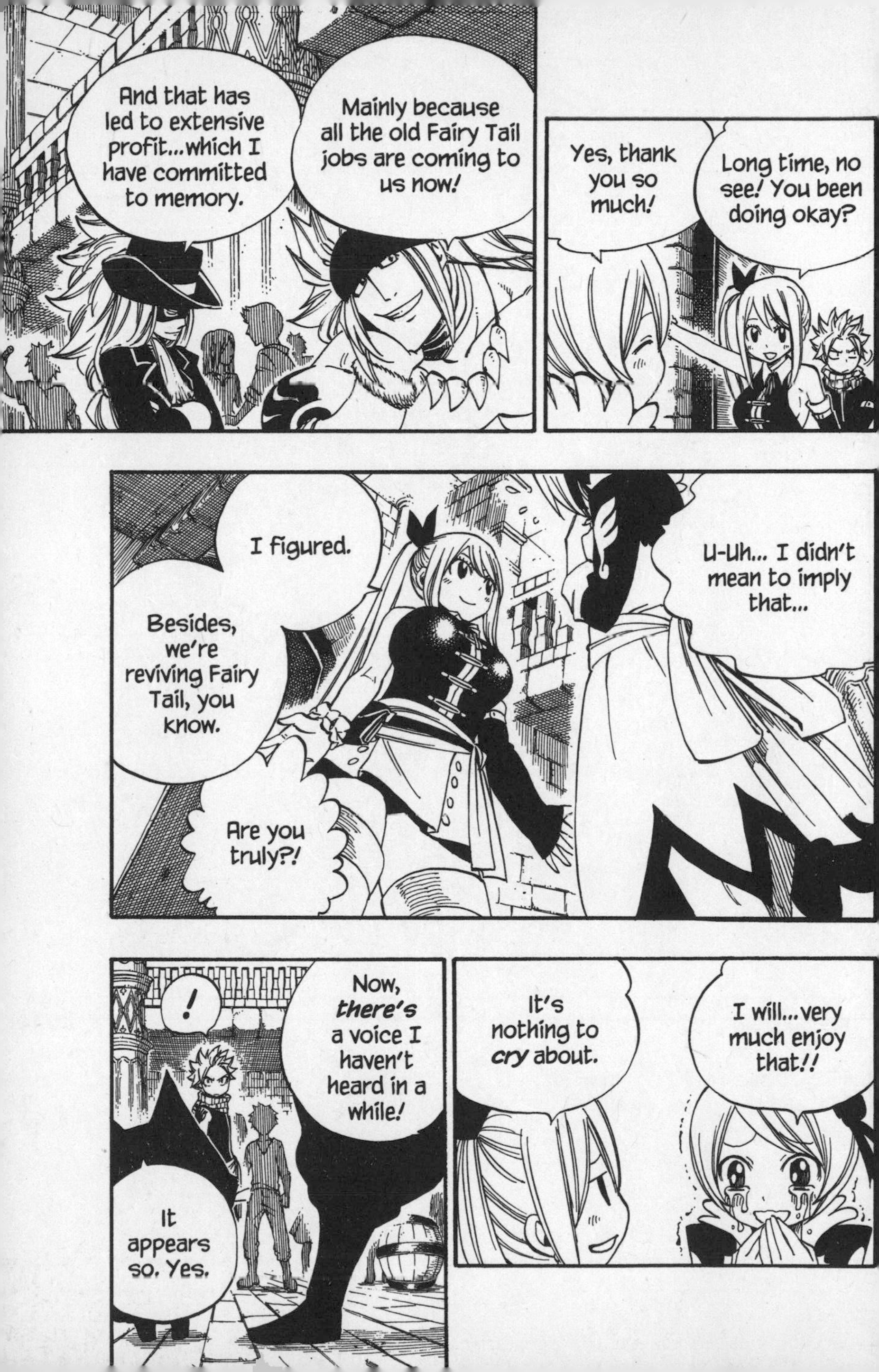
Long time, no see! You been doing okay?
Yes, thank you so much!
Mainly because all the old Fairy Tail jobs are coming to us now!
And that has led to extensive profit...which I have committed to memory.
U-Uh... I didn't mean to imply that...
I figured.
Besides, we're reviving Fairy Tail, you know.
Are you truly?!
I will...very much enjoy that!!
It's nothing to *cry* about.
!
Now, ***there's*** a voice I haven't heard in a while!
It appears so. Yes.

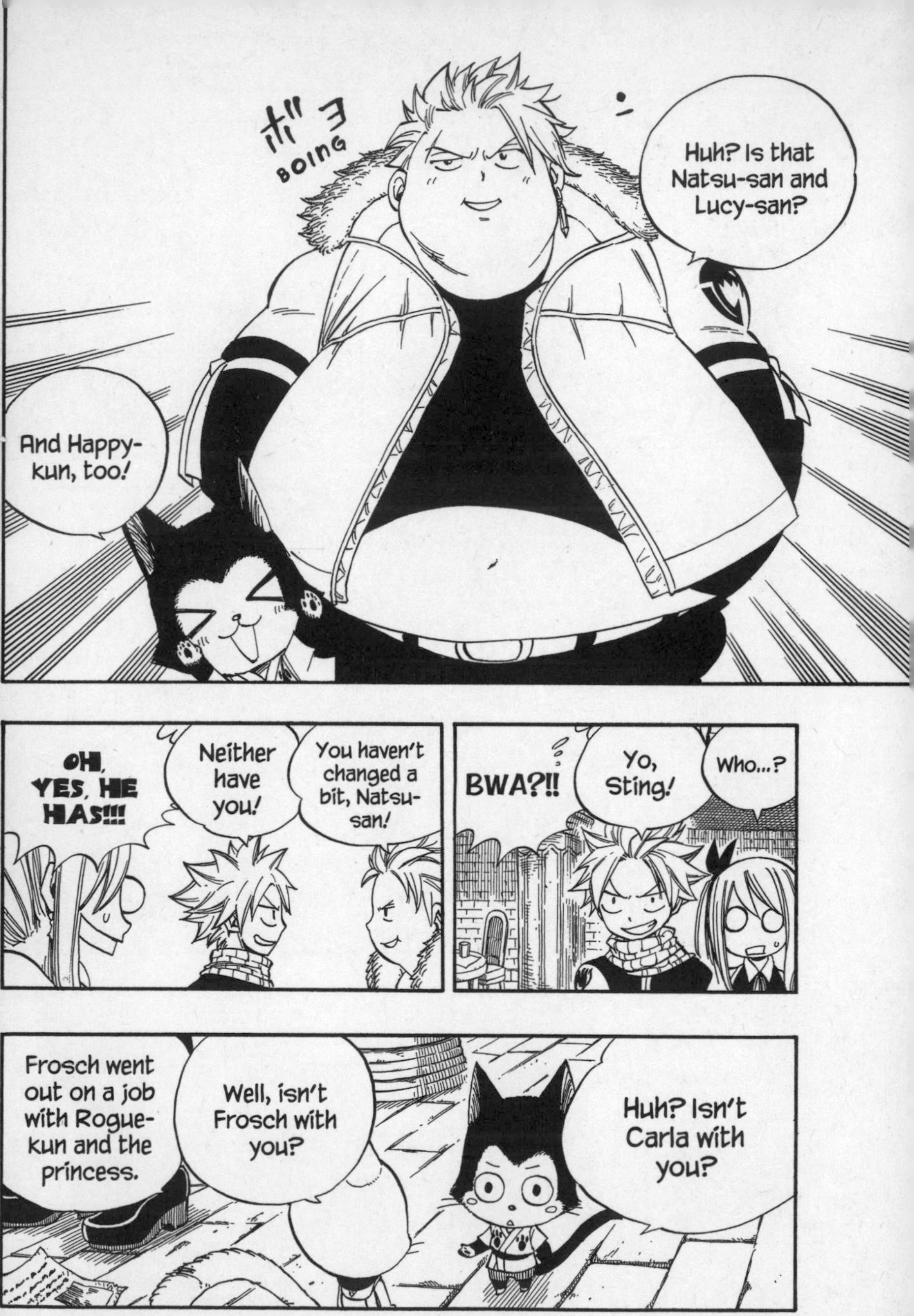
Huh? Is that Natsu-san and Lucy-san?
ボヨ
BOING
And Happy-kun, too!
Who...?
Yo, Sting!
BWA?!!
You haven't changed a bit, Natsu-san!
Neither have you!
OH, YES, HE HAS!!!
Huh? Isn't Carla with you?
Well, isn't Frosch with you?
Frosch went out on a job with Rogue-kun and the princess.

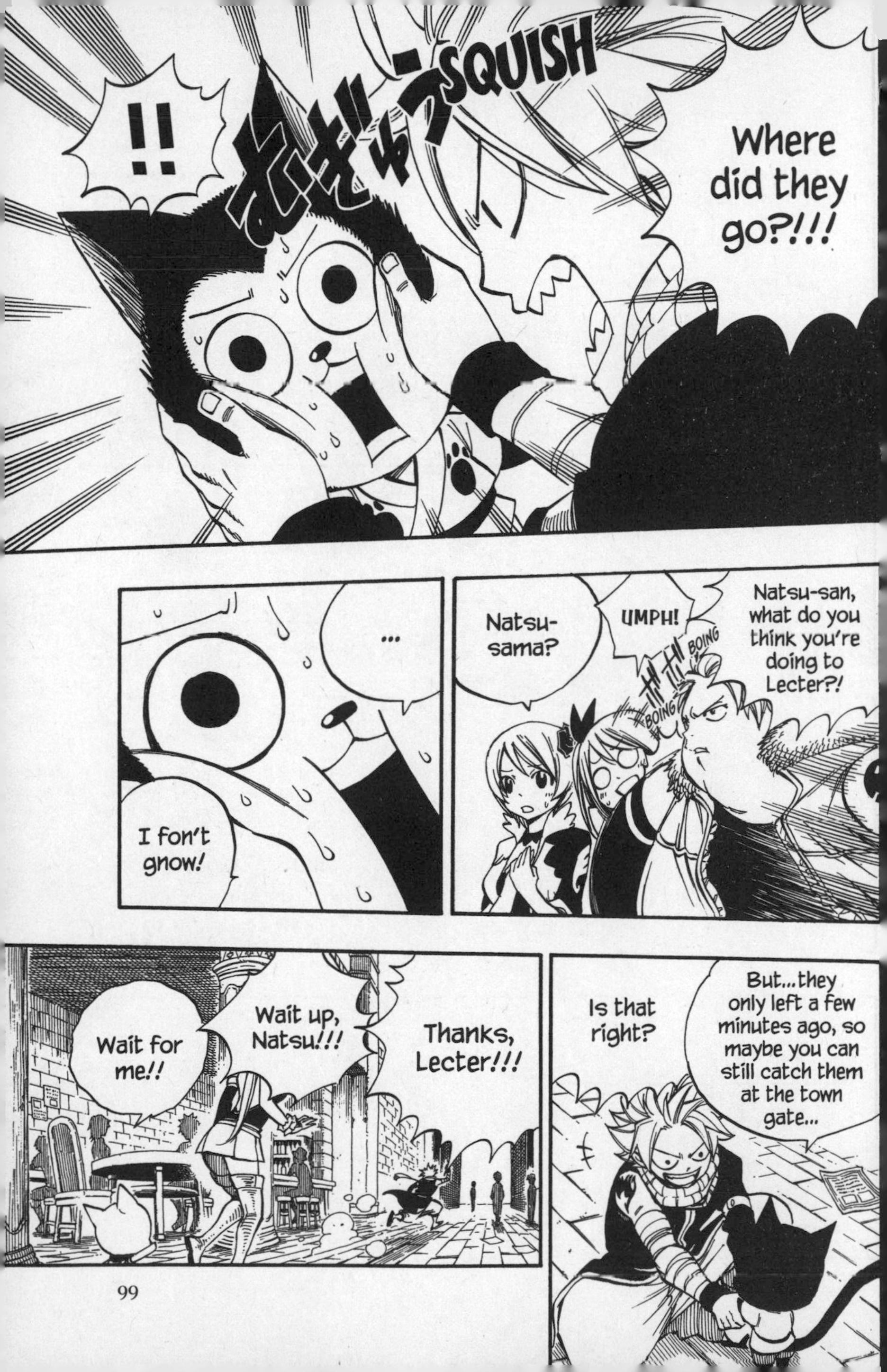
SQUISH
Where did they go?!!!
!!
Natsu-san, what do you think you're doing to Lecter?!
UMPH!
BOING
BOING
Natsu-sama?
...
I fon't gnow!
But...they only left a few minutes ago, so maybe you can still catch them at the town gate...
Is that right?
Thanks, Lecter!!!
Wait up, Natsu!!!
Wait for me!!

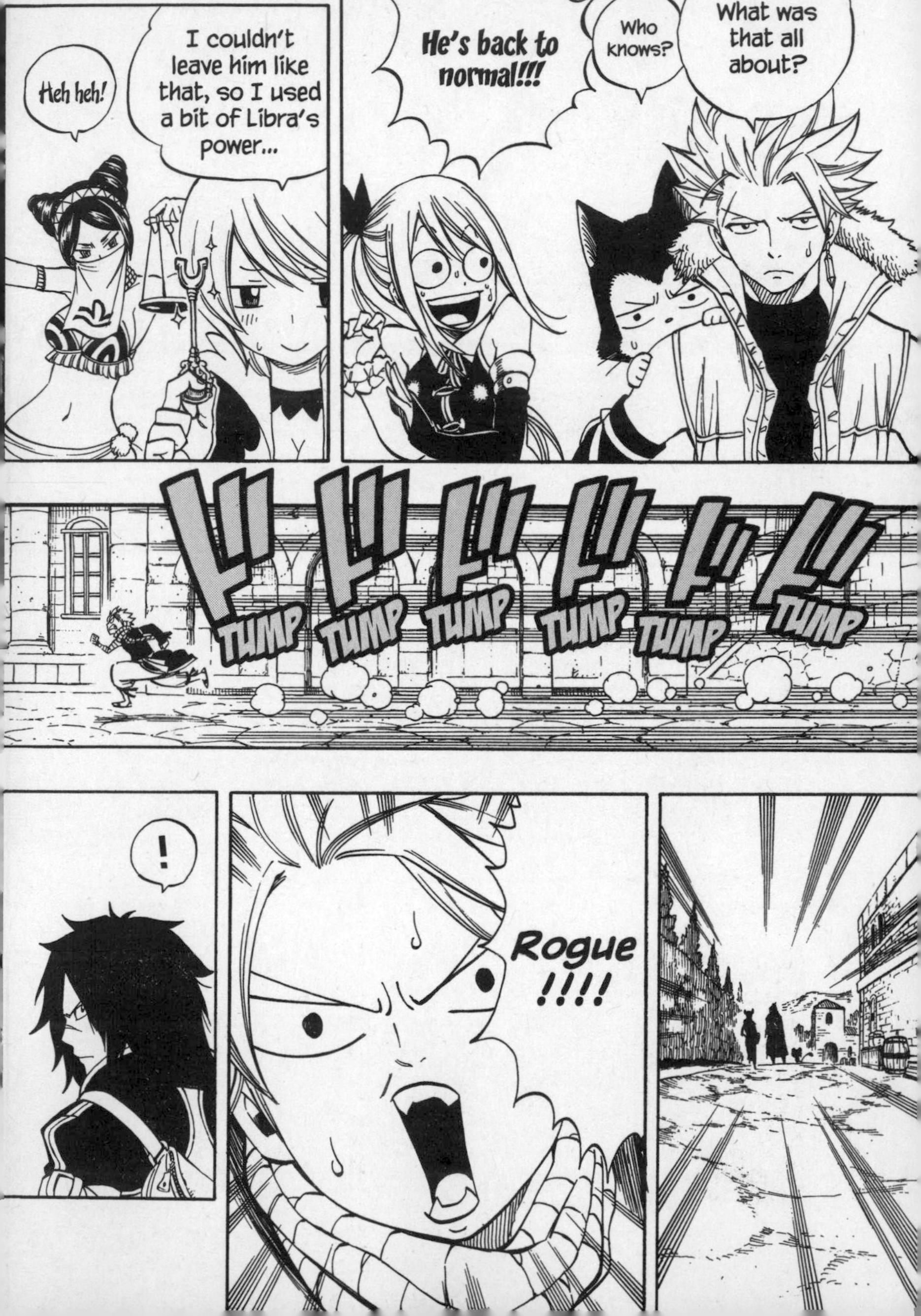
What was that all about?
Who knows?
He's back to normal!!!
I couldn't leave him like that, so I used a bit of Libra's power...
Heh heh!
TUMP
TUMP
TUMP
TUMP
TUMP
TUMP
Rogue!!!!
!

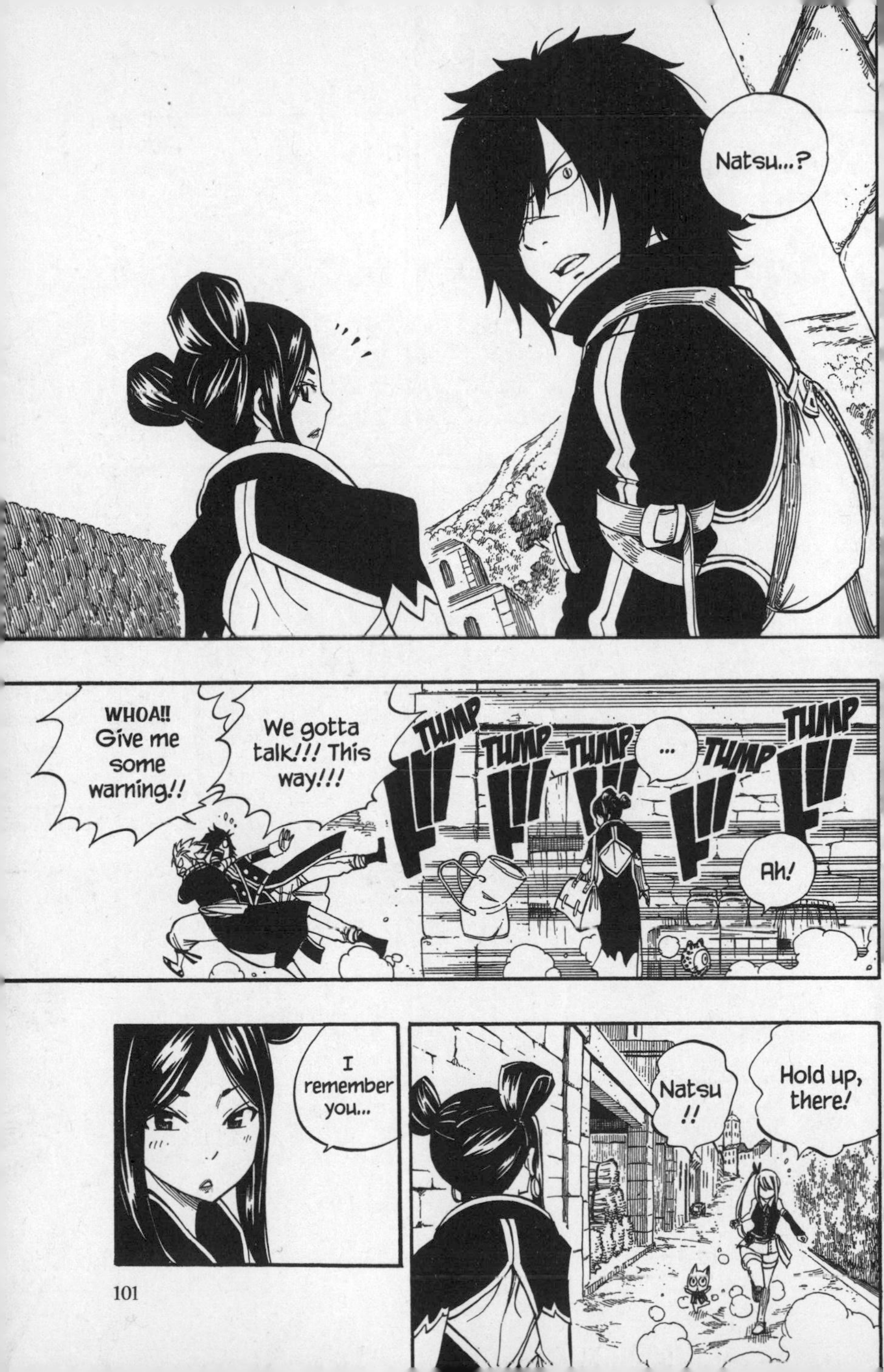
Natsu...?
TUMP
Ah!
TUMP
...
TUMP
TUMP
TUMP
We gotta talk!!! This way!!!
WHOA!! Give me some warning!!
Hold up, there!
Natsu !!
I remember you...

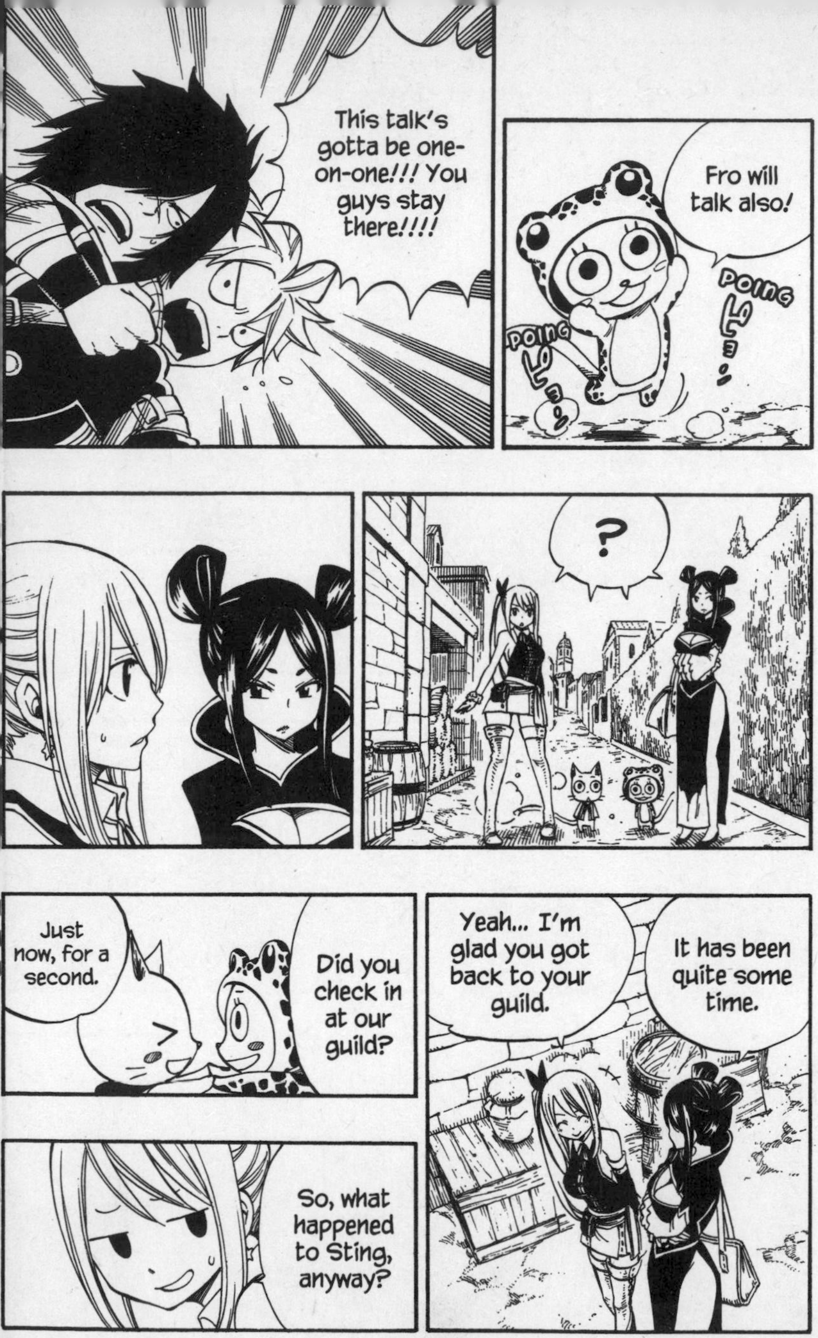
Fro will talk also!
POING
POING
This talk's gotta be one-on-one!!! You guys stay there!!!!
?
It has been quite some time.
Yeah... I'm glad you got back to your guild.
Did you check in at our guild?
Just now, for a second.
So, what happened to Sting, anyway?

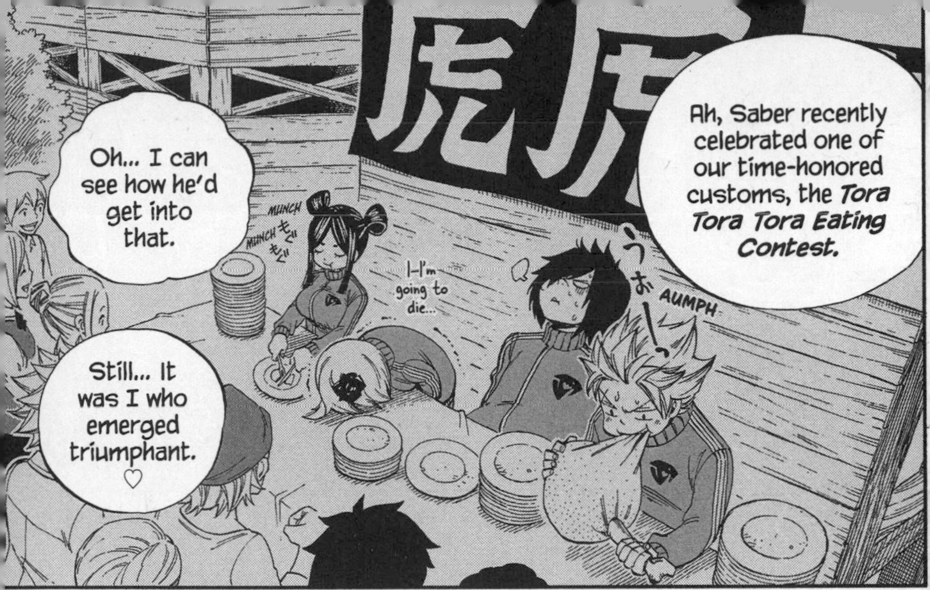
Ah, Saber recently celebrated one of our time-honored customs, the *Tora Tora Tora Eating Contest.*
AUMPH
I-I'm going to die...
MUNCH MUNCH
Oh... I can see how he'd get into that.
Still... It was I who emerged triumphant. ♡

Sign: Tora Tora Tora: "Tiger Tiger Tiger"

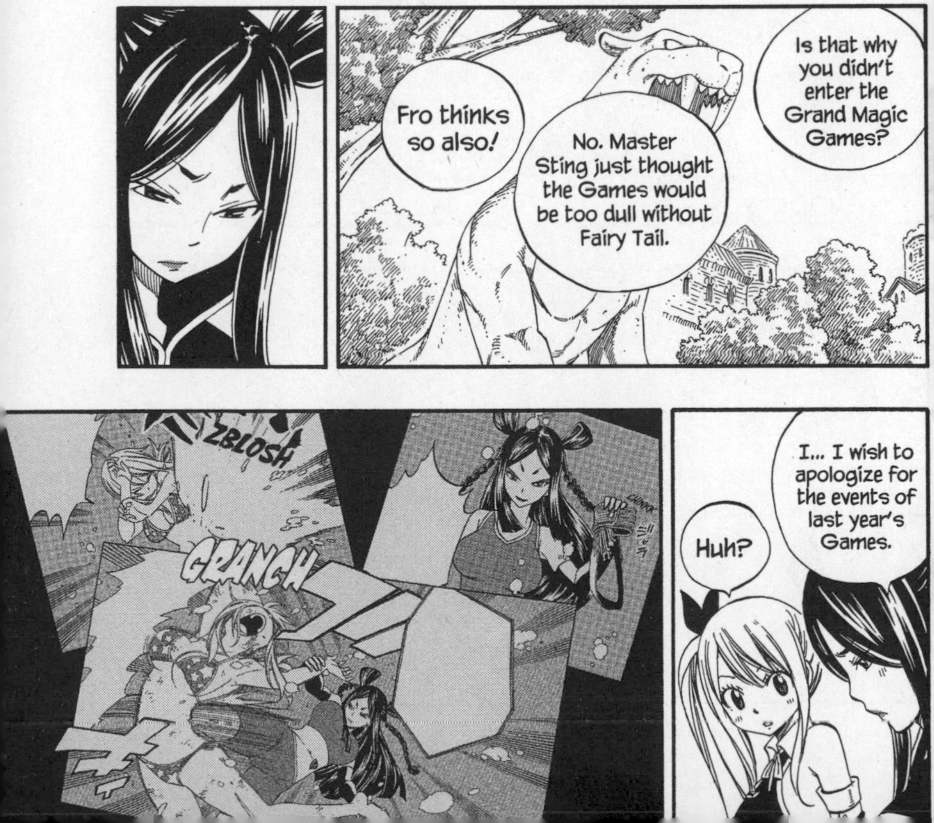
Is that why you didn't enter the Grand Magic Games?
No. Master Sting just thought the Games would be too dull without Fairy Tail.
Fro thinks so also!
I... I wish to apologize for the events of last year's Games.
Huh?
ZBLOSH
GRANCH

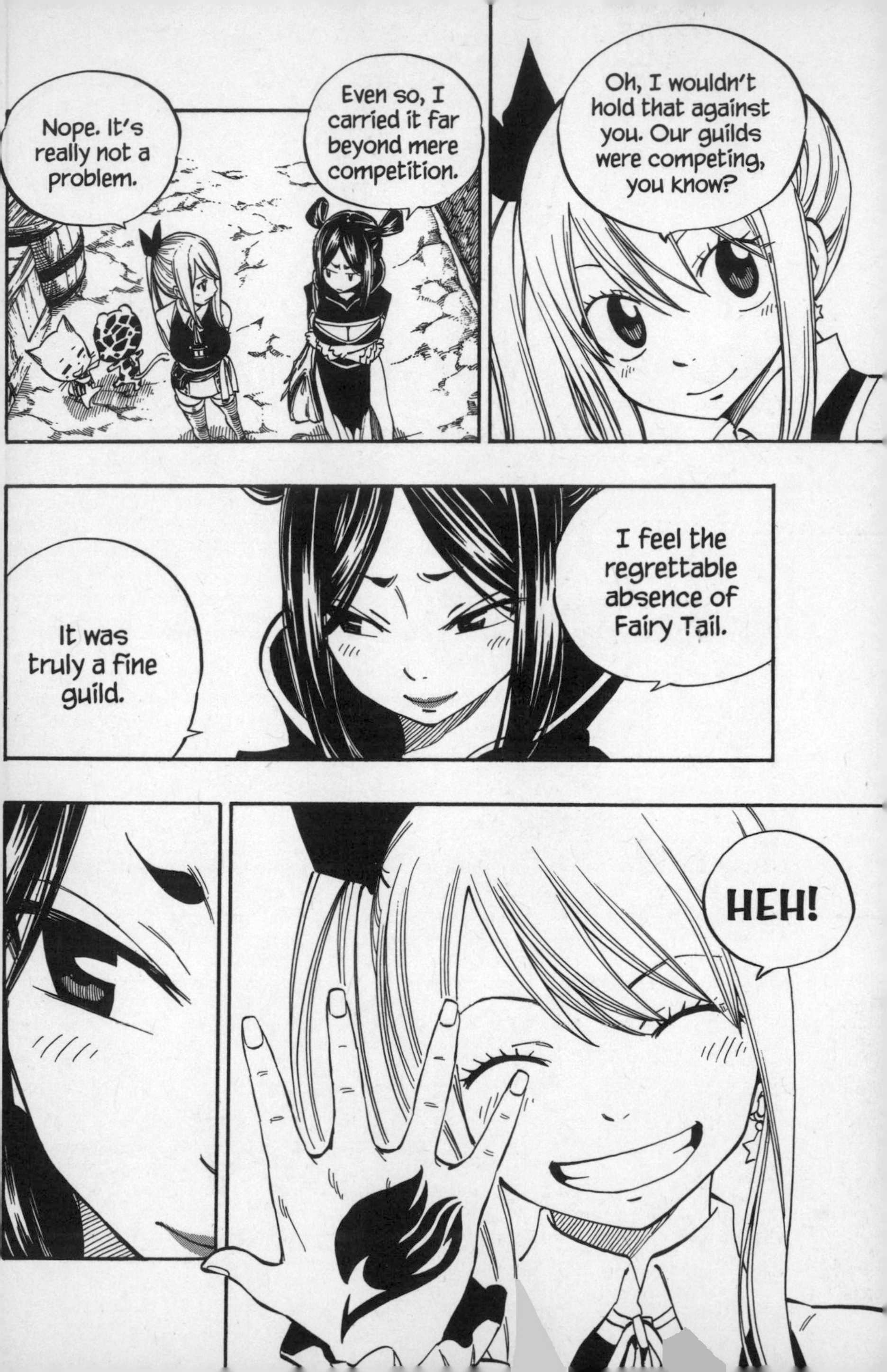
Oh, I wouldn't hold that against you. Our guilds were competing, you know?
Even so, I carried it far beyond mere competition.
Nope. It's really not a problem.
I feel the regrettable absence of Fairy Tail.
It was truly a fine guild.
HEH!

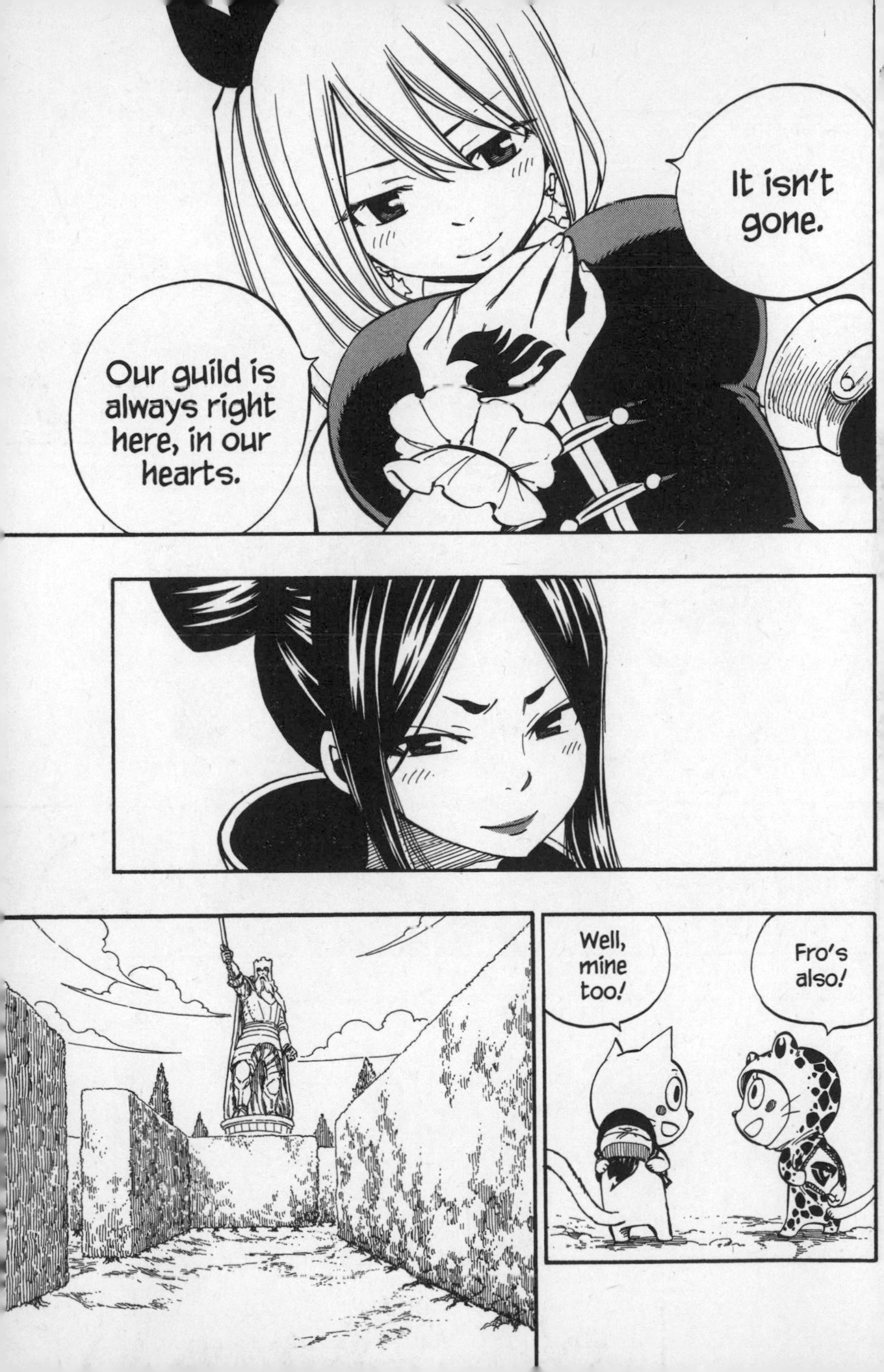
It isn't gone.
Our guild is always right here, in our hearts.
Fro's also!
Well, mine too!

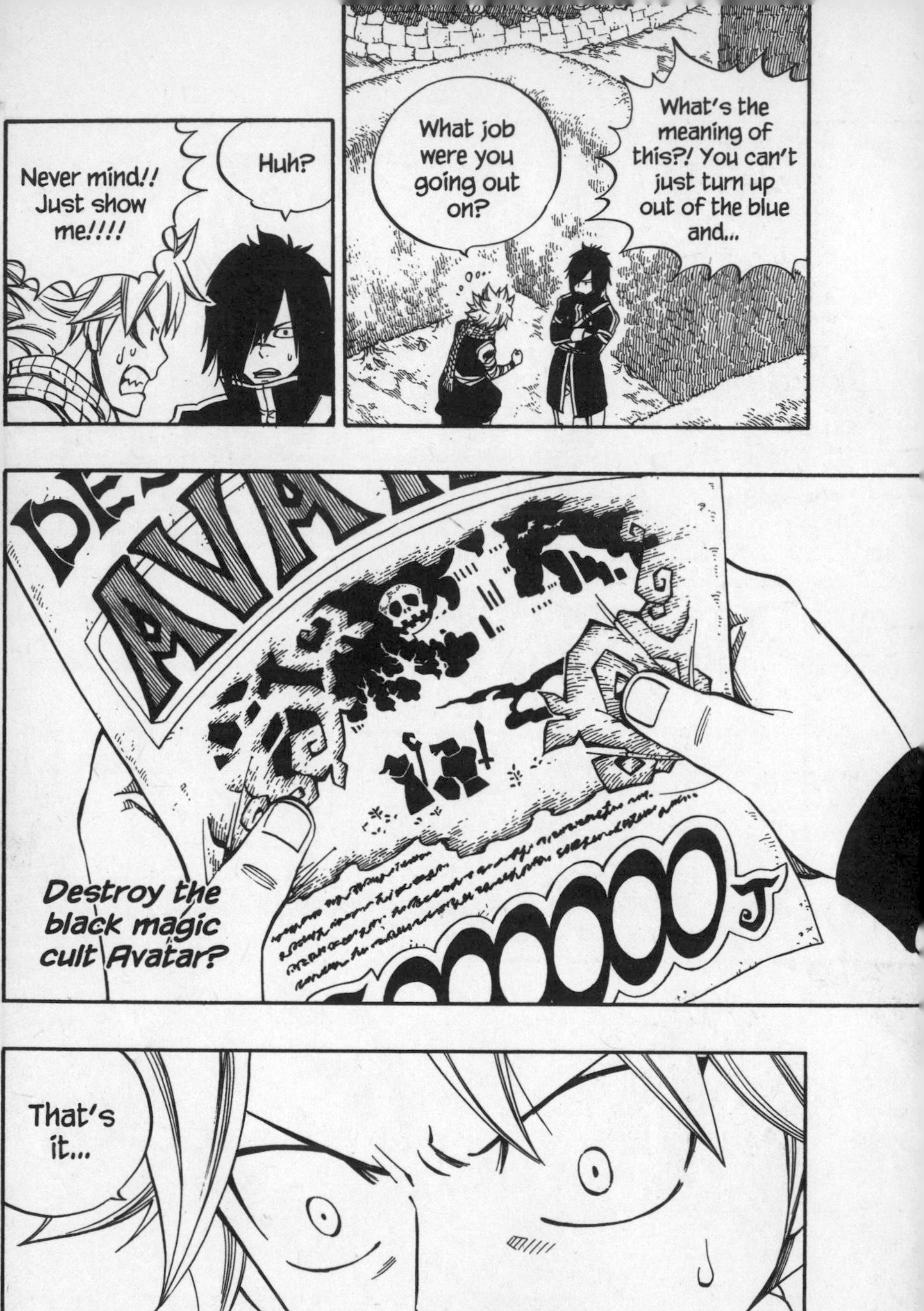
What's the meaning of this?! You can't just turn up out of the blue and...
What job were you going out on?
Huh?
Never mind!! Just show me!!!!
Destroy the black magic cult Avatar?
That's it...

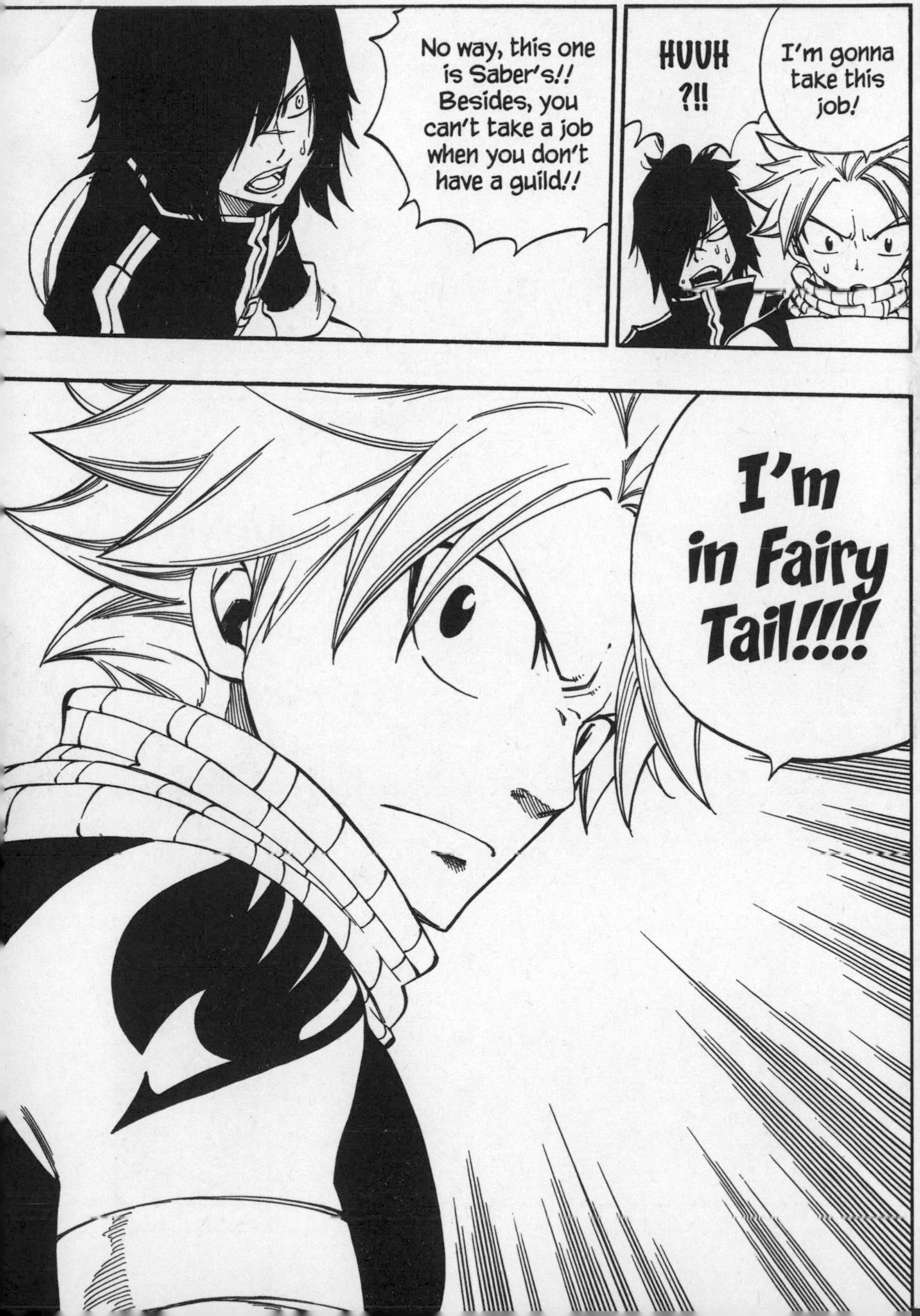
I'm gonna take this job!
HUUH ?!!
No way, this one is Saber's!! Besides, you can't take a job when you don't have a guild!!
I'm in Fairy Tail!!!!

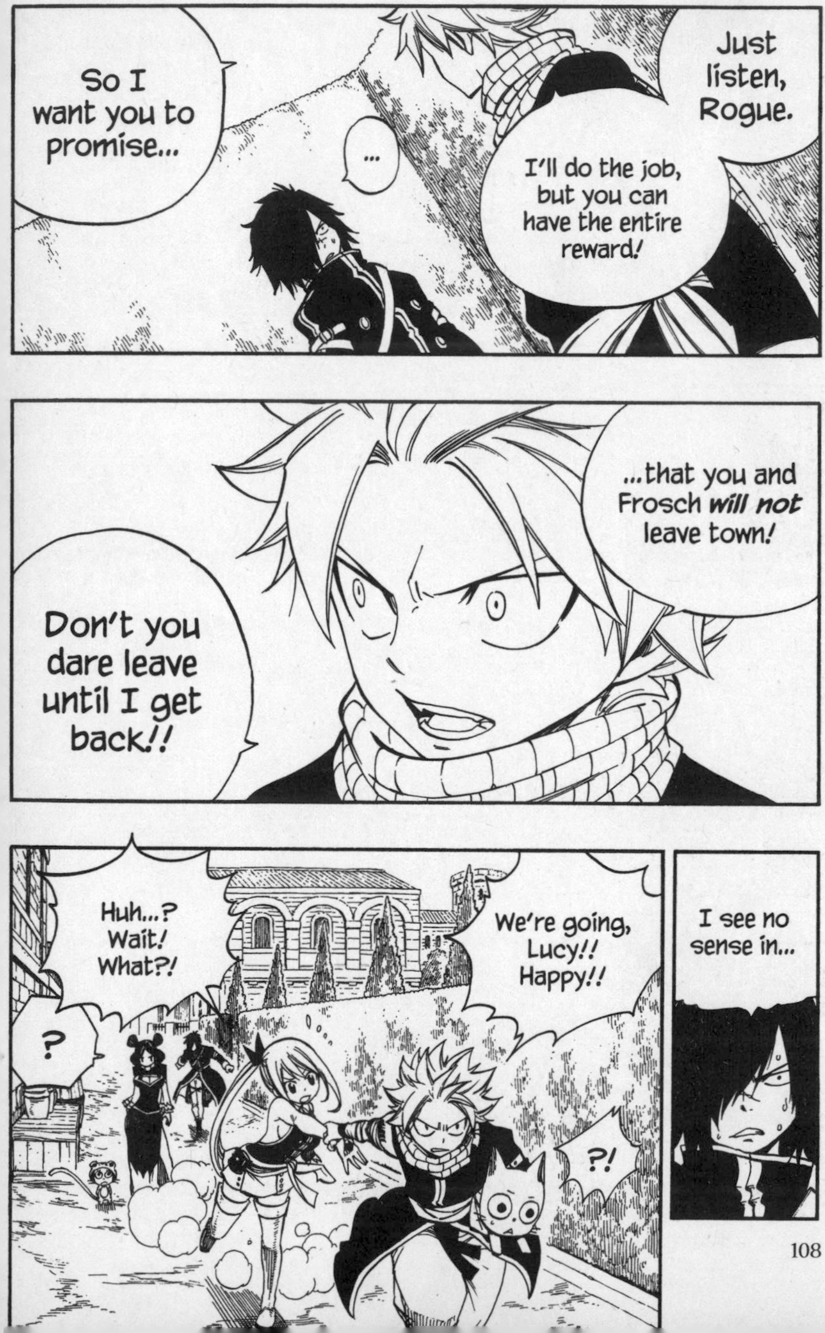
Just listen, Rogue.
I'll do the job, but you can have the entire reward!
...
So I want you to promise...
...that you and Frosch *will not* leave town!
Don't you dare leave until I get back!!
I see no sense in...
We're going, Lucy!! Happy!!
?!
Huh...? Wait! What?!
?

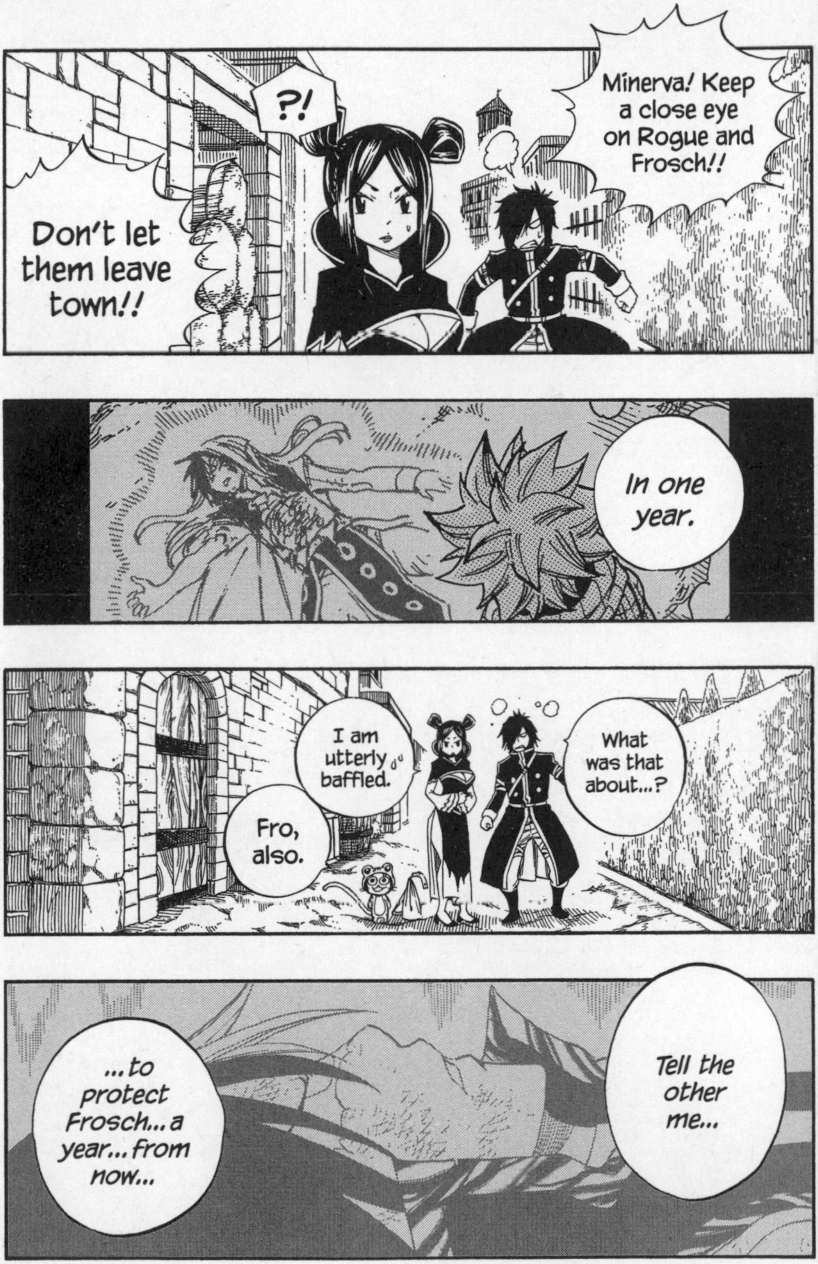
Minerva! Keep a close eye on Rogue and Frosch!!
?!
Don't let them leave town!!
In one year.
What was that about...?
I am utterly baffled.
Fro, also.
Tell the other me...
...to protect Frosch... a year... from now...

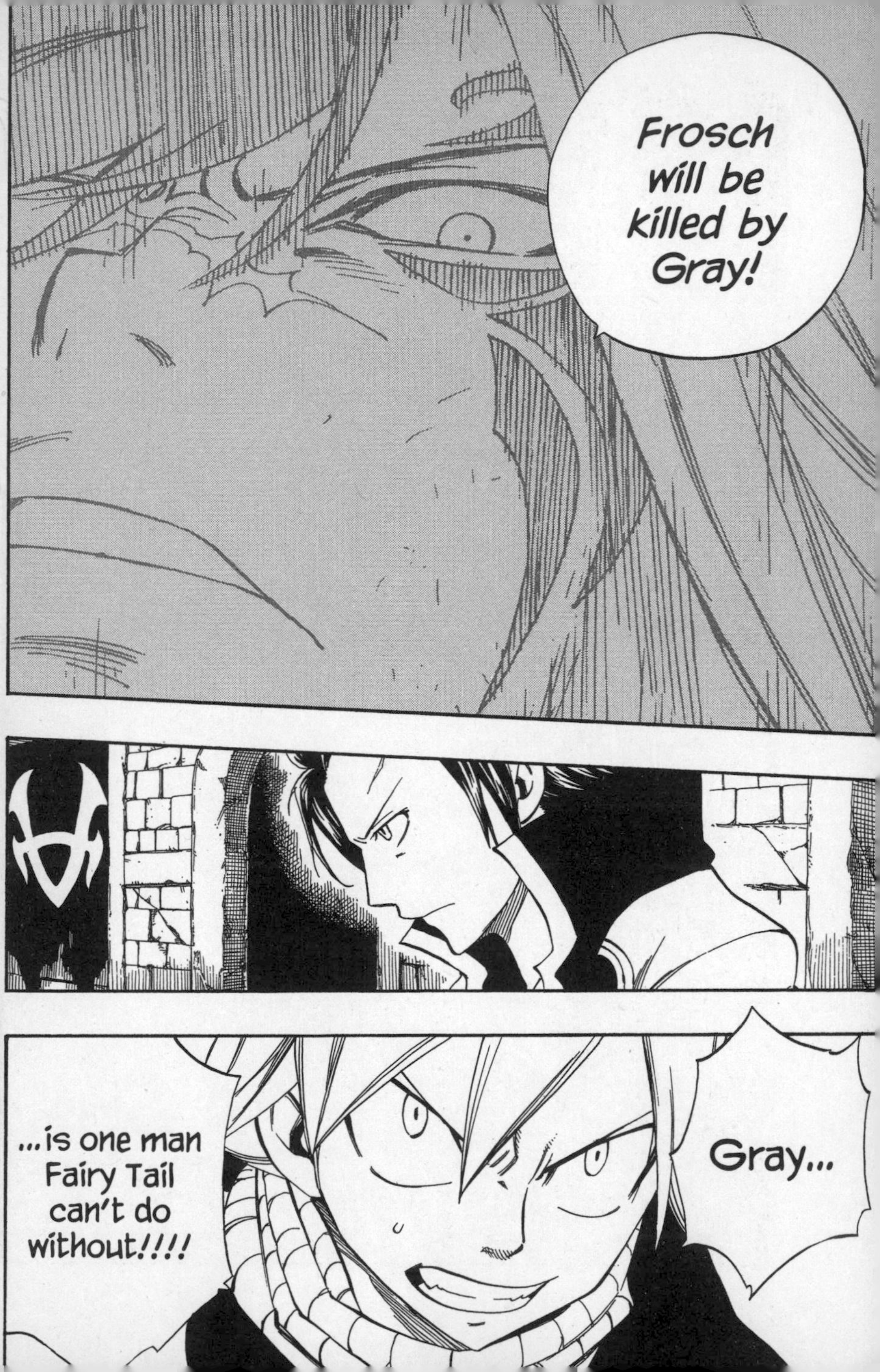
Frosch will be killed by Gray!
Gray...
...is one man Fairy Tail can't do without!!!!

FAIRY TAIL

フェアリーテイル

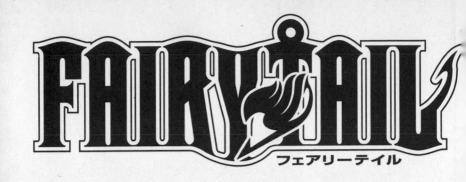

Chapter 426: Black Heart

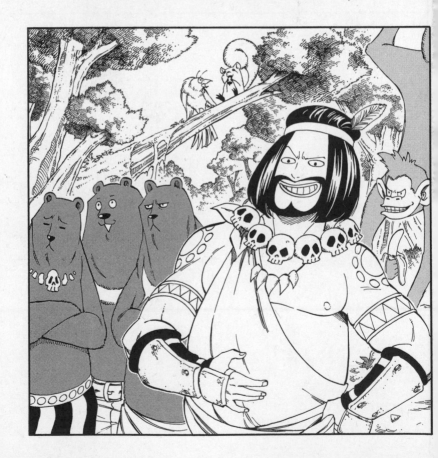

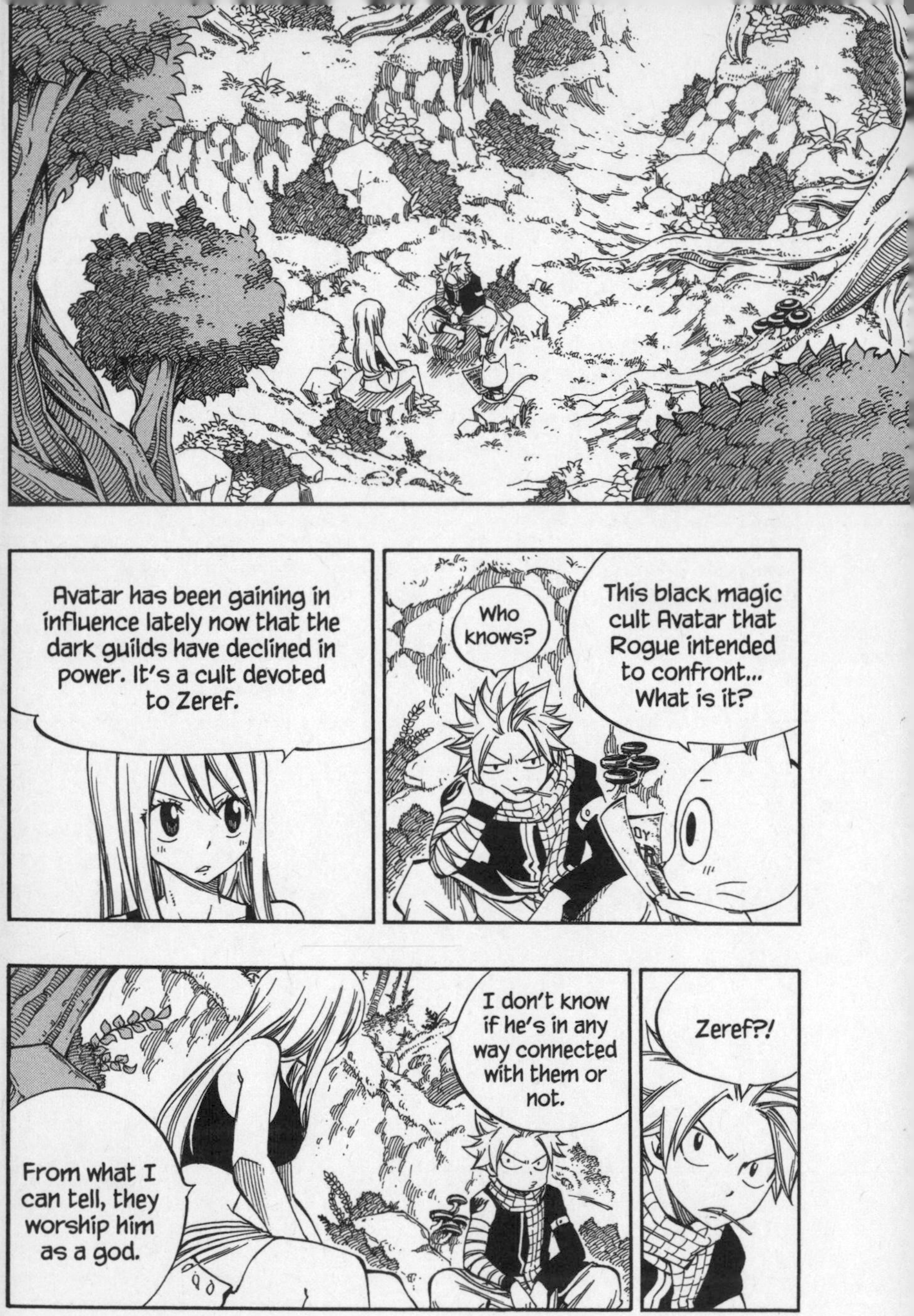
This black magic cult Avatar that Rogue intended to confront... What is it?
Who knows?
Avatar has been gaining in influence lately now that the dark guilds have declined in power. It's a cult devoted to Zeref.
Zeref?!
I don't know if he's in any way connected with them or not.
From what I can tell, they worship him as a god.

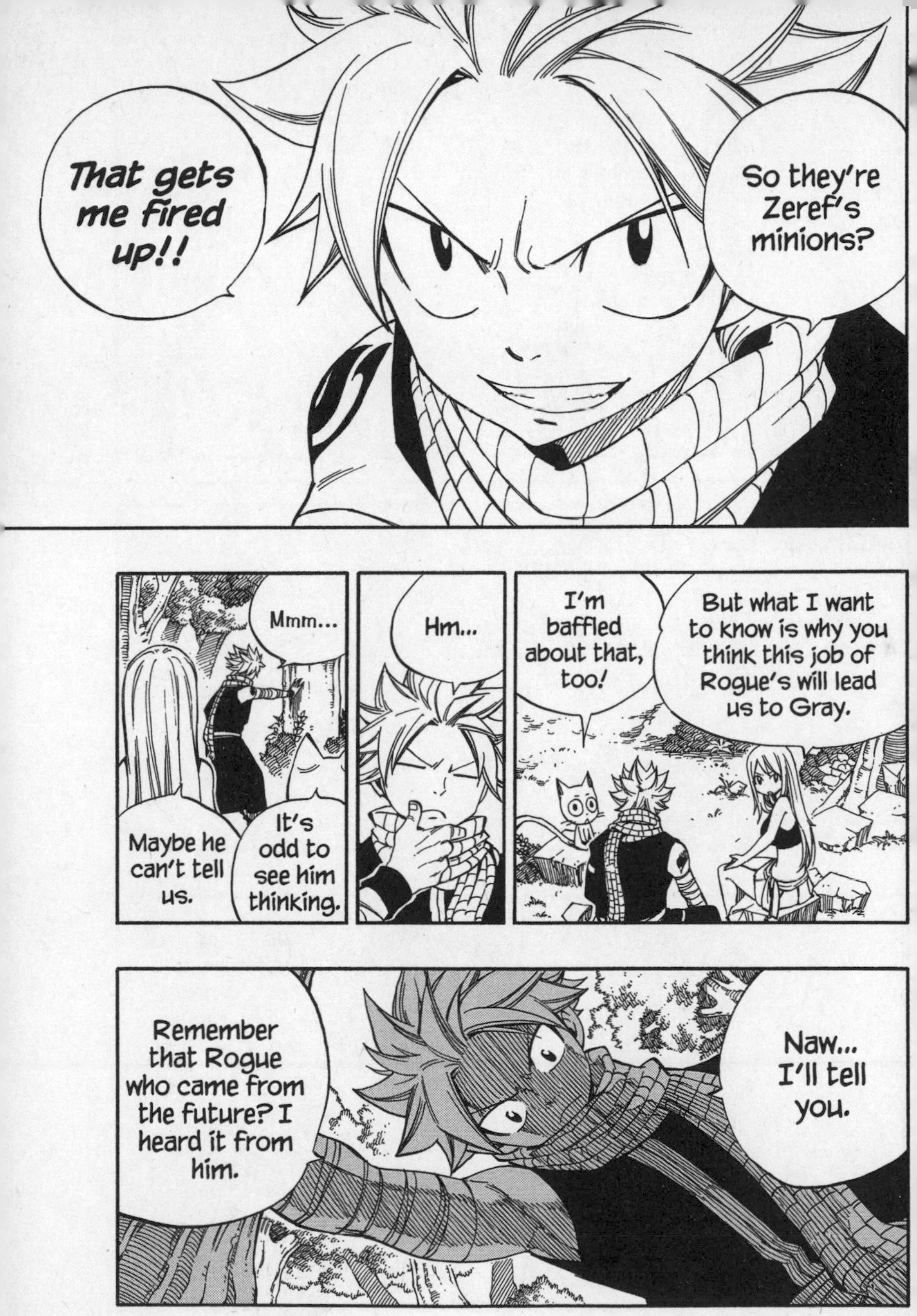
So they're Zeref's minions?
That gets me fired up!!
But what I want to know is why you think this job of Rogue's will lead us to Gray.
I'm baffled about that, too!
Hm...
Mmm...
It's odd to see him thinking.
Maybe he can't tell us.
Naw... I'll tell you.
Remember that Rogue who came from the future? I heard it from him.

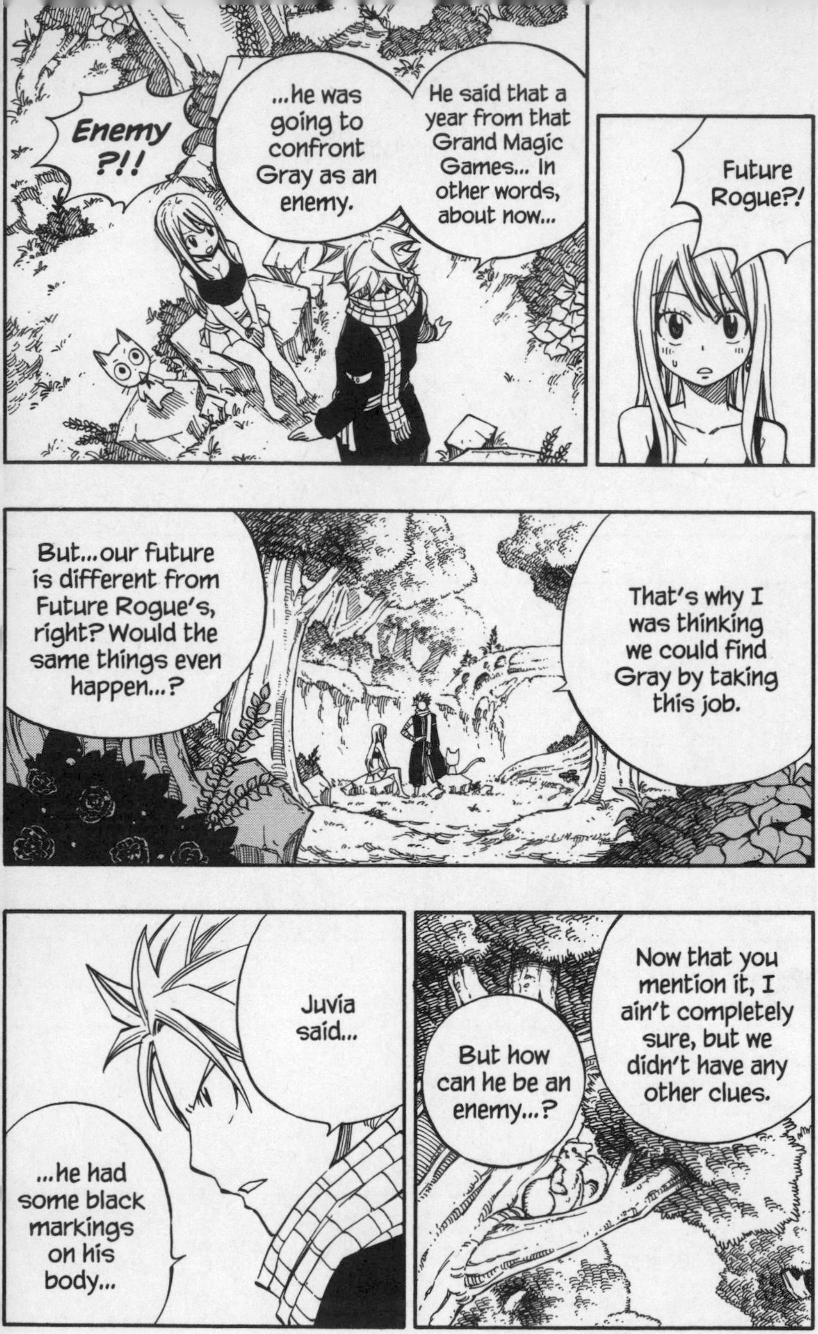
Future Rogue?!
He said that a year from that Grand Magic Games... In other words, about now...
...he was going to confront Gray as an enemy.
Enemy ?!!
That's why I was thinking we could find Gray by taking this job.
But...our future is different from Future Rogue's, right? Would the same things even happen...?
Now that you mention it, I ain't completely sure, but we didn't have any other clues.
But how can he be an enemy...?
Juvia said...
...he had some black markings on his body...

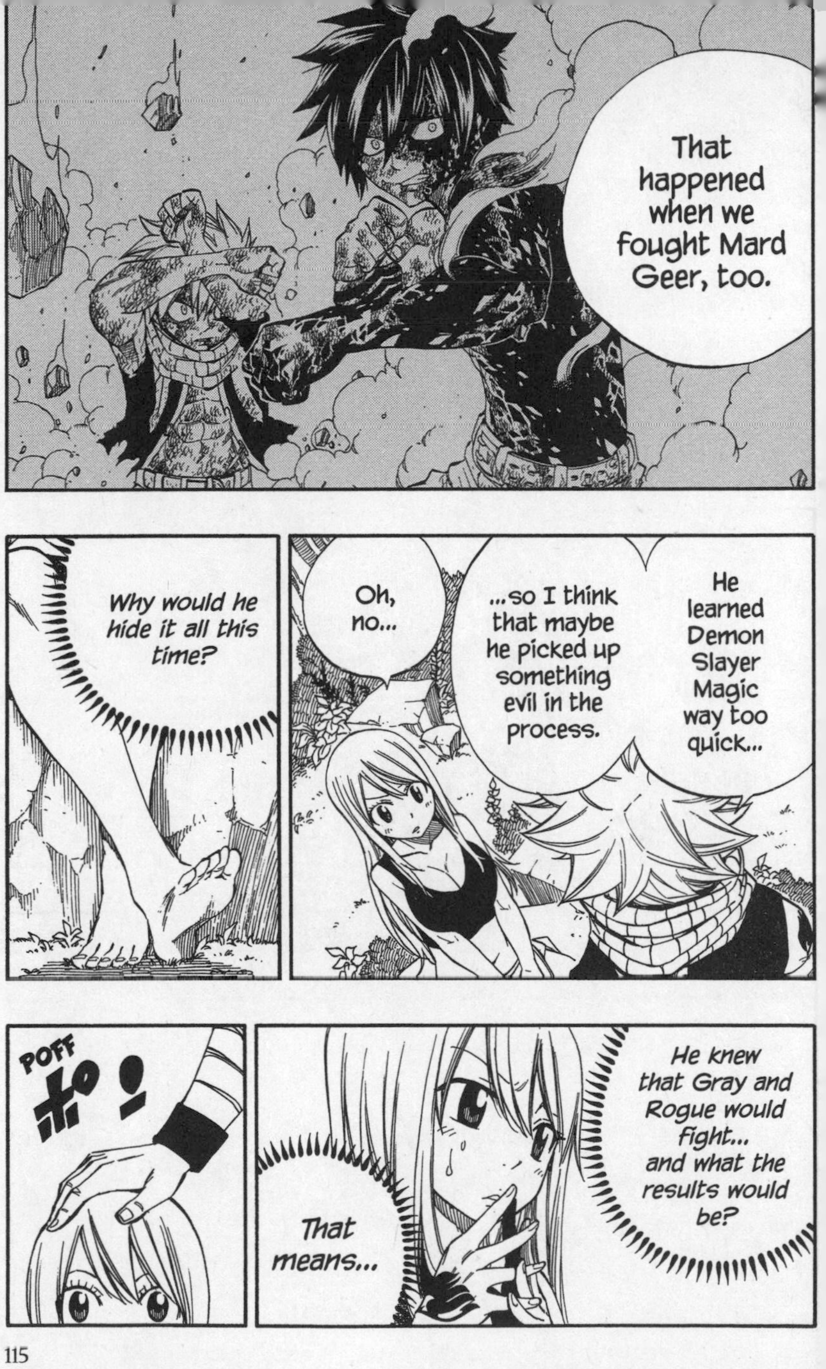

That happened when we fought Mard Geer, too.
He learned Demon Slayer Magic way too quick...
...so I think that maybe he picked up something evil in the process.
Oh, no...
Why would he hide it all this time?
He knew that Gray and Rogue would fight... and what the results would be?
That means...
POFF

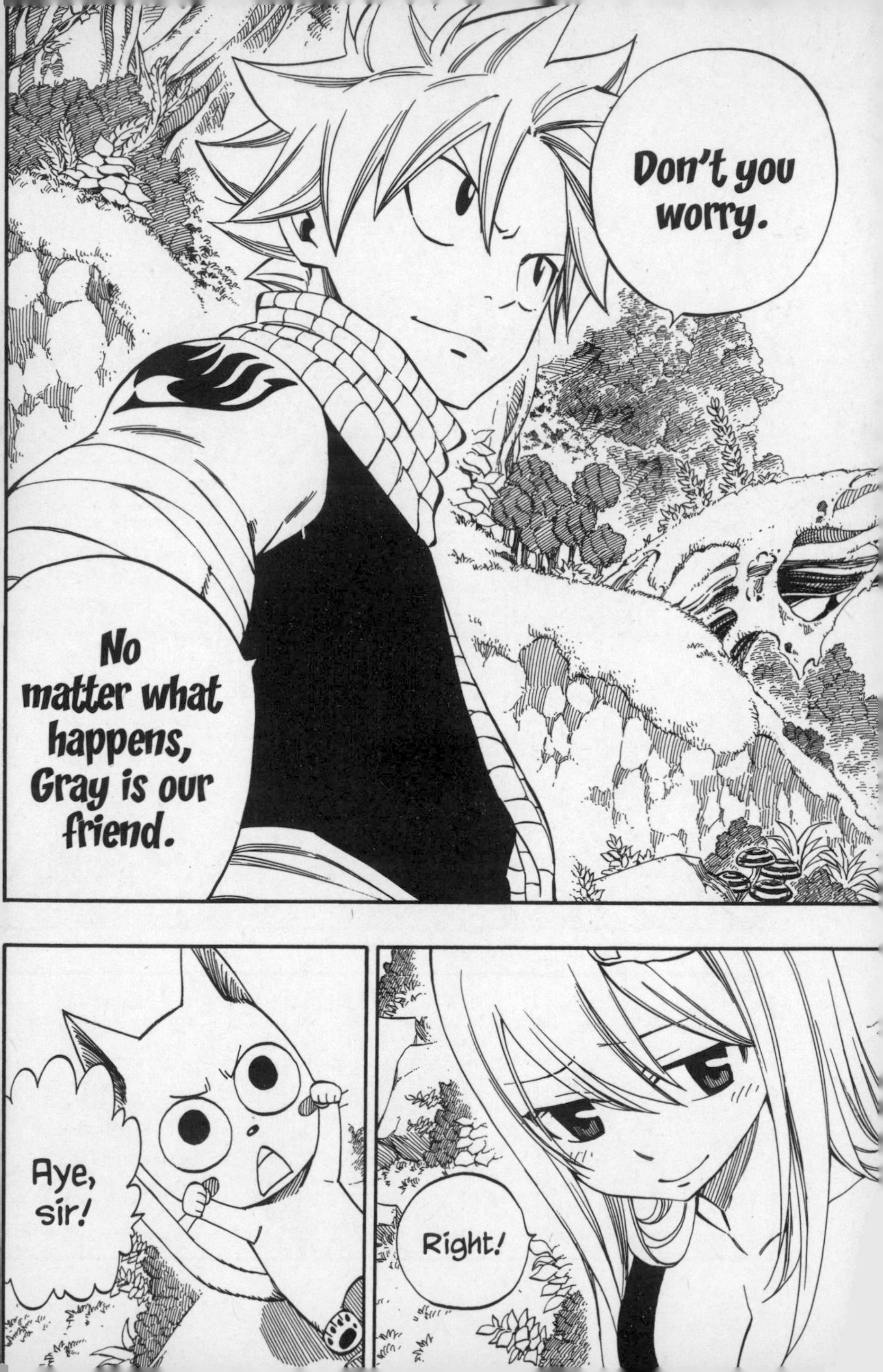
Don't you worry.
No matter what happens, Gray is our friend.
Right!
Aye, sir!

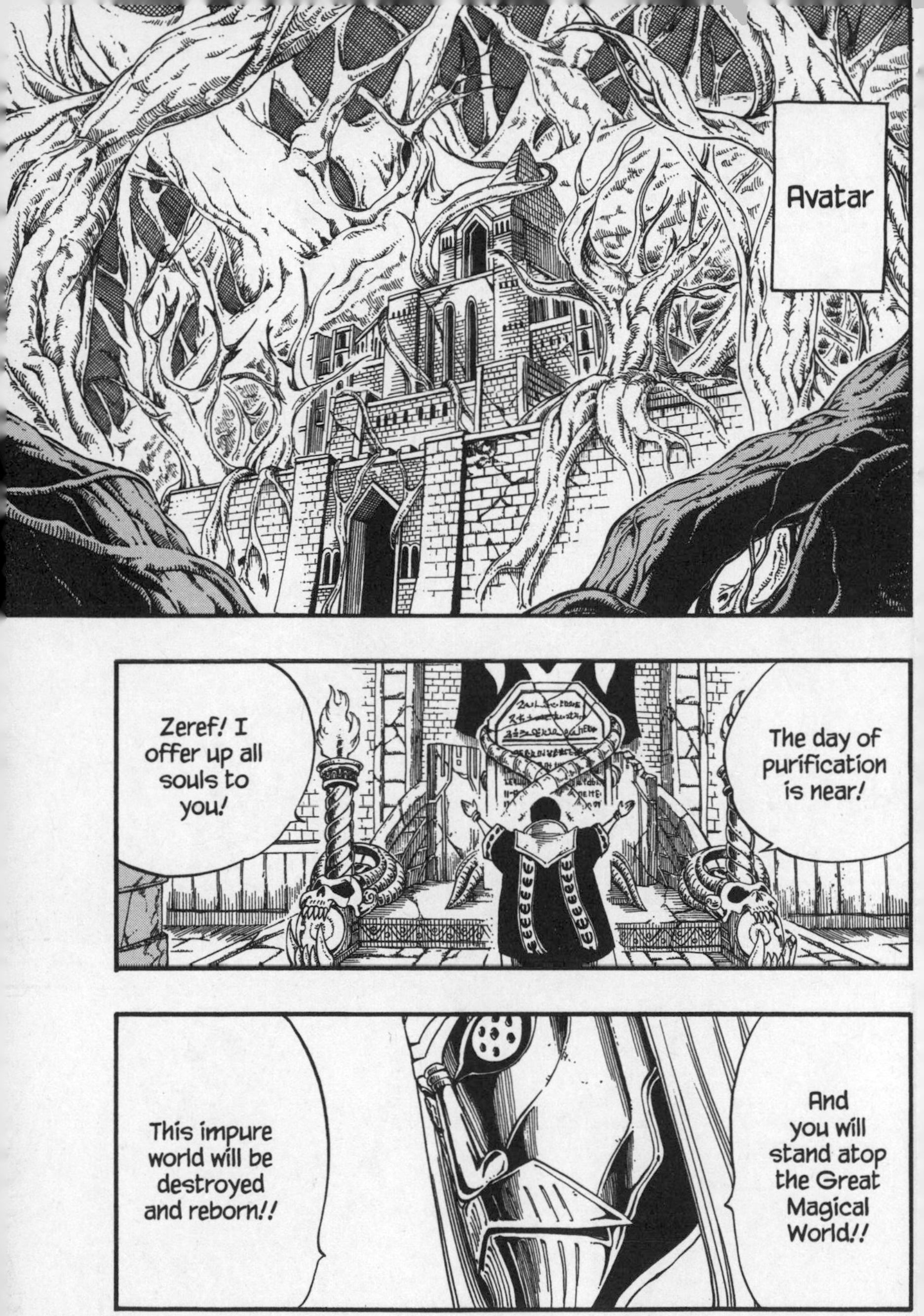
Avatar
The day of purification is near!
Zeref! I offer up all souls to you!
And you will stand atop the Great Magical World!!
This impure world will be destroyed and reborn!!

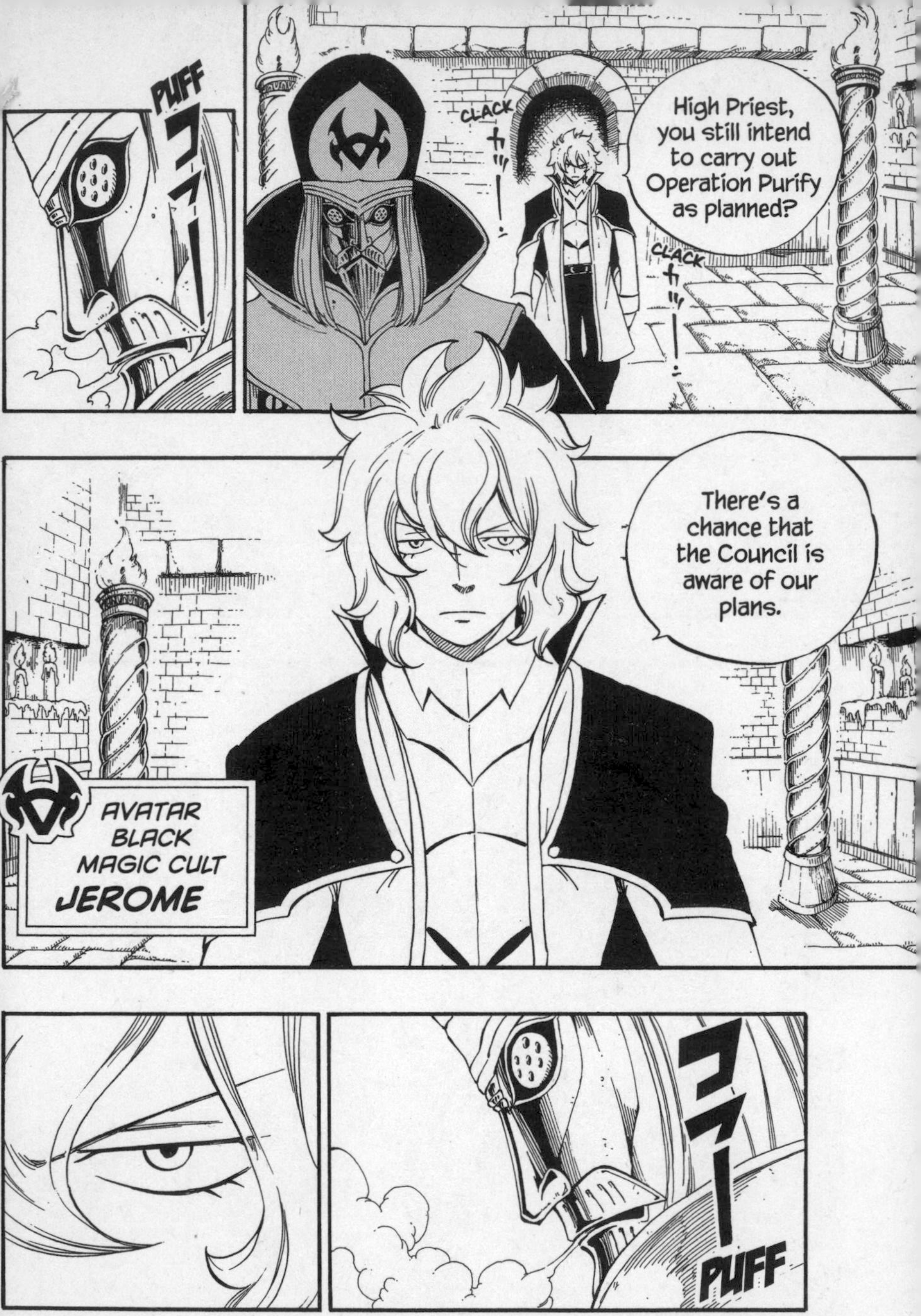
High Priest, you still intend to carry out Operation Purify as planned?
CLACK
CLACK
PUFF
There's a chance that the Council is aware of our plans.
AVATAR BLACK MAGIC CULT
JEROME
PUFF

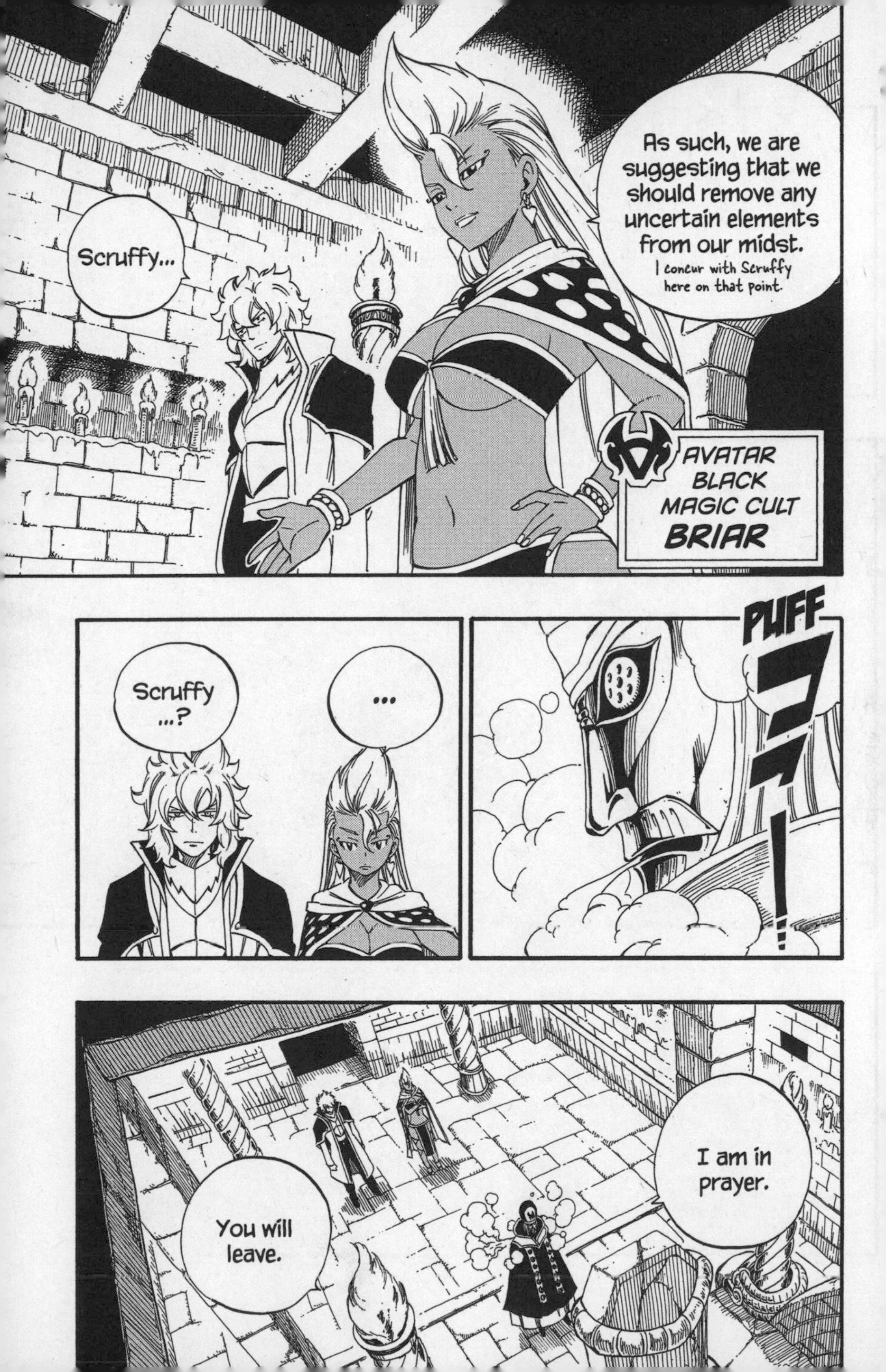
As such, we are suggesting that we should remove any uncertain elements from our midst.
I concur with Scruffy here on that point.
Scruffy...
AVATAR BLACK MAGIC CULT BRIAR
PUFF
...
Scruffy ...?
I am in prayer.
You will leave.

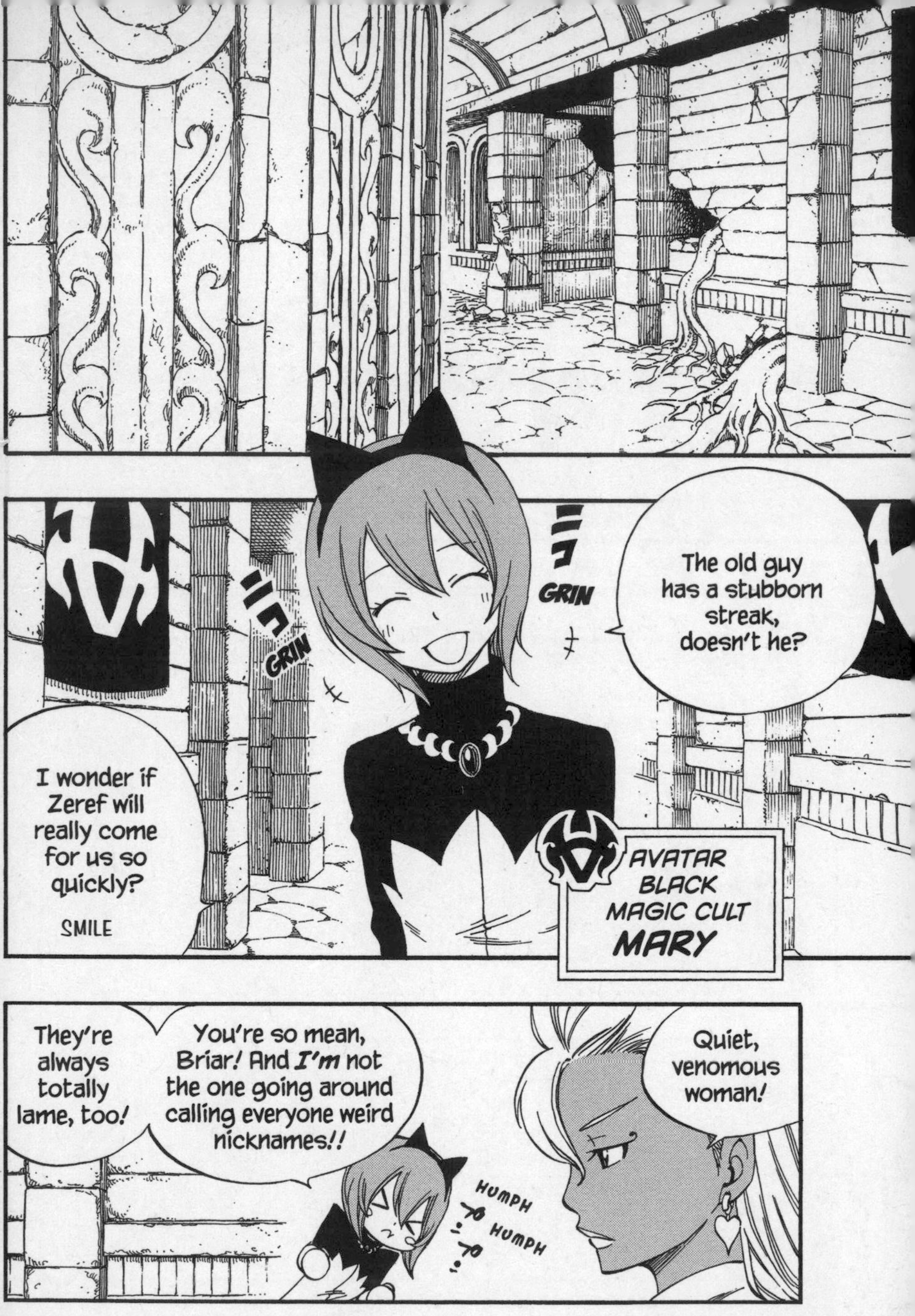

The old guy has a stubborn streak, doesn't he?
GRIN
GRIN
AVATAR BLACK MAGIC CULT MARY
I wonder if Zeref will really come for us so quickly?
SMILE
Quiet, venomous woman!
You're so mean, Briar! And *I'm* not the one going around calling everyone weird nicknames!!
They're always totally lame, too!
HUMPH
HUMPH

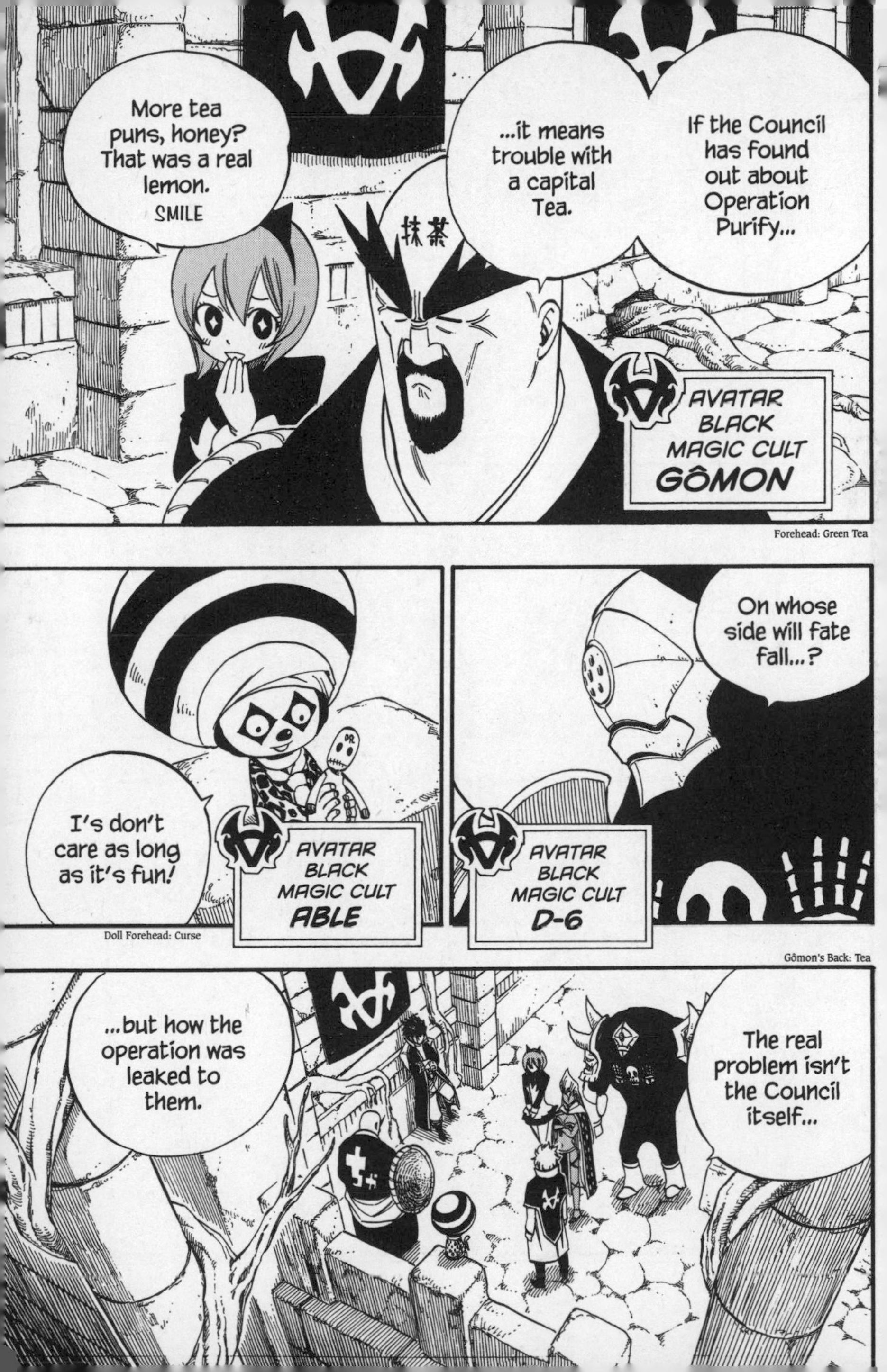
If the Council has found out about Operation Purify...
...it means trouble with a capital Tea.
抹茶
More tea puns, honey? That was a real lemon.
SMILE
AVATAR BLACK MAGIC CULT GÔMON
On whose side will fate fall...?
AVATAR BLACK MAGIC CULT D-6
I's don't care as long as it's fun!
AVATAR BLACK MAGIC CULT ABLE
The real problem isn't the Council itself...
...but how the operation was leaked to them.
Forehead: Green Tea
Gômon's Back: Tea
Doll Forehead: Curse

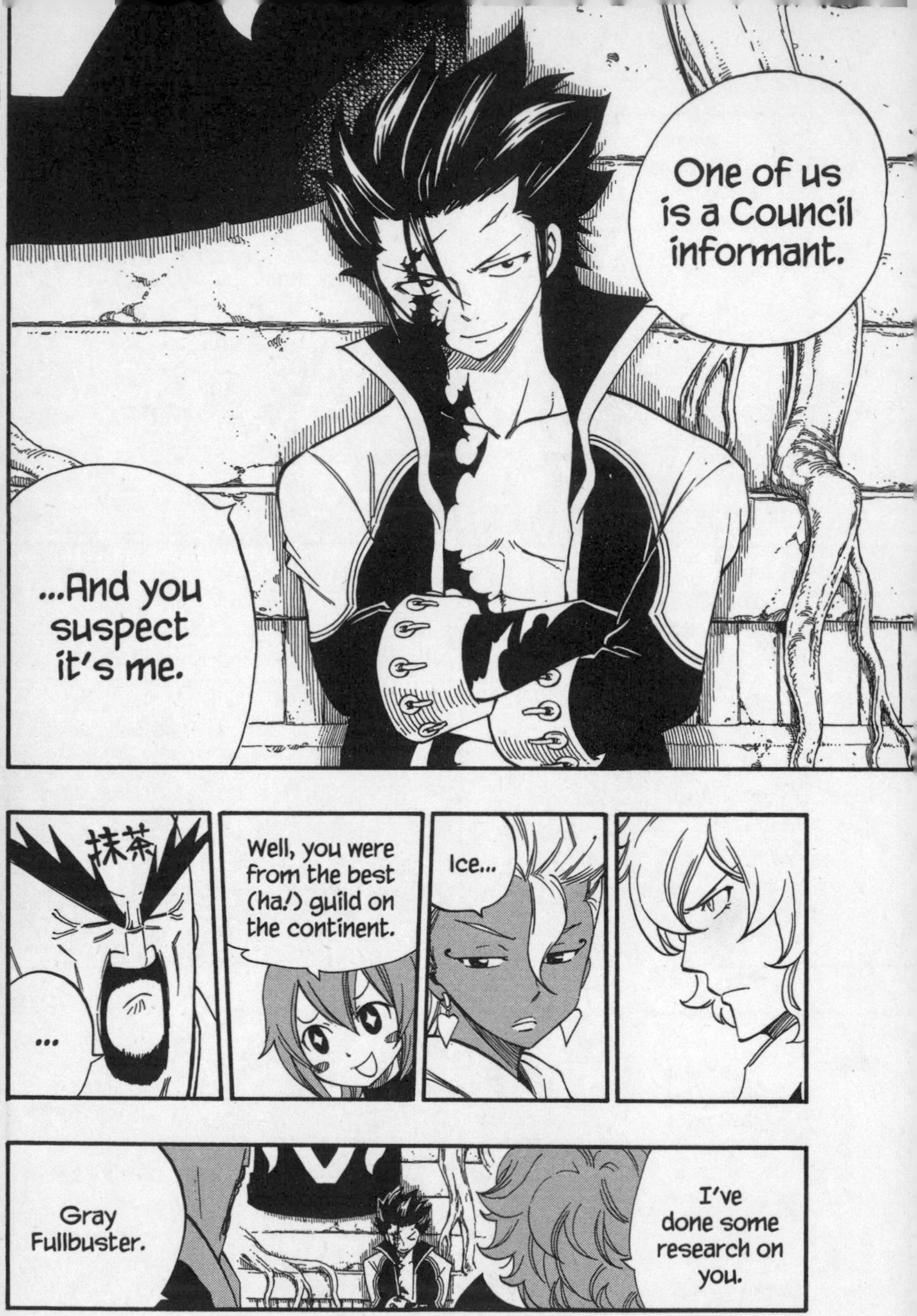
One of us is a Council informant.
...And you suspect it's me.
Ice...
Well, you were from the best (ha!) guild on the continent.
抹茶
...
I've done some research on you.
Gray Fullbuster.

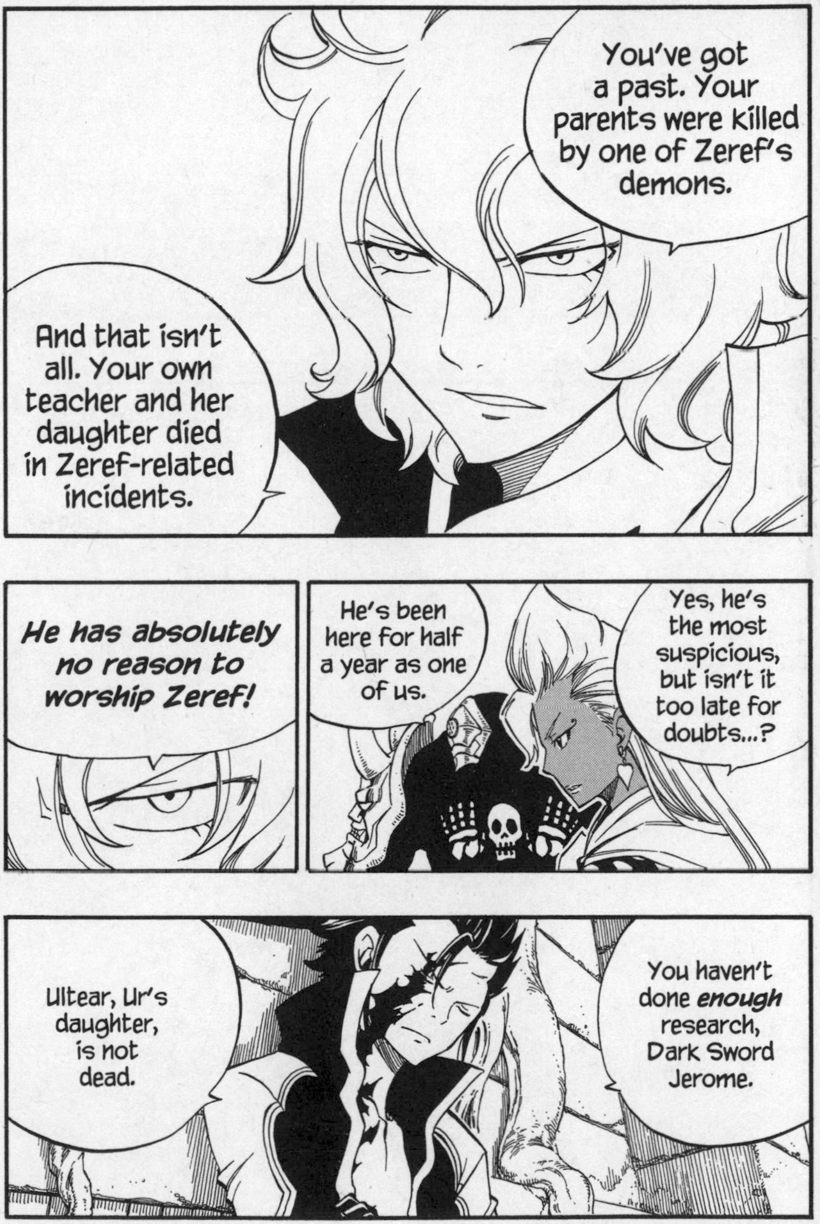
You've got a past. Your parents were killed by one of Zeref's demons.
And that isn't all. Your own teacher and her daughter died in Zeref-related incidents.
Yes, he's the most suspicious, but isn't it too late for doubts...?
He's been here for half a year as one of us.
He has absolutely no reason to worship Zeref!
You haven't done *enough* research, Dark Sword Jerome.
Ultear, Ur's daughter, is not dead.

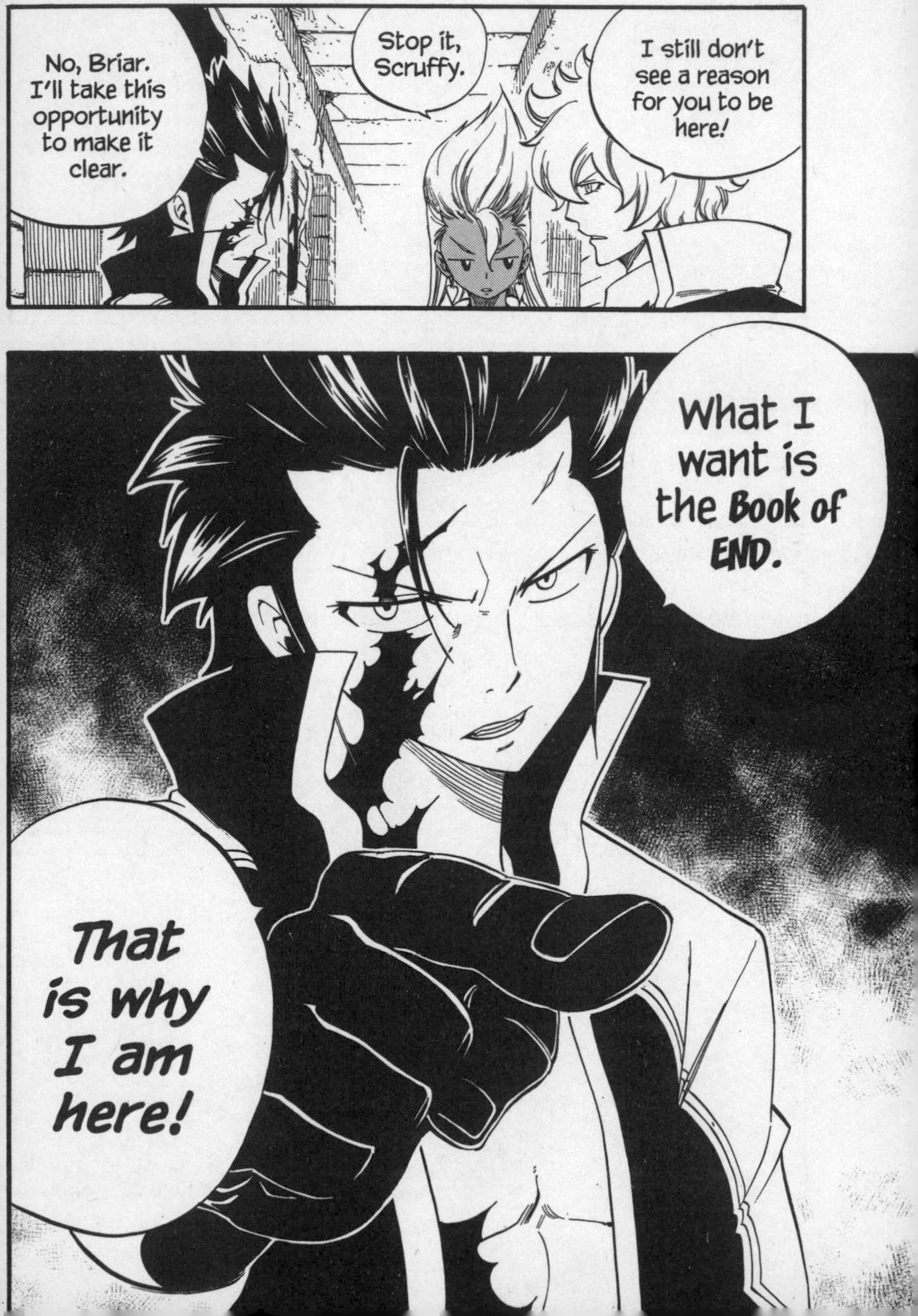
I still don't see a reason for you to be here!
Stop it, Scruffy.
No, Briar. I'll take this opportunity to make it clear.
What I want is the Book of END.
That is why I am here!

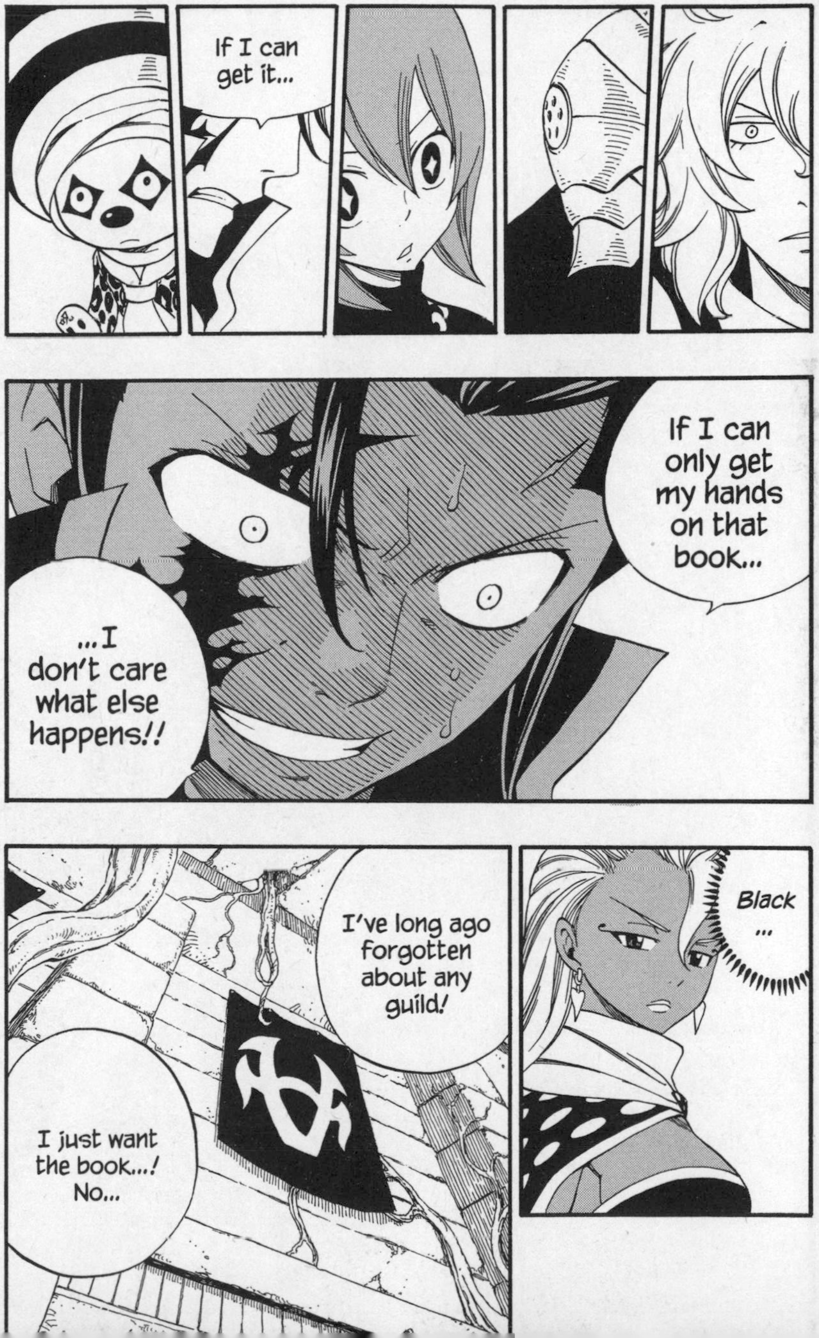
If I can get it...
If I can only get my hands on that book...
...I don't care what else happens!!
Black ...
I've long ago forgotten about any guild!
I just want the book...! No...

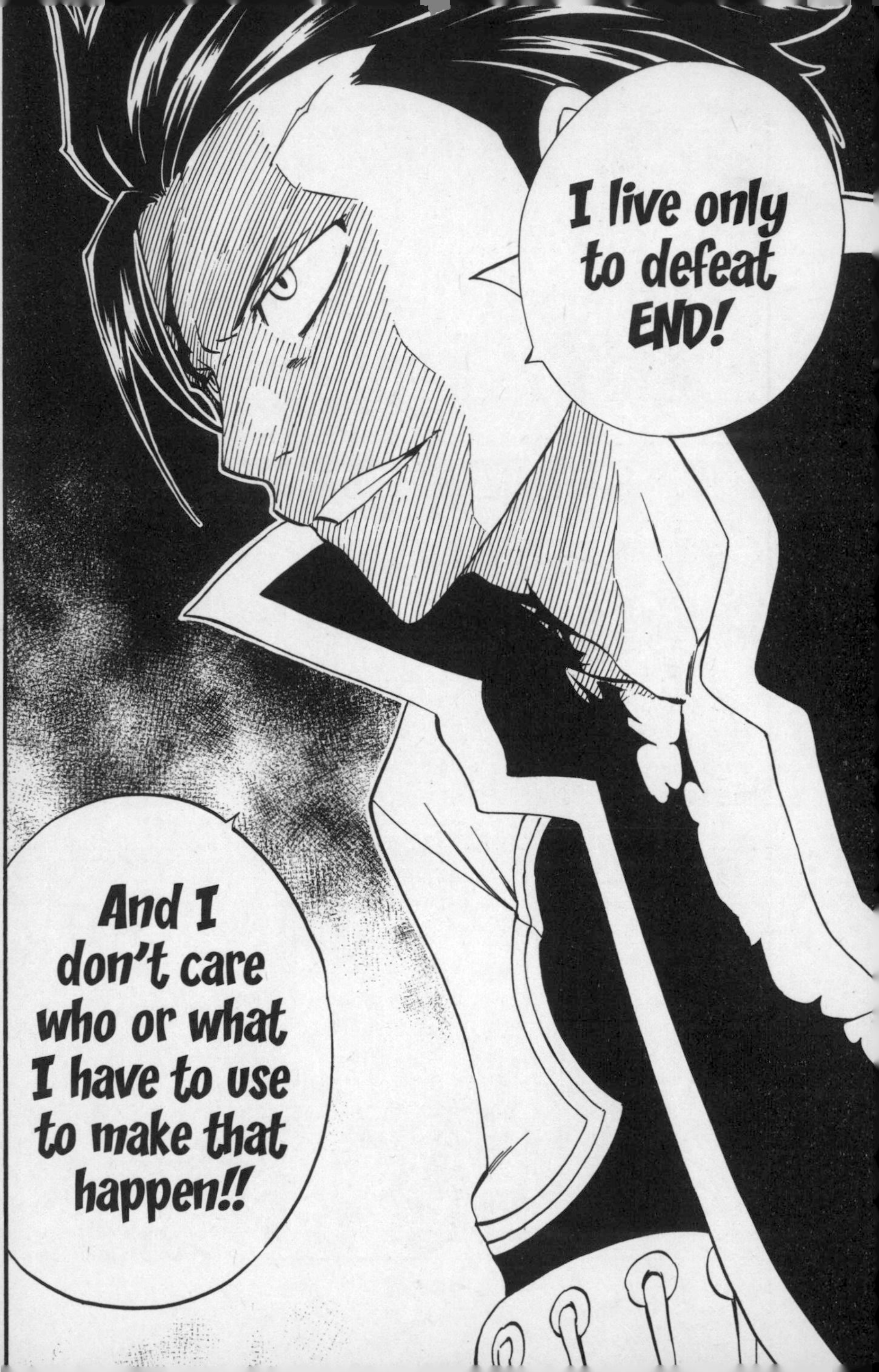
I live only to defeat END!
And I don't care who or what I have to use to make that happen!!

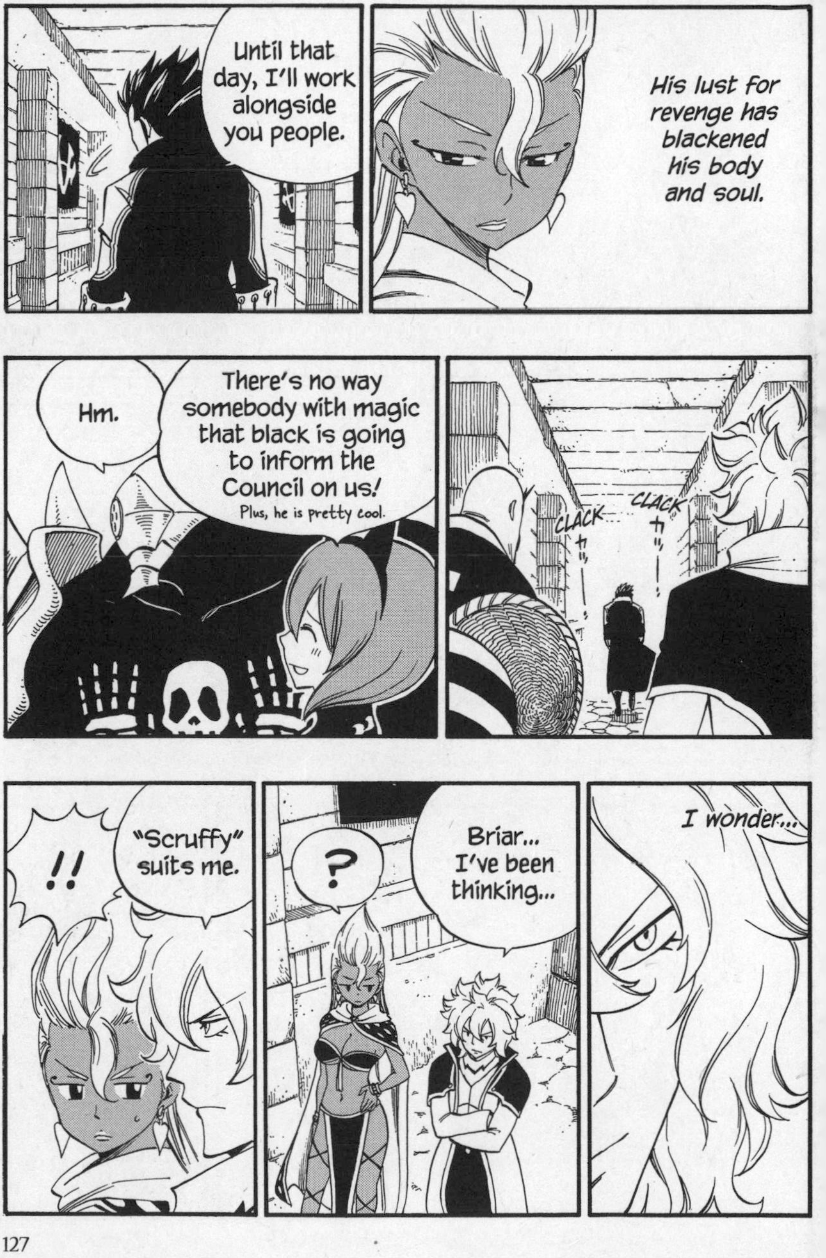
His lust for revenge has blackened his body and soul.
Until that day, I'll work alongside you people.
CLACK
CLACK
There's no way somebody with magic that black is going to inform the Council on us!
Plus, he is pretty cool.
Hm.
I wonder...
Briar... I've been thinking...
?
"Scruffy" suits me.
!!

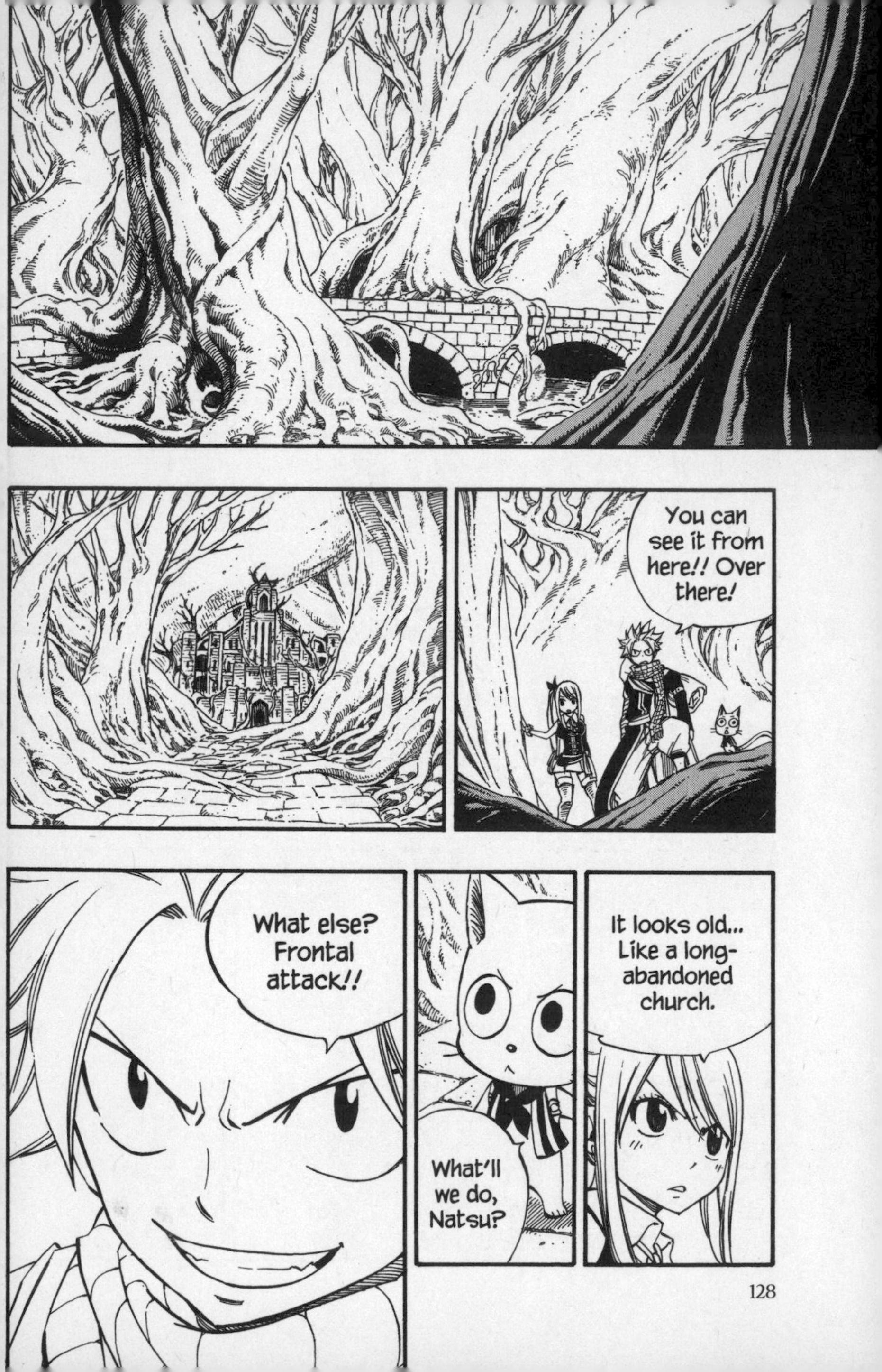
You can see it from here!! Over there!
It looks old... Like a long-abandoned church.
What'll we do, Natsu?
What else? Frontal attack!!

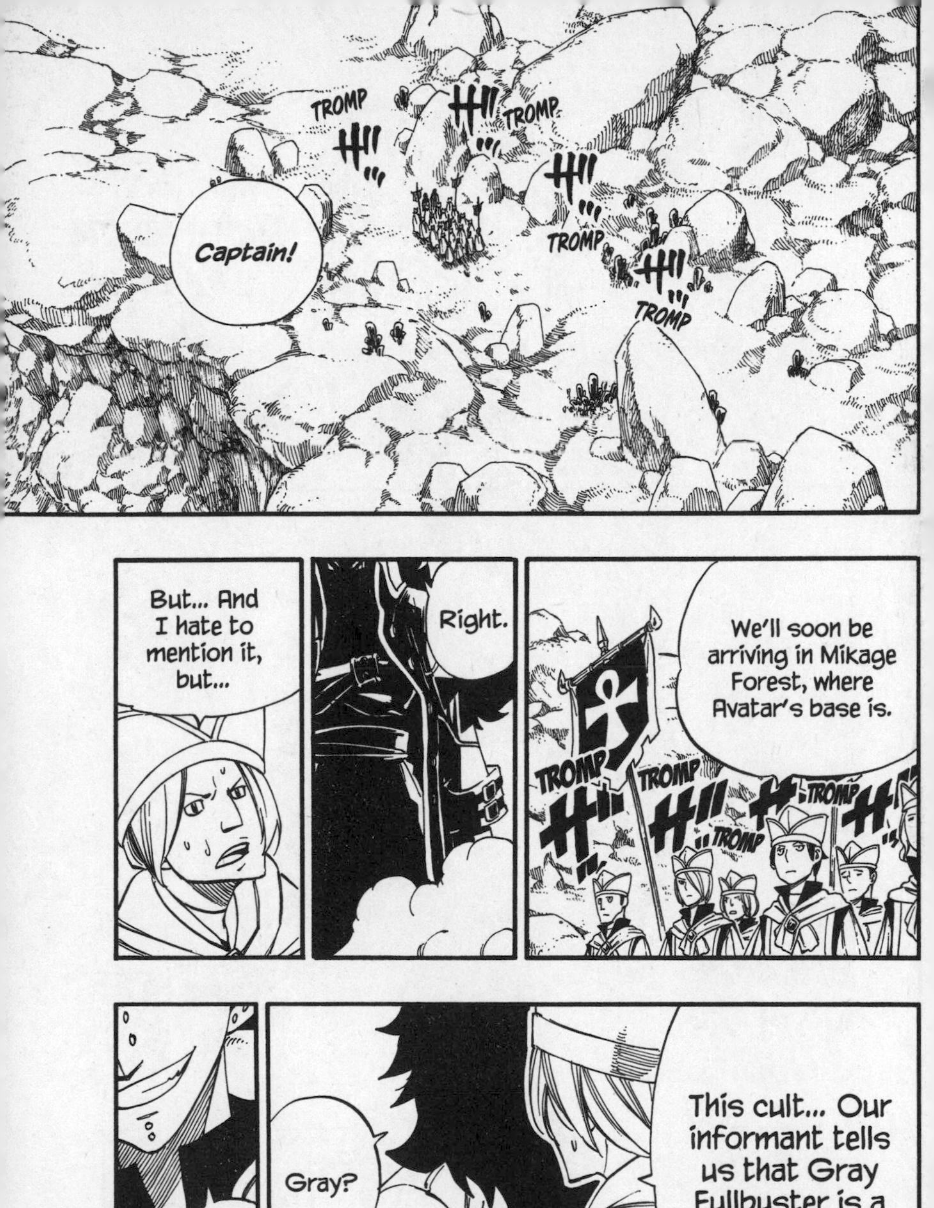
TROMP
TROMP
TROMP
TROMP
Captain!
We'll soon be arriving in Mikage Forest, where Avatar's base is.
TROMP
TROMP
TROMP
TROMP
Right.
But... And I hate to mention it, but...
This cult... Our informant tells us that Gray Fullbuster is a member of it...
Gray?
GEE HEE!

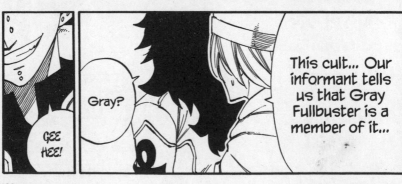

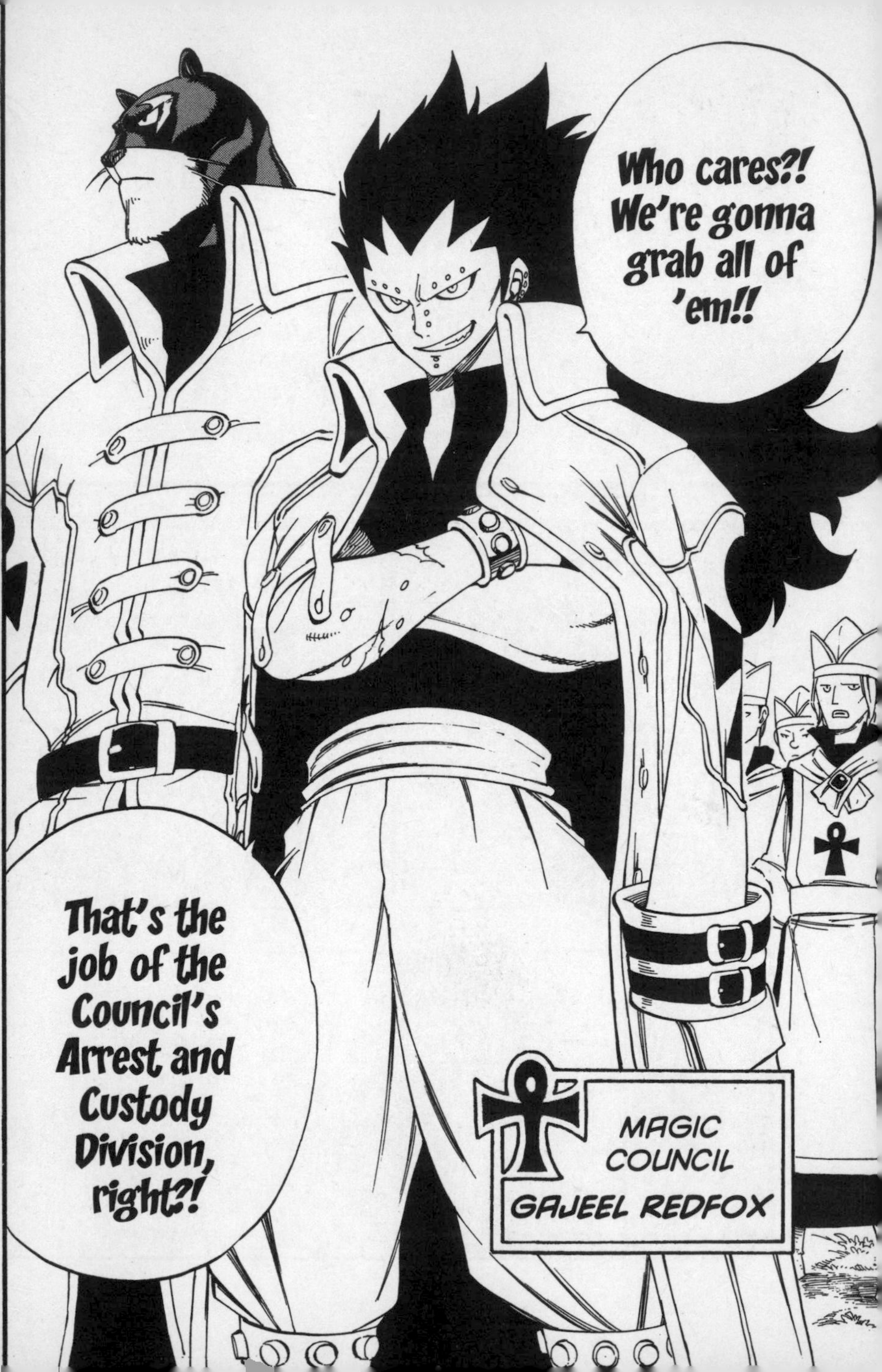
Who cares?! We're gonna grab all of 'em!!
That's the job of the Council's Arrest and Custody Division, right?!
MAGIC COUNCIL
GAJEEL REDFOX

Chapter 427: Pitched Underground Battle

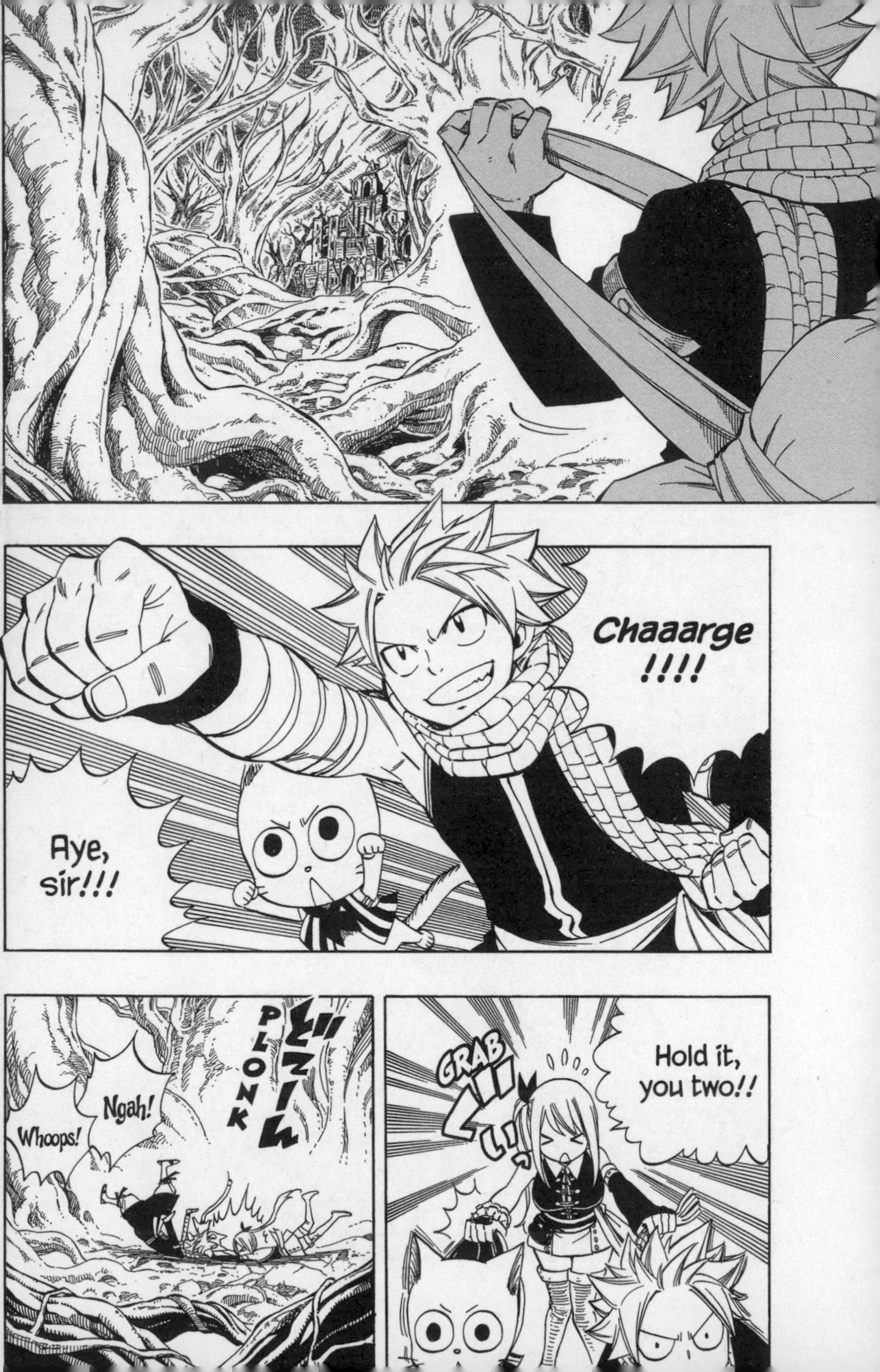
Chaaarge!!!!
Aye, sir!!!
GRAB
Hold it, you two!!
PLONK
Ngah!
Whoops!

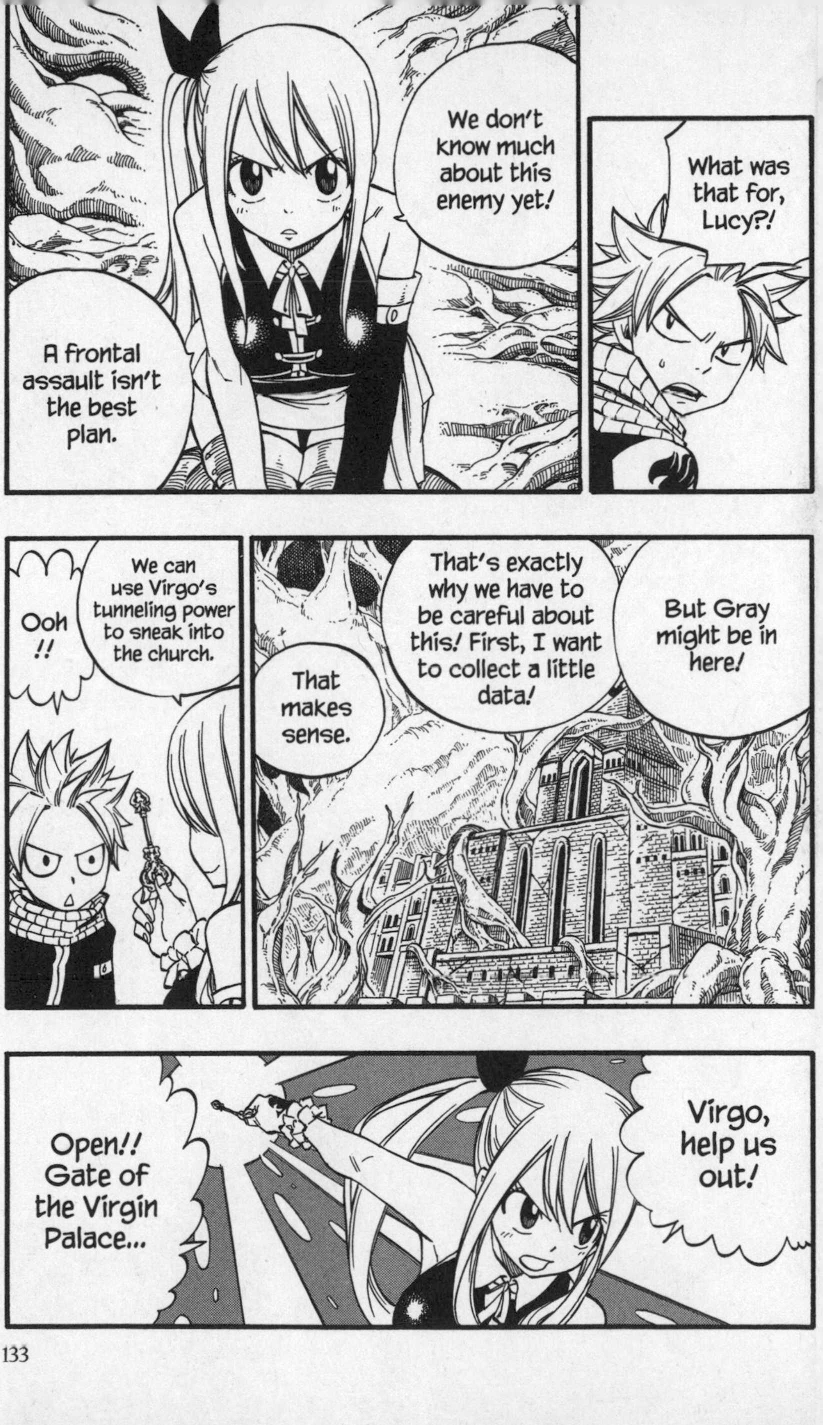
What was that for, Lucy?!
We don't know much about this enemy yet!
A frontal assault isn't the best plan.
But Gray might be in here!
That's exactly why we have to be careful about this! First, I want to collect a little data!
That makes sense.
We can use Virgo's tunneling power to sneak into the church.
Ooh !!
Virgo, help us out!
Open!! Gate of the Virgin Palace...

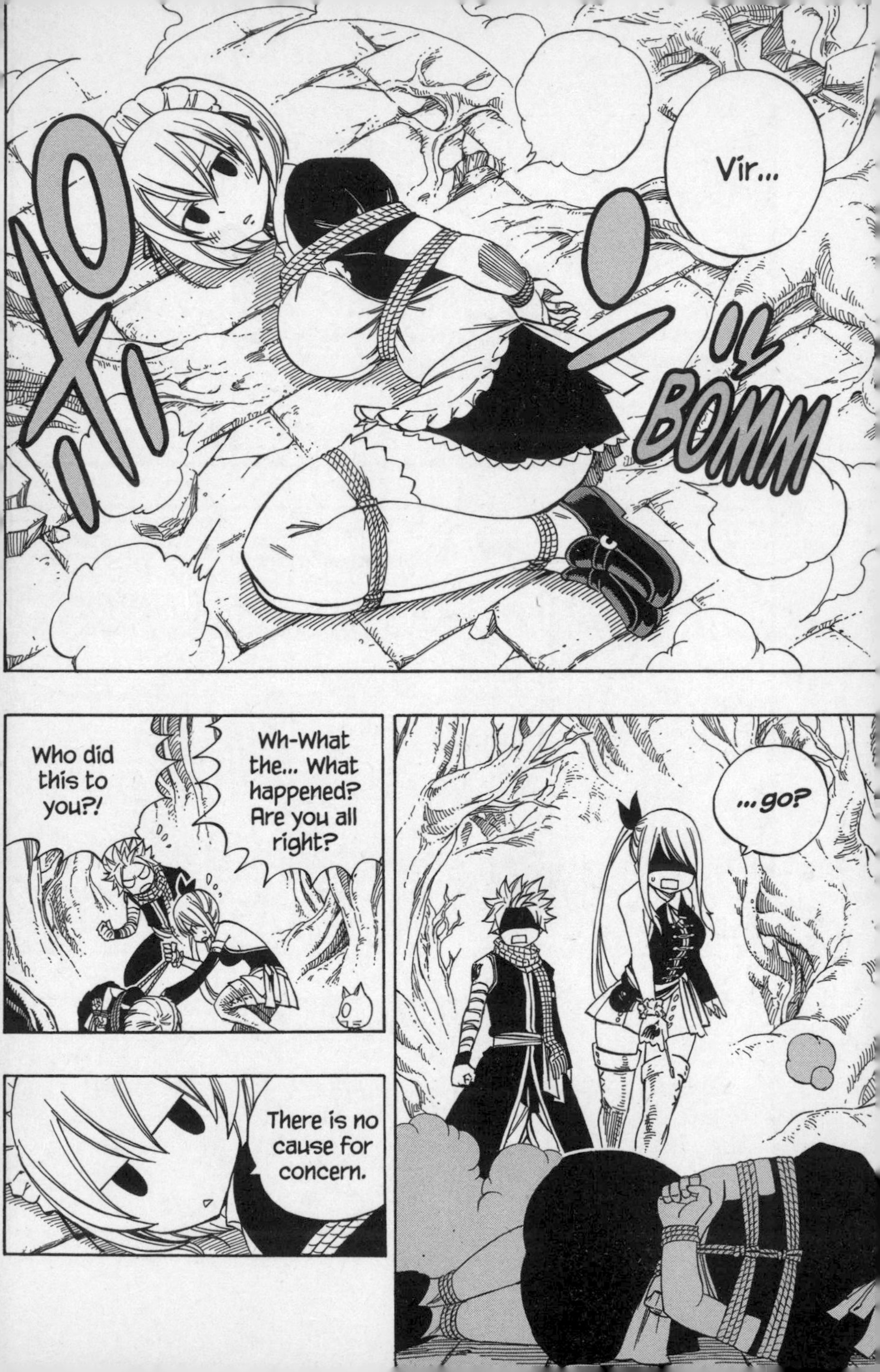
Vir...
BOMM
...go?
Wh-What the... What happened? Are you all right?
Who did this to you?!
There is no cause for concern.

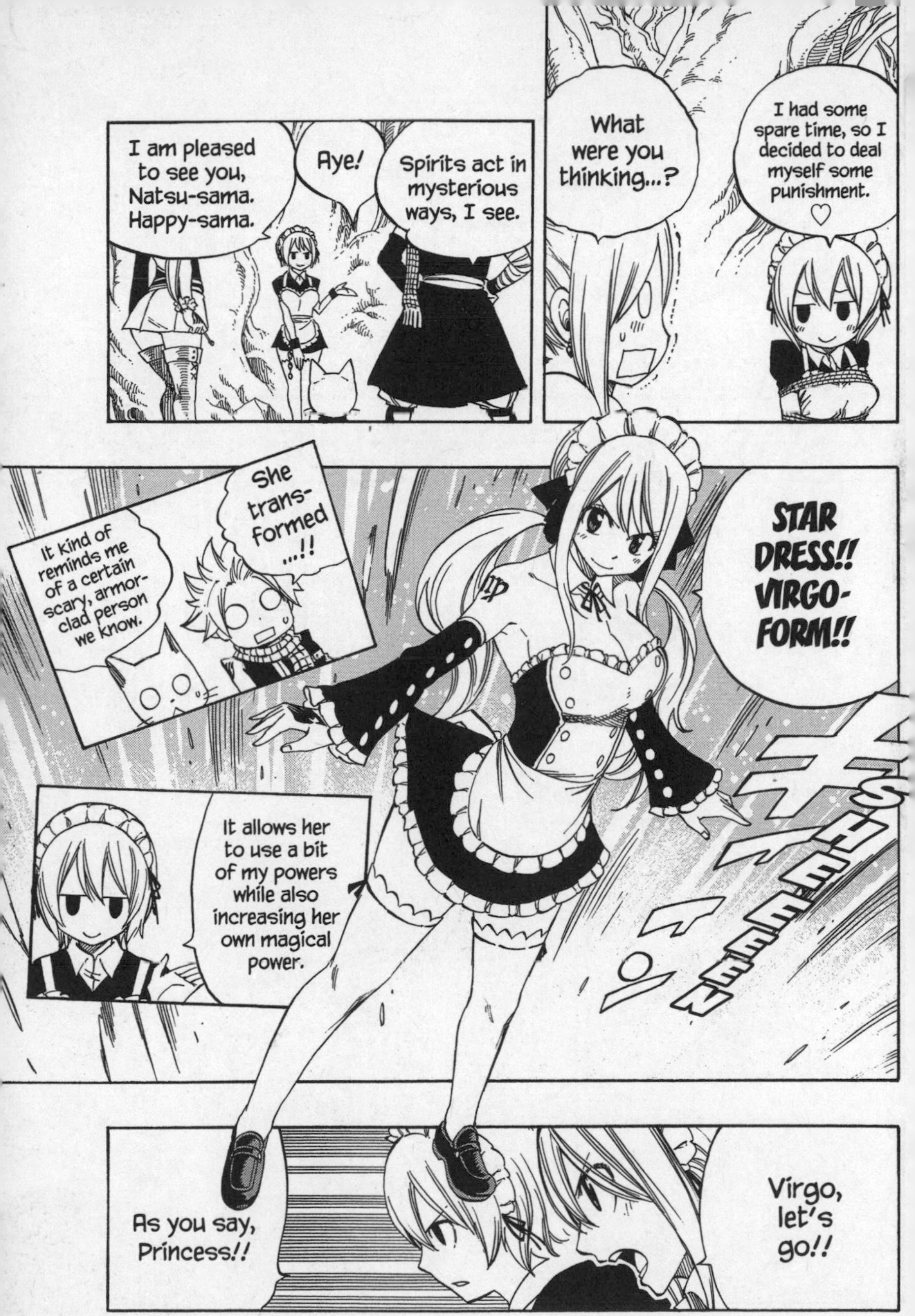
What were you thinking...?
I had some spare time, so I decided to deal myself some punishment. ♡
Spirits act in mysterious ways, I see.
Aye!
I am pleased to see you, Natsu-sama. Happy-sama.
STAR DRESS!! VIRGO-FORM!!
SHEEEEN
She transformed...!!
It kind of reminds me of a certain scary, armor-clad person we know.
It allows her to use a bit of my powers while also increasing her own magical power.
Virgo, let's go!!
As you say, Princess!!

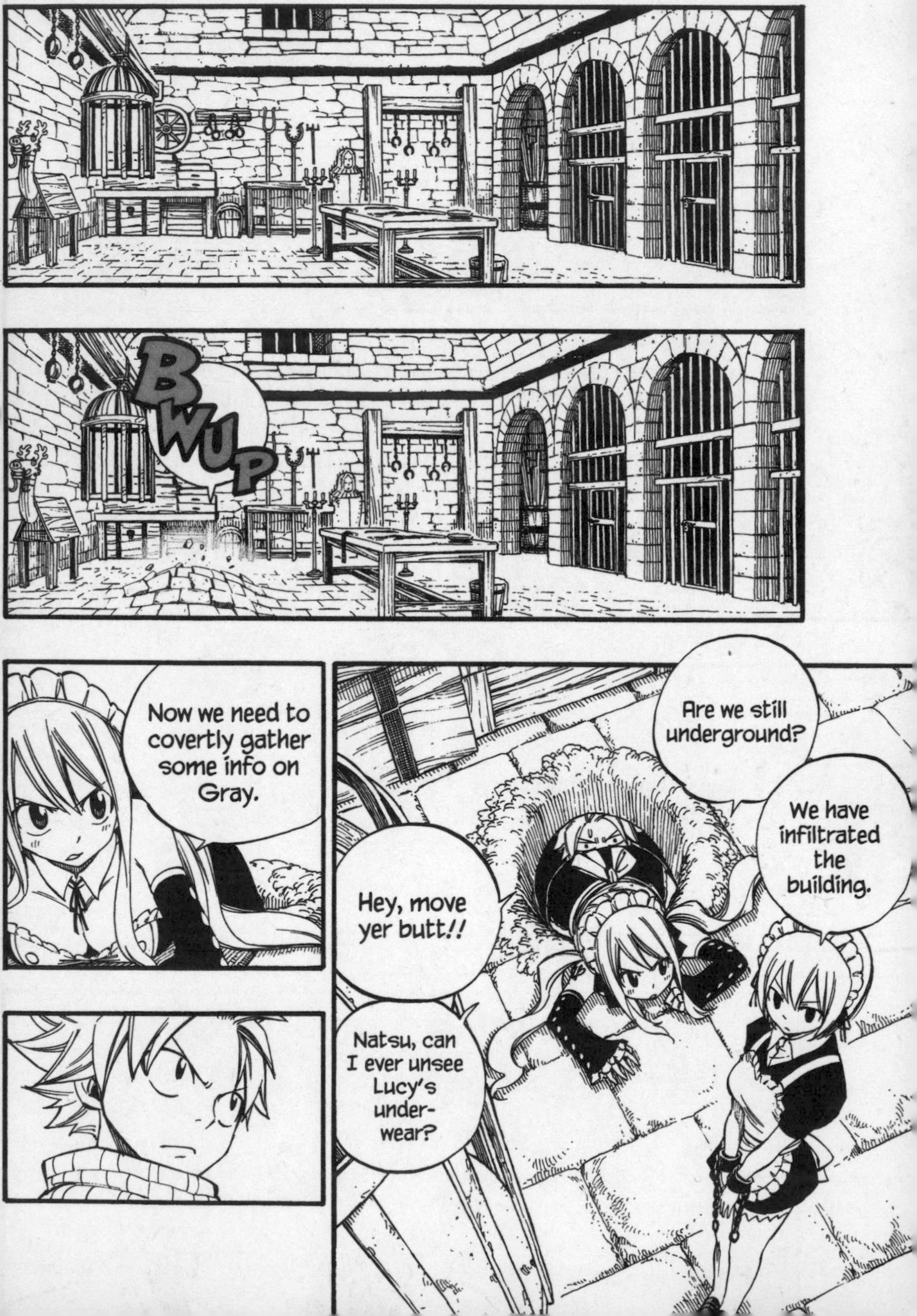
BWUP
We have infiltrated the building.
Are we still underground?
Hey, move yer butt!!
Natsu, can I ever unsee Lucy's underwear?
Now we need to covertly gather some info on Gray.

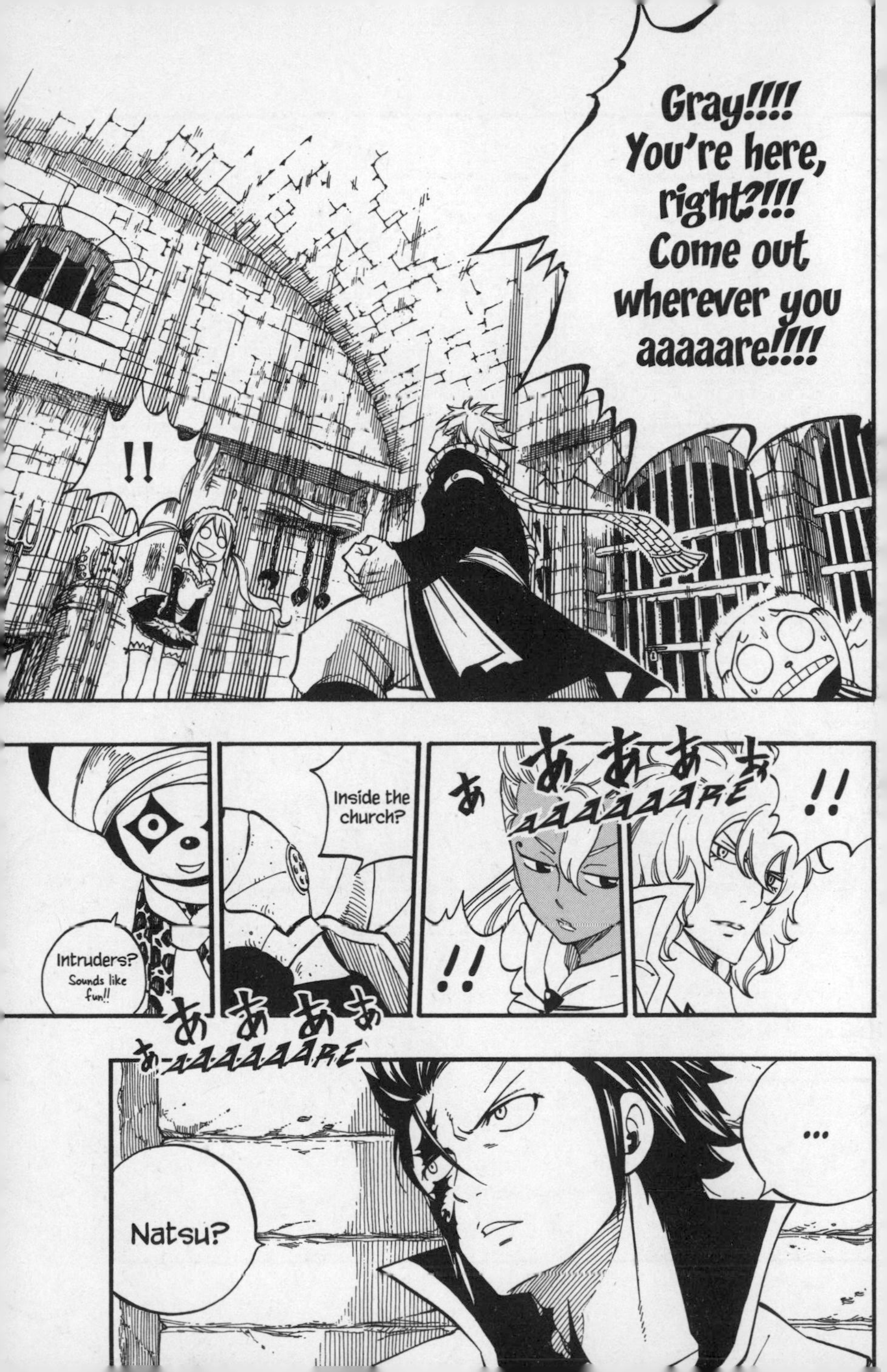
Gray!!!! You're here, right?!!! Come out wherever you aaaaare!!!!
!!
!!
ああああ AAAAAAARE
!!
Inside the church?
Intruders? Sounds like fun!!
ああああ AAAAAAARE
...
Natsu?

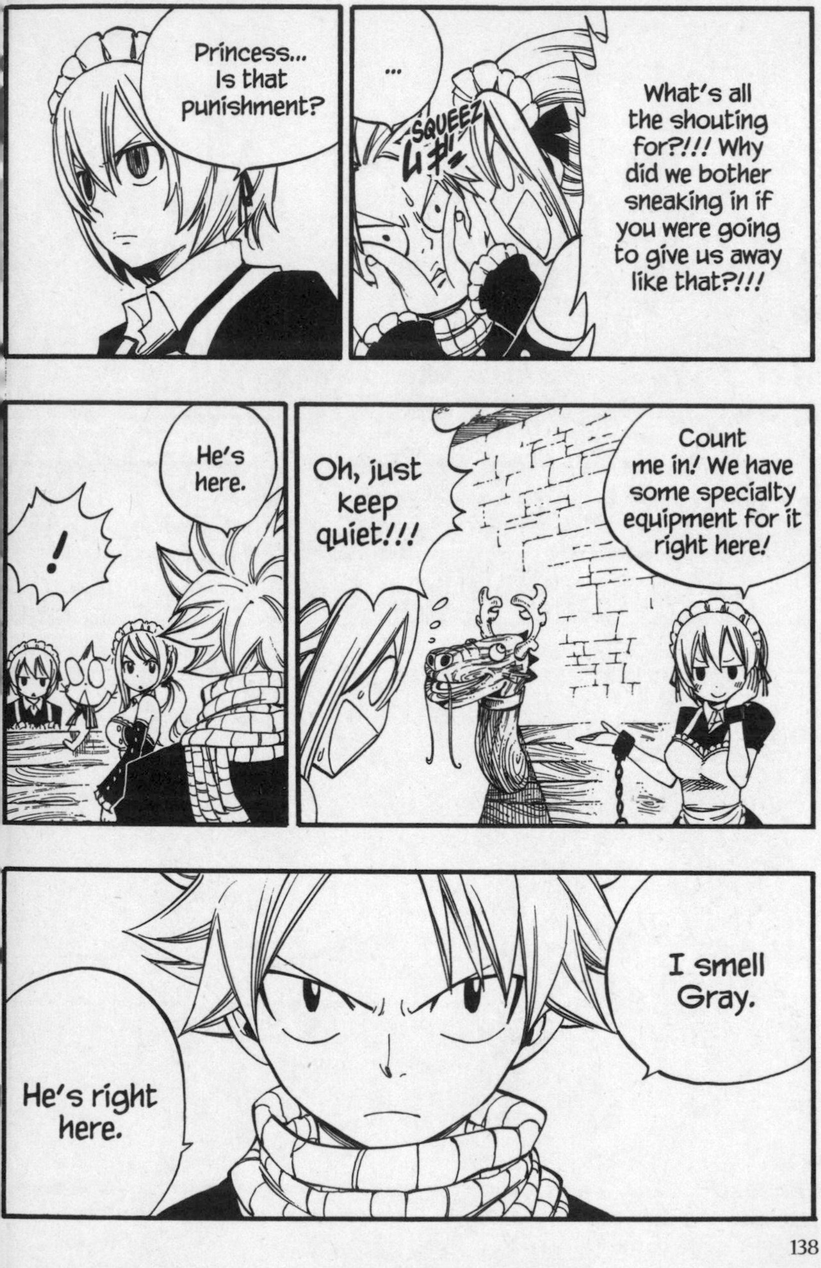
What's all the shouting for?!!! Why did we bother sneaking in if you were going to give us away like that?!!!
...
SQUEEZ
Princess... Is that punishment?
Count me in! We have some specialty equipment for it right here!
Oh, just keep quiet!!!
He's here.
!
I smell Gray.
He's right here.

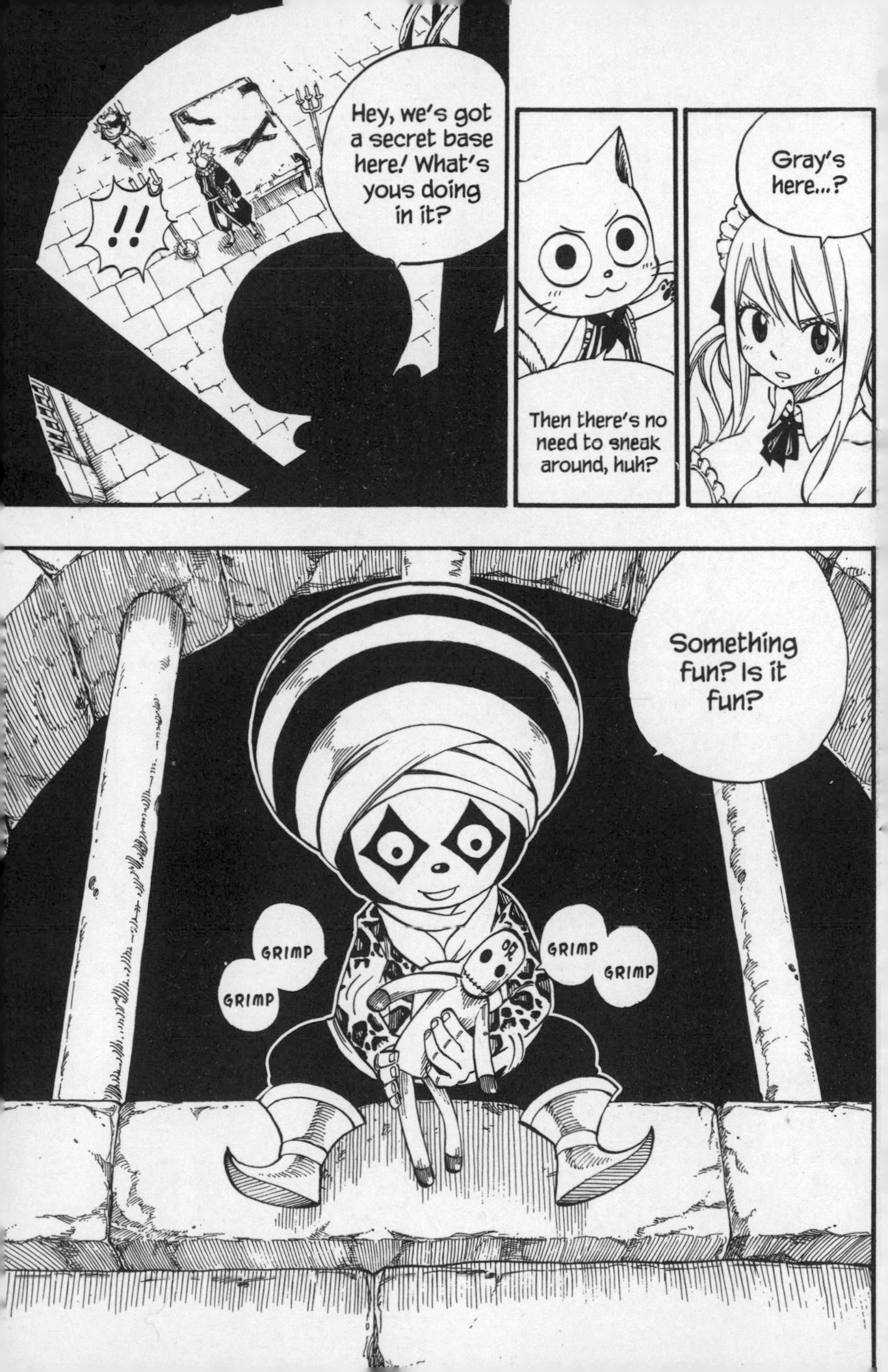
Gray's here...?
Then there's no need to sneak around, huh?
Hey, we's got a secret base here! What's yous doing in it?
!!
Something fun? Is it fun?
GRIMP
GRIMP
GRIMP
GRIMP

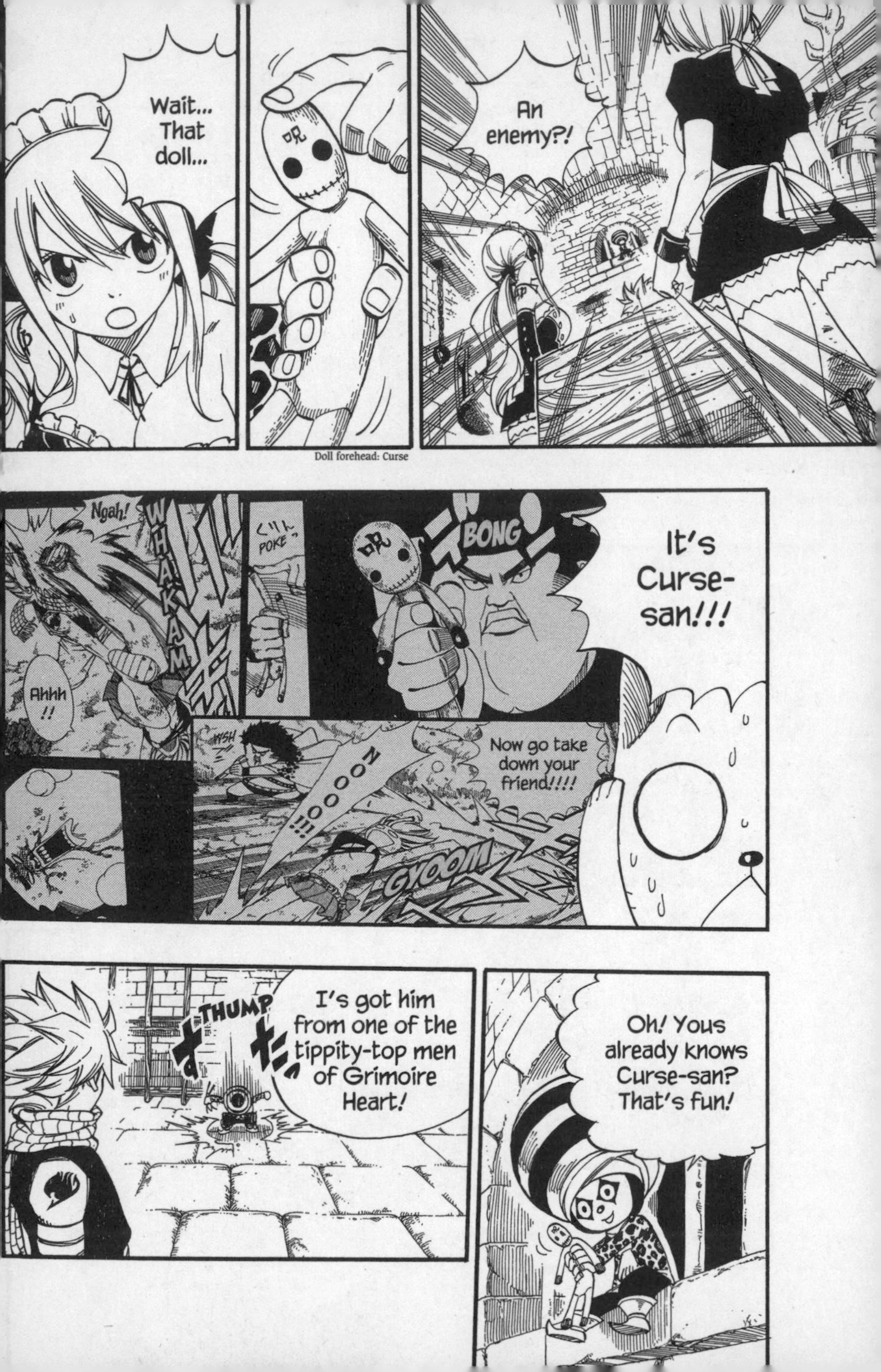
An enemy?!
Wait... That doll...
Doll forehead: Curse
It's Curse-san!!!
BONG
くりん POKE
Ngah!
WHAKAM
Ahhh!!
Now go take down your friend!!!!
WYSH
NOOOO!!!
GYOOM
Oh! Yous already knows Curse-san? That's fun!
THUMP
I's got him from one of the tippity-top men of Grimoire Heart!

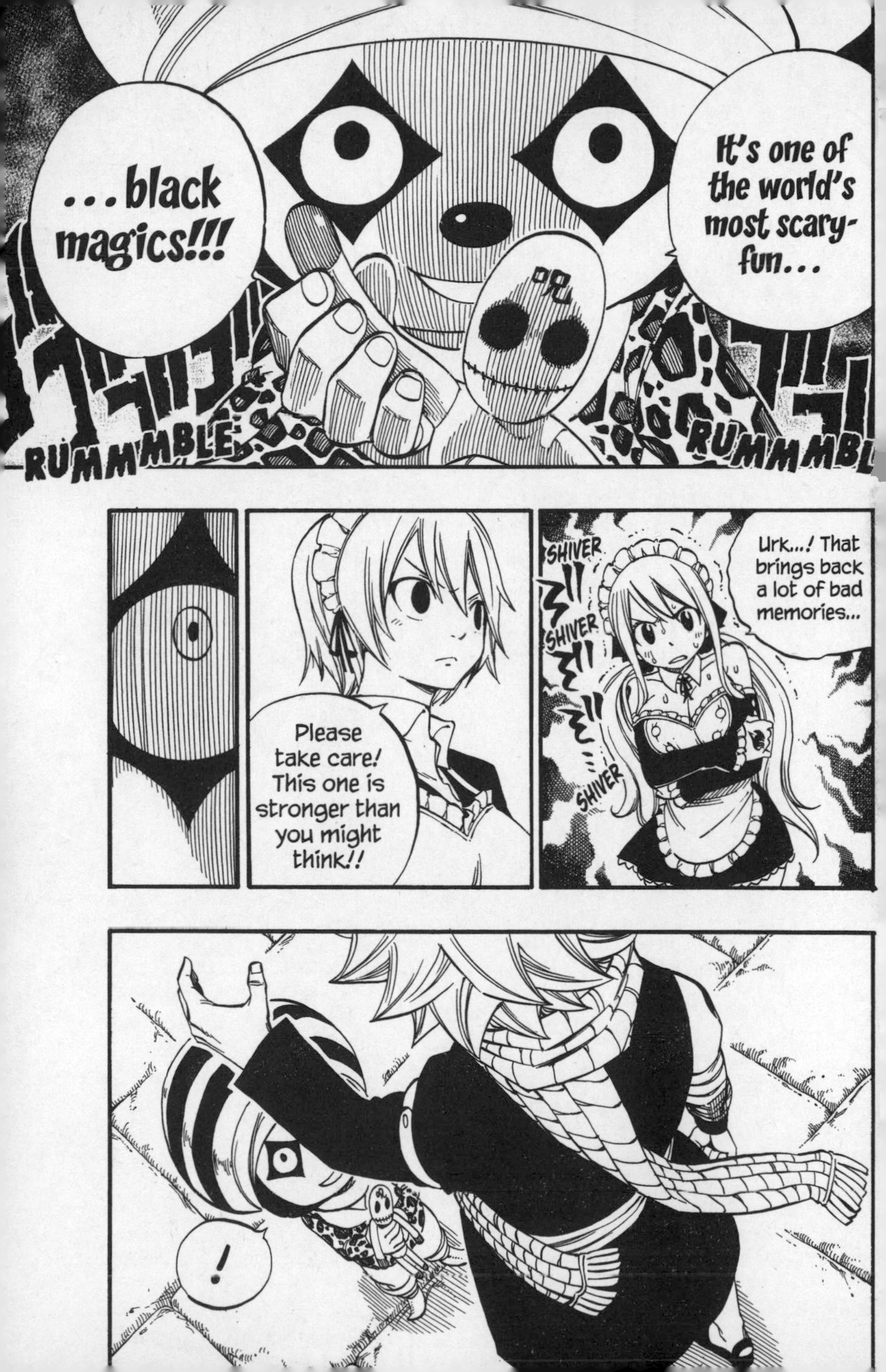
It's one of the world's most scary-fun...
...black magics!!!
RUMMMBL
RUMMMBLE
SHIVER
SHIVER
SHIVER
Urk...! That brings back a lot of bad memories...
Please take care! This one is stronger than you might think!!
!

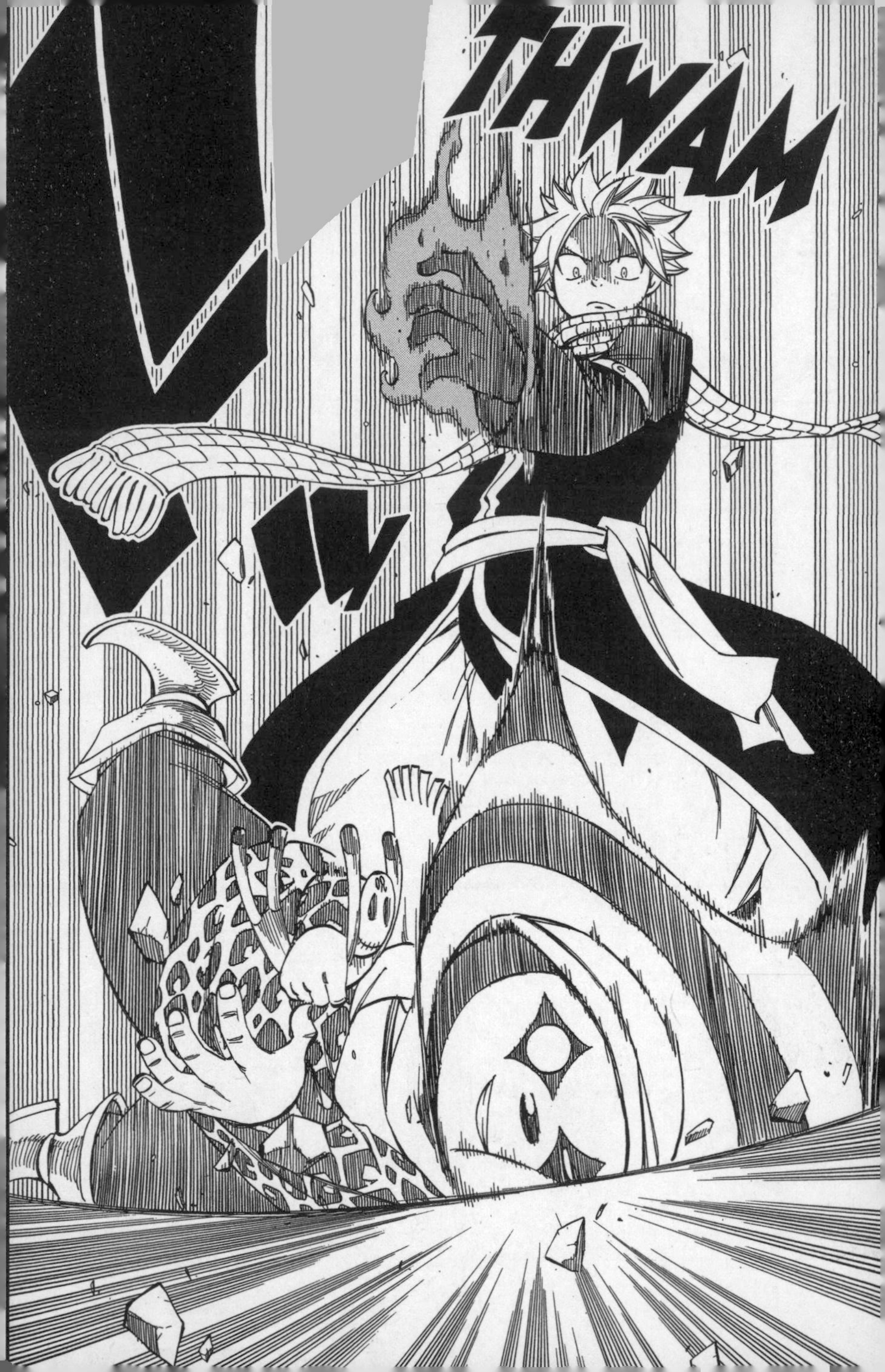
THWAM

Ah...

Ahhh ...

Huh?

Sorry, but I got no use for anybody here but Gray.

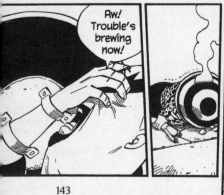

Aw! Trouble's brewing now!

Able!!

TUMP

TUMP

TUMP

TUMP

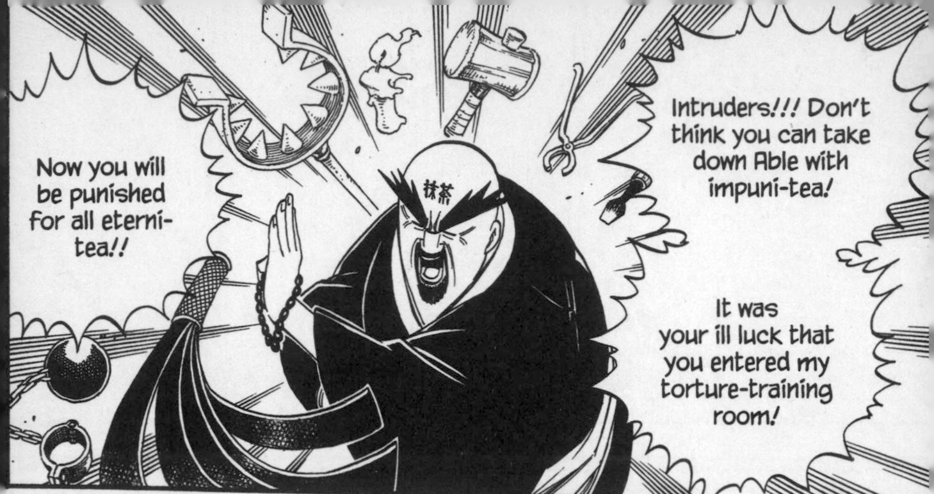
Intruders!!! Don't think you can take down Able with impuni-tea!
It was your ill luck that you entered my torture-training room!
Now you will be punished for all eterni-tea!!
Forehead: Green Tea

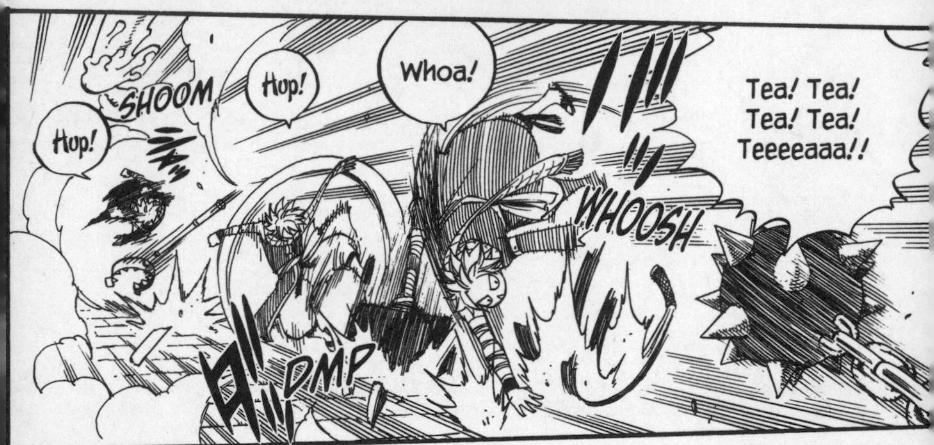
Tea! Tea! Tea! Tea! Teeeeaaa!!
WHOOSH
Whoa!
Hop!
SHOOM
Hop!
DMP
*A variation on the Spanish Donkey torture device.

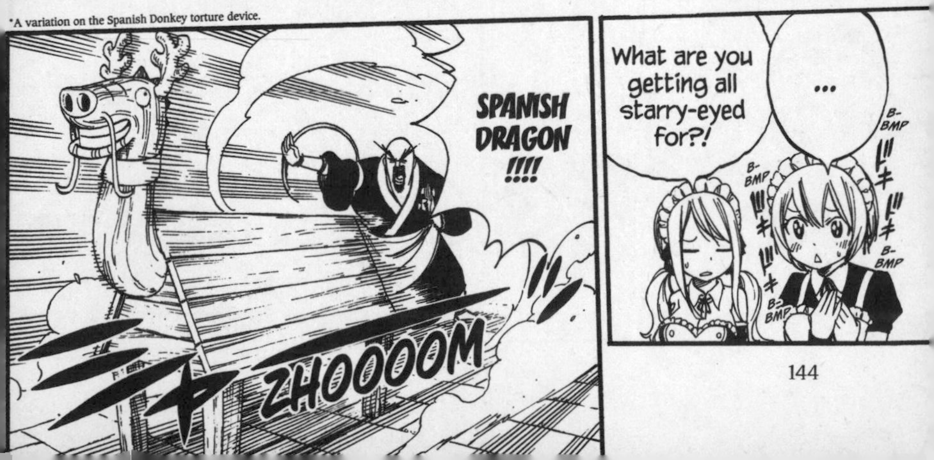
...
B-BMP
What are you getting all starry-eyed for?!
B-BMP
B-BMP
B-BMP
SPANISH DRAGON!!!!
ZHOOOOM

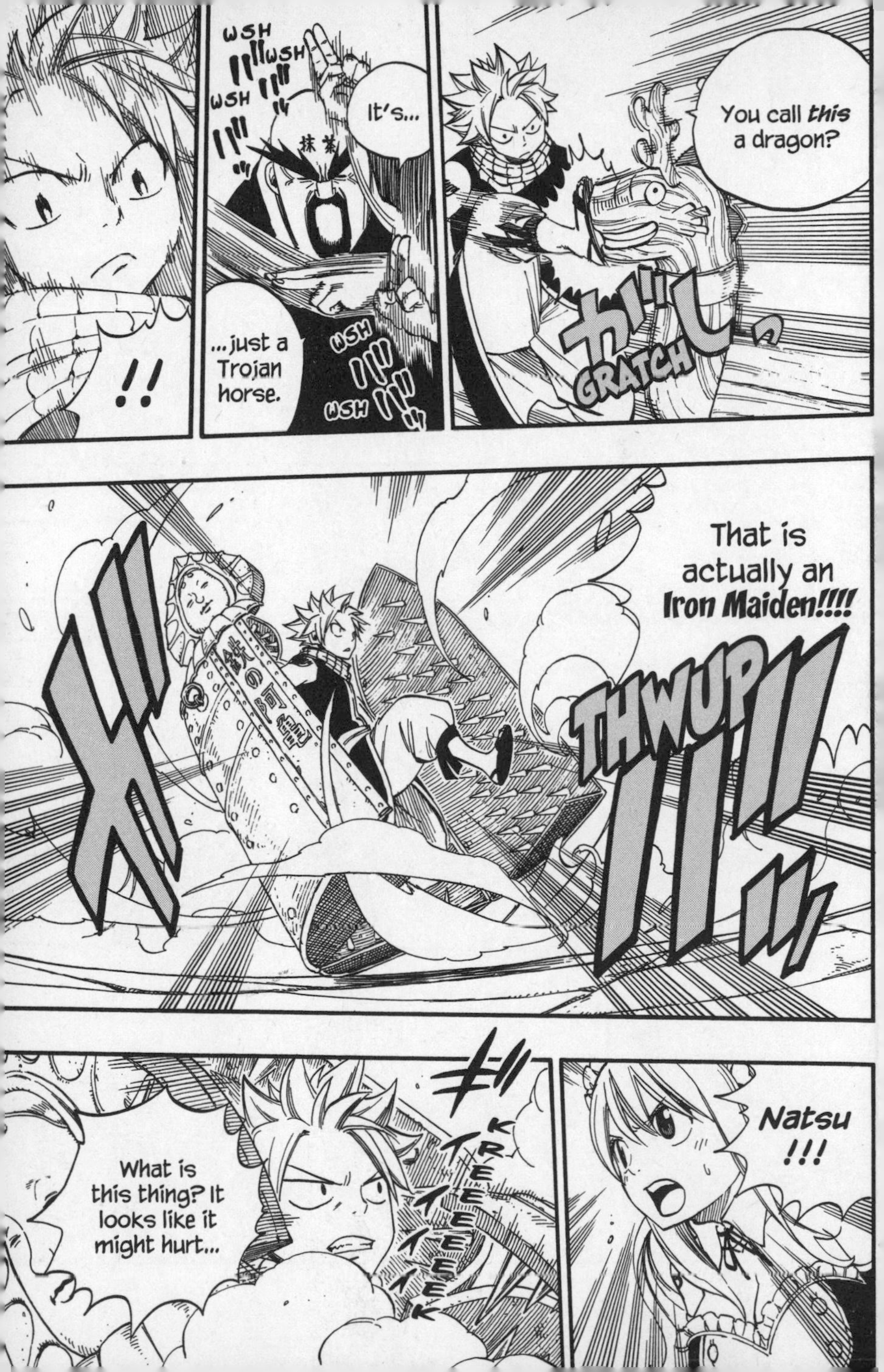

You call *this* a dragon?
GRATCH
WSH WSH WSH
It's...
...just a Trojan horse.
WSH WSH
!!
That is actually an **Iron Maiden!!!!**
THWUP
Natsu !!!
KREEEEEEEK
What is this thing? It looks like it might hurt...

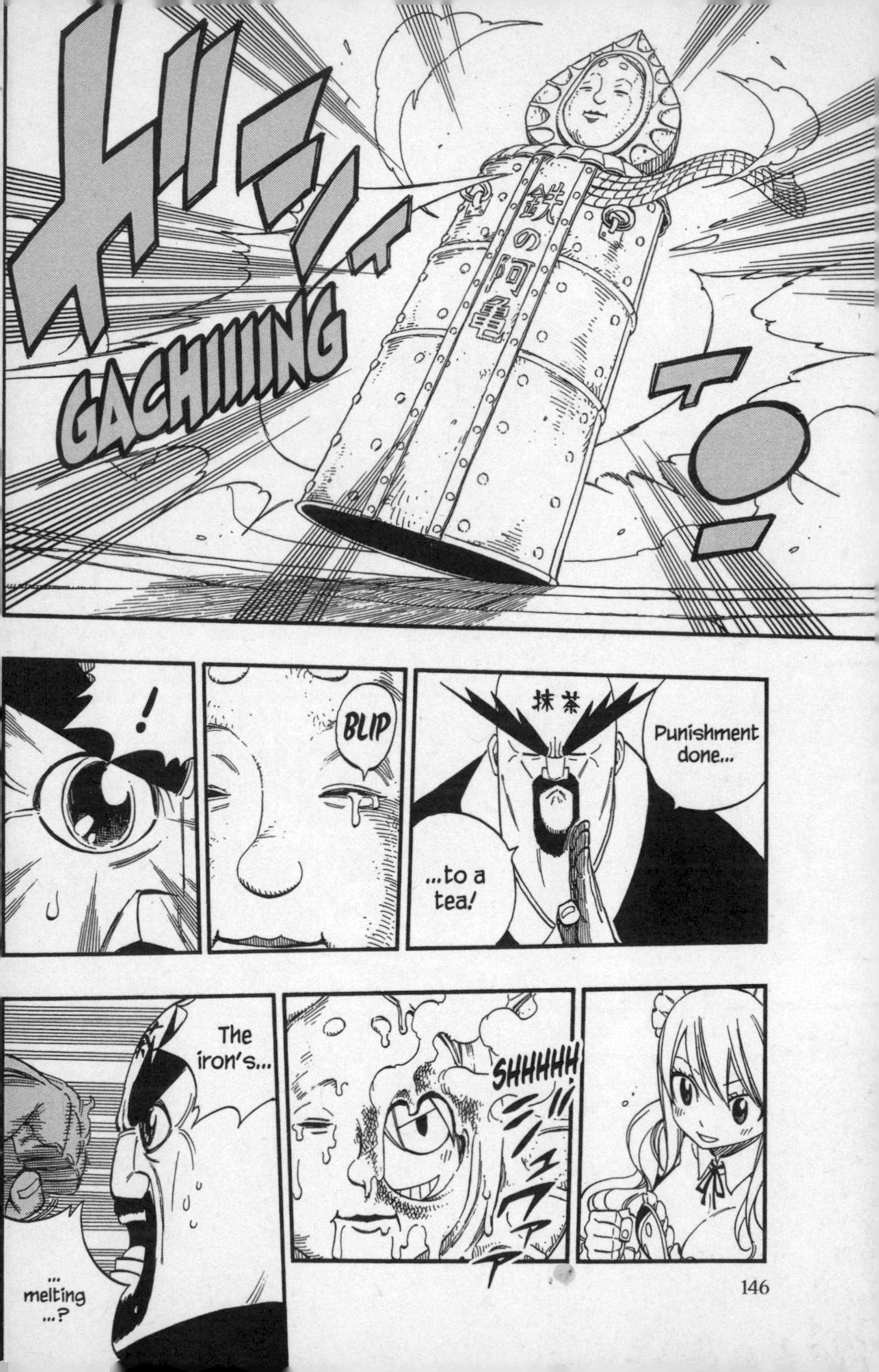
鉄の阿呆
GACHIIIING
抹茶
Punishment done...
...to a tea!
BLIP
!
SHHHHH
The iron's...
...melting...?

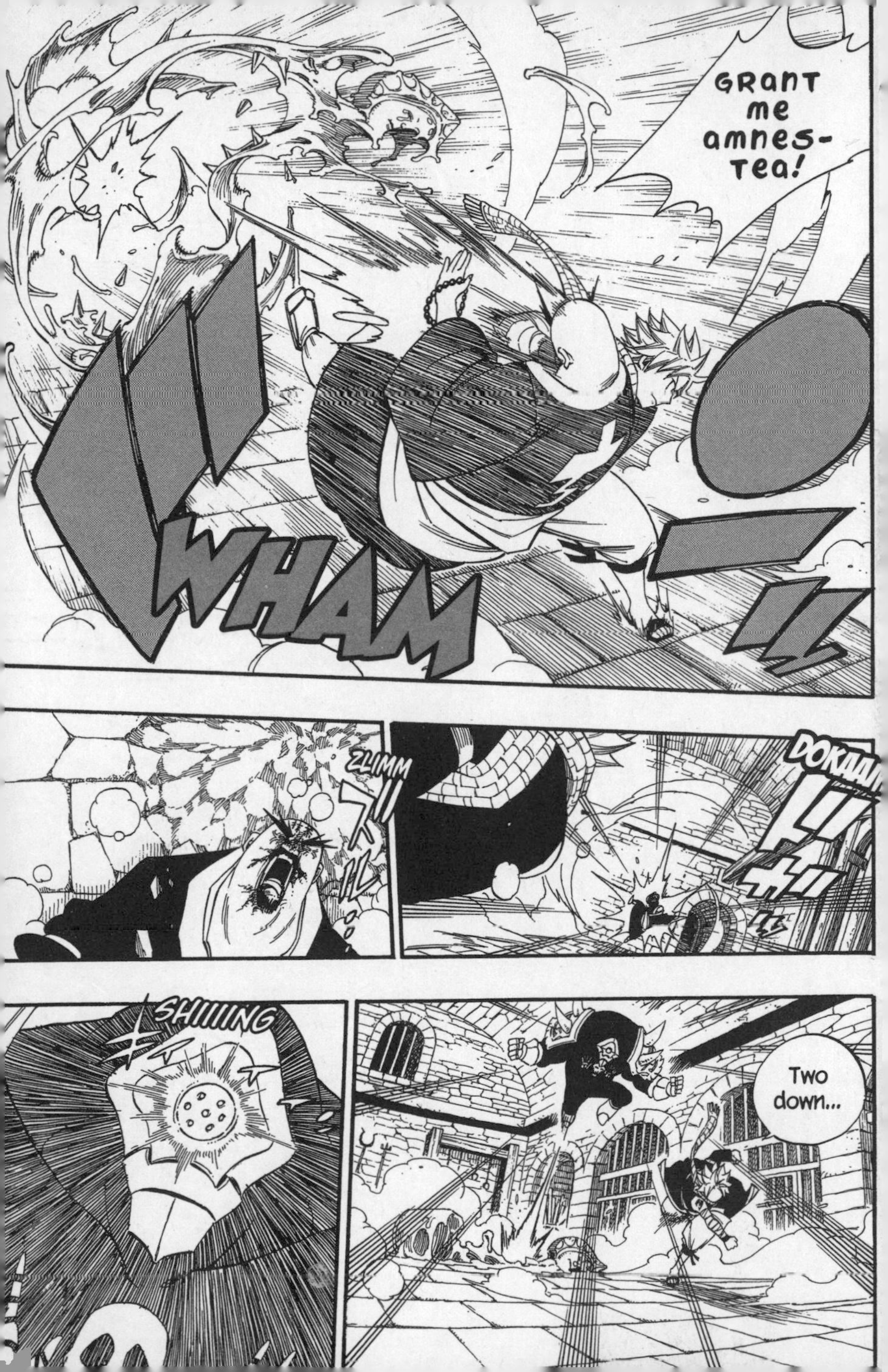
GRANT me amnes-tea!
WHAM
DOKAAA
ZLIMM
Two down...
SHIIIING

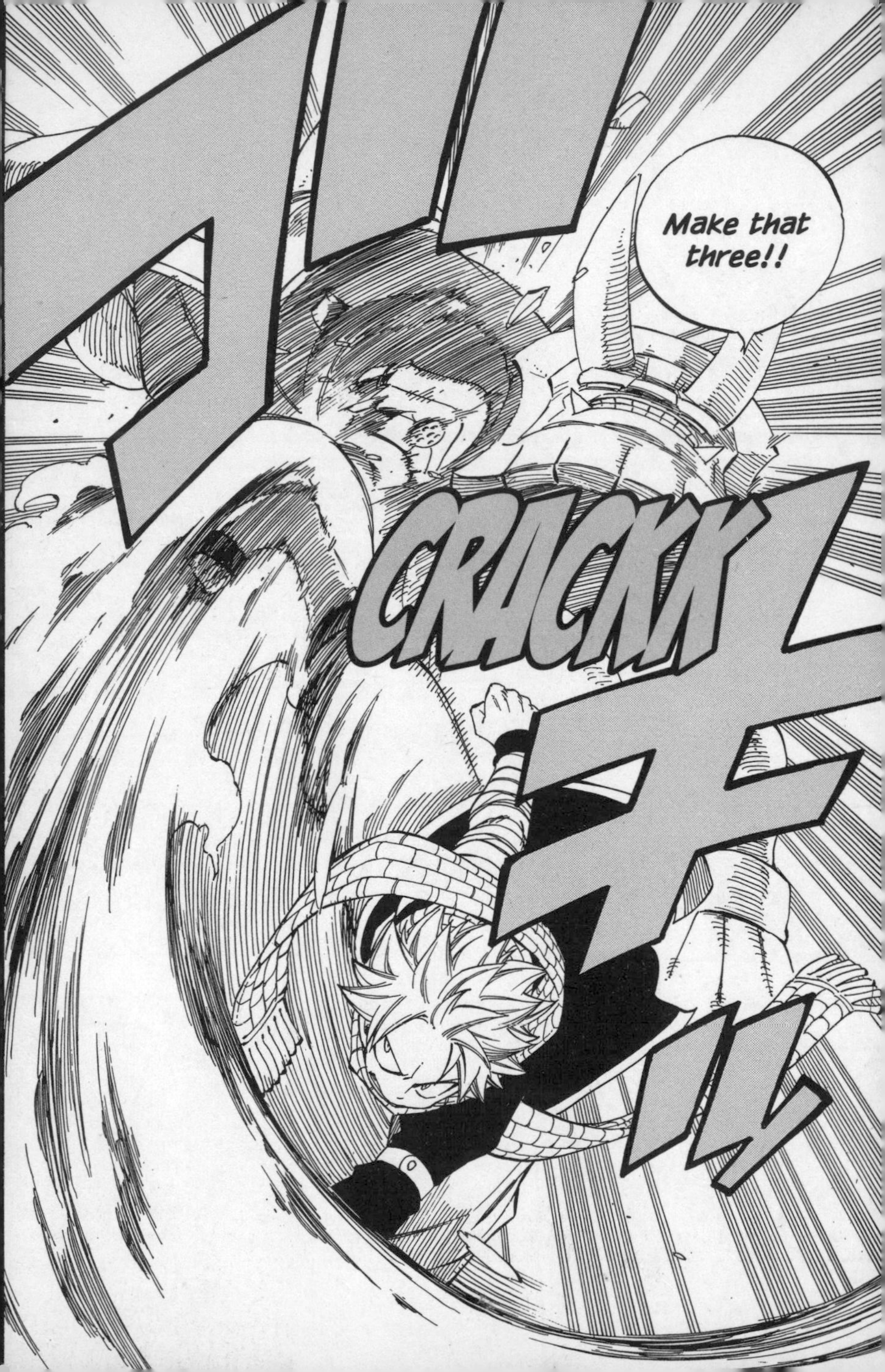
Make that three!!
CRACKK

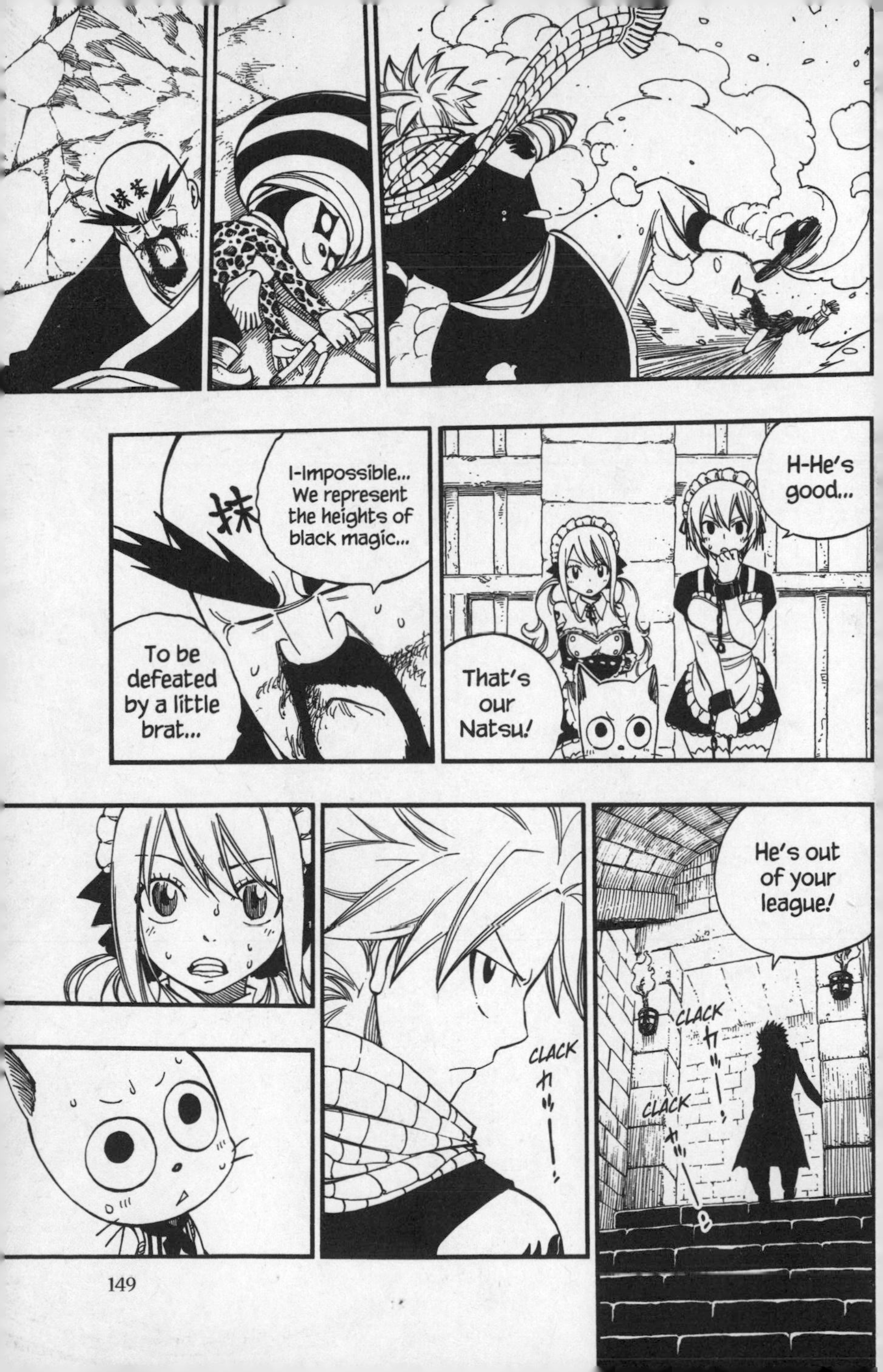
H-He's good...
That's our Natsu!
I-Impossible... We represent the heights of black magic...
To be defeated by a little brat...
He's out of your league!
CLACK
CLACK
CLACK

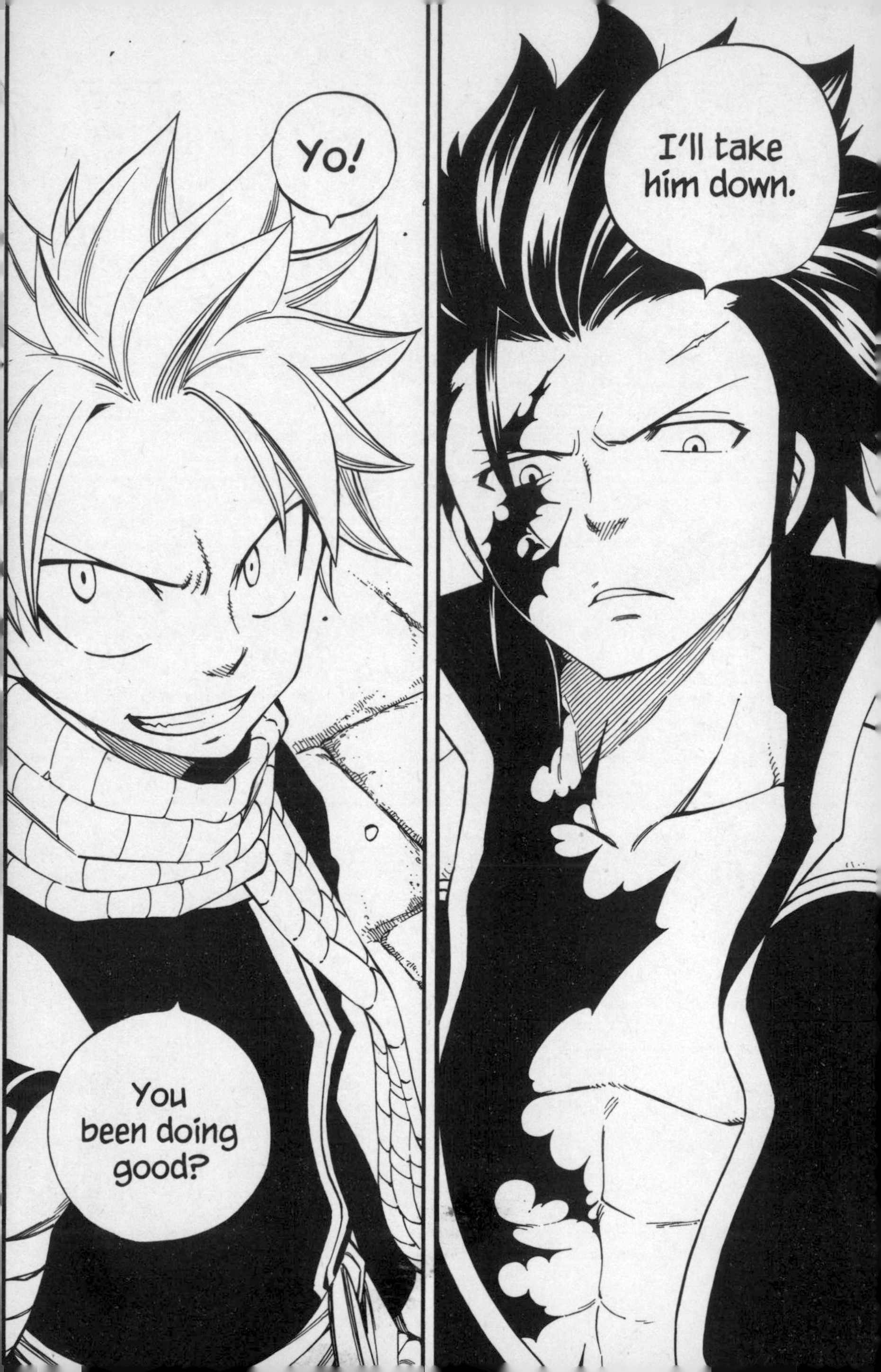
I'll take him down.
Yo!
You been doing good?

FAIRY TAIL

フェアリーテイル

Chapter 428: When We Take Different Paths

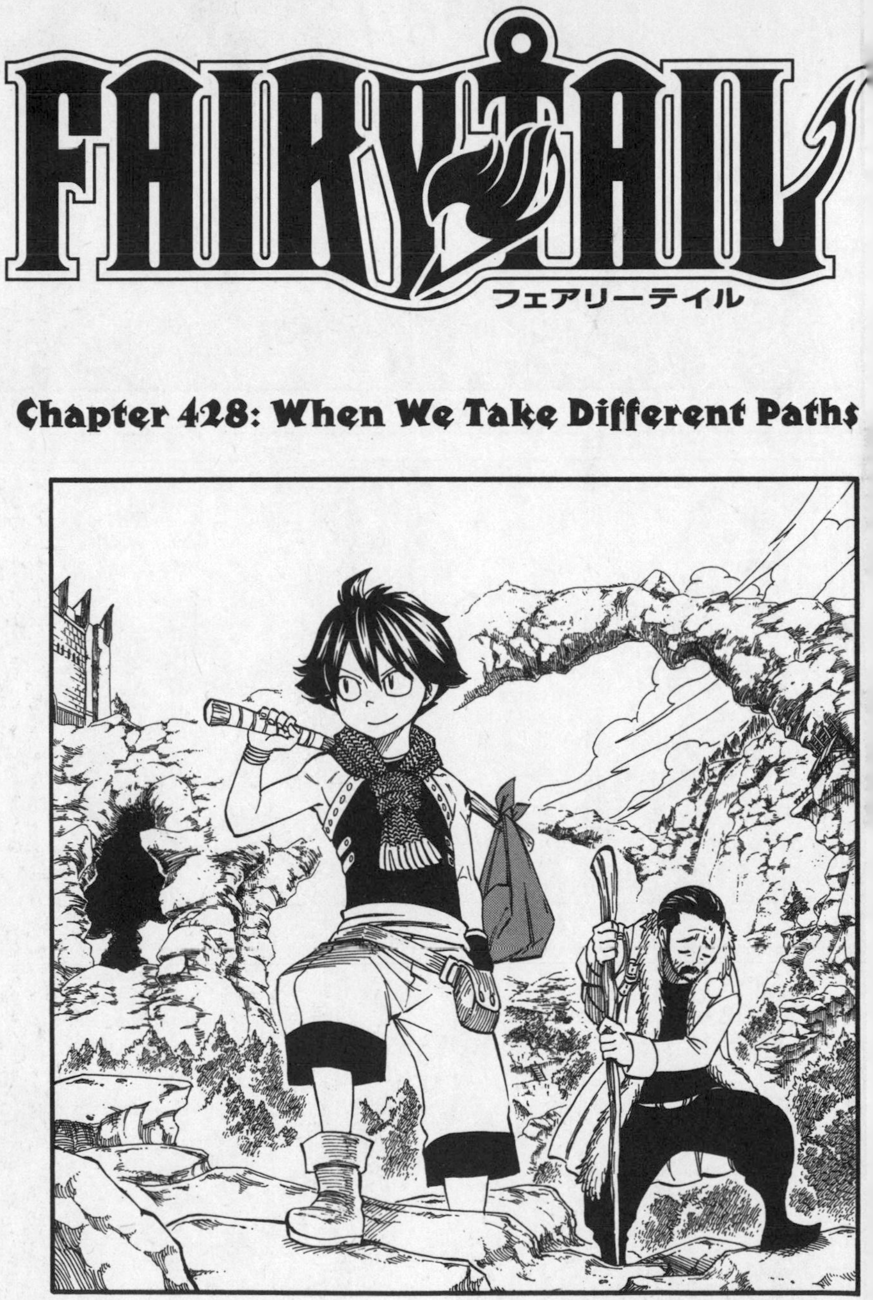

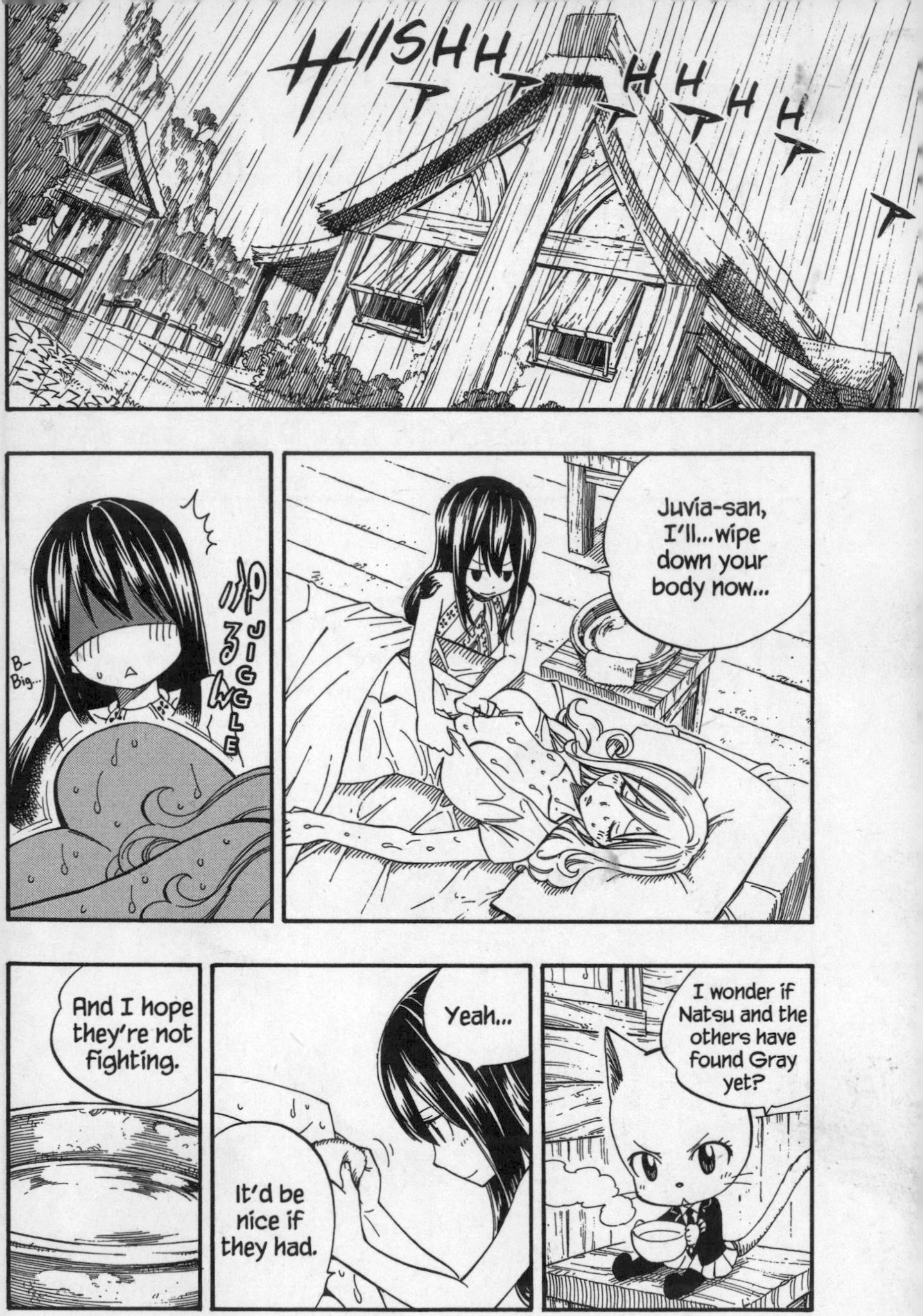
HISSHH
HHHH
Juvia-san, I'll...wipe down your body now...
JIGGLE
B-Big...
I wonder if Natsu and the others have found Gray yet?
Yeah...
It'd be nice if they had.
And I hope they're not fighting.

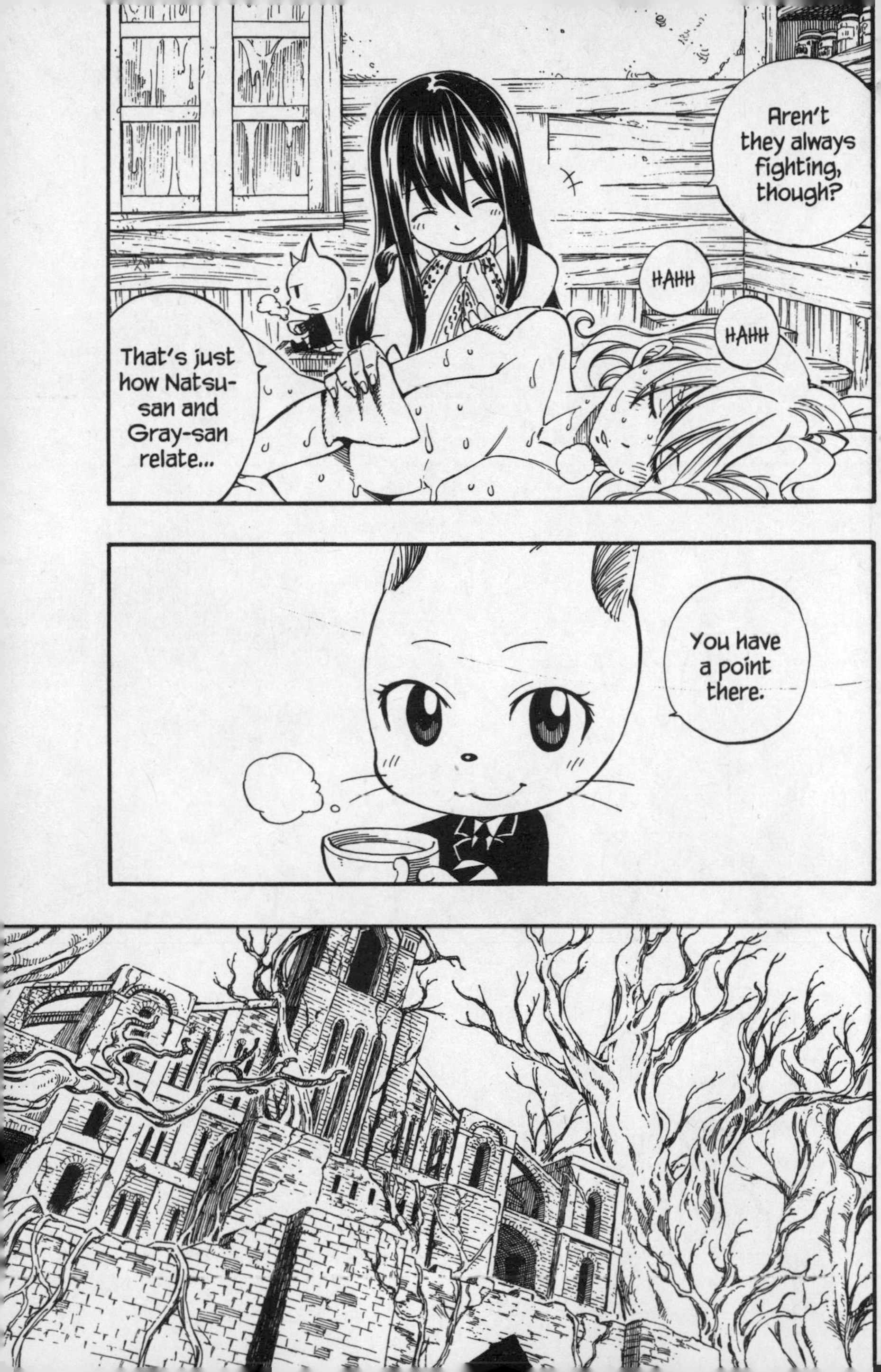
Aren't they always fighting, though?
HAHH
HAHH
That's just how Natsu-san and Gray-san relate...
You have a point there.

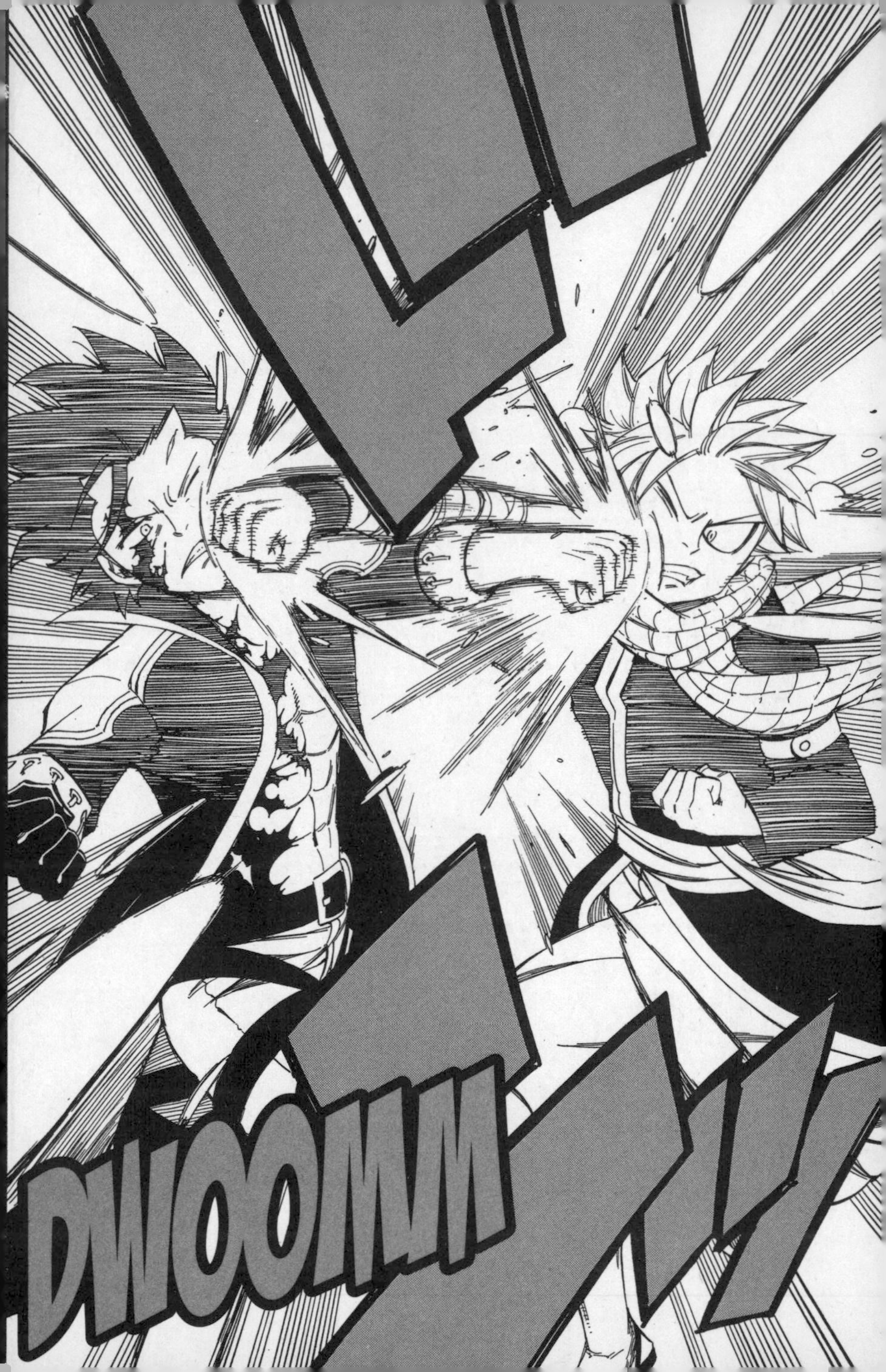
DWOOMM

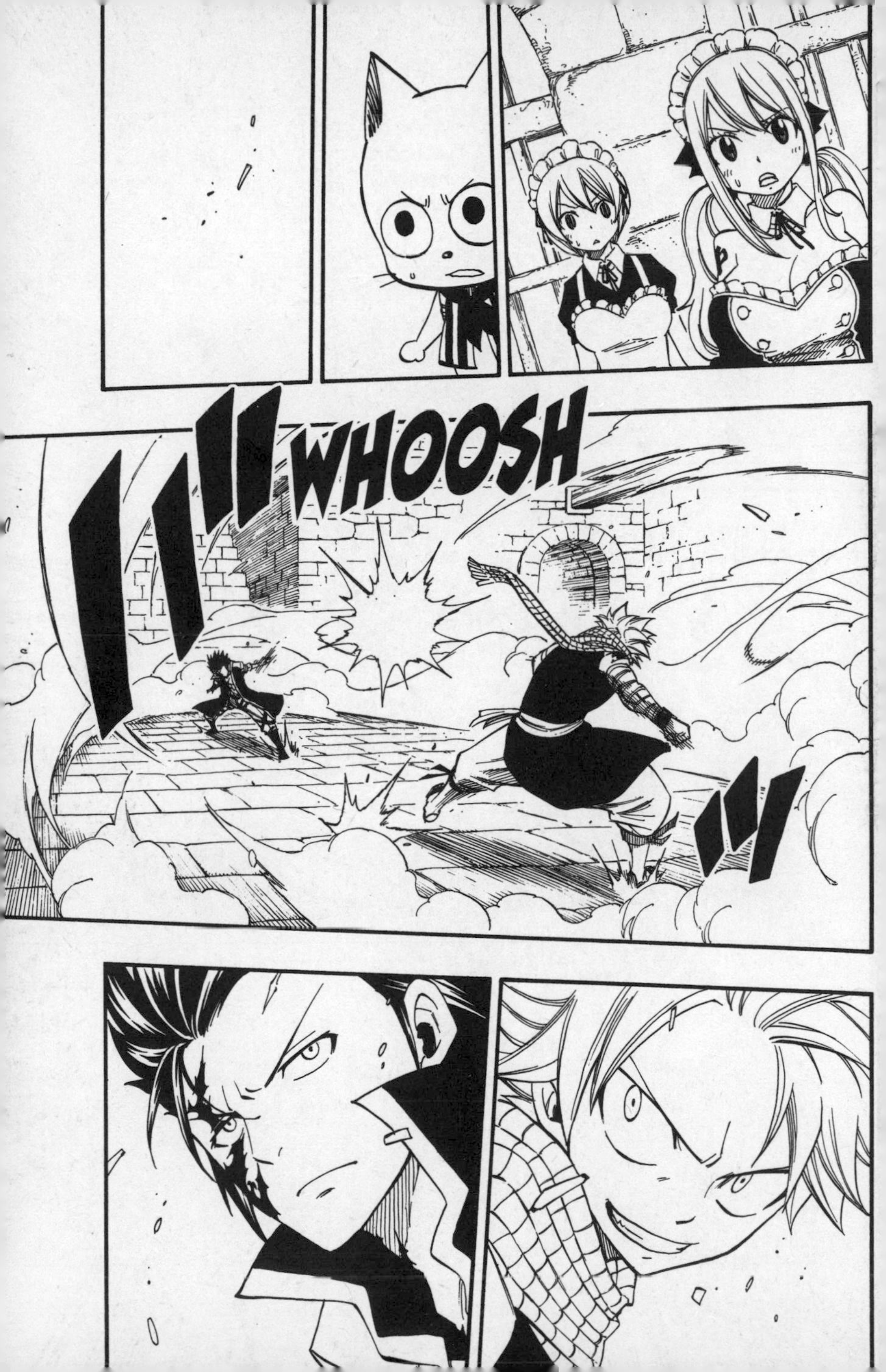
WHOOSH

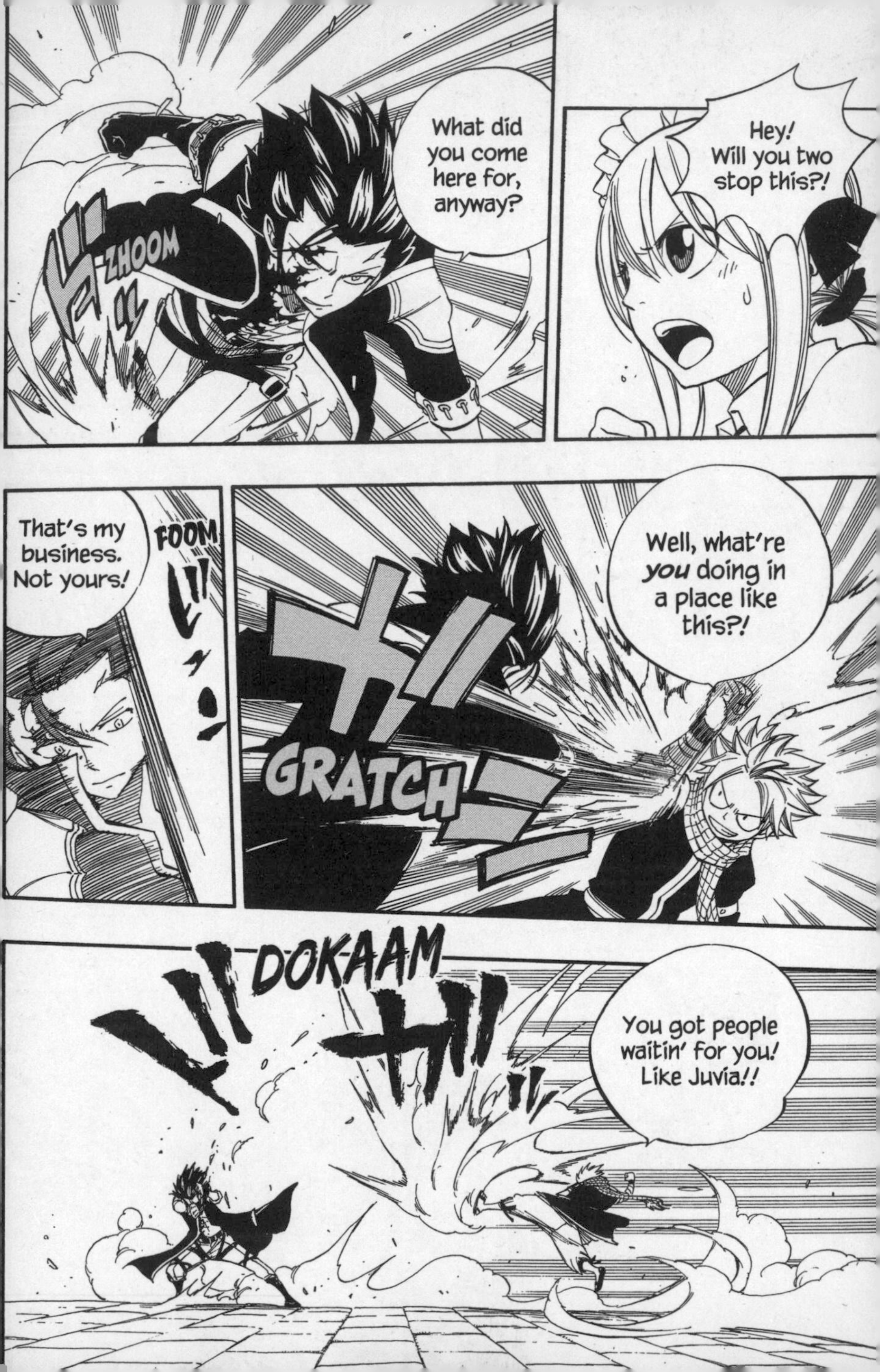
Hey! Will you two stop this?!
What did you come here for, anyway?
ZHOOM
Well, what're *you* doing in a place like this?!
GRATCH
FOOM
That's my business. Not yours!
You got people waitin' for you! Like Juvia!!
DOKAAM

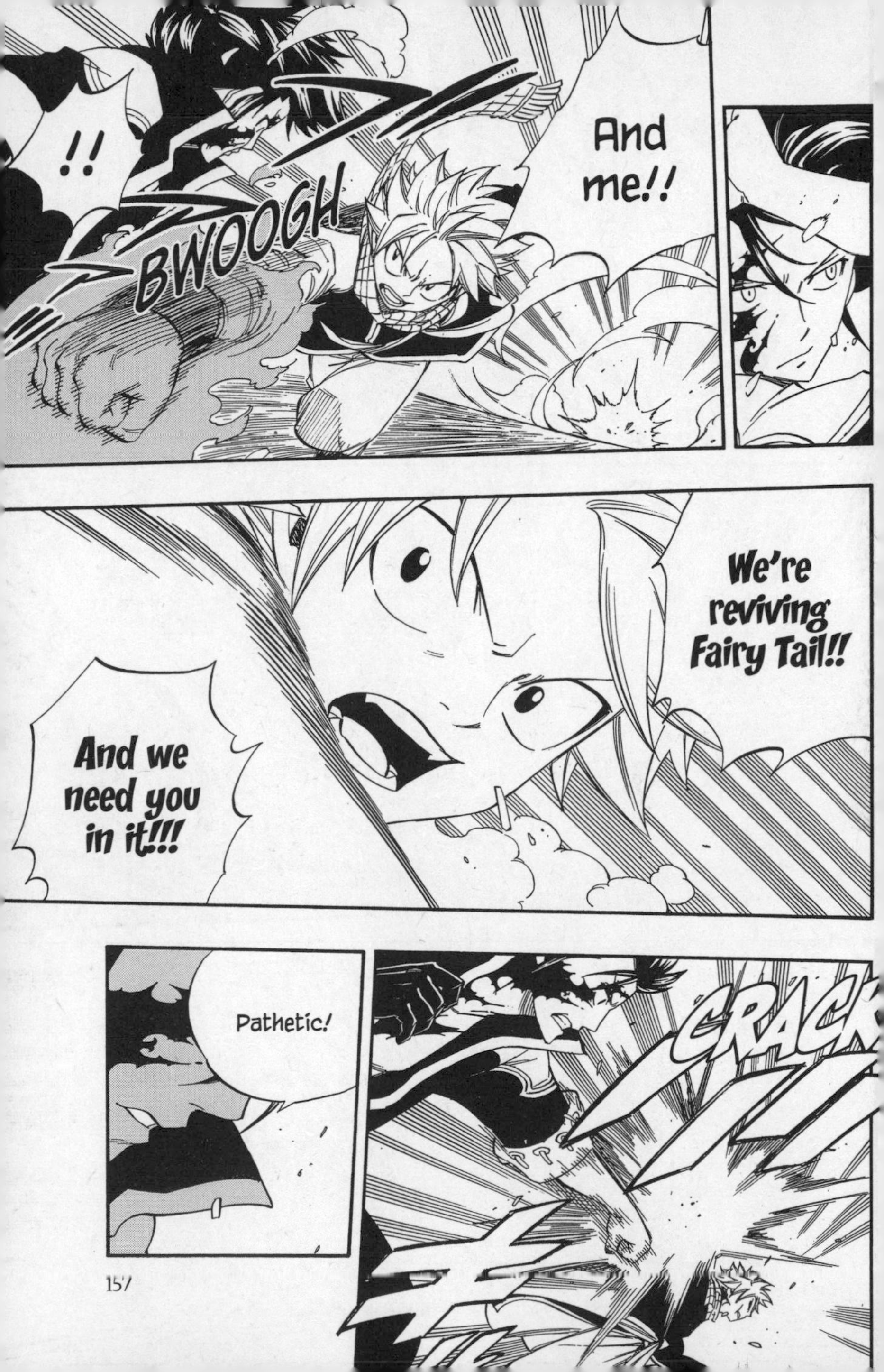
And me!!
!!
BWOOGH
We're reviving Fairy Tail!!
And we need you in it!!!
CRACK
Pathetic!

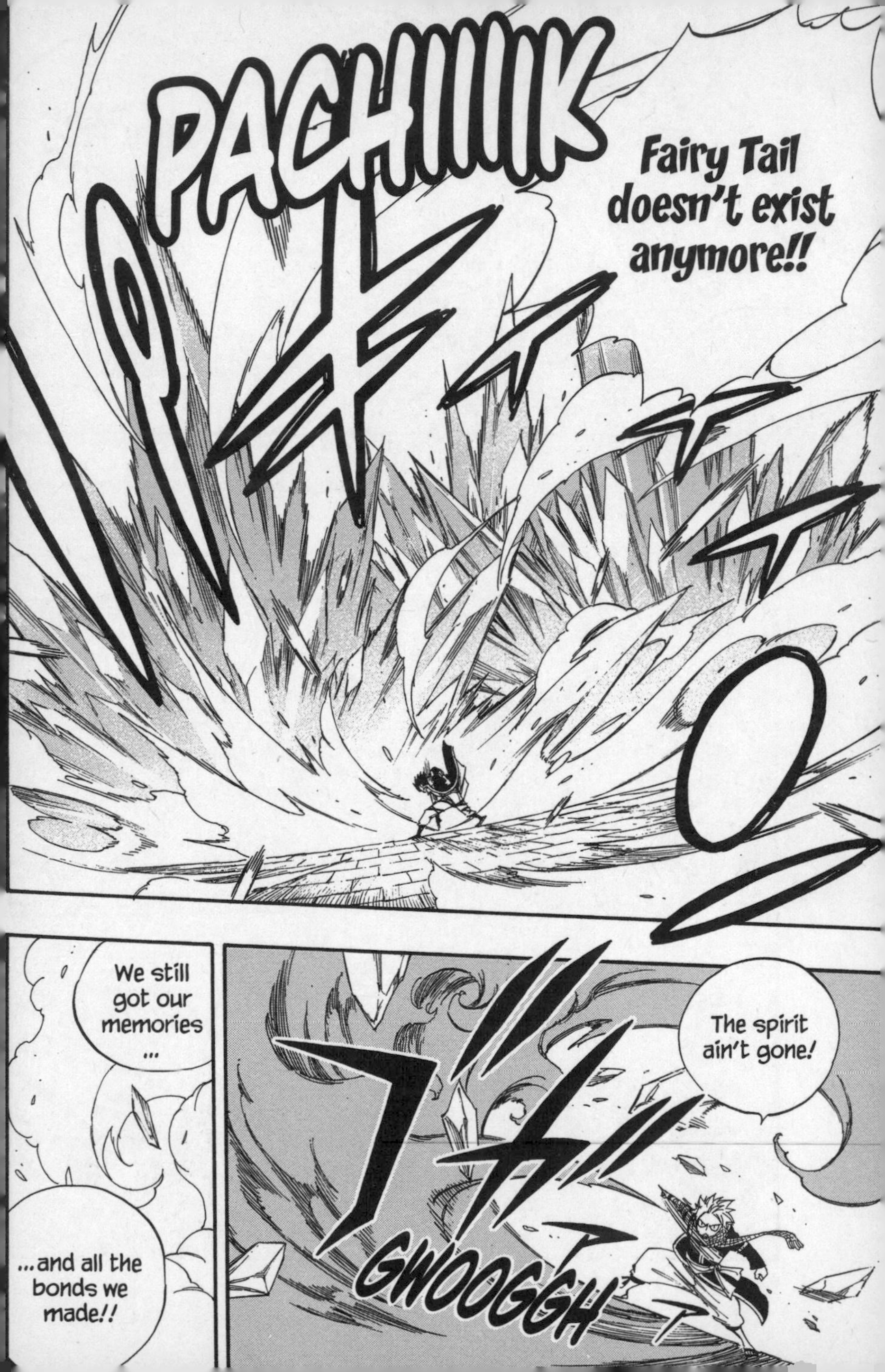
Fairy Tail doesn't exist anymore!!
PACHIIIK
The spirit ain't gone!
GWOOGGH
We still got our memories ...
...and all the bonds we made!!

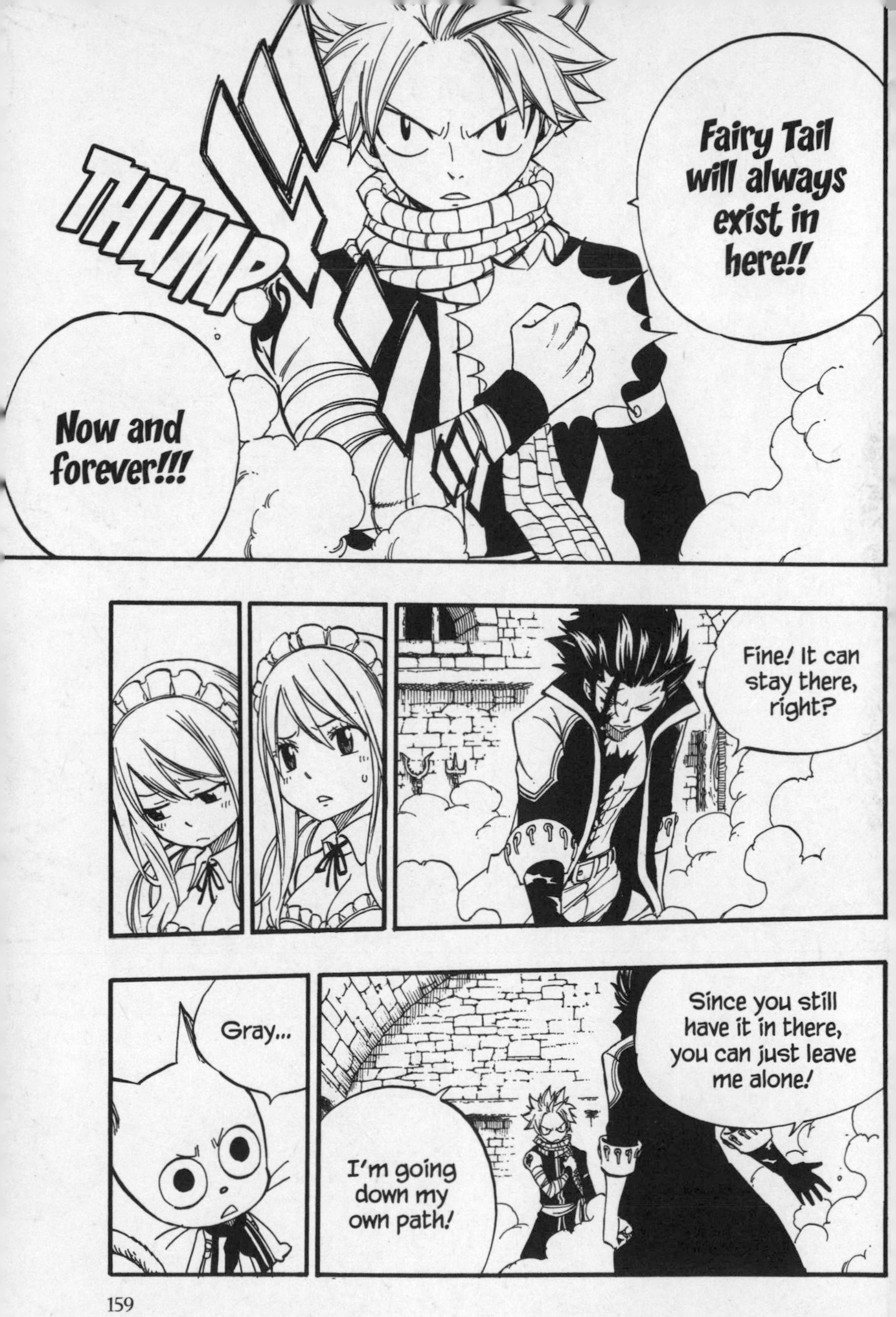
Fairy Tail will always exist in here!!
THUMP
Now and forever!!!
Fine! It can stay there, right?
Since you still have it in there, you can just leave me alone!
I'm going down my own path!
Gray...

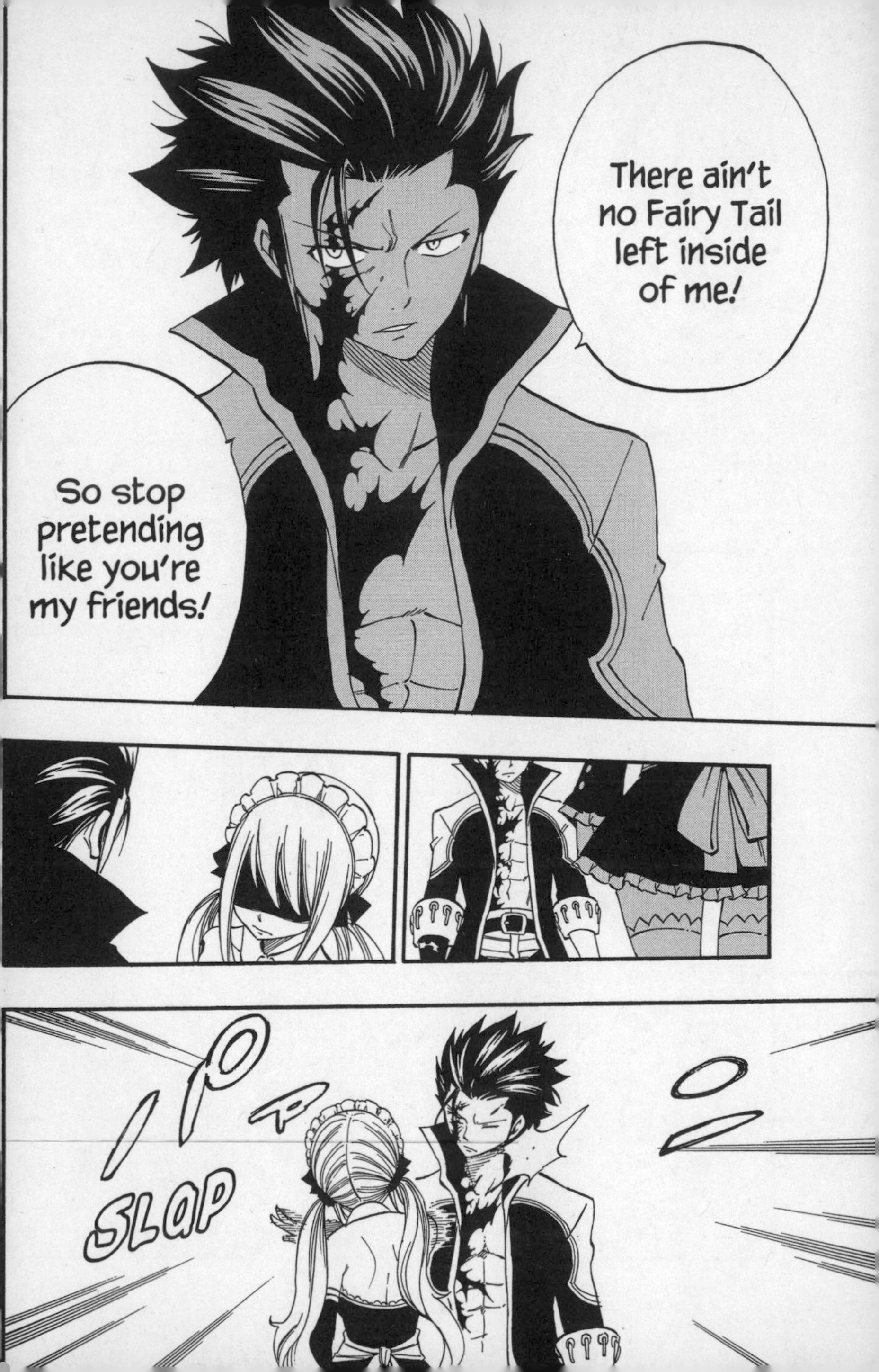
There ain't no Fairy Tail left inside of me!
So stop pretending like you're my friends!
SLAP

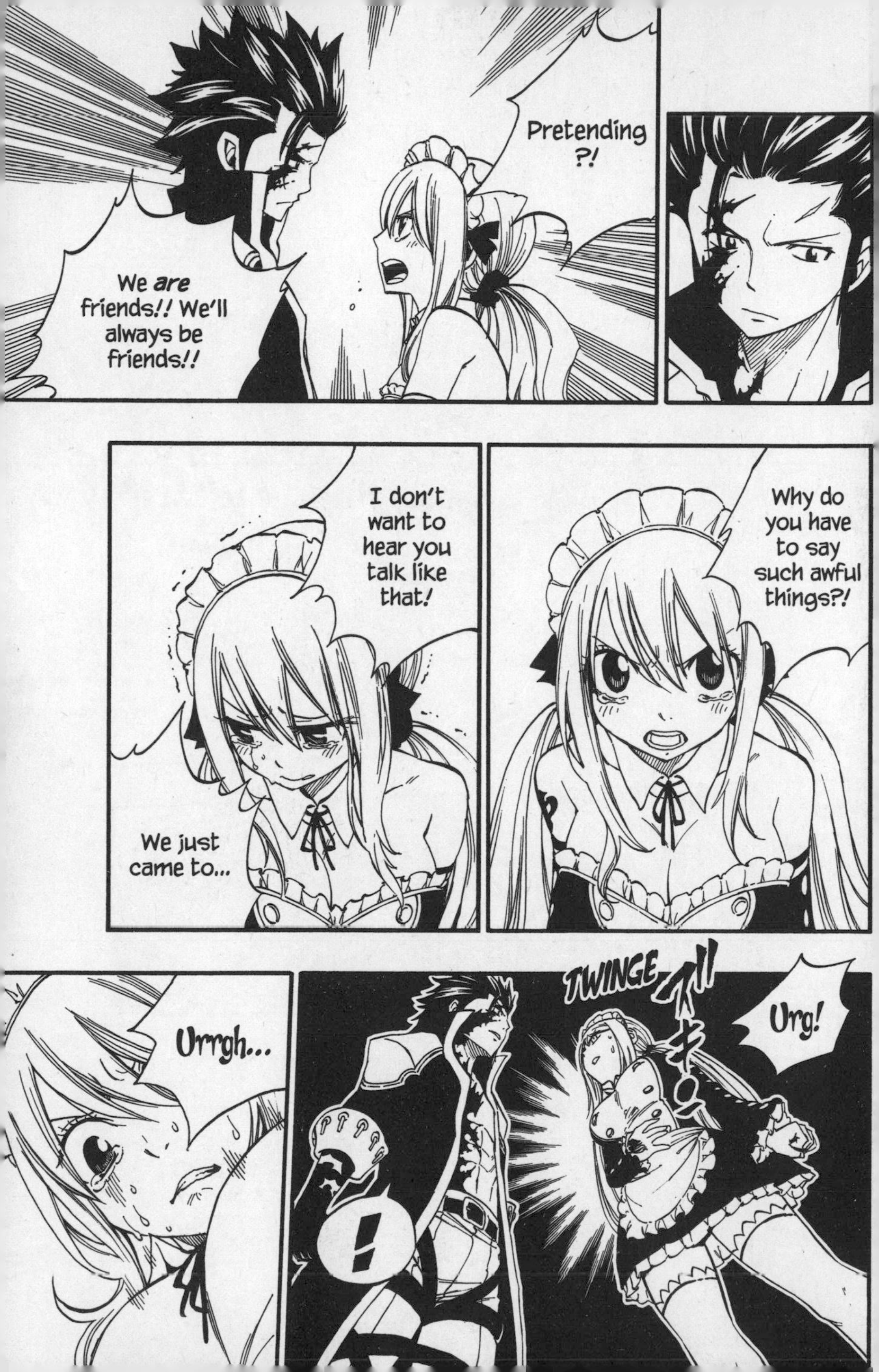
Pretending ?!
We are friends!! We'll always be friends!!
Why do you have to say such awful things?!
I don't want to hear you talk like that!
We just came to...
TWINGE
Urg!
!
Urrgh...

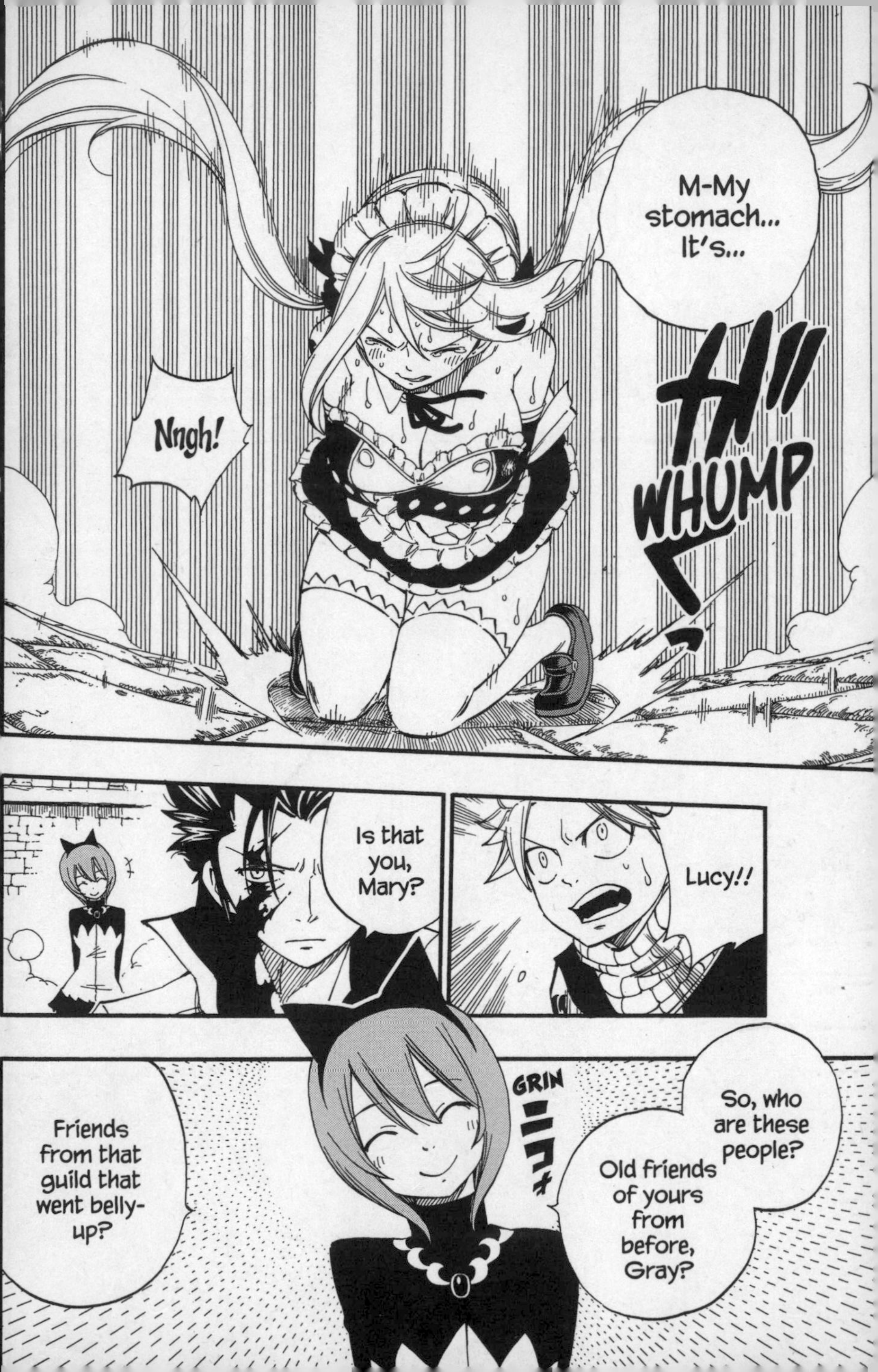
M-My stomach... It's...
WHUMP
Nngh!
Lucy!!
Is that you, Mary?
So, who are these people?
Old friends of yours from before, Gray?
GRIN
Friends from that guild that went belly-up?

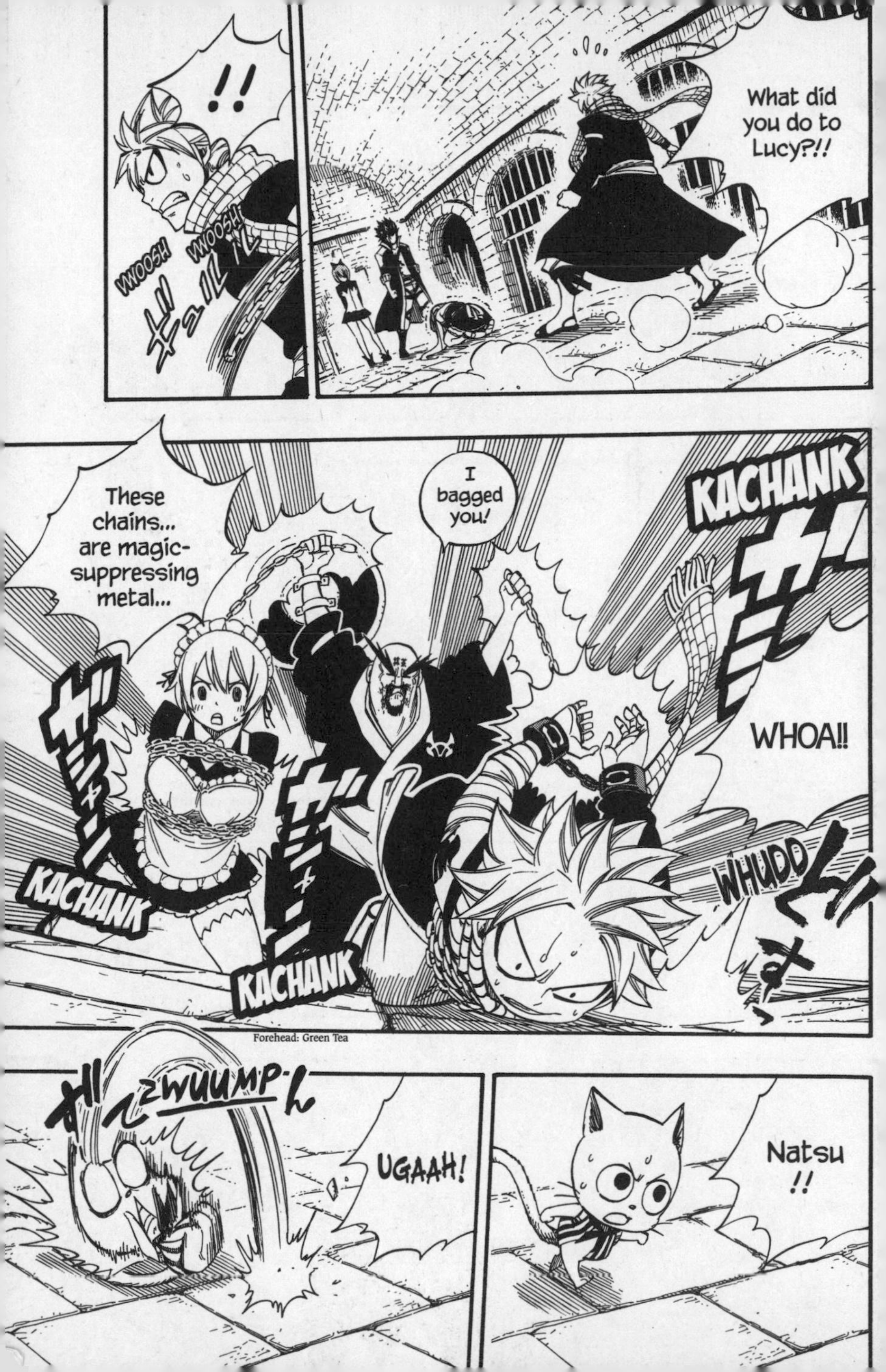
What did you do to Lucy?!!
!!
WOOSH
WOOSH
KACHANK
WHOA!!
I bagged you!
These chains... are magic-suppressing metal...
WHUDD
KACHANK
KACHANK
Natsu !!
UGAAH!
WUUMP
Forehead: Green Tea

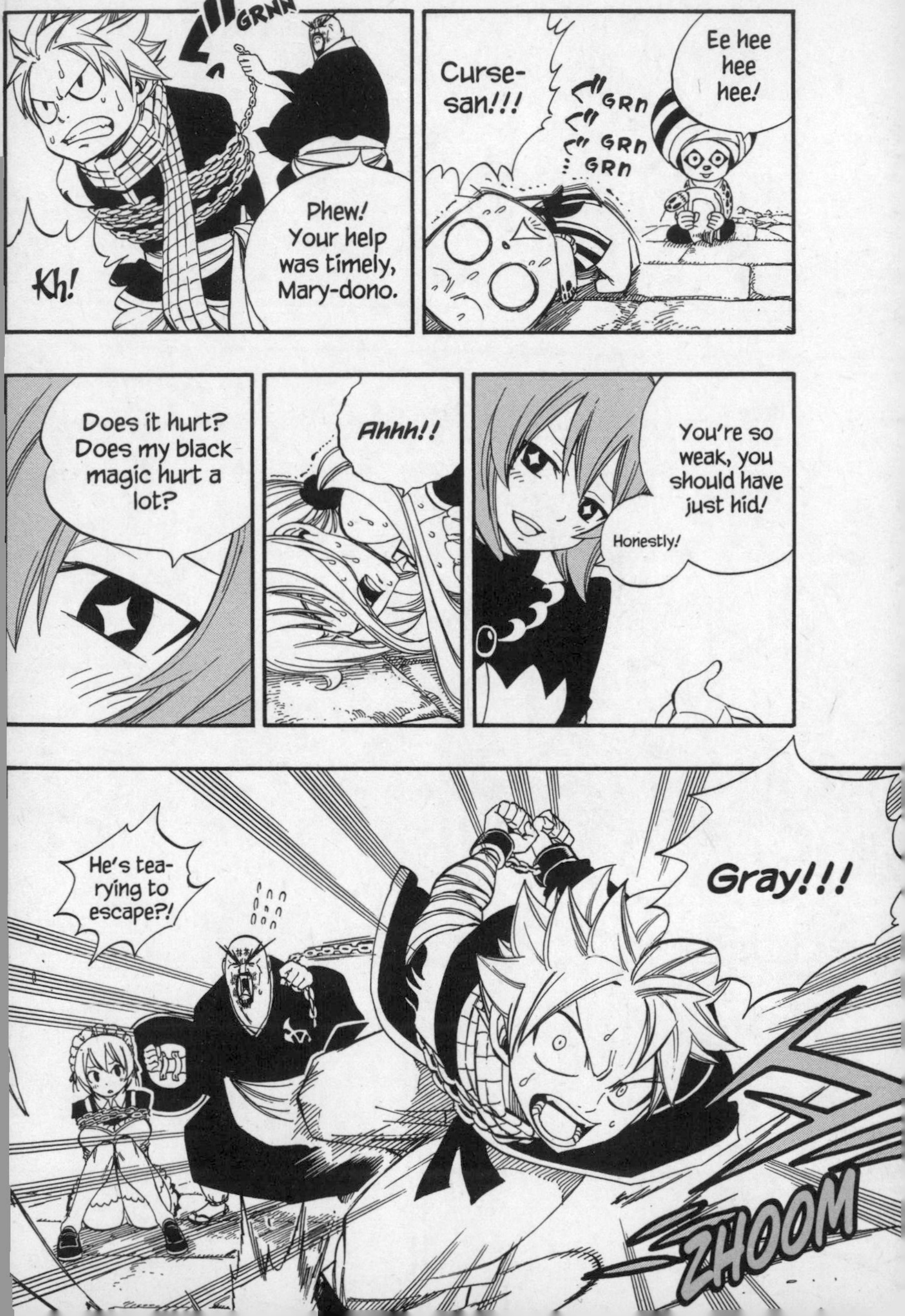
Ee hee hee hee!
Curse-san!!!
GRN GRN GRN
GRNN
Phew! Your help was timely, Mary-dono.
Kh!
You're so weak, you should have just hid!
Honestly!
Ahhh!!
Does it hurt? Does my black magic hurt a lot?
Gray!!!
He's tea-rying to escape?!
ZHOOM

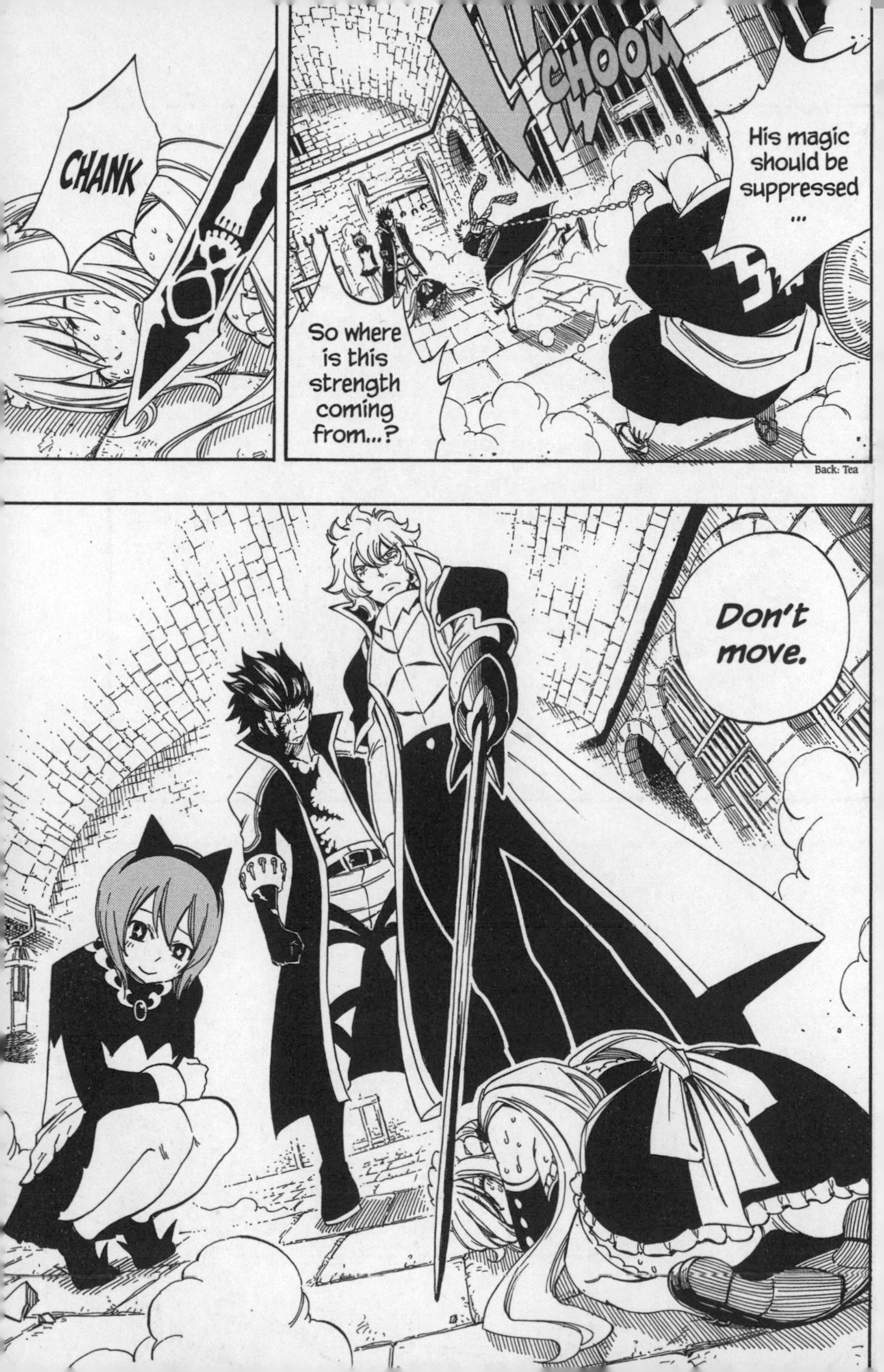
CHOOM
His magic should be suppressed ...
So where is this strength coming from...?
CHANK
Don't move.

Back: Tea

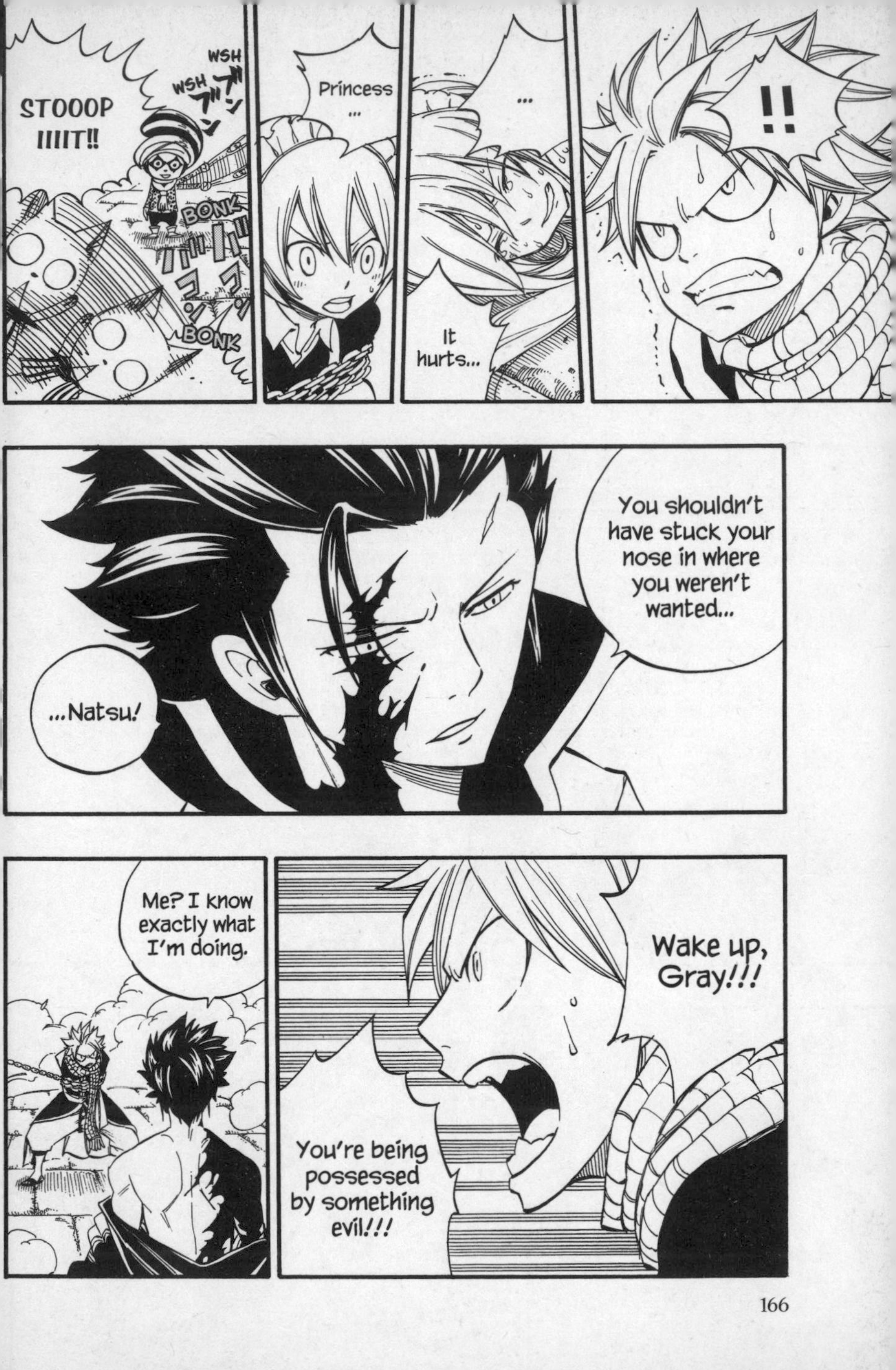
!!
...
It hurts...
Princess ...
WSH
WSH
STOOOP IIIIT!!
BONK
BONK
You shouldn't have stuck your nose in where you weren't wanted...
...Natsu!
Wake up, Gray!!!
You're being possessed by something evil!!!
Me? I know exactly what I'm doing.

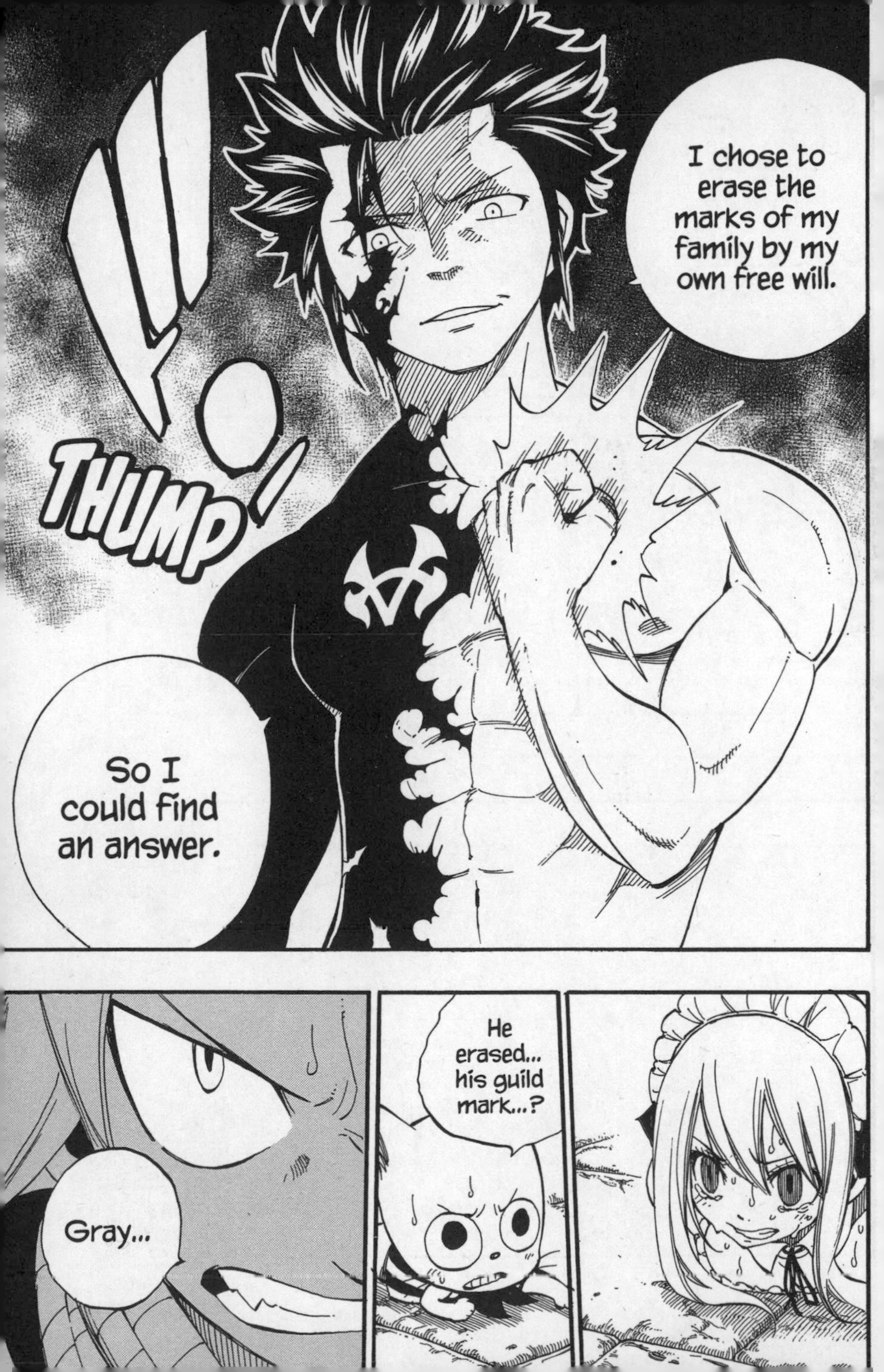
I chose to erase the marks of my family by my own free will.
THUMP
So I could find an answer.
He erased... his guild mark...?
Gray...

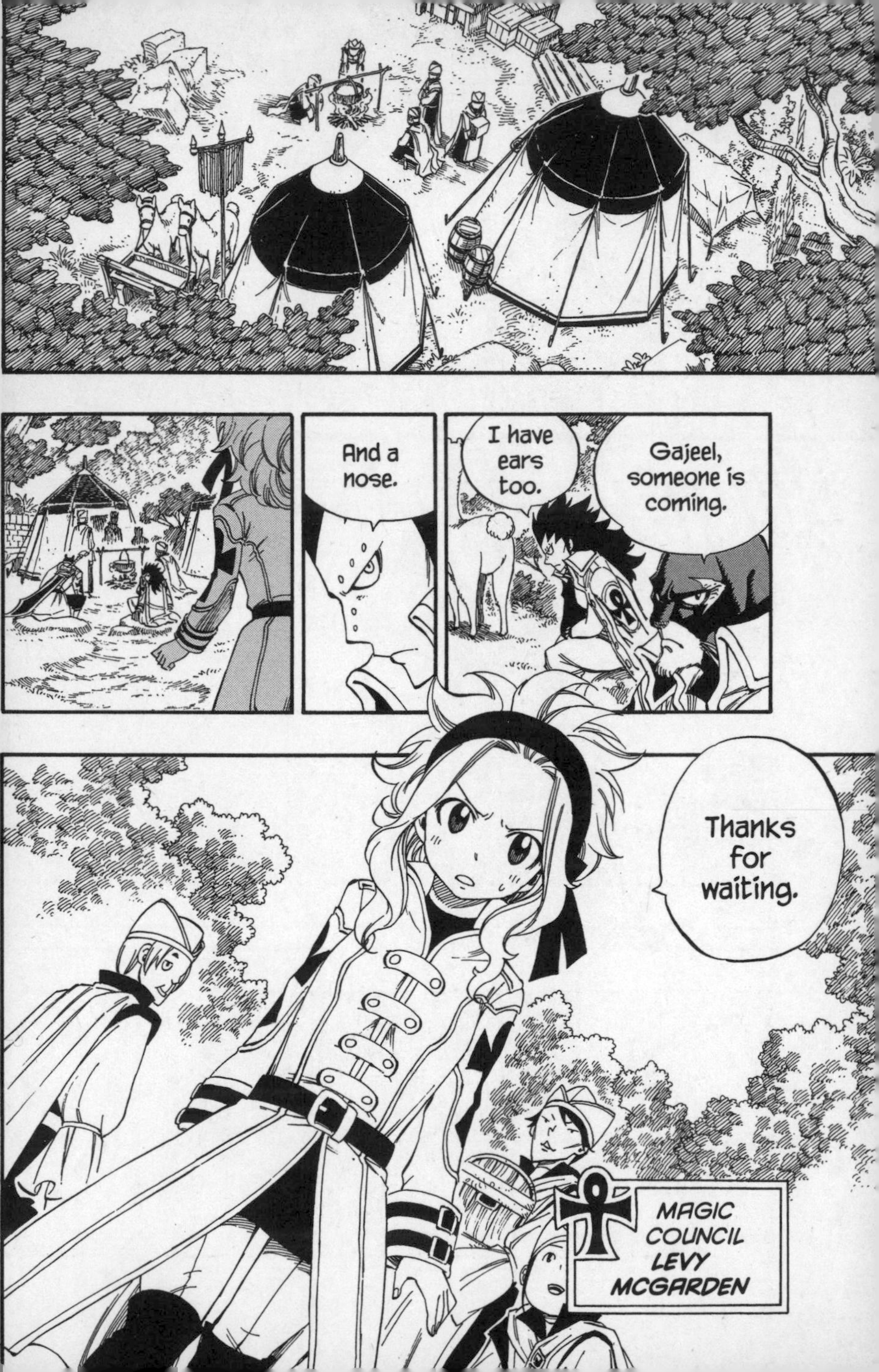
Gajeel, someone is coming.
I have ears too.
And a nose.
Thanks for waiting.
MAGIC COUNCIL LEVY MCGARDEN

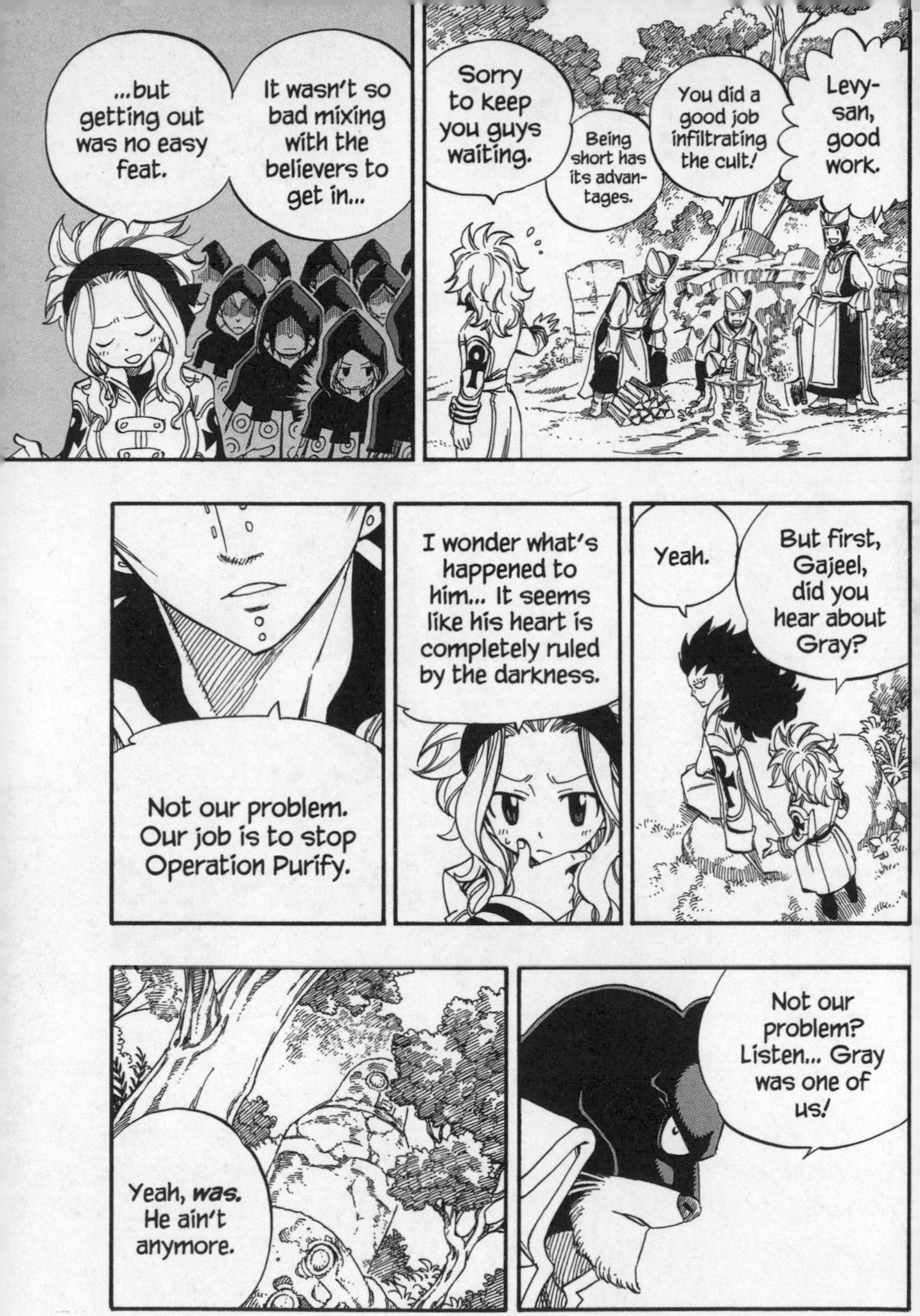
Levy-san, good work.
You did a good job infiltrating the cult!
Being short has its advantages.
Sorry to keep you guys waiting.
It wasn't so bad mixing with the believers to get in...
...but getting out was no easy feat.
But first, Gajeel, did you hear about Gray?
Yeah.
I wonder what's happened to him... It seems like his heart is completely ruled by the darkness.
Not our problem. Our job is to stop Operation Purify.
Not our problem? Listen... Gray was one of us!
Yeah, *was.* He ain't anymore.

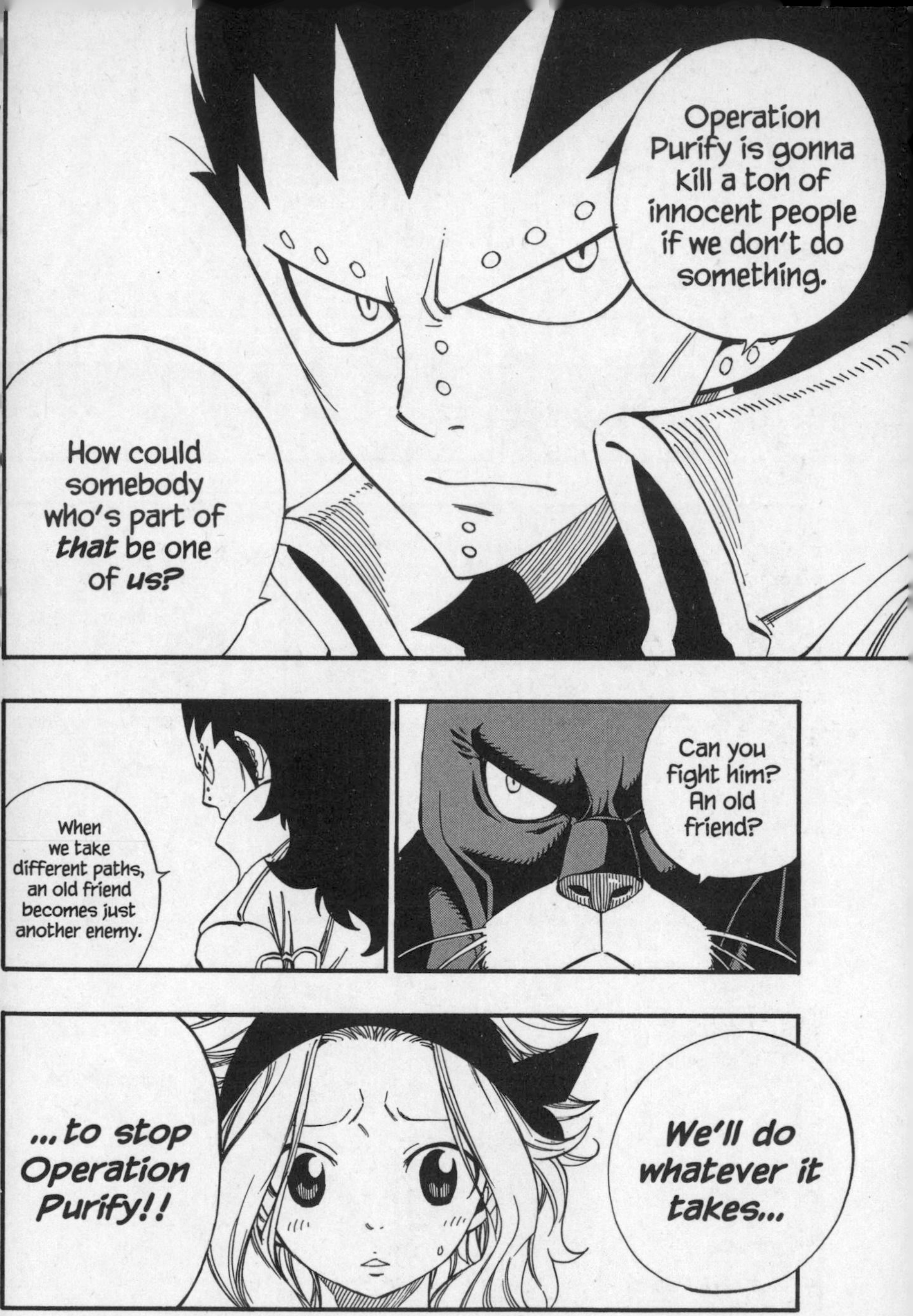
Operation Purify is gonna kill a ton of innocent people if we don't do something.
How could somebody who's part of *that* be one of *us?*
Can you fight him? An old friend?
When we take different paths, an old friend becomes just another enemy.
We'll do whatever it takes...
...to stop Operation Purify!!

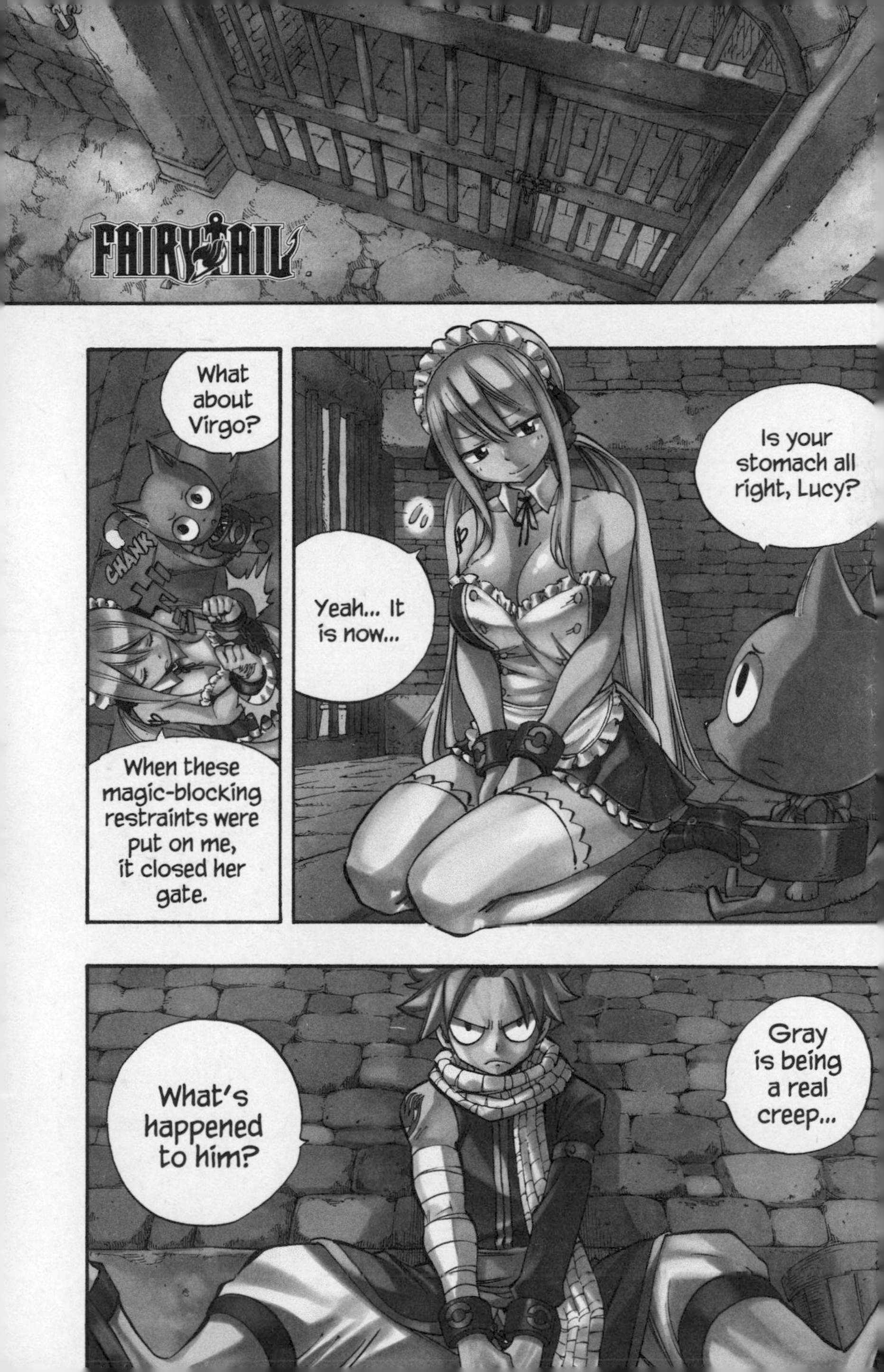
FAIRY TAIL
Is your stomach all right, Lucy?
Yeah... It is now...
What about Virgo?
CHANK
When these magic-blocking restraints were put on me, it closed her gate.
Gray is being a real creep...
What's happened to him?

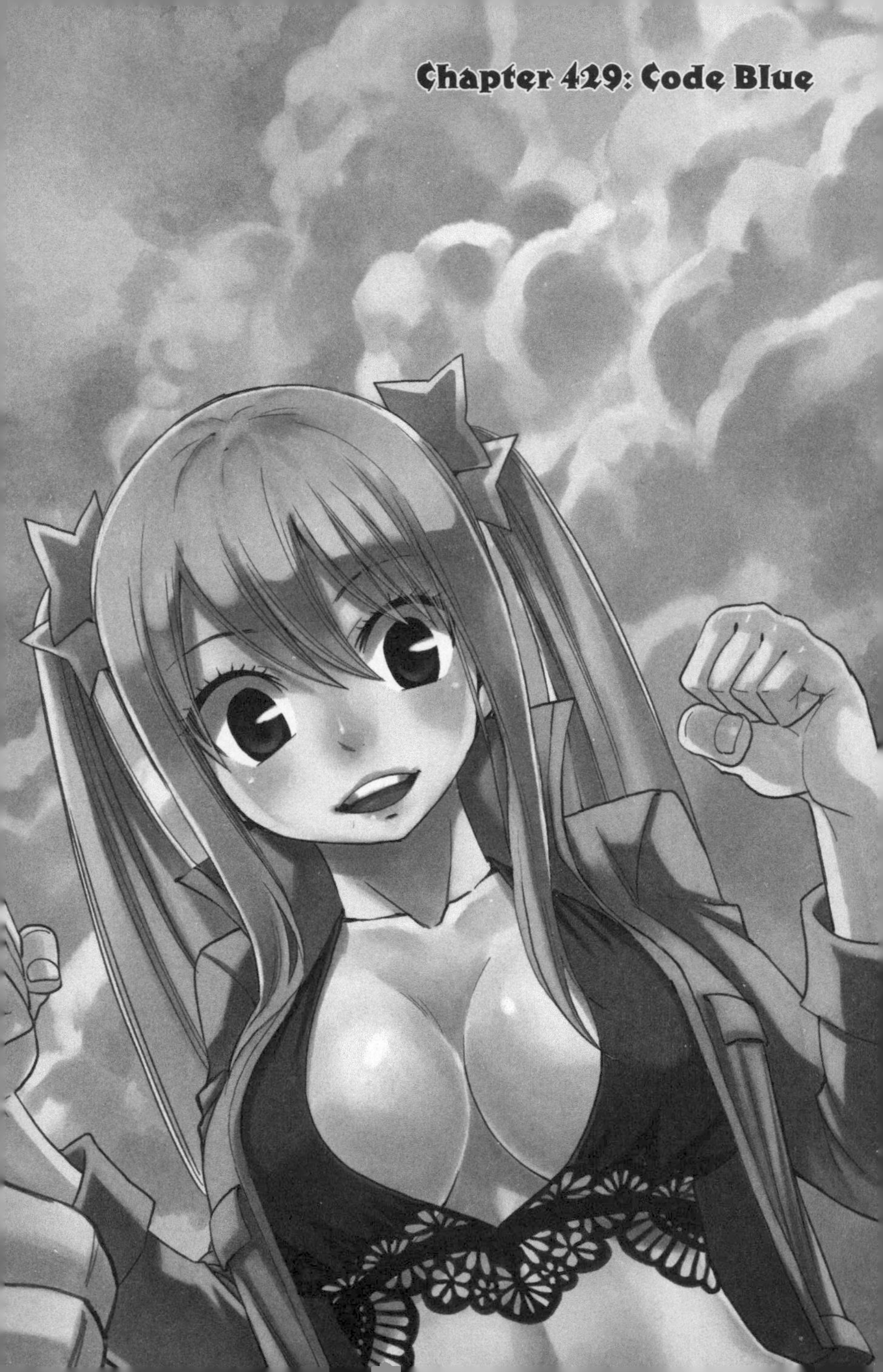
Chapter 429: Code Blue

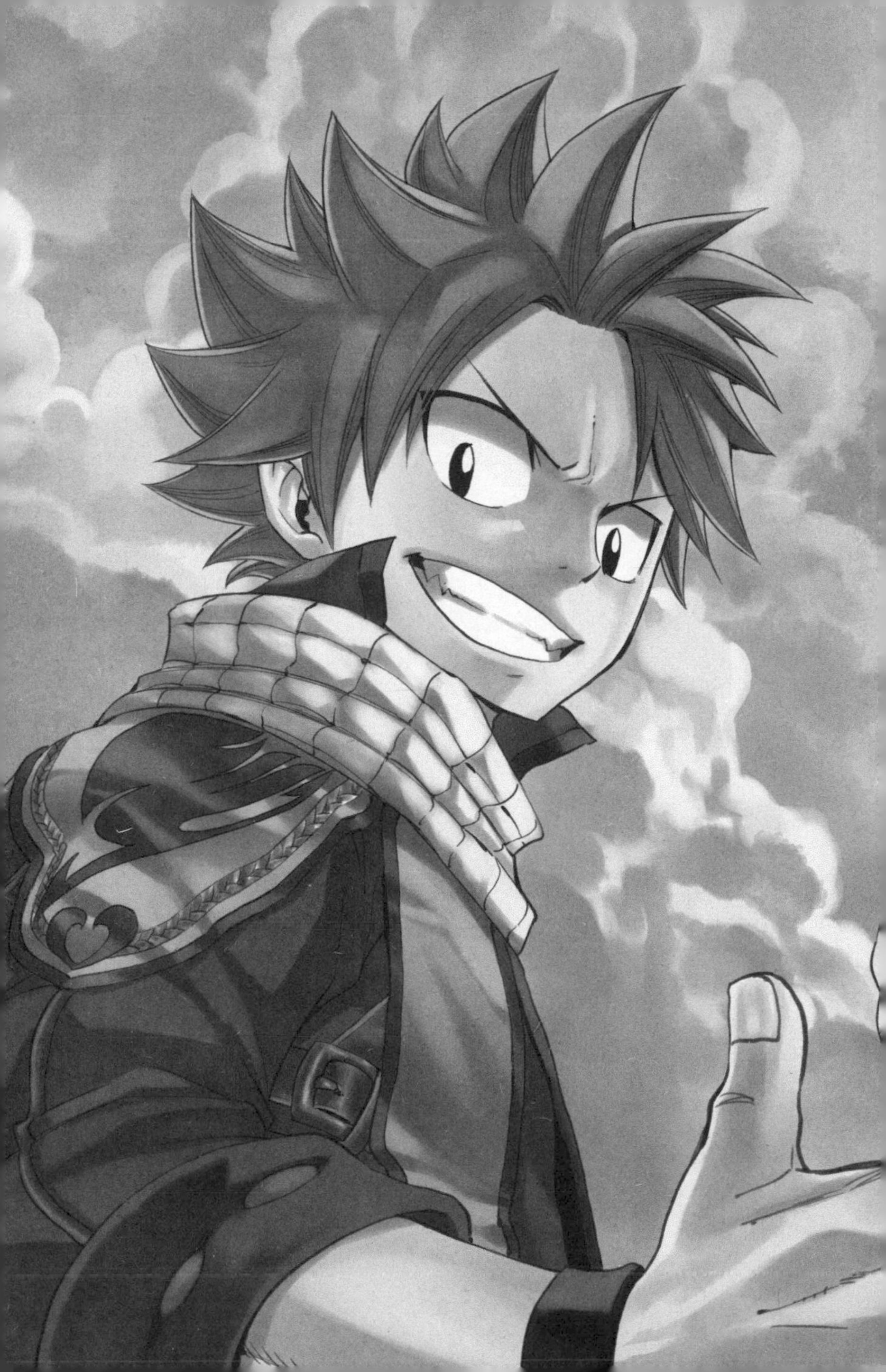

FAIRY TAIL
フェアリーテイル

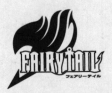

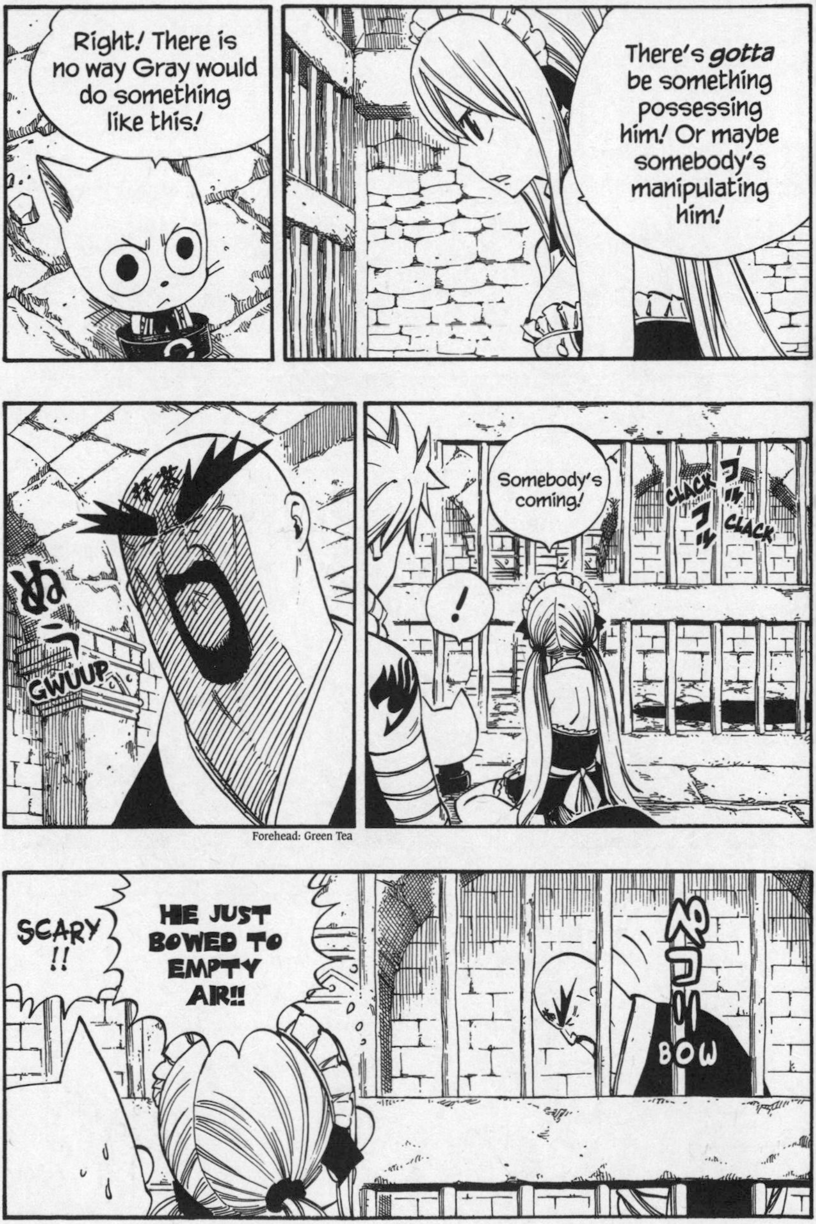
There's *gotta* be something possessing him! Or maybe somebody's manipulating him!
Right! There is no way Gray would do something like this!
Somebody's coming!
!
コツ コツ
CLACK CLACK
ぬっ
GWUUP
ペコーリ
BOW
HE JUST BOWED TO EMPTY AIR!!
SCARY!!

Forehead: Green Tea

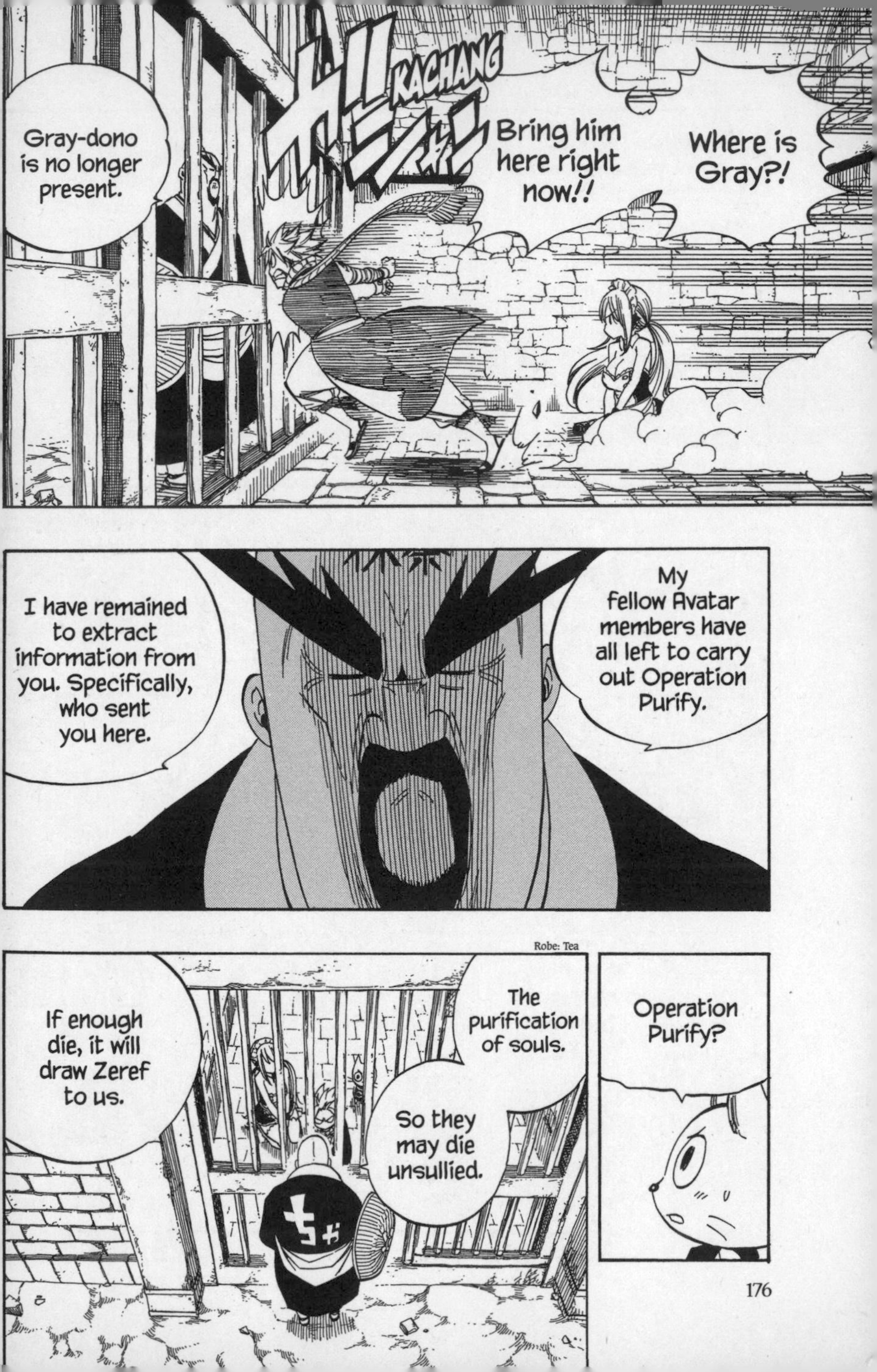
Where is Gray?!
Bring him here right now!!
KACHANG
Gray-dono is no longer present.
My fellow Avatar members have all left to carry out Operation Purify.
I have remained to extract information from you. Specifically, who sent you here.
Operation Purify?
Robe: Tea
The purification of souls.
So they may die unsullied.
If enough die, it will draw Zeref to us.

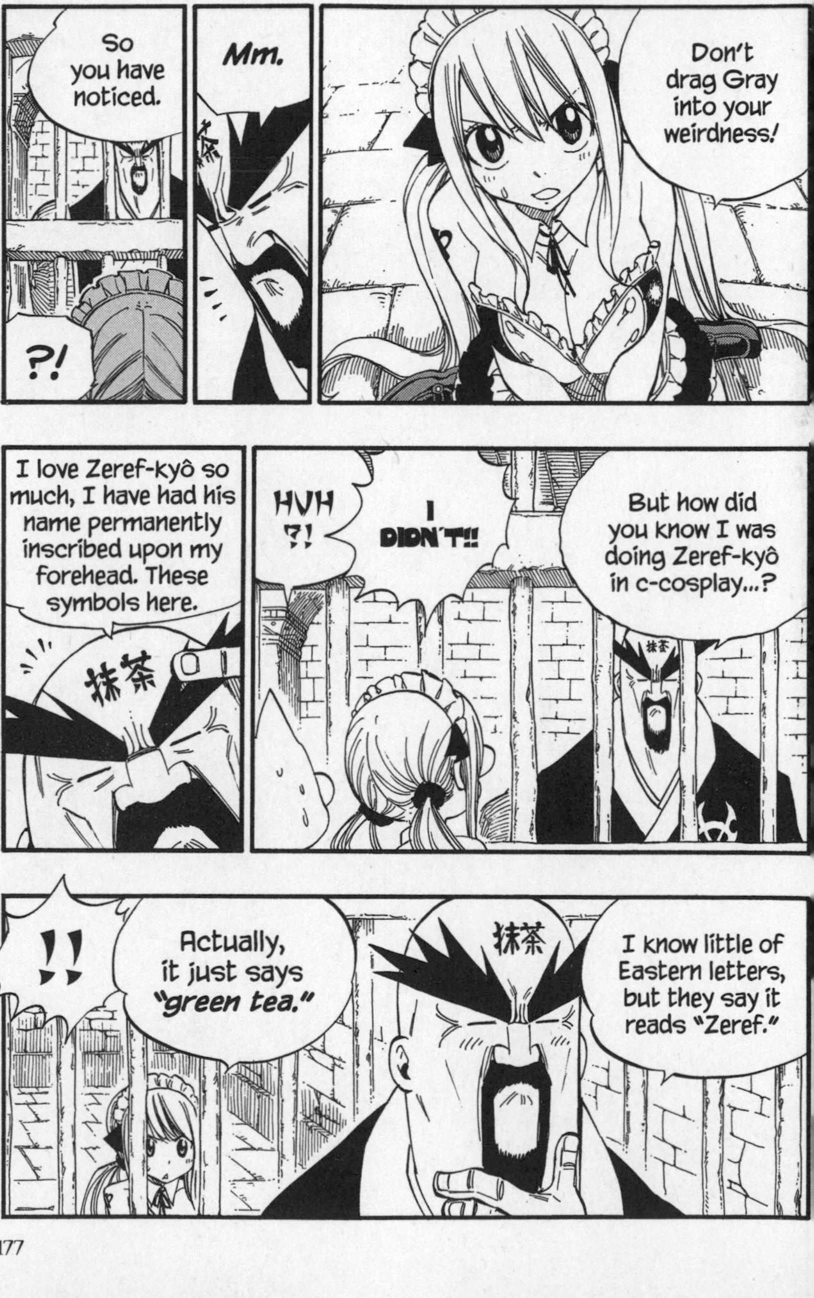
Don't drag Gray into your weirdness!
Mm.
So you have noticed.
?!
But how did you know I was doing Zeref-kyô in c-cosplay...?
抹茶
I DIDN'T!!
HUH ?!
I love Zeref-kyô so much, I have had his name permanently inscribed upon my forehead. These symbols here.
抹茶
I know little of Eastern letters, but they say it reads "Zeref."
抹茶
Actually, it just says "green tea."
!!

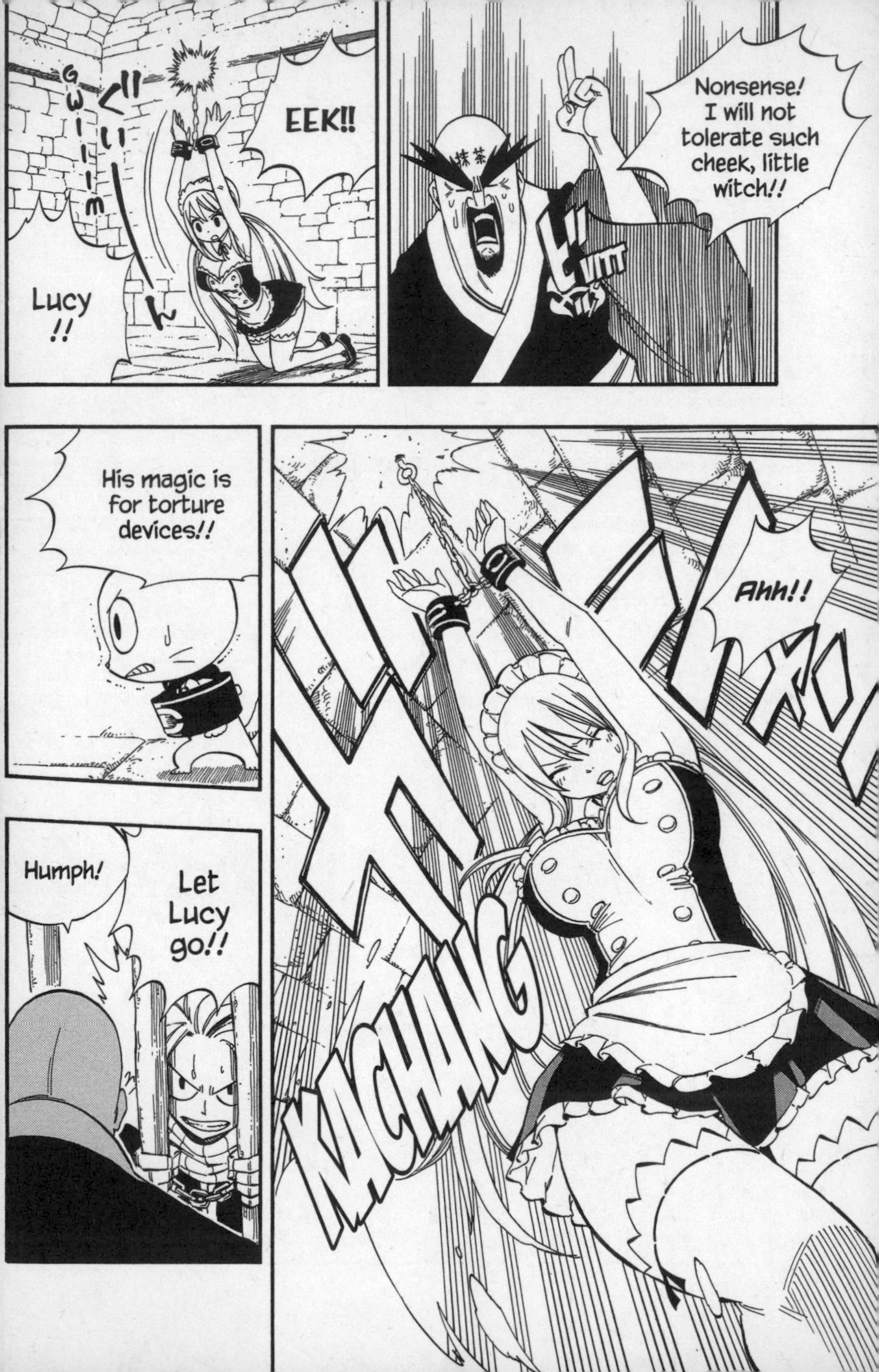
Nonsense! I will not tolerate such cheek, little witch!!
VITT
EEK!!
Lucy!!
Ahh!!
KACHANG
His magic is for torture devices!!
Humph!
Let Lucy go!!

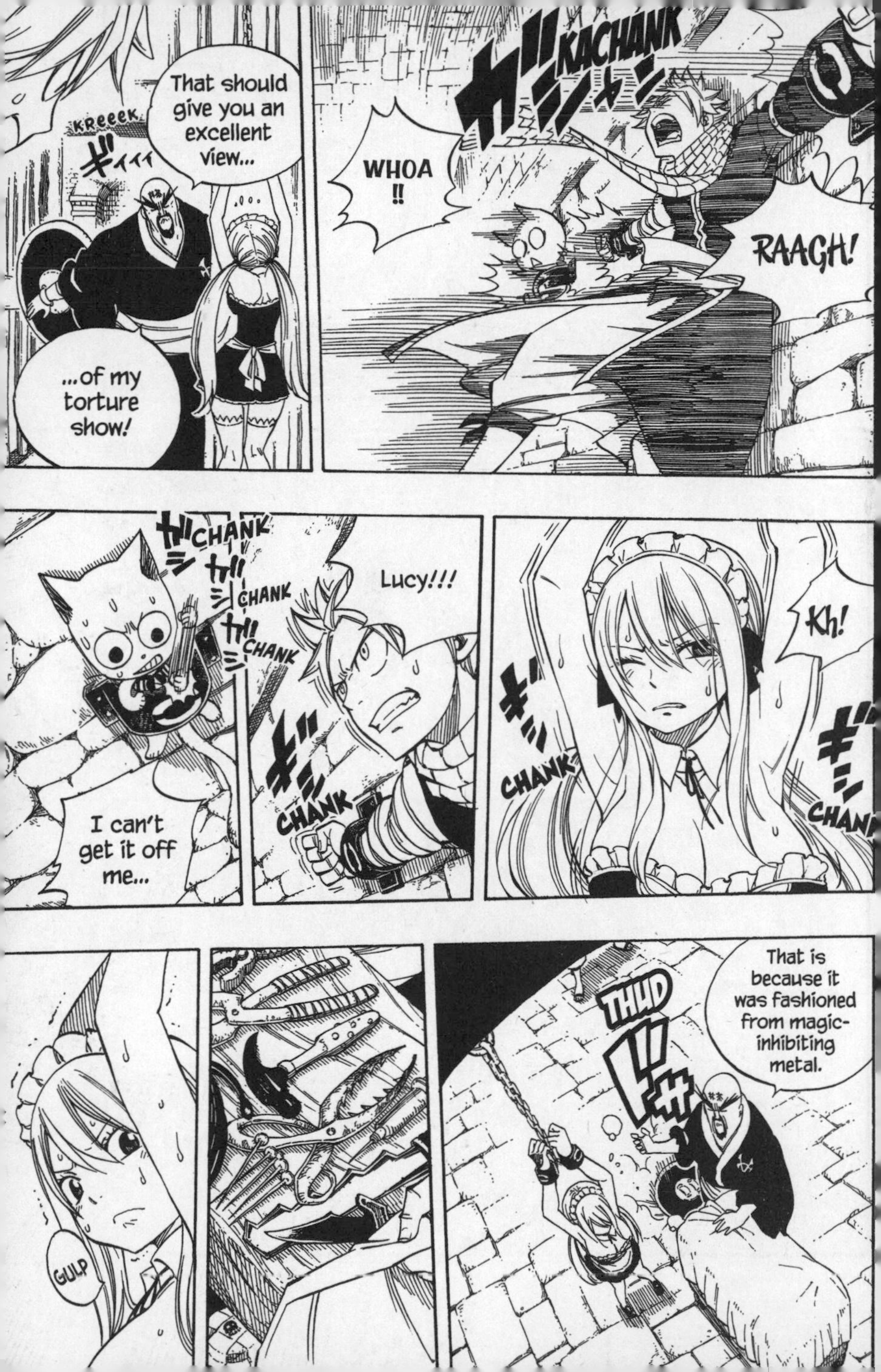
KACHANK
WHOA!!
RAAGH!
KREEEK
That should give you an excellent view...
...of my torture show!
Kh!
CHANK
CHAN
Lucy!!!
CHANK
CHANK
CHANK
CHANK
I can't get it off me...
THUD
That is because it was fashioned from magic-inhibiting metal.
GULP

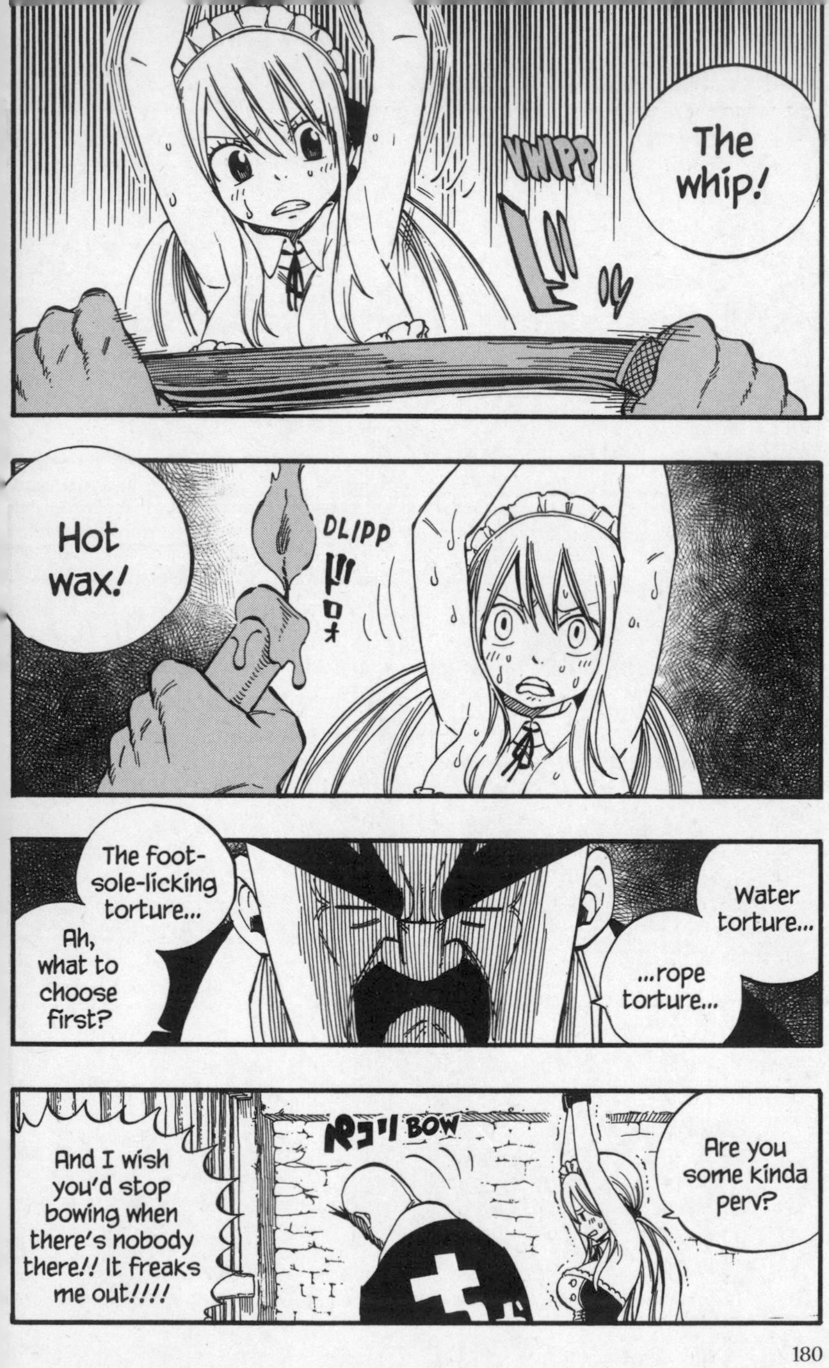
The whip!
VWIPP
Hot wax!
DLIPP
ドロォ
Water torture...
...rope torture...
The foot-sole-licking torture...
Ah, what to choose first?
Are you some kinda perv?
ペコリ BOW
And I wish you'd stop bowing when there's nobody there!! It freaks me out!!!!

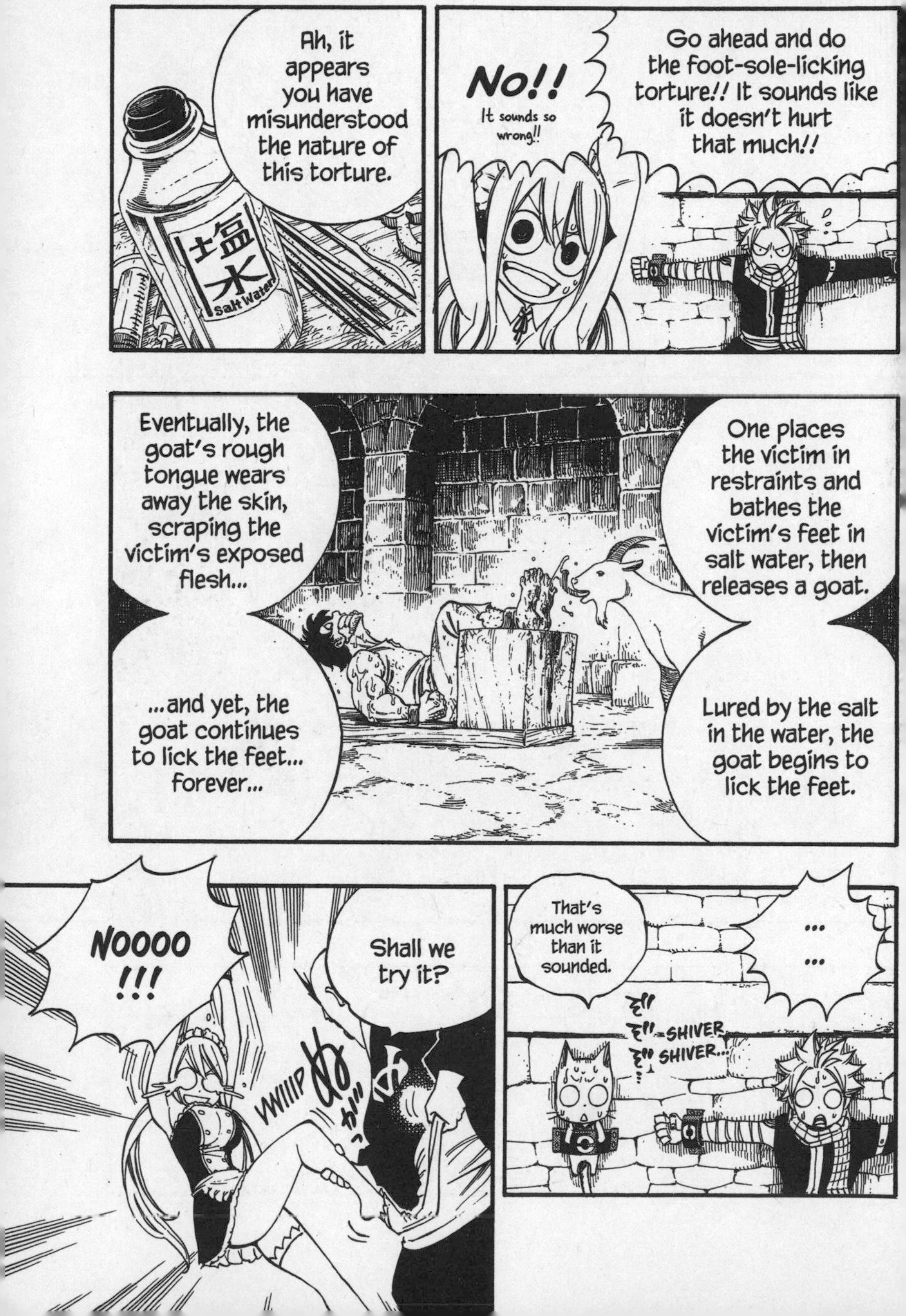
Go ahead and do the foot-sole-licking torture!! It sounds like it doesn't hurt that much!!
No!!
It sounds so wrong!!
Ah, it appears you have misunderstood the nature of this torture.
塩水
Salt Water
One places the victim in restraints and bathes the victim's feet in salt water, then releases a goat.
Lured by the salt in the water, the goat begins to lick the feet.
Eventually, the goat's rough tongue wears away the skin, scraping the victim's exposed flesh...
...and yet, the goat continues to lick the feet... forever...
...
...
That's much worse than it sounded.
SHIVER SHIVER...
Shall we try it?
NOOOO!!!
VWIIIP

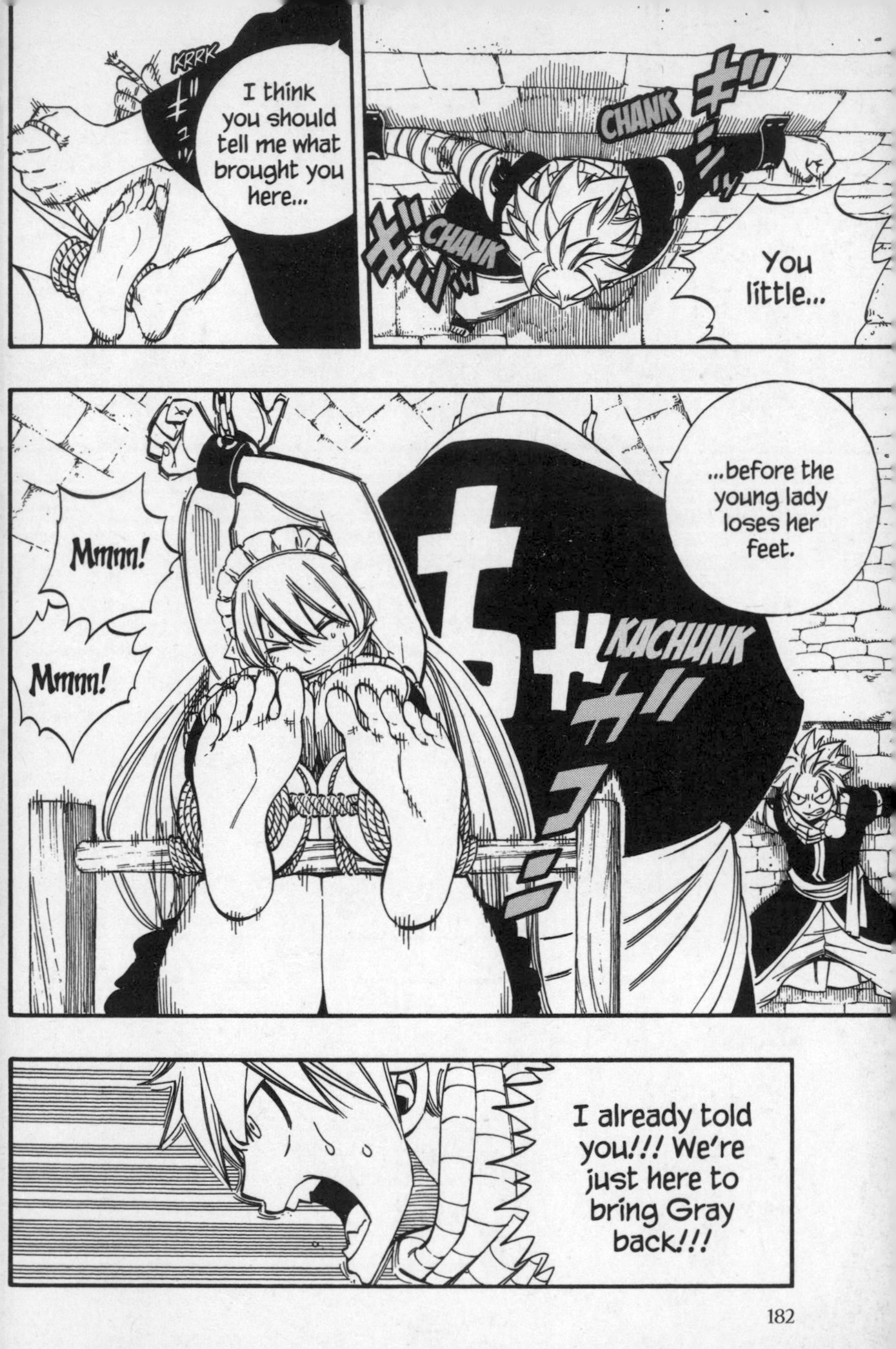
CHANK
CHANK
You little...
KRRK
I think you should tell me what brought you here...
...before the young lady loses her feet.
KACHUNK
Mmnn!
Mmnn!
I already told you!!! We're just here to bring Gray back!!!

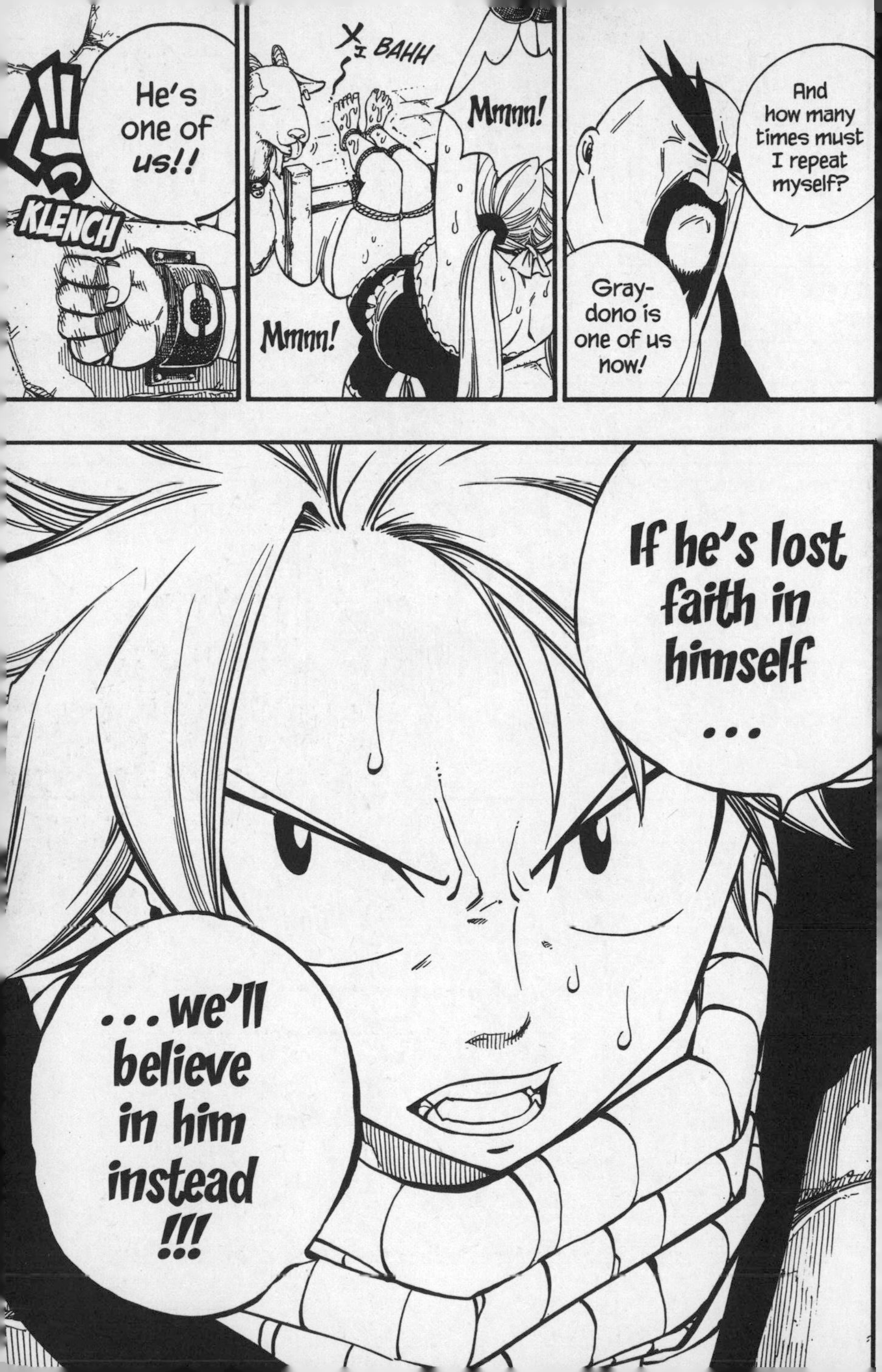
And how many times must I repeat myself?
Gray-dono is one of us now!
Mmnn!
BAHH
Mmnn!
He's one of us!!
KLENCH
If he's lost faith in himself ...
...we'll believe in him instead!!!

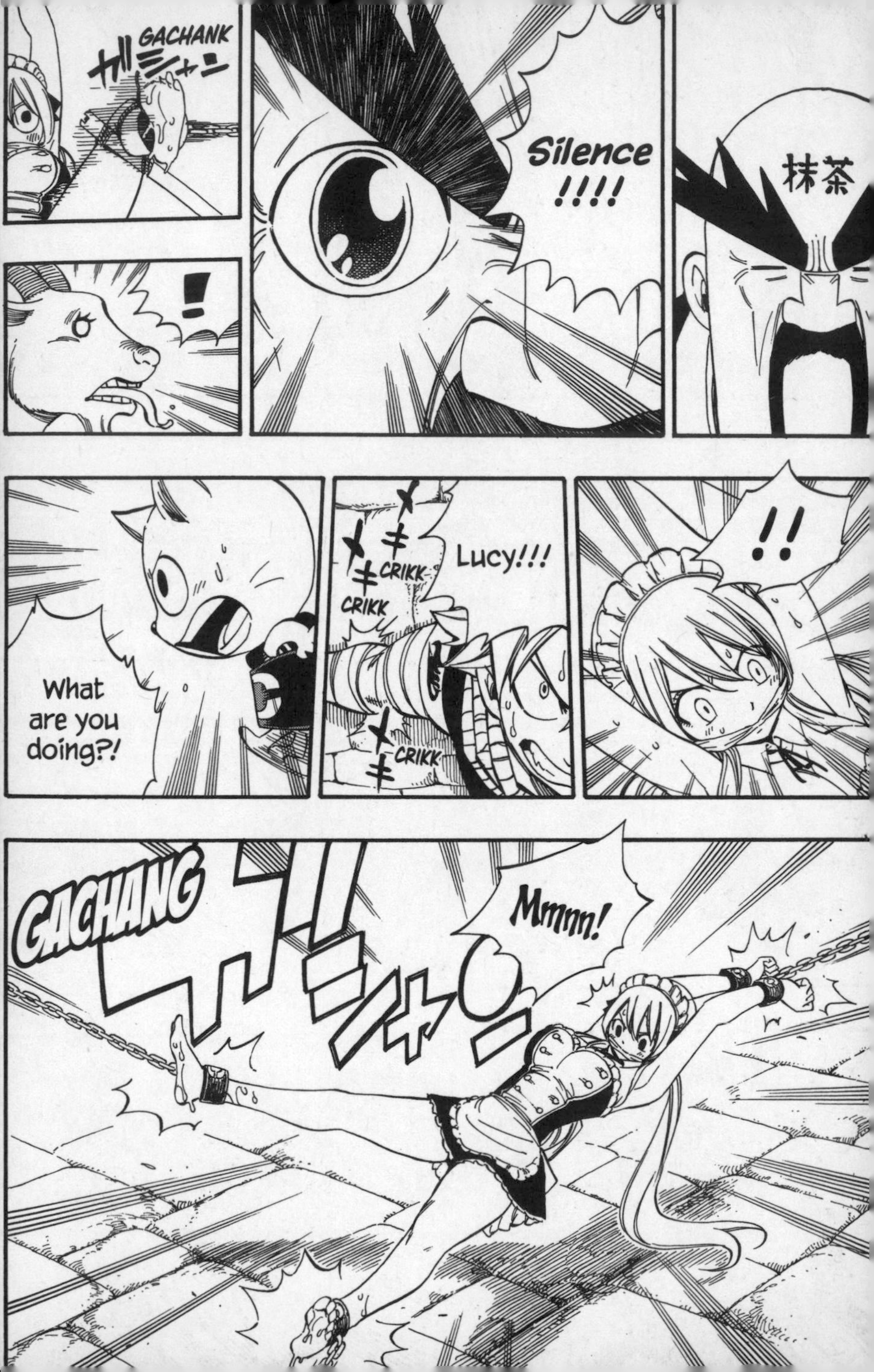
抹茶
Silence !!!!
GACHANK
ガシャン
!
!!
Lucy!!!
CRIKK
CRIKK
CRIKK
What are you doing?!
Mmmm!
GACHANG
ガシャン

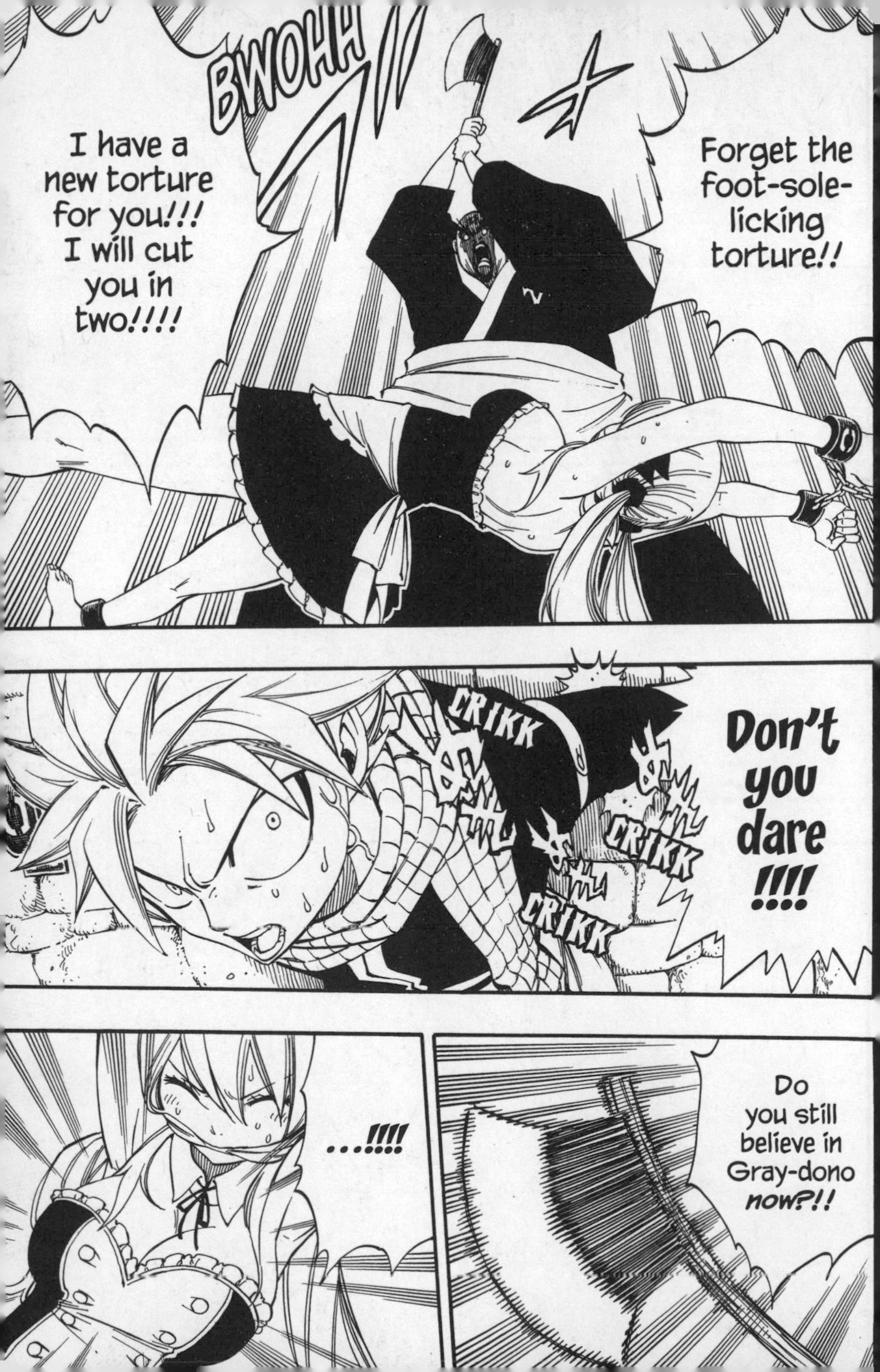
Forget the foot-sole-licking torture!!
BWOHH
I have a new torture for you!!! I will cut you in two!!!!
Don't you dare!!!!
CRIKK
CRIKK
CRIKK
Do you still believe in Gray-dono now?!!
...!!!!

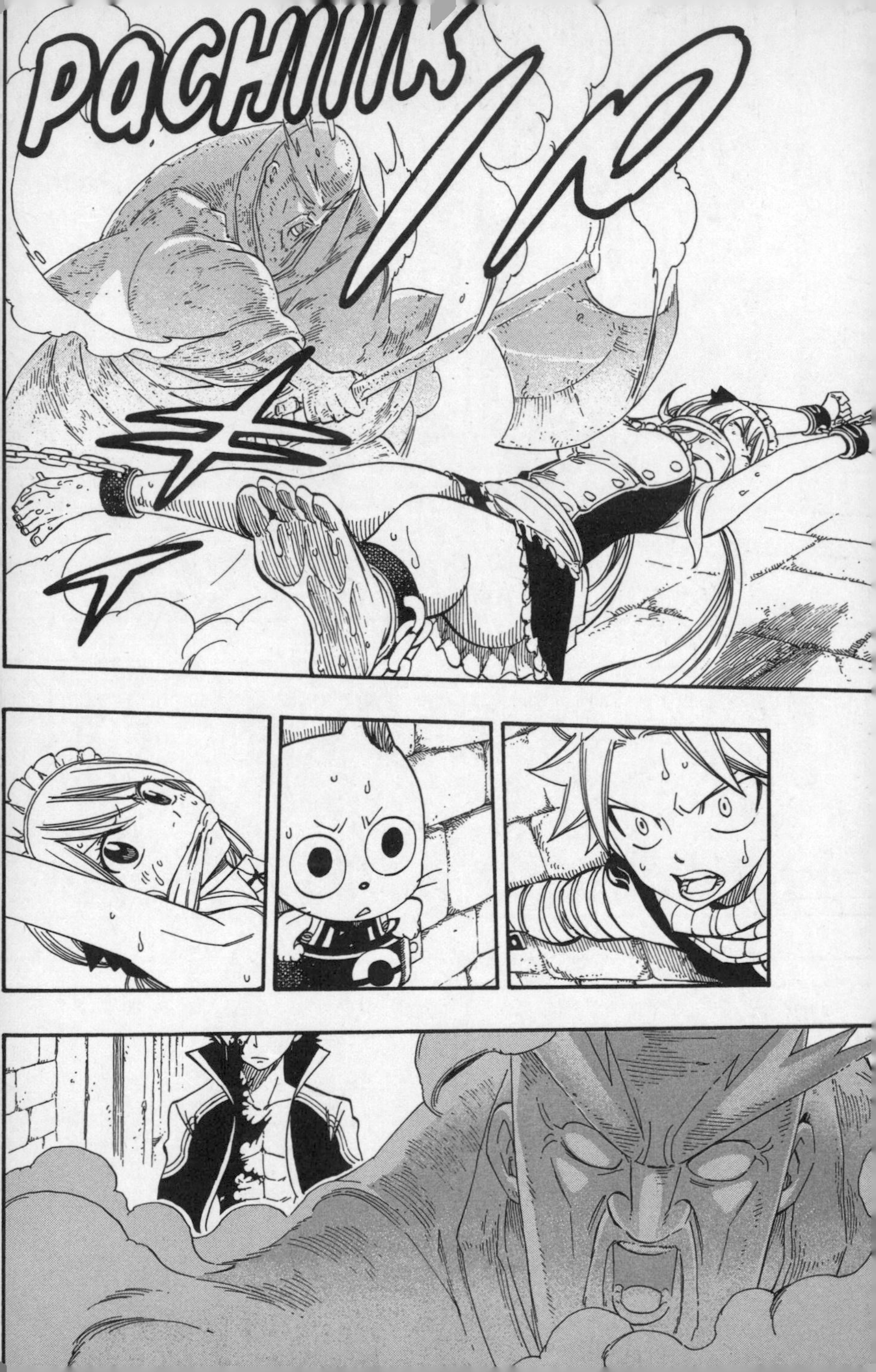
PACHIIIN

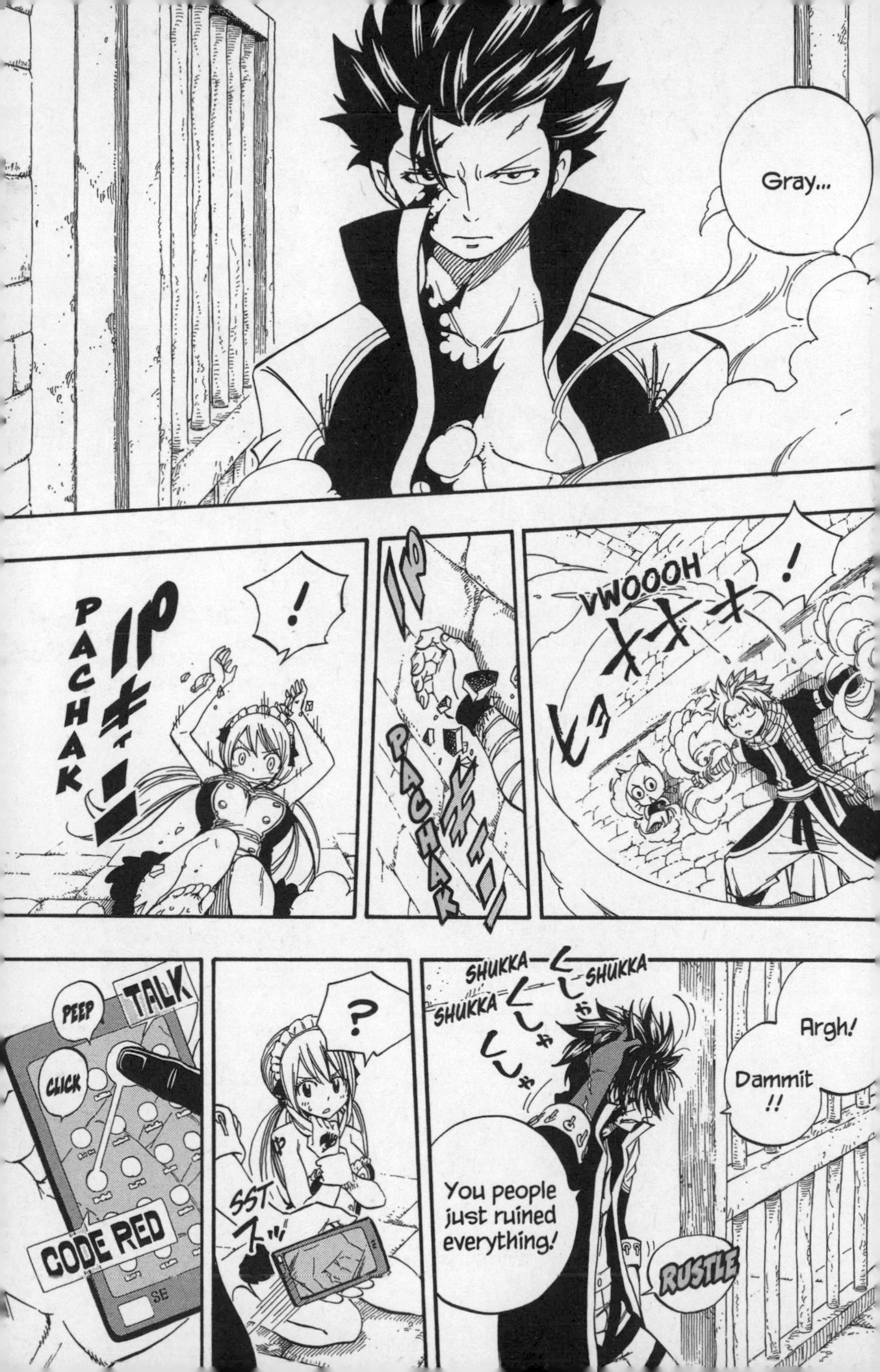
Gray...
VWOOOH
!
PACHAK
PACHAK
!
Argh!
Dammit!!
SHUKKA
SHUKKA
SHUKKA
You people just ruined everything!
RUSTLE
?
SST
TALK
PEEP
CLICK
CODE RED
SE

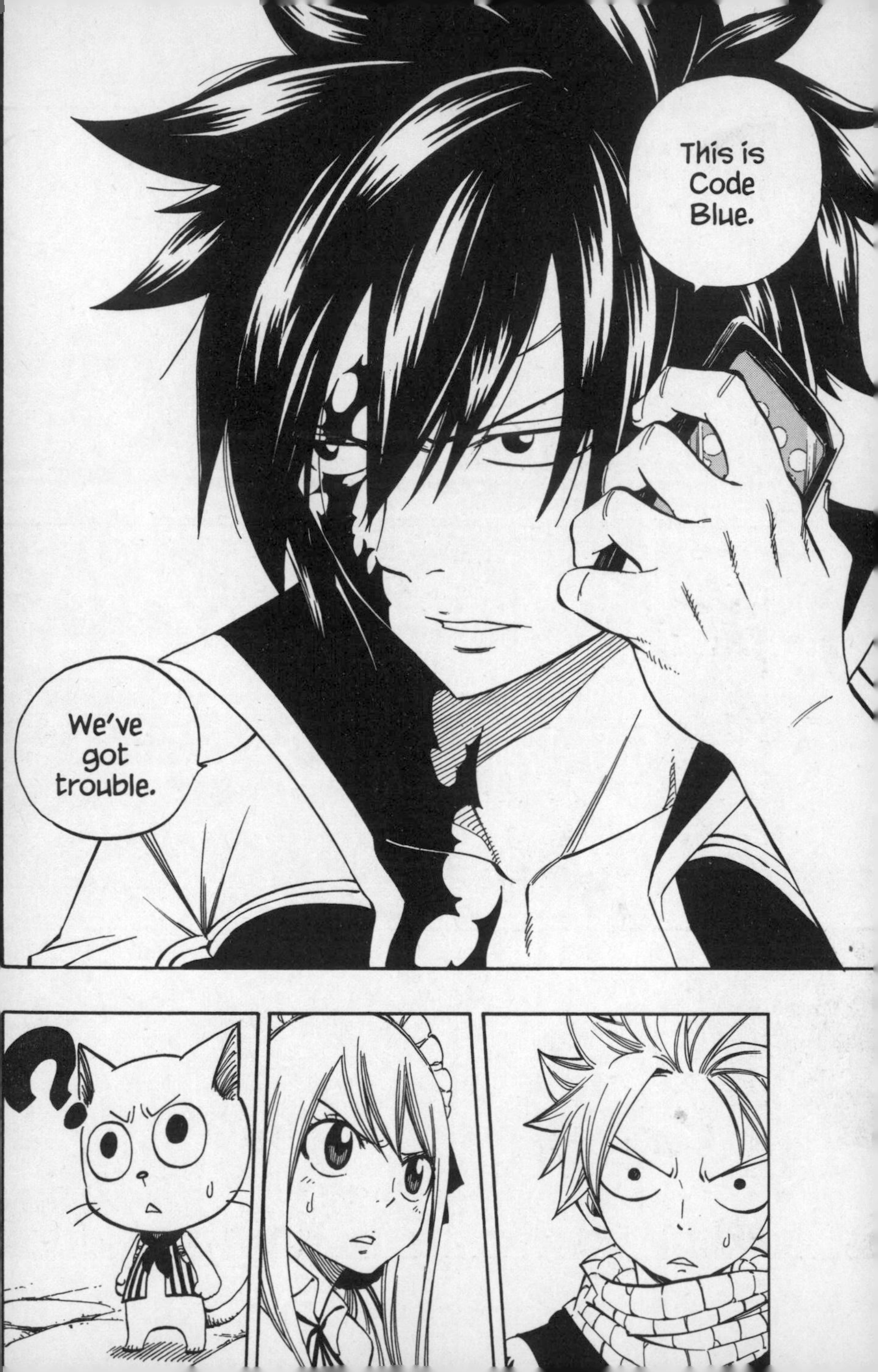
This is Code Blue.
We've got trouble.

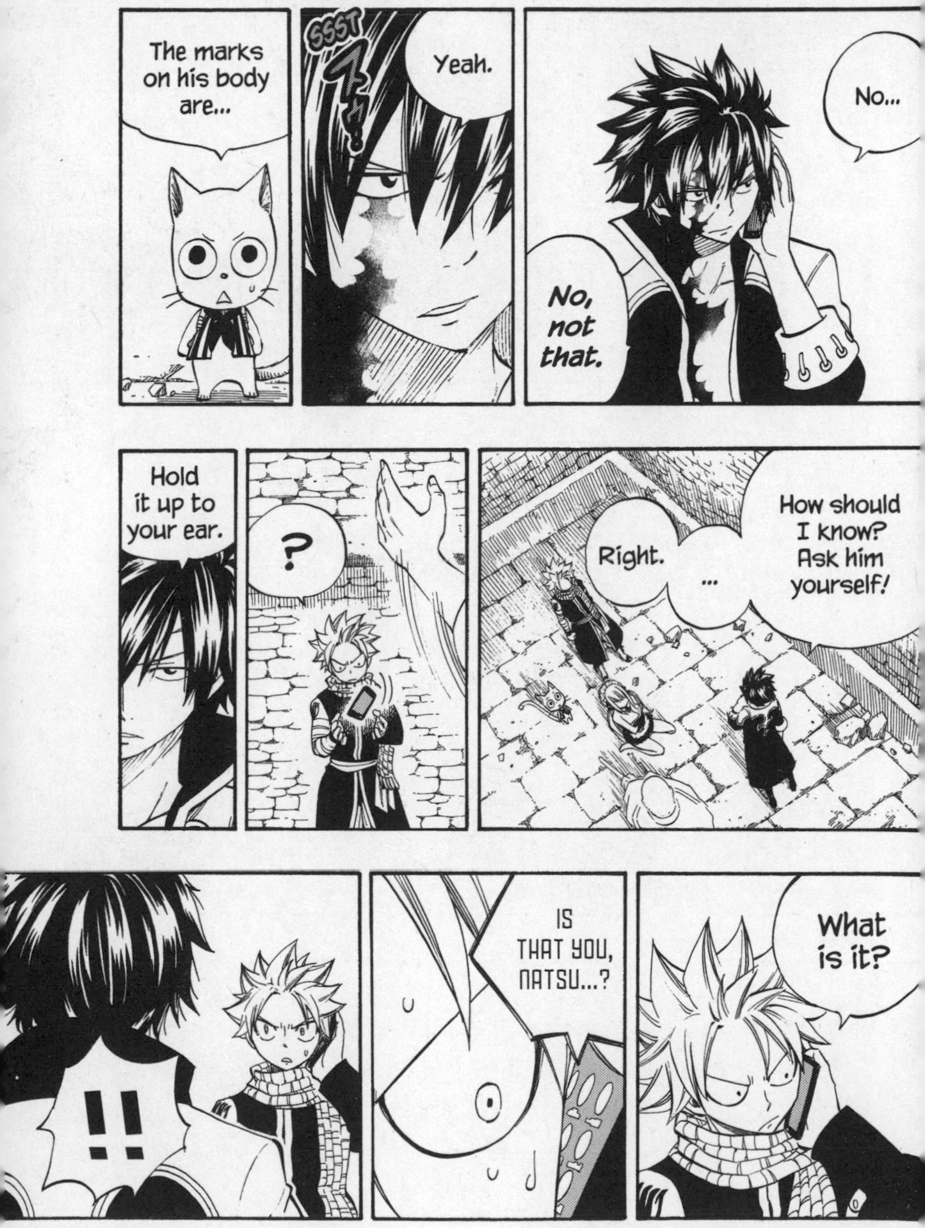
No...
No, not that.
SSST
Yeah.
The marks on his body are...
How should I know? Ask him yourself!
...
Right.
?
Hold it up to your ear.
What is it?
IS THAT YOU, NATSU...?
!!

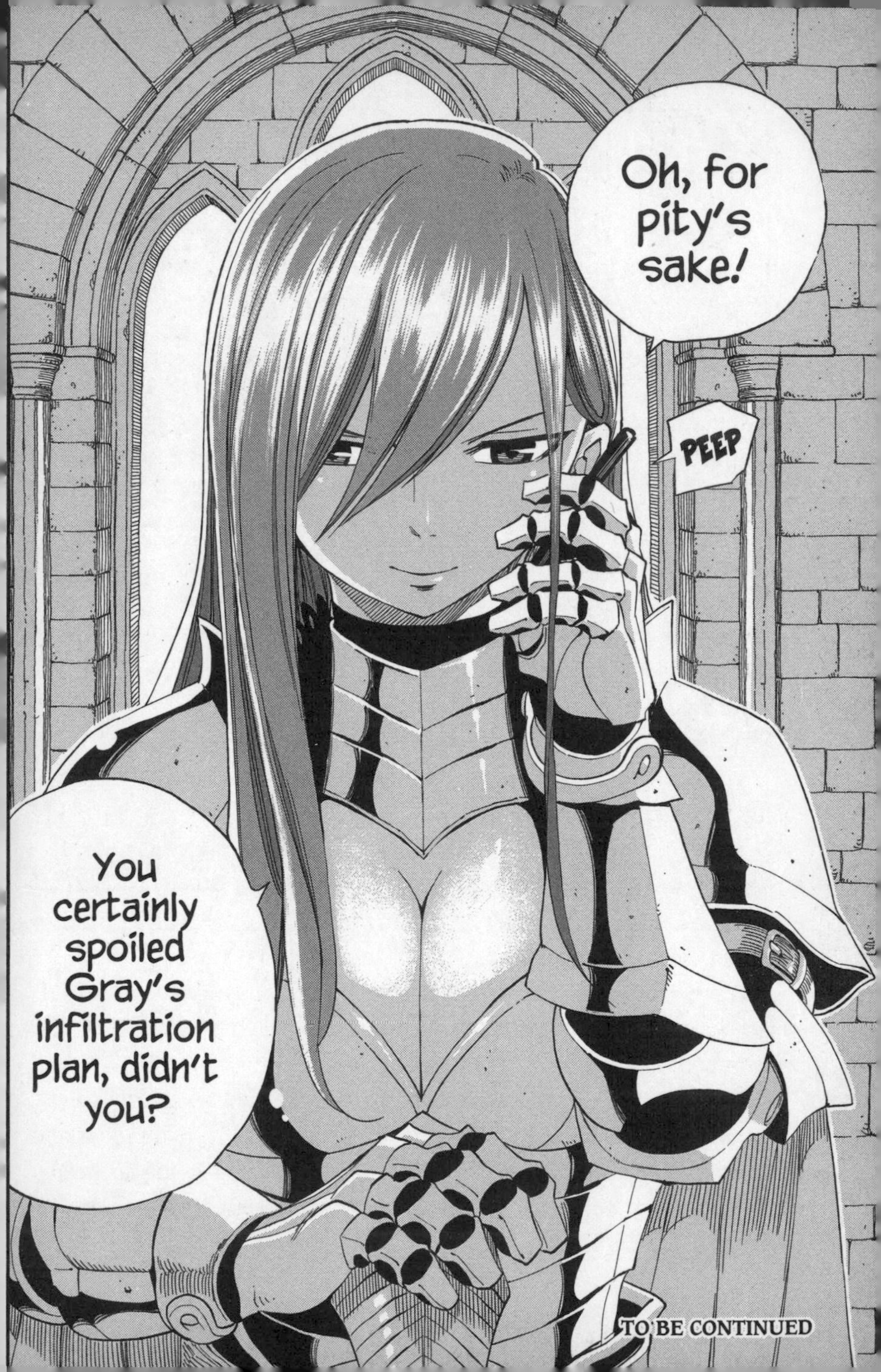
Oh, for pity's sake!
PEEP
You certainly spoiled Gray's infiltration plan, didn't you?
TO BE CONTINUED

あとがき
Afterword

Let's celebrate!! We've gone 50 volumes!! Clap clap!! The day I said that I would probably end it after 10 volumes seems like forever ago! Fifty volumes!! Well, first, I'd like to express my thanks to all of you readers. Thank you so much for your unwavering support! The only reason I was able to go 50 volumes is definitely the support of you readers! Thank you so much for reading this manga!!

Next, thank you to the editor!! He came right on board with my never-take-a-holiday style, and he battled right along with me, never taking a break, all this time! When I got stuck trying to come up with the rough story, he'd come in with all kinds of advice. When I'd get a little down, he'd inspire me! I really appreciate him every day.

And a big thank you to everyone in the editorial department who supported me!

Also there's my staff, who work under terrible workloads without a word of complaint! They're great friends! They don't just fill in backgrounds, they love Fairy Tail too, and help me out with all kinds of story ideas! You people don't know how grateful I am!

Then there are my family, friends, people connected with the anime, games, and merchandise!! Tons of gratitude their way!! Well, everybody! Thank you!!

According to what I've heard, this 50th volume brings my page count to a total of 9,487 pages. Which means that in three more volumes, I'll have passed 10,000 pages!! Well, I'm going to keep giving it everything I got. So please, everybody, keep cheering me on!!

FROM HIRO MASHIMA

What with one thing and another, I was at 50 volumes before I really knew it. And it's all thanks to you!
I'm as surprised as anyone that it went on this long!
And from now on, too…
If you'd patiently watch over me, it'd make me happier than anything else I can imagine!

Original Jacket Design: Hisao Ogawa

FAIRY TAIL
フェアリーテイル

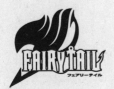

Thanks for all your support!

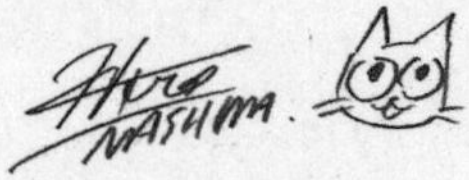
Hiro MASHIMA.

FAIRY TAIL

フェアリーテイル

50

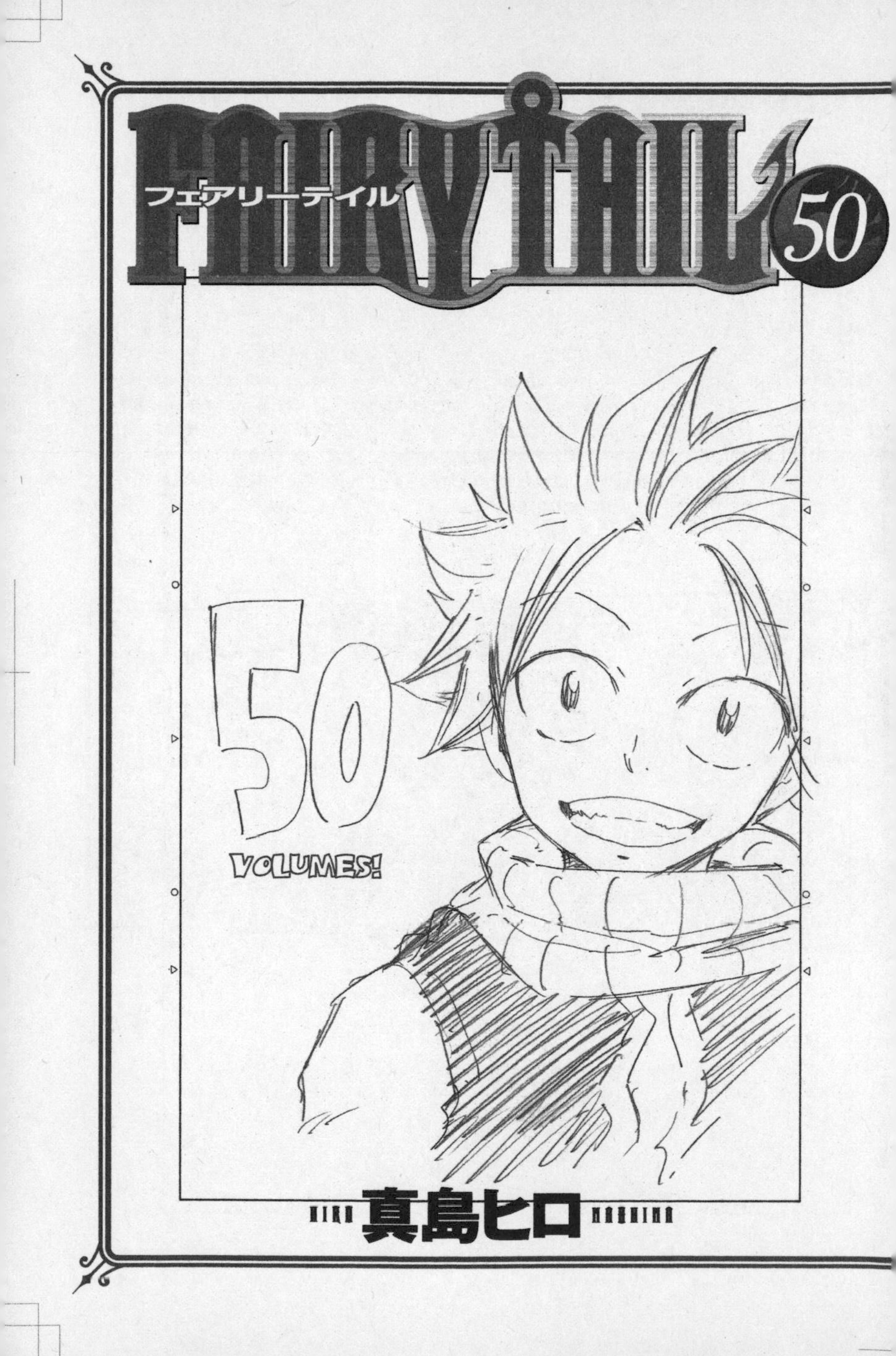

50
VOLUMES!

HIRO 真島ヒロ MASHIMA

Translation Notes:

Japanese is a tricky language for most Westerners, and translation is often more art than science. For your edification and reading pleasure, here are notes on some of the places where we could have gone in a different direction with our translation of the work, or where a Japanese cultural reference is used.

Page 18, Orochi's Fin

Yamata no Orochi is the eight-headed, eight-tailed serpent of Japanese legends. The *Nihon Shoki* (*Chronicles of Ancient Japan*) uses *kanji* for it that translate out to the "Giant Snake of Yamata." It was a maiden-devouring serpent from ancient legends that was slain by the expelled god Susanoo. There are quite a few snake references here, including not only the Viper Inn, but also Lamia Scale itself. Lamia is a woman out of Greek legend who was transformed by a jealous Hera into a half-woman, half-snake monstrosity who devours children.

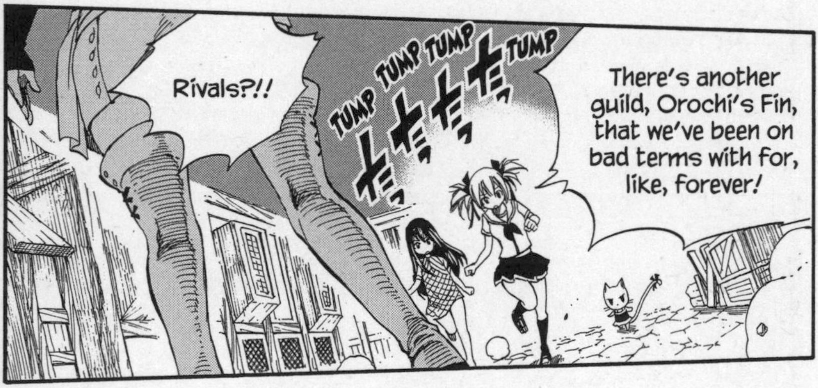
There's another guild, Orochi's Fin, that we've been on bad terms with for, like, forever!
TUMP TUMP TUMP TUMP
Rivals?!!

Page 121, Gômon

The *kanji* for Gômon's name mean "excellent" and "gate," but when different kanji are used, gômon means "torture." This will become important in a few pages.

Page 129,
Mikage Forest

Although no kanji is given for Mikage, the term is used for a Buddhist deity, but it also a term for a god of death.

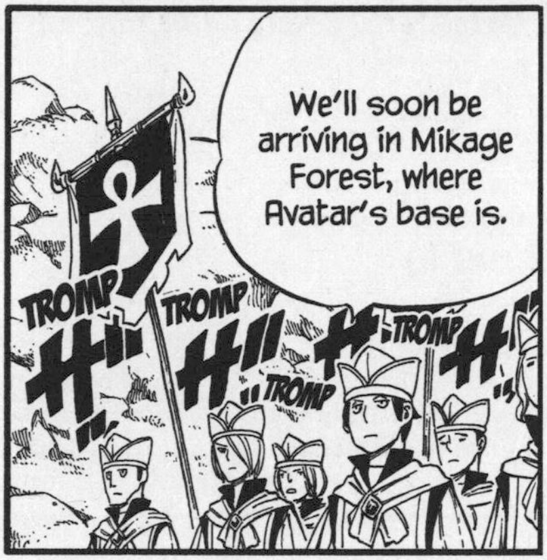
We'll soon be arriving in Mikage Forest, where Avatar's base is.
TROMP
TROMP
TROMP
TROMP

Page 145,
Iron maiden

Perhaps most people know the phrase as the name of the British metal band, but they got the name from a torture device. Though it might have been a real torture device, experts now believe it was more likely a hoax created in the late 1700s. Apparently, sources describing it only date back to 1793. The Japanese letters on the iron maiden in the manga are "*tetsu no okame.*" *Tetsu* means "iron," and an *okame* is a traditional Japanese mask depicting a round-faced young woman. So it would translate out to, "iron maiden mask."

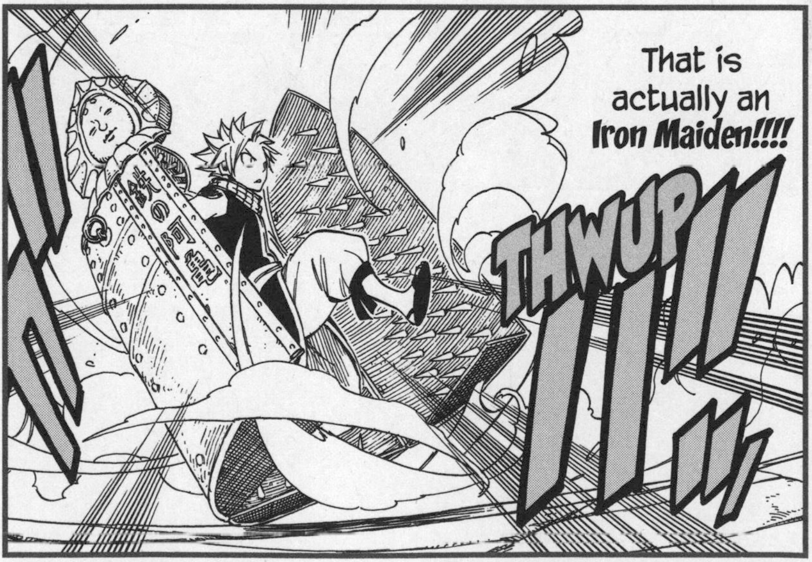
That is actually an Iron Maiden!!!!
THWUP!!

Page 165,
-dono

As described in the notes way back in Volume 16, "*-dono*" is an archaic honorific that is much like "*-sama*," which is used for Japanese lords.

Page 177,
Zeref-kyô

Like *-dono*, *-kyô* is also an archaic honorific that is not used today, but is still well known to the Japanese. *–kyô* is also a respectful honorific, but it shows an even higher level of respect than *–dono*.

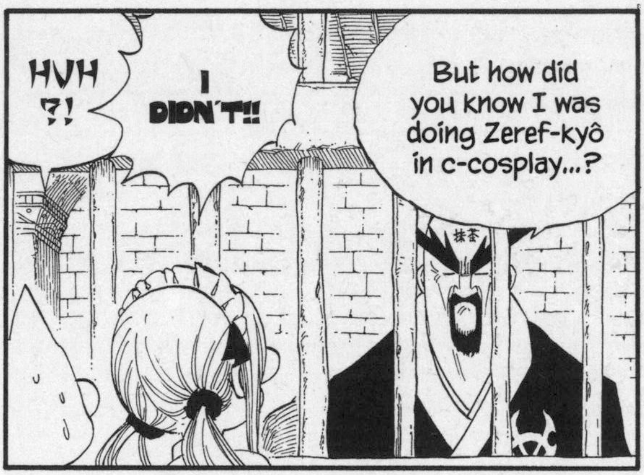
But how did you know I was doing Zeref-kyô in c-cosplay...?
I DIDN'T!!
HUH ?!

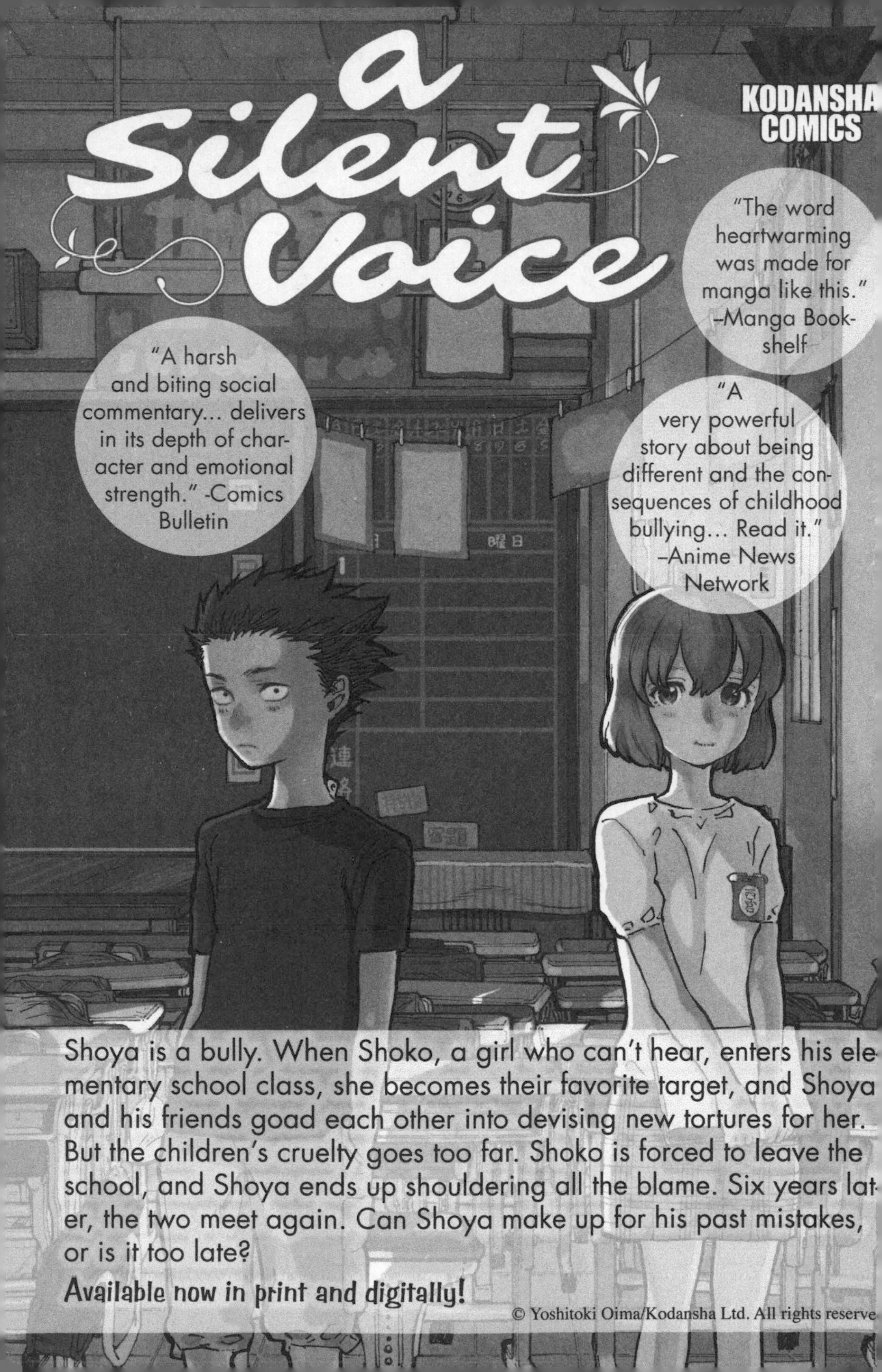

a Silent Voice
KODANSHA COMICS
"The word heartwarming was made for manga like this." –Manga Bookshelf
"A harsh and biting social commentary... delivers in its depth of character and emotional strength." -Comics Bulletin
"A very powerful story about being different and the consequences of childhood bullying… Read it." –Anime News Network
Shoya is a bully. When Shoko, a girl who can't hear, enters his elementary school class, she becomes their favorite target, and Shoya and his friends goad each other into devising new tortures for her. But the children's cruelty goes too far. Shoko is forced to leave the school, and Shoya ends up shouldering all the blame. Six years later, the two meet again. Can Shoya make up for his past mistakes, or is it too late?
Available now in print and digitally!
© Yoshitoki Oima/Kodansha Ltd. All rights reserve

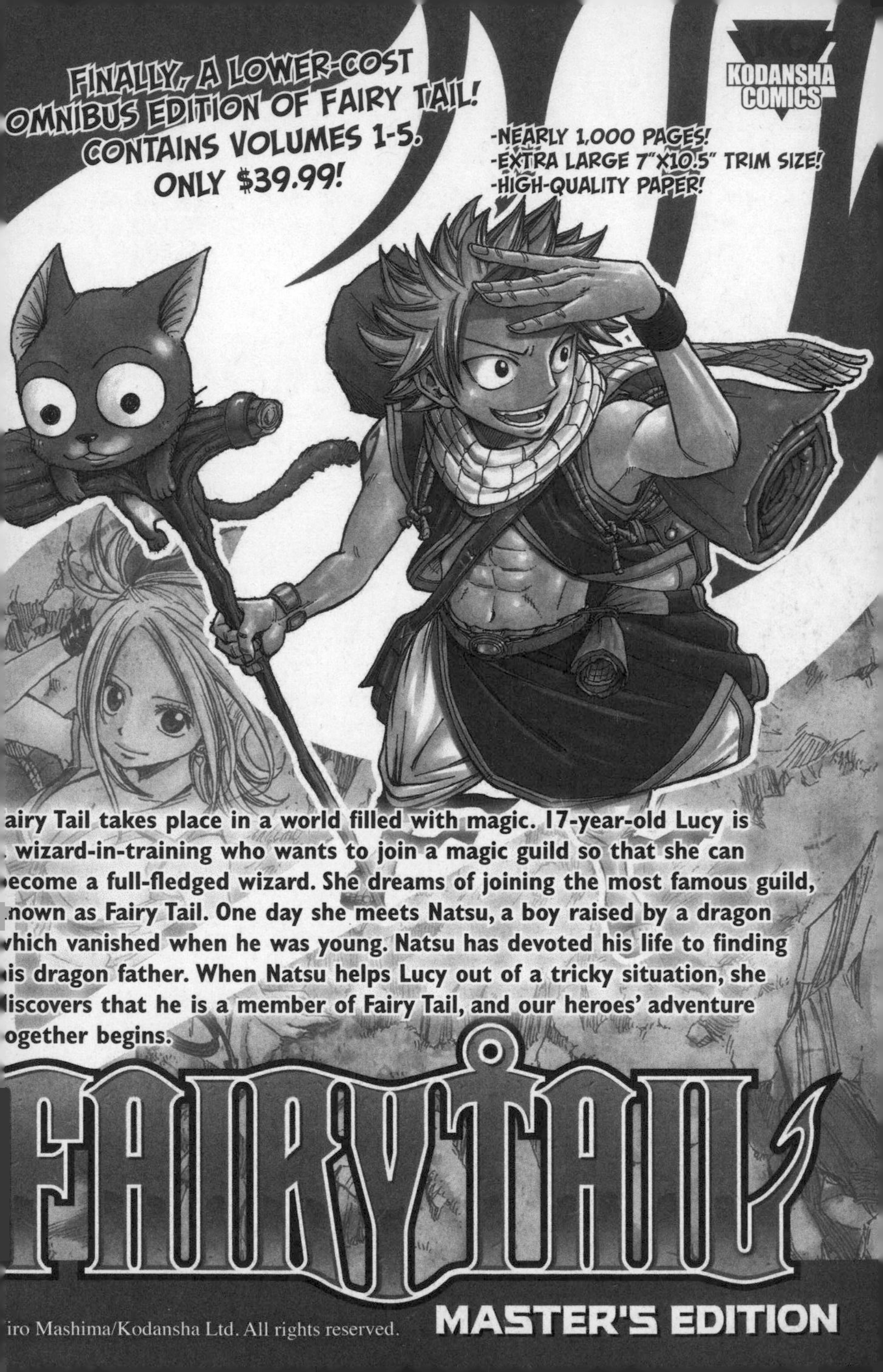
KODANSHA COMICS
FINALLY, A LOWER-COST OMNIBUS EDITION OF FAIRY TAIL! CONTAINS VOLUMES 1-5. ONLY $39.99!
-NEARLY 1,000 PAGES!
-EXTRA LARGE 7"X10.5" TRIM SIZE!
-HIGH-QUALITY PAPER!
airy Tail takes place in a world filled with magic. 17-year-old Lucy is wizard-in-training who wants to join a magic guild so that she can ecome a full-fledged wizard. She dreams of joining the most famous guild, nown as Fairy Tail. One day she meets Natsu, a boy raised by a dragon hich vanished when he was young. Natsu has devoted his life to finding is dragon father. When Natsu helps Lucy out of a tricky situation, she iscovers that he is a member of Fairy Tail, and our heroes' adventure ogether begins.
FAIRY TAIL
MASTER'S EDITION
iro Mashima/Kodansha Ltd. All rights reserved.

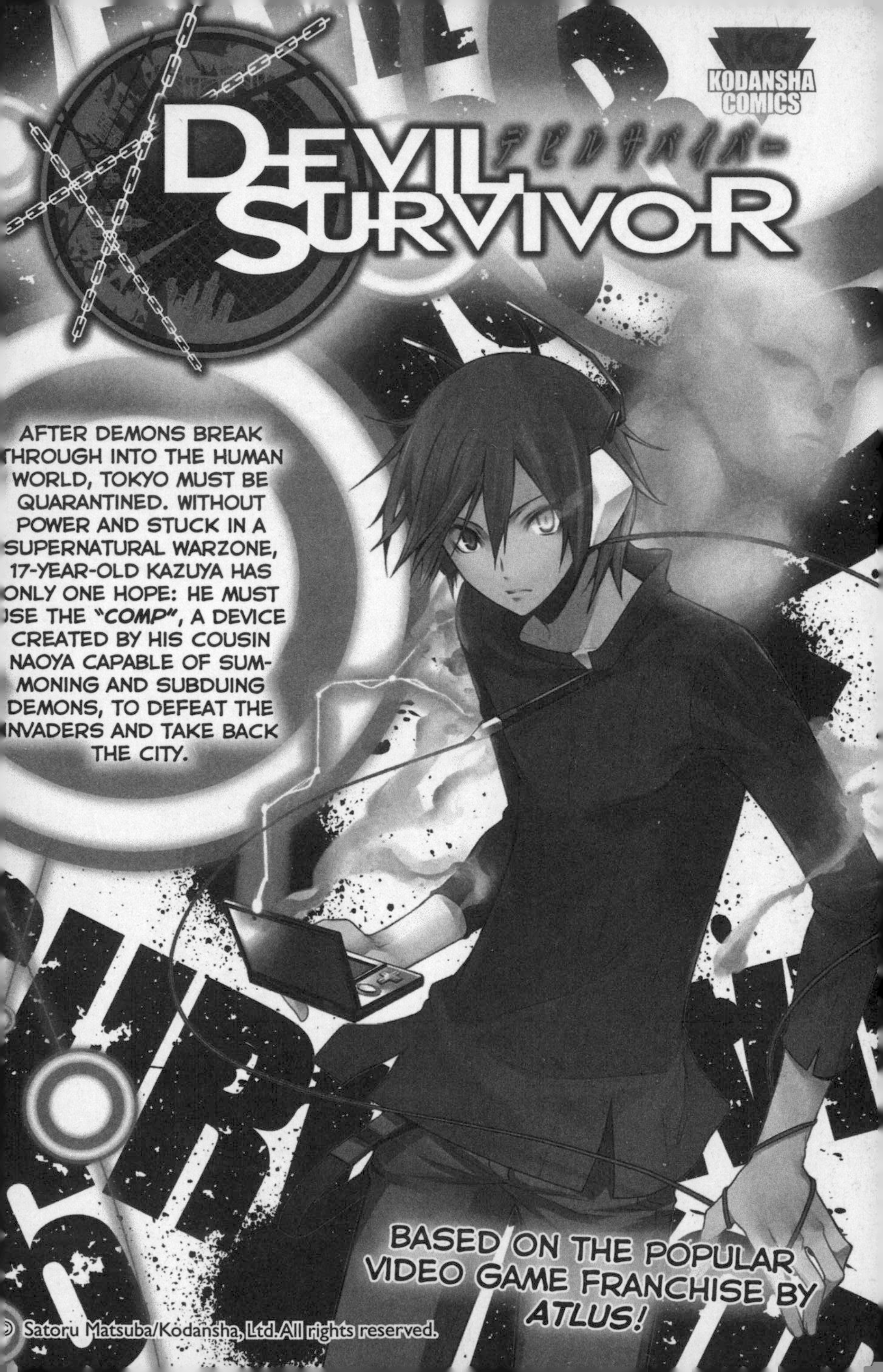
KODANSHA COMICS
DEVIL SURVIVOR
AFTER DEMONS BREAK THROUGH INTO THE HUMAN WORLD, TOKYO MUST BE QUARANTINED. WITHOUT POWER AND STUCK IN A SUPERNATURAL WARZONE, 17-YEAR-OLD KAZUYA HAS ONLY ONE HOPE: HE MUST USE THE "*COMP*", A DEVICE CREATED BY HIS COUSIN NAOYA CAPABLE OF SUMMONING AND SUBDUING DEMONS, TO DEFEAT THE INVADERS AND TAKE BACK THE CITY.
BASED ON THE POPULAR VIDEO GAME FRANCHISE BY *ATLUS!*
© Satoru Matsuba/Kodansha, Ltd. All rights reserved.

INUYASHIKI

A superhero like none you've ever seen, from the creator of "Gantz"!

Ichiro Inuyashiki is down on his luck. He looks much older than his 58 years, his children despise him, and his wife thinks he's a useless coward. So when he's diagnosed with stomach cancer and given three months to live, it seems the only one who'll miss him is his dog.

Then a blinding light fills the sky, and the old man is killed... only to wake up later in a body he almost recognizes as his own. Can it be that Ichiro Inuyashiki is no longer human?

comes in extra-large editions with color pages!

KODANSHA COMICS

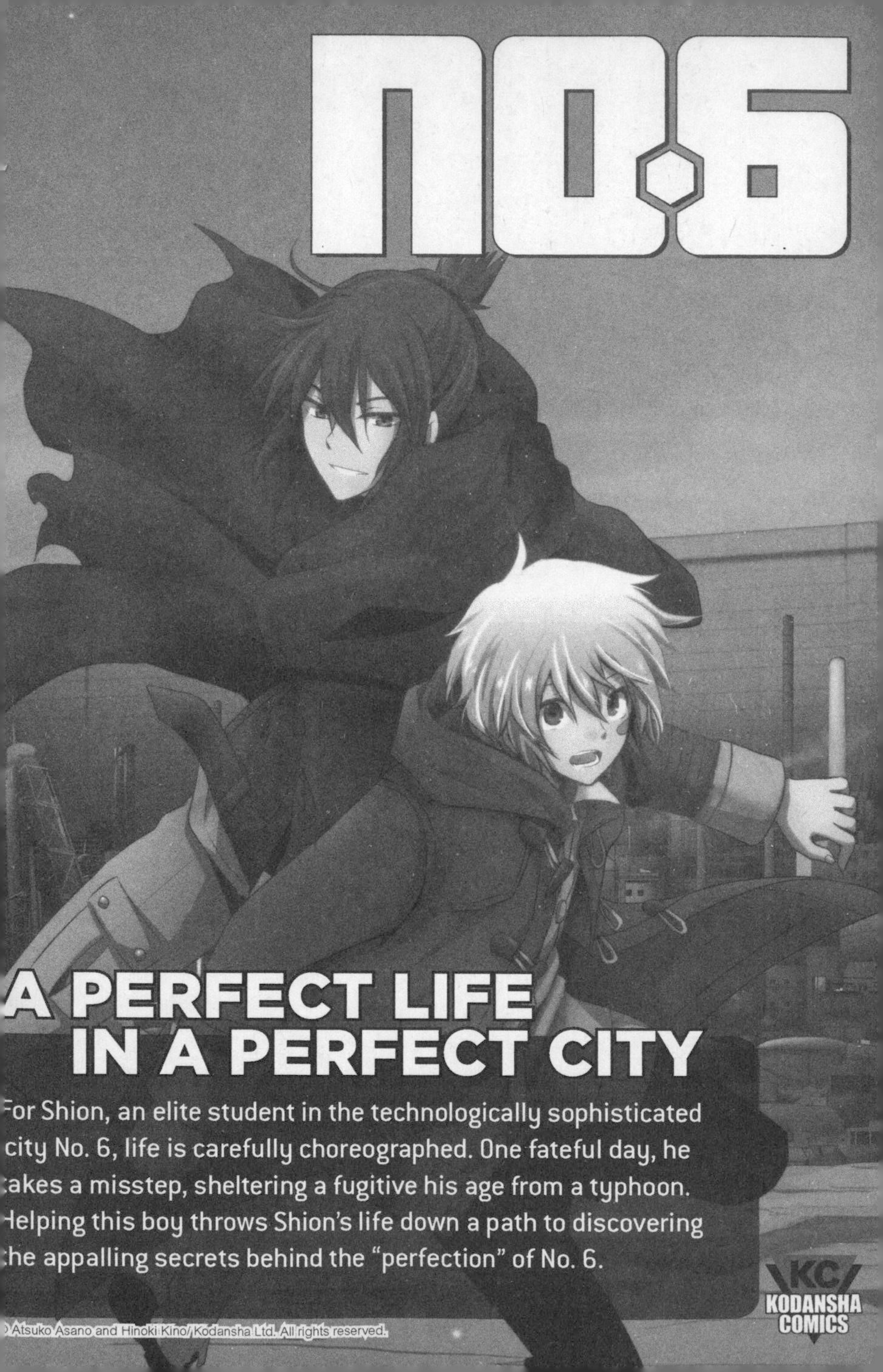
NO.6
A PERFECT LIFE
IN A PERFECT CITY
For Shion, an elite student in the technologically sophisticated city No. 6, life is carefully choreographed. One fateful day, he takes a misstep, sheltering a fugitive his age from a typhoon. Helping this boy throws Shion's life down a path to discovering the appalling secrets behind the "perfection" of No. 6.
KC
KODANSHA COMICS
© Atsuko Asano and Hinoki Kino/ Kodansha Ltd. All rights reserved.

Maria
THE VIRGIN WITCH

PURITY AND POWER

As a war to determine the rightful ruler of
medieval France ravages the land, the witch
Maria decides she will not stand idly by as
men kill each other in the name of God and
glory. Using her powerful magic, she summons
various beasts and demons —even going as far
as using a succubus to seduce soldiers into sub-
mission under the veil of night— all to stop the
needless slaughter. However, after the Arch-
angel Michael puts an end to her meddling, he
curses her to lose her powers if she ever gives
up her virginity. Will she forgo the forbidden
fruit of adulthood in order to bring an end to
the merciless machine of war?
Available now in print and digitally!

KODANSHA
COMICS